AN UNSTOPPABLE FORCE
The Scottish Exodus to Canada

Lucille H. Campey

BIRLINN

This edition published in 2008 by
Birlinn Limited
West Newington House
10 Newington Road
Edinburgh EH9 1QS

www.birlinn.co.uk

ISBN10: 1 84158 773 7
ISBN13: 978 1 84158 773 8

British Library Cataloguing-in-Publication Data
A catalogue record for this book is available from the British Library

Front cover: *A Coronach in the Backwoods*, oil painting by George W. Simson (1791–1862)
dated 1859. *Courtesy of National Museums of Scotland 000-000-574-758-0.*

Back cover: *Curling on the Lakes, near Halifax, Nova Scotia*, by Lawrence Henry Buckton
(active 1866–68) Photogravure published c. 1867 by Thomas McLean. *Courtesy of Library
and Archives Canada, Acc. No. 1970-188-2074, W.H. Coverdale Collection of Canadiana.*

Cover design by Erin Mallory
Text design by Heidy Lawrance, WeMakeBooks.ca
Edited by Jane Gibson
Printed by Transcontinental
Printed and bound in Canada

To Geoff

Also by Lucille H. Campey

"A Very Fine Class of Immigrants":
Prince Edward Island's Scottish Pioneers, 1770–1850

"Fast Sailing and Copper-Bottomed":
Aberdeen Sailing Ships and the Emigrant Scots
They Carried to Canada, 1774–1855

The Silver Chief:
Lord Selkirk and the Scottish Pioneers of Belfast,
Baldoon and Red River

After the Hector:
The Scottish Pioneers of Nova Scotia and Cape Breton, 1773–1852

The Scottish Pioneers of Upper Canada, 1
784–1855: Glengarry and Beyond

Les Écossais:
The Scottish Pioneers of Lower Canada, 1763–1855

With Axe and Bible:
The Scottish Pioneers of New Brunswick, 1784–1874

All published by Natural Heritage Books,
A Member of The Dundurn Group, Toronto

Lucille Campey has her own Web site: www.scotstocanada.com

TABLE OF CONTENTS

TABLES AND FIGURES

Tables

Figures

ACKNOWLEDGEMENTS

I AM INDEBTED TO MANY PEOPLE. I wish first of all to thank Mrs Betty R.L. Rhind (née Brown) of Montreal, for her generous permission to use John Rhind's superb account of the *Jane Boyd*'s crossing from Aberdeen to Montreal in 1854. I am also extremely grateful to Gail Dever for bringing John Rhind's diary to my attention. I also thank Andrew Laing of Peterborough, Ontario, for sending me his mother's copy of yet another splendid ship's diary. This one, produced by John Hart, describes the *Carleton*'s crossing from Glasgow to Quebec in 1842. I am also very grateful to Claire Banton of Library and Archives Canada and Tim Sanford of the Archives of Ontario for their help during my recent visits.

Thanks are due particularly to the staff members at the National Archives of Canada for their help in obtaining manuscript and published sources, as well as in locating material for illustrations. As ever I thank staff members at the National Library of Scotland and the National Archives of Scotland for their assistance. I also wish to thank the staff at the Toronto Reference Library and the Aberdeen University Library for kind help on my various visits.

I am very grateful, as well, to the people who have helped me to obtain illustrations. I thank Margaret Wilson of the National Museums of Scotland for her help in obtaining the right to reproduce the magnificent "A Coronach in the Backwoods" painting, on the front cover of this book. I thank Pam Williams of the Central Library, Birmingham, England, Mike Craig of the University of Aberdeen, and Wanda Lyons of the Public Archives of New Brunswick for their help in locating illustrations. I also thank Jill MacMicken Wilson of the Public Archives and Records Office of Prince Edward Island and Deborah Holder of the Archives of Ontario for their assistance in resolving copyright issues. I am also very grateful to the Most Reverend Vernon Fougere, bishop of Charlottetown, for his permission to reproduce a portrait of Bishop Angus MacEachern.

I would also like to acknowledge the part played by my own family roots. My great-great-grandfather William Thomson left Drainie (Lossiemouth area) in Morayshire in the early 1800s and, but for a last-minute change, would have settled in Prince Edward Island. Instead he and his family went to Digby, Nova Scotia, and later to Antigonish, where he established Maple Grove Farm at West River. I mention him because my search for him in Scotland and Nova Scotia inspired my interest in early Scottish emigration and greatly influenced my approach to the subject.

As ever I am indebted to Jane Gibson for her painstaking work during the editing phase and much-appreciated encouragement and support. I wish also to thank my friend Jean Lucas for reading the original manuscript and providing me with such helpful comments. Most of all I thank my husband, Geoff, for cheering me on while giving me so much practical help. He has produced all of the tables, figures, and appendices, located or produced the illustrations, and carried out background research. I rely on Geoff more than words can say.

PREFACE

I HAD TWO OBJECTIVES IN WRITING THIS book. Having previously studied Scottish emigration from a provincial perspective, I was aware of the many positive factors that drew emigrant Scots to particular provinces in Canada. My first objective in the current book has been to build on these regional studies and assess the overall impact of Canada's enormous pulling power in directing emigrant streams from Scotland. I have therefore examined the progress of Scottish colonization across Canada, in the context of both the factors that caused people to leave Scotland and the factors in Canada that attracted them. My second objective, which I develop in later chapters of the book, has been to challenge the popular misconception that this emigration was driven principally by dire happenings in Scotland.

The exodus of people from Scotland to Canada continues to be enveloped in a great deal of negative imagery, much of it undeserved. This seems especially strange given the enormous success that Scots achieved in Canada, not just as pioneer farmers but in every field of endeavour. However, for people who mourn their loss to Scotland, the happy ending is irrelevant. The doleful scene on the front cover of this book typifies the sadness that is easily engendered by the subject. Why did people tear themselves away from their loved ones in Scotland and endure the discomforts and expense of a sea crossing just to come to a gloomy wilderness like this? But of course this artist's interpretation is intended to arouse sympathy. There is another side to pioneer life that is not shown. Scots began with wildernesses but ended up as prosperous farmers. The happy curling scene that is depicted on the back cover of this book more accurately reflects the outcome of this emigration saga.

Despite having a happy ending, the Scots to Canada story is clouded by a victim culture that concentrates on Highland emigration and its

alleged associations with forced expulsions and wicked landlords. The fact
that the exodus came primarily from the Lowlands is ignored. This distorted picture arises in part from the fierce anti-emigration campaigns of the
late eighteenth and early nineteenth centuries, which were run by Highland
landlords, seeking to hold on to their tenantry, and by the scheming of
Highland politicians in later years, who discredited emigration in pursuit of
domestic land reform objectives. While most Highlanders eagerly grasped
the escape route from extreme poverty that emigration offered them, the
passionate rhetoric of anti-emigration campaigners ensured that their
departure would always be viewed in the worst possible light.

Emigrant sea crossings have also attracted much negative publicity,
most of it ill-founded. Fortunately, the quality of the shipping used to take
emigrants across the Atlantic can be determined from the *Lloyd's Shipping
Register*. Still in use today, it provides irrefutable evidence that Scots sailed
in highly seaworthy ships. Far from being put on rickety old barges, as is
frequently alleged, they had access to the best shipping of their day. Yet the
myth that emigrant Scots endured wretched ships, manned by rum-soaked
crews, continues to be perpetuated through innuendo and anecdote.

Two recurring themes in the book are the importance that Scots placed
on their culture and on their religion. Follow-on emigration usually came
from areas that had fostered the original settlement footholds, creating
highly distinctive Scottish communities in British North America/Canada.
Presbyterians and Roman Catholics expanded their territories quite separately, leaving many parts of Canada with clear religious demarcations. The
clergymen sent out from Scotland were a valuable religious and cultural lifeline, and the extensive visit reports that they left behind are packed full of
details on the progress being made by the early-nineteenth-century Scottish
colonizers.

The inescapable conclusion of this study is that most emigration was
voluntary and self-financed. The determination to emigrate became an
unstoppable force. A combination of push and pull factors brought thousands of Scots to Canada. They laid down a rich and deep seam of Scottish
culture, which continues to enrich Canada's present-day society.

ABBREVIATIONS

AR	*Acadian Recorder*
ACA	Aberdeen City Archives
AJ	*Aberdeen Journal*
AO	Archives of Ontario, Toronto
AU	Aberdeen University
CM	*Caledonian Mercury*
DC	*Dundee Courier*
DCA	Dundee City Archives
DCB	*Dictionary of Canadian Biography*
DGC	*Dumfries and Galloway Courier*
DWJ	*Dumfries Weekly Journal*
EA	*Edinburgh Advertiser*
EU	Edinburgh University Special Collection
GA	*Greenock Advertiser*
GC	*Glasgow Chronicle*
GH	*Glasgow Herald*
IA	*Inverness Advertiser*
IC	*Inverness Courier*
IJ	*Inverness Journal*
JJ	*John O'Groats Journal*
LAC	Library and Archives Canada, Ottawa
ML	Mitchell Library, Glasgow
MM	McCord Museum, Montreal
NAB	National Archives of Britain, Kew
NAS	National Archives of Scotland
NBC	*New Brunswick Courier*
NLS	National Library of Scotland

NSARM Nova Scotia Archives and Record Management
OLA   Orkney Library and Archives
PAM   Public Archives of Manitoba, Winnipeg
PANB   Public Archives of New Brunswick, Fredericton
PAPEI   Public Archives and Records Office of Prince Edward Island, Charlottetown
PC   *Perth Courier*
PEIG   *Prince Edward Island Gazette*
PEIRG   *Prince Edward Island Royal Gazette*
PP   *Parliamentary Papers*
QM   *Quebec Mercury*
RG   *Royal Gazette*
SA   *Statistical Account of Scotland*
SCA   Scottish Catholic Archives, Edinburgh
SCRO   Staffordshire County Record Office
SG   *Scottish Genealogist*
SH   *Scottish Highlander*
SM   *Scots Magazine*
SRA   Strathclyde Regional Archives
UBSC   University of Birmingham Special Collections
UNBA   University of New Brunswick Archives, Fredericton

One

CANADA'S APPEAL

*There cannot be ... a scene more totally new to a
native of these kingdoms than the boundless forests of America.
An emigrant set down in such a scene feels
almost the helplessness of a child.*[1]

AS THE LARGE GROUP OF PEOPLE WHO had sailed from the Isle of Skye edged closer to Orwell Bay in Prince Edward Island in the summer of 1803, a vast forest came into view. Lord Selkirk, who accompanied the emigrants, recorded their bewilderment and dismay as their ship approached the harbour. Coming from nearly treeless islands, they had few axe skills and yet their first task would be to hack their way through what must have seemed impenetrable forests. It was a daunting prospect.

In his much-celebrated Gaelic poem, "A' Choille Ghruamach" ("The Gloomy Forest"), John MacLean would express the great foreboding felt by Hebridean islanders at such moments. Written in 1819, the poem caused great consternation in his native Tiree. As people learned of MacLean's anguish and despair at being enveloped in one of Nova Scotia's great wildernesses, those who might have considered emigrating had second thoughts.[2] When a copy of MacLean's poem was read aloud at a wedding in Tobermory, in nearby Mull, such was the sympathy felt for MacLean that his friends decided there and then to help him return home. But when they offered him the money for an expenses-paid return trip, he declined it.[3] He did so because mentally he had passed the point of no return. Having recoiled initially at the sight of the great forests, he now accepted them. MacLean's gloom had lifted, and his poetry would now relate the greater freedoms and better livelihoods to be had through emigration. His reactions were typical of what most newly arrived Highlanders and Islanders experienced.

How can it be that people so easily traumatized by the sight of large trees succeeded in such difficult circumstances? They actually became Canada's foremost pioneers. Highlanders were novices at tree felling, but, when it came to coping with the privations, drudgery, and isolation of pioneer life, they were in a league of their own. Lord Selkirk's group from Skye certainly rose to the occasion. Within eight months of landing at Orwell Bay, sixty-three families were planting crops on newly cleared land, a truly heroic achievement.[4] Together they formed the hugely important Belfast settlements. Their dogged determination to succeed was matched by the enthusiasm of the Skye followers who joined them. People came in spite of raging wars between Britain and France, escalating sea transport costs, and the vicious anti-emigration campaigns being waged in Scotland to stop them from leaving. Yet the exodus from the Highlands and Islands of Scotland could not be stopped.

In the late eighteenth and early nineteenth centuries Scotland's ruling classes strongly opposed emigration. They feared that the growing exodus was depleting Scotland's workforce and armed forces. Owners of Highland estates were particularly aggrieved at the loss of their tenants and put up fierce resistance to their going. Because they did not understand the ordinary person's longing for a decent living, the elite never appreciated the extent of Canada's appeal. In a nutshell, Canada offered Scotland's poor and oppressed an escape route to a better world. Although those who emigrated were not just the poor and dispossessed, they were the ones who had most to gain initially. By emigrating, people could enjoy greater prosperity and aspire to owning their own land.[5] There was no pecking order in the New World. There were no landlords demanding high rents and no factory owners paying starvation wages for labour. They could be free-thinking individuals seeking what was best for their families, rather than serfs and wage slaves living under an oppressive regime.

Thus, by emigrating, people could gain materially while enjoying the freedom and benefits of a more egalitarian society. And by emigrating in large groups and settling together, they could transfer their way of life and traditions to their new communities. Poor economic prospects in Scotland combined with this heady mix of rewards fuelled the zeal to emigrate and propelled the movement into an unstoppable force.

Highlanders were the largest ethnic group to arrive in North America from Britain between 1775 and 1815, greatly outnumbering Lowlanders at this stage.[6] And being some of the earliest immigrants, they had a profound impact on Canada's early settlement pattern. Major Highland population

The Indian Point pioneer cemetery at West Mabou, Cape Breton, which overlooks the sea. The cemetery is dedicated to the early Catholic Highlanders, mainly from west Inverness-shire, who came to the area from the early 1800s. *Photograph by Geoff Campey.*

centres began taking shape from the late eighteenth century in Prince Edward Island, Cape Breton, eastern Nova Scotia, and eastern Upper Canada (later Ontario). Although Highlanders dominated initially, they were quickly dwarfed numerically by the much larger influx of Lowlanders, which began when the Napoleonic Wars were coming to an end in 1815.

With the deepening economic depression throughout Scotland, enthusiasm for emigration rose, and, after 1815, a growing number of Lowlanders were taking their chances in the wilds of Canada. Conditions were particularly desperate in the Clyde region's textile districts. With the invention of the power loom, handloom weavers were having to cope with redundancy and extreme destitution. Although factory jobs were plentiful in cities such as Glasgow, they were badly paid. But, by taking advantage of a subsidized emigration scheme that was being promoted by the government in 1815, redundant weavers could establish settlements for themselves in the Rideau Valley of eastern Upper Canada. Having been employed as weavers in sedentary jobs, they too lacked axe skills and had little farming experience. Nevertheless they cheerfully relinquished their trades and against all the odds became highly successful colonizers. Group after group from the textile districts in and around Glasgow and Paisley came to the Rideau Valley over the following decades, often settling as whole communities. As a former weaver later explained to the 1827 Emigration Select Committee, many of the Rideau Valley communities were composed "of the neighbours and friends who had once lived in close proximity back in Scotland."[7]

John Hart sailed with a group of around four hundred fellow weavers from Glasgow in 1842. He certainly had no intention of ever returning. Standing on the deck of his ship, he watched Scotland disappear into the distance, "I was going to make some remarks upon the last sight of the land that

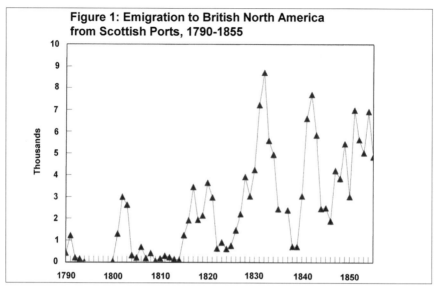

Figure 1: Emigration to British North America from Scottish Ports, 1790-1855

Sources: Pre-1825 figures have been computed from customs records and newspaper shipping reports. Data for 1825–1855 is taken from the British Parliamentary Papers: Emigration Returns from British North America, 1839–1840; Colonial Land and Emigration Commissioners, Annual Reports, 1841–1855.

gave me birth but again, when I thought that it was a land that denied me bread and forced me to leave it for another, the impression soon left me."[8]

There were plenty of people like John Hart who felt a twinge of bitterness towards Scotland for failing to give them a sustainable living. The favourable reports sent by the previous arrivals had no doubt led his group to the Rideau Valley. The cycle would continue, creating a recurring pattern. Once the first arrivals had attracted followers from their part of Scotland to a region of Canada, each successive wave of emigrants did the same. Distinctive emigrant streams were thereby created. In many cases the chain of people following each other from Scotland to Canada persisted for decades.

Despite breaking their links with Britain by emigrating, most Scots remained loyal to the British Crown, making Canada their preferred choice over the United States. But, while Scots were the predominant group in the earliest emigration waves, they quickly lost ground numerically to the Irish and English, who followed them in far greater numbers. Scots ranked first before 1825, then were second to the Irish until 1830, but after this they were also outnumbered by the English. The early Scottish influx was at its height between 1830 and 1855, but even then it accounted for only 11 per cent of the total immigration from Britain to Canada (Figure 1).[9] With its stronger economy and better climate, the United States rose in popularity from the mid-1850s on, but preferences changed again in the early twentieth century when, with the prairies being opened up, Canada once again became the favoured choice.[10] In the fourteen years from 1901 to 1914, nearly 170,000 Scots arrived at Canadian ports – about 65 per cent as many as the estimated total for the previous century.[11] Nearly all of the emigration in this later period was to Ontario and the prairie provinces. Thus, while Scots played a vital role in creating early settlement footholds, their numbers were never very large in relation to other ethnic groups. It was their early arrival and not their overall numbers that made them so important

The 190 Highlanders who sailed to mainland Nova Scotia in 1773 in the famous *Hector* were the first group to arrive directly from Britain. However, the "New Scotland" that they saw before them was Scottish in name only. They were greatly outnumbered by the 8,000 New Englanders, who had been moved to the province between 1759 and 1762 at government expense. And to make way for them, the government had forcibly removed 13,000 French-speaking Acadians from their lands in two separate deportations, carried out in 1755 and 1758.[12] Through these extreme and brutal measures the British government removed the indigenous population, which

The arrival in 1761 of Captain John Nairne of the Fraser's Highlanders (78th) at the seigneury of Murray Bay (la Malbaie) in 1761. Nairne's regiment had played a key role in the capture of Quebec two years earlier. Although this remote region, some ninety miles northeast of Quebec City, attracted few Scots, it has a special place in Canada's history, for being the earliest of its Scottish settlements. *Courtesy of Library and Archives Canada C-040583, W. H. Coverdale Collection of Canadiana.*

it feared would side with France, and brought in loyal settlers of British extraction to take their place. The hunting and fishing territories of the Native Peoples had also been seized to assist the process of colonization.[13]

Britain's treatment of Quebec's French Canadians could not have been more different. Having defeated France in the Seven Years' War, which ended in 1763, the old province of Quebec became a British possession, but the captives of this conquest were handled cautiously. Given its considerable population, deportations were out of the question.[14] And with ongoing fears over an imminent American invasion, there was merit in trying to court favour with French Canadians. So instead of forced removals there was appeasement. The French-speaking Roman Catholic population was given the right to follow its traditional practices and laws, and Quebec became the only place in the entire British Empire where Catholics and Protestants had equal status.[15] The strategy brought its rewards. Quebec remained neutral when the Americans attacked during the War of Independence in 1783 and staunchly supported the British side in the American War of 1812–14.[16]

Britain's colonization policy, such as it was, relied initially on a vain hope that wealthy merchants and landowners in Britain would finance emigration schemes to North America, but in reality few did. Through this policy vast tracts of land went to privileged individuals, thereby giving land speculators a field day while ordinary settlers were left with a bureaucratic muddle.[17] But the government was adamant that little or no public money be spent on emigration. However, the situation changed dramatically with Britain's defeat in the American War of Independence. Fearing a further loss of territory, in 1784 it relocated 40,000 Loyalists from the United States to key river and coastal boundaries in the northern colonies that remained under British control (now Canada).[18] Thirty-five thousand of them were granted land along both sides of the Bay of Fundy in the Maritime region, while most of the remainder were assigned land along the St. Lawrence River, with the rest being scattered in the Gaspé Peninsula, Prince Edward Island, and Cape Breton.[19] As a result of this action, Loyalists swelled the population of the Nova Scotia peninsula and gave the newly created province of New Brunswick an instant population. The smaller group of Loyalists who were sent to stretches along the St. Lawrence gave Upper Canada its earliest immigrant communities, which were concentrated at the eastern end of the province.[20]

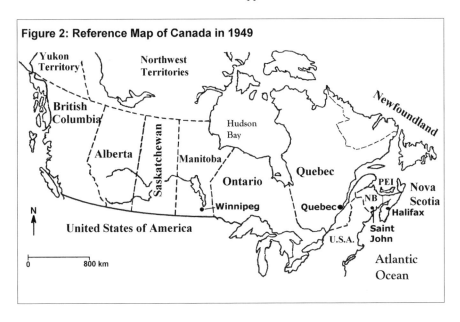

Figure 2: Reference Map of Canada in 1949

Included among Upper Canada's Loyalist communities was the remarkable contingent from Glengarry in Inverness-shire, which had travelled north from New York state. Having moved it to its new location on the St. Lawrence, the government inadvertently created a great stimulus for further emigration from the northwest Highlands. Despite the difficulties and high cost of reaching this inland location, Highlanders rushed forward in droves to join their compatriots.

However, a totally different situation emerged around the Bay of Fundy. Faced with the knowledge that the Maritime provinces' valuable timber trade with Britain was developing on the east side of Nova Scotia, in and around Pictou, Scottish Loyalists promptly moved east. The *Hector* settlers had exported timber from Pictou as early as 1775. Then, when a large number of ex-soldiers from two disbanded Scottish regiments – the Duke of Hamilton's (82nd) and the Royal Highland Emigrants (the 84th) – were allocated land in Pictou, during the Loyalist influx ten years later, its future as the region's major timber port became secure.[21] Having financed their relocation to the west of the province so that they could bolster the population of this key region, the government was powerless to stop the Scottish Loyalists from moving east. Scottish initiative and entrepreneurial zeal took precedence over the government's defence concerns. As they moved across, Scottish Loyalists contributed to the fast-growing population that was being replenished directly from Scotland. By the 1820s, when large

Scottish enclaves had been established in the eastern counties of Pictou, Antigonish, Colchester, and Guysborough, Nova Scotia really could live up to its name.

Immigrant Scots were driven entirely by their own priorities and objectives and saw nothing wrong in defying the government or breaking the law. Despite government restrictions that banned settlers from entering Cape Breton, large numbers of Highlanders snapped up its best river and coastal frontages. Having previously settled in Prince Edward Island, they had become disenchanted with its devilish land-tenure arrangements. The fact that they were most unwelcome, since they were considered to be a possible threat to Britain's coal-mining interests in Cape Breton, was of no consequence. Pictou's development as a major timber port had swept Cape Breton into its path. Spotting the enormous timber-trade potential, wave after wave of Highlanders came to the Island. Lowlanders followed from 1816 on, and, by the 1820s, Scots were the predominant ethnic group in Cape Breton. As a final touch of irony, Pictou had become a Highland success story only because the Hector arrivals had refused to accept the inferior, inland locations that had been allocated to them by the Philadelphia Land Company. With typical Highland panache they grabbed the best coastal and river sites by the harbour. The process was repeated again in Cape Breton. In both cases the land was taken illegally by squatting.

It was a similar story in New Brunswick. Having been granted land by the Crown in 1784 along the Nashwaak River north of Fredericton, men of the disbanded Royal Highland Regiment (42nd) uprooted themselves and moved northward to the Miramichi region.[22] As was the case with the Nova Scotia Loyalists, they followed the hub of the timber trade. With his founding of the Miramichi's lumbering and shipbuilding industries nineteen years earlier, the Morayshire-born William Davidson had created yet another Scottish magnet. From Davidson's time on, the Scottish influx to New Brunswick mirrored the steady progression of the timber trade as it moved northward and westward. The trade's principal financiers and merchants were Scottish, and in the forefront were Alan Gilmour and Alexander Rankin, both of whom became great timber barons.

The eastern Martime provinces were extremely attractive to early Scottish arrivals. One obvious reason was their relative proximity to Scotland. This translated into cheaper fares for Atlantic crossings. Another factor was their burgeoning timber trade. There was another important consideration as well. Although most Highlanders and Islanders could cope well with a cold climate, the endless, dreary forests were much harder to bear. Because they were used to living by the sea, the miles of splendid coastline offered by Prince Edward Island, Cape Breton, and peninsular Nova Scotia gave them a semblance of a home away from home. By the same token, New Brunswick's massive forests and land-locked position were far less appealing to the eye, as were the vast inland stretches of Upper and Lower Canada.[23] Meanwhile, although Newfoundland had its important fisheries, it attracted very few emigrant Scots, who preferred to follow the fortunes of the timber trade.[24]

Royal Highland Regiment (42nd) uniform in 1768. It is believed that curling was first introduced to New Brunswick by officers of the 42nd who were stationed at Saint John in 1853. *Courtesy of Library and Archives Canada, C-043324.*

Having initially condemned emigration as detrimental to the country's interests, people in authority had a rude shock when Britain nearly lost Canada to the United States in the hard-fought War of 1812–14. Such were the government's defence concerns that the previously unthinkable idea of using public funds to subsidize emigration suddenly became official policy. Assisted emigration schemes were offered to some five hundred Scots, divided equally between Lowlanders and Highlanders, who were relocated to the Rideau Valley region at the Crown's expense. Their role was to form a civilian defence line between the St. Lawrence and Ottawa rivers. However, Highlanders were unimpressed with these objectives. They would accept the funds being offered to emigrate only on condition that they could join their compatriots in the already established Highland settlements at Glengarry, just to the east of the Rideau Valley settlements. Being desperate to find obliging settlers at this time, the authorities accepted this condition. Meanwhile, hard-pressed handloom weavers living in and around Glasgow and Paisley continued to stream into the Rideau Valley, although they had to go almost through hoops of fire to raise their funds. Responding to intense public pressure, the government offered limited help, while money was also raised from private benefactors.

By the 1820s, Scotland's poor and dispossessed were in a wretched state. The on-going process of removing Highland estate tenants from their lands to make way for sheep farms was intensifying, while the decline of kelp production in the Western Isles had brought extreme destitution there.[25] Lowlanders too were feeling the strain. As the situation worsened, the government came under increasing public pressure to provide subsidized emigration. Petitions streamed into the Colonial Office requesting help to emigrate. A Glasgow tailor asked for "a free passage to Upper Canada, as the want of employment and high price of the necessaries of life prevented him [from] supporting his family, whom he trusts will become successful." Seventeen families from West Kilbride in Ayrshire were desperate to leave. "Owing to the badness of the trade, thousands are thrown out of employment and reduced to a state of wretchedness hitherto unknown." Four thousand Glasgow families appealed for assistance in another petition, and so it went on. But such requests were always ignored by the government.[26]

Although the government could not be persuaded to part with public money to subsidize emigration to Canada, beyond what it had spent on the Rideau Valley schemes, there was growing public awareness of its benefits. Highland landlords, who had formerly fought hard to retain their tenants, swung around in favour of emigration. By the time that the great famine struck the Highlands and Islands in the mid-1840s, they faced mounting debts, and their tenants, near-starvation. Both sides had a common interest in finding a solution. But, although landlord-assisted emigration was a logical response to the growing humanitarian crisis, it attracted considerable negative publicity. The fact that landlords were putting up their own money in these circumstances led to the accusation that tenants were being forced to leave against their will. While this interpretation suits present and past commentators who mourn the loss of Highlanders from Scotland, it is ludicrous to argue that it was only the landlords who benefited from these arrangements. The tenants would have been well aware of the harsh realities that they faced. They had long pleaded for the funds to emigrate because they wanted something better than the suffering and hopelessness that their homeland offered them. That financial help was now on offer.

For people raising their own resources to emigrate, reaching Upper Canada was a particularly difficult challenge. The inland journey was cumbersome and lengthy. In the 1820s it could be as costly as the sea crossing.[27] Nevertheless Upper Canada rose sharply in popularity from 1830 on, when internal communications improved. Its fertile lands, better climate, and good trading prospects with the United States made it the most desirable of destinations. Lowlanders from Aberdeenshire and Dumfriesshire and Highlanders from Sutherland and Perthshire ended up being near neighbours in the heart of the peninsula. Because they were some of the earliest arrivals, they had sufficient land to expand as distinct communities. And once the Canada Company's vast Huron Tract was opened up, it also became a great magnet for Scots. In fact, such was the appeal of the western peninsula to Scots that it soon generated a major east to west migration from the Maritime provinces to Upper Canada. However, despite the region's plentiful attractions, many Western Isles settlers rejected Upper Canada and still insisted on maintaining their long-standing links with Cape Breton. Even at the depths of the Cape Breton potato famine, they actually had to be stopped from migrating by the order of the lieutenant-governor.

View of Galt in 1857. It was named after John Galt, the famous Scottish novelist, who became the first commissioner of the Canada Company. Drawn by Alice E. Brown. *Courtesy of Archives of Ontario C 281–0–0–0–11.*

But for Canada's timber trade with Britain, this great exodus of Scots could not have happened. The doubling of the already high duties on Baltic timber in 1811 had the effect of pricing it out of the British market and making North American timber the cheaper alternative.[28] As the trade soared, regular and affordable sea crossings came within the reach of the average emigrant. The timber trade provided the ships that carried emigrant Scots to Canada, and it also gave recently arrived settlers a market for their felled trees. And as new arrivals sought the best locations along coastal frontages near timber bays and their river tributaries, the trade actually determined where each new community would be formed.[29] The commercial links established by Scottish timber merchants also influenced events. When Dumfriesshire's textile and agricultural districts experienced an economic downturn from 1817, local people emigrated to Prince Edward Island and New Brunswick because those were the two provinces from which Dumfries's timber merchants were importing their timber.[30]

Religious observance was a valuable support mechanism for uprooted Scots who were coming to terms with what was to them a strange environment. In tending to the religious needs of the large numbers of Roman Catholic Highlanders in Prince Edward Island, Cape Breton, and eastern Nova Scotia, Father Angus MacEachern (later bishop) needed to cover vast

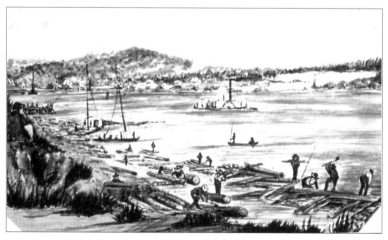

Steam Ferry Boat and Rafting Timber on the St. John River near Fredericton, New Brunswick, watercolour by William Smyth Maynard Wolfe (1831–72). *Courtesy of Library and Archives Canada, Acc. No. 1985–3–70.*

Outdoor Communion of Presbyterians, 1863, pen and ink drawing by Charles William Jefferys (1869–1951). *Courtesy of Library and Archives Canada, Acc. No. 1972-26-1402.*

distances.[31] Travelling usually by boat, he would attend to baptisms, weddings, and the dying as required and would make annual visits to his scattered congregations.[32] The Presbyterian clergymen of the Established Church of Scotland sent out by the Glasgow Colonial Society also constituted a crucial religious and cultural lifeline.[33] Trudging phenomenal distances to scattered communities, the ministers gave sermons to crowds of Scots who themselves had walked many miles to hear the word of God. It helped them to survive the rigours and feelings of isolation of pioneer life. The Reverend John Clugston, who was based in Quebec City, achieved great feats of endurance in tending to scattered congregations in the Eastern Townships and the Gaspé region, while the Reverend Alexander MacLean thought nothing of travelling from one end of New Brunswick to the other. He set up various Sabbath schools, sampled a lumber camp for a few days, and turned up at Miramichi Bay at the time of the great fire in 1825 to help organize relief efforts there.

Belonging to a Canadian Presbyterian sect, not the established Kirk, William Bell, the Rideau Valley's first minister at Perth, was very much his own man. Serving his congregation for forty years, he found his endurance always tested to the full:

No person who has never lived in a new settlement can conceive how fatiguing and unpleasant it is to wade through swamps and bushes,

and climb over rocks and fallen timber, under a burning sun, and surrounded by clouds of mosquitoes. Every night when I reached home
I was ready to drop down with corporeal and mental fatigue.[34]

He preached on the first Sunday after his arrival, in 1817, renting "the large
upper room of an Inn," and by the second Sunday he had opened a Sunday
school "with five children only."[35] He founded temperance societies, Sunday
schools, and Bible classes and helped to form Presbyterian congregations
across the Rideau Valley. Such men were in a class of their own when it
came to dogged determination and diligence.

As was the case at Perth in eastern Upper Canada, the Established
Church of Scotland met with severe competition in Prince Edward Island.[36]
It struggled to survive there because of the much greater appeal of the independent sects and the newly formed Scotch Baptists.[37] However, the Presbyterianism of the Established Church had a great following in Cape Breton
thanks to the fund-raising efforts of Mrs. Isabella MacKay, a wealthy lady
of Highland extraction who lived in Edinburgh. Although she had never set
foot in Cape Breton, she dedicated her life to supporting its Presbyterian
congregations. Founding the Edinburgh Ladies Association in 1831 to raise
funds, she recruited Glasgow Colonial Society missionaries and school-
teachers herself and, by so doing, spread religion and education throughout
Cape Breton.

For nearly a century Scots fled their country in search of the better life
that Canada could offer. Such was the zeal for emigration that no harsh
words, interference, or dire events could stop it. The unstoppable force, once
unleashed, attracted wave after wave of emigration. However, a limiting
factor was the emigrant's ability to finance the Atlantic crossings and acquire
suitable land. When James Brown, New Brunswick's emigration agent,
undertook a promotional tour of Scotland to sell the province's merits, he
made much of his penniless arrival there and subsequent rise to prosperity.[38]
It sounded like a dream come true for his audiences, yet few people
responded. As Brown ruefully acknowledged, had he the ability to authorize
public funds for sea crossings "we could get as many as we want."[39]

Isabella MacKenzie, who had friends in New Brunswick, wanted to emigrate so badly in 1834 that she falsely claimed to the Colonial Office that
her stepson Donald had served in the Sutherland Regiment (93rd), when,

Clearing Town Plots at Stanley, New Brunswick. The New Brunswick and Nova Scotia
Land Company established the town of Stanley on the Nashwaak River in 1834. Lith-
ograph, October 1834, by W. P. Kay, printed by Day and Haghe of London, England,
and published by George Ackerman & Co., London, England. *Courtesy of Library and
Archives Canada, C–000017.*

in fact, he was only a boy of seventeen. However small the land grant, it
"would be a great blessing to my family," she wrote, but this plea from a
destitute widow went unheeded.[40] The Colonial Office correspondence
files are full of letters like this from all over Scotland, each pleading for
financial aid to emigrate.

It was the prospect of such assistance that tempted a group from Skye to
sign up with the New Brunswick and Nova Scotia Land Company in 1836.
They had jumped at the offer of free passages, but it turned out to be bogus.
The land company brought great notoriety upon itself for its shameful treatment of these Skye crofters, who came to grief in their settlement near
Stanley, in York County, New Brunswick.[41] Inadequate accommodation and
provisions caused the spread of "a most fatal disease" that claimed about
forty lives.[42] However, despite these fatalities, Skye people continued to emigrate with increasing gusto to Prince Edward Island and Cape Breton, both
places having long-standing Skye communities.

Emigration was always going to be risky. The sea crossing was fraught with
dangers, and harrowing conditions awaited the first clearers of the forests.
Success was certainly not a foregone conclusion. The operation had to be
planned in great detail beforehand.[43] Janet McCuaig's preparation before
leaving Islay for Upper Canada just after 1815 was exemplary. Following the

death of her husband, John Campbell, she decided to emigrate. She "wisely determined to learn all the skills possible in Scotland." To do this she took her children to Glasgow and "apprenticed them for seven long years." Two sons worked in shipyards to acquire carpentry, and three "went to sea as sailors, spending their spare time on land to learn farming." Meanwhile, two daughters "trained as house makers with special attention to spinning and weaving." Being Gaelic speakers, they also took the opportunity to learn English. And when it came time to board ship for Quebec, "the sailor sons signed on as crew."[44]

Despite a happy ending, this emigration saga is shrouded in a victim culture that is preoccupied mainly with wicked landlords, forced expulsions, and emotional horror stories. The myth that the Highlands could have gone on supporting its people is perpetuated, in spite of the hard facts to the contrary. The loss of Highlanders is mourned sentimentally, while the much larger exodus of Lowlanders is ignored. Such a distorted picture owes much to the machinations of Highland politicians in the 1880s, who heaped great odium on emigration in pursuit of their own domestic land reforms.

Because the age-old problems of unproductive land, overpopulation, and atrocious poverty always remained, the rational case for emigration could never be defeated. That was why Highlanders emigrated in such great numbers in the early twentieth century. Over one hundred years earlier, the battle had just begun. As an emigration fever rampaged through the Highlands of Scotland, the ruling classes had formulated a plan to stop it in its tracks, but they never stood a chance.

Two

EMIGRATION FRENZY

*The rapid strides which emigration is daily making
demands the speediest interposition of government
to stop and impede its progress.*[1]

T HE *Edinburgh Advertiser's* PLEA FOR government action in 1773
reflected the great disquiet throughout Scotland over the acceler-
ating exodus of people to North America. If the situation went
unchecked, warned the newspaper, the nation would soon be "drained of
many labouring people, as well as artificers and manufacturers." Poor and
uncertain economic prospects at home, coupled with glowing reports of the
better life in North America, had led many people to opt for emigration.
There was no real threat of depopulation, but the rising numbers of emigrants were nevertheless regarded as a dangerous development. Despite the
mounting furor over emigration, it took another thirty years before the British
government actually intervened and introduced legislation that was
designed to limit the numbers who could leave the country. However, this
provided only a temporary bar to emigration, which resumed with a
vengeance with the ending of the Napoleonic Wars in 1815.

It was argued by most people in authority that emigration was highly
detrimental to Scotland's interests. Men were being lost who would otherwise be in the workforce or armed services. Fearing the loss of so many
tenants from their estates, some Highland landlords ran frenzied campaigns
to halt the exodus. But the "epidemical fever" that Dr. Samuel Johnson first
witnessed in the Western Isles in 1773 had quickly developed an uncontrol-
lable momentum. Although the so-called fever was raging throughout Scotland, it was claiming far more people from the Highlands and Islands than

from the Lowlands.[2] And there was certainly no question of anyone being forced to emigrate. Quite the contrary. People emigrated in spite of the criticisms hurled at them and the barriers being placed in their way.

Table 1

Report of Emigration from Various Highland Areas to North America, 1772–73 (taken from the Lord Justice Clerk's report to the Earl of Suffolk in April 1774) [NAS RH1/2/933(10)(12)(13)]

Argyll and Bute

	men	women	children	total
Conival Presbytery				
Dunoon				0
Kilmodan				0
Kilfinan				0
Lochgoilhead				0
Strachur				0
Rothsay				0
Kingarth	1			1
Inverchaolin				0
Kintyre Presbytery				
Campbeltown and Southend				60
Killean	14	10	23	47
Kilcalmonell	25			25
Kilbride in Arran				0
Kilmory in Arran			No return	
Gigha	7			7
Jura				20
Skipness				0
Kilarrow in Islay	1			1
Kildalton in Islay				0
Kilchomen in Islay	3			3
Inverary Presbytery				
Inverary				0
North Knapdale	1	2	3	6
South Knapdale	2	2	6	10
Craignash			No return	
Glassary			No return	
Kilmartin			No return	
Lorn Presbytery				
Kilbrandon				0
Ardchattan			No return	
Kilninver				0

	men	women	children	total
Kilchrenan			No return	
Glenorchy	2			2
Lismore	2	1	1	5
Kilmore			No return	

Mull Presbytery

Coll			No return	
Torosay			No return	
Tiree			No return	
Morvern			No return	
Ardnamurchan			No return	
Kilfinichan			No return	
Kilninian			No return	
			Total	187

By a subsequent report from the Sheriff, from the Parish of Kilmory

	58	43		
			Total	288

<u>Ross-shire</u>

	men	women	children	total
Contin	2	1	2	5
Fodderty	1		2	3
Dingwall	1	1	2	4
Killearnan	4	3	5	12
Alness	9	3	4	16
Rosskeen	4	4	11	19
Kilmuir Easter	1	1	4	6
Tarbat	4	3	7	14
Edderton	3	2	5	10
Kincardine	20	19	37	76
Loch Broom	9	7	23	39

[N.B. of the above number of 39 who have emigrated from the Parish of Loch Broom 26 persons have gone from Coigach a part of the annexed estates of Cromarty and eleven families more in Coigach have quitted their possessions at Whitsunday last and sold their cattle and effects in order to be ready to sell [sail] out for America at the first opportunity.]

	men	women	children	total
Gairloch	4	4	5	13
Applecross	1	1	3	5
Loch Carron	25	17		42
Lochalsh	12	4	19	35
Letterfearn	8	6	8	22

	men	women	children	total
Croe	11	10	11	32
Uig, Island of Lewis	27	18	40	85
Barvas, Island of Lewis	72	71	134	277
Lochs, Island of Lewis	6	7	5	18
Stornoway, Island of Lewis	36	33	29	98
Total	260	215	356	831

Morayshire

Elgin Presbytery

Elgin	2	3	2	7
Duffus	4	4	6	14

Forres Presbytery

Forres	6	1		7
Dyke	2	2	7	11
Edinkillie	11	7	20	38
Dallas	1	1	2	4

Aberdour Presbytery

Knockando	1	1	5	7
Dundurcas (Rothes)	7	7	29	43
Inveravon (Banffshire)	1			1

Abernethy Presbytery

Abernethy (Inverness-shire)	3	1	4	8
Cromdale	1			1
Duthhill (Inverness-shire)	3			3

Nairnshire

Nairn Presbytery

Nairn	2	2	7	11
Ardclach	17	12	24	53
Auldearn	4	2		6
Cawdor	4		2	6
Croy (Inverness-shire)	1	1	5	7
Total of both shires	70	44	113	227

The *Scot's Magazine*'s close monitoring of emigrant departures and official government surveys carried out between 1770 and 1775 reveal that
Highlanders were leaving primarily from mainland areas in Argyll, Inverness-shire, Sutherland, Caithness, and Wester Ross and from the Hebridean
islands of Lewis, Skye, Jura, Islay, and Arran (Table 1).[3] Most of them were
heading for North Carolina and New York. However, some Highlanders
opted instead for the Island of St. John (later Prince Edward Island) and
Pictou, Nova Scotia, although their numbers were relatively small. But following Britain's defeat in the American War of Independence, the situation
reversed dramatically.

Most of the Highland emigration in the late eighteenth and early nineteenth centuries was directed towards the colonies to the north, which
remained under British control. Highland communities were formed in the
Glengarry district of eastern Upper Canada immediately after the American
war ended in 1783, and they, together with the established settlements in
the Maritimes provinces, continued to attract large groups of Highlanders
over the following decades. As the influx grew, Prince Edward Island, Nova
Scotia, Cape Breton, and eastern Upper Canada would each develop major
centres of Highland culture. Although some Lowlanders arrived during this
early period, their numbers were relatively small. Newspaper shipping
reports, customs records, and other documentary evidence can account for
about 15,500 Scots who emigrated to British America between 1770 and
1815, and of this total some 79 per cent came from the Western Highlands
and Western Isles.[4]

The upheaval caused by the introduction of large, commercial sheep farms
in the Highlands was one of the main driving forces behind emigration. Estate
tenants were being evicted from the late eighteenth century to make way for
sheep, and understandably they felt alarmed over what the future held for
them. In addition to being displaced, many of them also had to endure poor
working conditions and oppressive landlords. Yet their landlords required their
labour and had no wish to lose them. Sheep farming was a new venture, but
traditional Highland products, such as kelp, fish, cattle, and timber, were
ongoing sources of profit and required an extensive workforce.[5]

Perthshire and Argyll were in the forefront of the movement towards
sheep farming, having large operations in place from the 1770s (Figure 3).
When sheep reached the parish of Callander in Perthshire, "the small

Figure 3: Reference Map of Scotland

◆ Embarkation Port

possessors were swept entirely away and all the business of the farm was managed by a shepherd or two and three or four dogs."[6] According to the Presbyterian minister, "those with money to pay their passage" to North America were emigrating in great numbers by the early 1790s, "carrying away their riches. Some, who had no money, bartered their services for a number of years, to obtain a passage; and others of less spirit, the dregs of the people in this predicament, have remained at home and sought asylum in the villages."[7]

Although much of the Highland exodus was a reaction to large-scale clearances that were making way for sheep farms, a minister from Knoydart pointed out that "this is not the only cause; the high rents demanded by landlords, the increase of population and the flattering accounts received from friends in America do also contribute to the evil."[8] By 1802, sheep farming extended into large inland stretches of Perthshire, Argyll, and Inverness-shire, taking in the entire west coast from Oban to Loch Broom, including much of Mull, but it arrived in Sutherland only after the turn of the century.[9] Thus were set in motion the time sequences that would trigger major emigration surges from different parts of the Highlands. Few Highlanders had the option available to Lowlanders in the more fertile regions of the country of finding alternative agricultural work near home. Some Highlanders reacted to their changed circumstances by supplementing their incomes with seasonal employment, particularly in lowland towns and cities, but relatively fewer migrated to other parts of Britain permanently.[10]

Meanwhile, in the kelp-making Hebridean islands and in parts of the west coast mainland, the opposite was happening. Landlords sought to retain their tenantry to produce kelp, and so population grew with rising demand for the product. Here, land was being sub-divided into ever smaller lots to accommodate the large numbers of people who were employed extracting kelp from seaweed.[11] While the manufacture of kelp, which was used in the production of soap and glass, was highly profitable for landlords, it provided unpleasant and poorly paid jobs to the people who did the work. Kelp-making was, according to Robert Brown, the factor of Clanranald's Uist estates, "a dirty and disagreeable employment" that required a man "to go out at the ebb of the sea to his middle in salt water" to cut seaweed, then to go "up to his neck in that element" to drag it ashore on the incoming tide. "From that extreme he is obliged to go and suspend himself over the burning [of the kelp]" as the ash is extracted from a kelp kiln.[12]

No wonder that in a kelp-making area like Skye Dr. Samuel Johnson found so much interest in emigration when he visited in 1773. He heard songs in "words which I did not understand. I inquired the subjects of the songs, and was told of one ... composed by one of the Islanders that was going in this epidemical fury of emigration to seek his fortune in America."[13]

Gribune-head in Mull. The smoke shown was produced by the burning of seaweed to make kelp. From William Daniell, *Voyage Round Great Britain,* Volume III (1818). *Courtesy of Birmingham Central Library, United Kingdom.*

He later saw in Portree harbour – "waiting to dispeople Skye by carrying the natives away to America" – the *Nestor,* one of two vessels that took nearly four hundred people to North Carolina in that year.[14] And in 1790, when he recalled the exodus since 1771, the Reverend William Bethune, minister of Duirinish, described the eight ships "which have sailed from this Island [Skye] with emigrants ... at very moderate computation carried away ... 2,400 souls and £24,000 sterling, ship freights included."[15]

The zeal to emigrate had also taken hold in Lewis, another kelp-producing island, especially in the parishes of Uig, Barvas, and Stornoway.[16] Some 840 people were being lost to North America in 1773, and far more were expected to follow.[17] When he heard of these developments, Lord Seaforth,[18] their landlord, rushed to Lewis from his London home "to treat with the remainder of his tenants" that summer, but to no avail.[19] After learning that some Lewis people had got as far as Dorset in May of the following year, he consulted his advisers about "stopping the emigrations at London."[20] The plan was to prevent people with outstanding debts from leaving the country. Later that summer his managers were hoping that "the proper letter will be wrote to the Collector and Controller [of Customs] at Stornoway about the emigrants."[21] However, Lord Seaforth's factor advised him that "fair words and mild usage is much recommended to be used to those who are thought to be at the point of emigration," and this message seems to have stopped his lordship from being overly coercive.[22]

It was a similar story in North Uist, from where two hundred people were reported to have emigrated to North Carolina and New York between 1771 and 1775. Their letters back home spoke of "living in a state of much greater affluence with less labour, having the facility of procuring a property for a small sum of money, and the produce they can call their own, and from which their removal does not depend on the will of capricious masters."[23] Writing twenty years later, a disapproving Presbyterian minister observed that "the implicit faith given to these accounts made them [the North Uist people] resolve to desert their native land and to encounter the dangers of crossing the Atlantic to settle in the wilds of America."[24]

In some Roman Catholic districts of the Western Isles and in west Inverness-shire, religious persecution was yet another factor that drove the growing exodus. When MacDonald of Clanranald put his Roman Catholic tenantry under pressure to convert to Presbyterianism, he stimulated large numbers to leave. The ill-feeling he engendered, together with rising rents, caused many people to emigrate. Sympathizing with the tenants and feeling aggrieved about his own prospects in the Clanranald estates, John MacDonald of Glenaladale, a prominent tacksman, organized their departures with the assistance of the Scottish Catholic Church.[25] Following the introduction of the new farming methods, the tacksman's traditional social and military roles were becoming increasingly

Scotchfort Monument at Prince Edward Island commemorating the arrival of a large group of Roman Catholic Highlanders in 1772. *Courtesy of PEI Public Archives and Records Office, Charlottetown Camera Club Collection Acc. 2320/3–9.*

obsolete.[26] Having a reduced status and higher rents to pay, many of them emigrated, taking with them large numbers of tenants from their former estates. In MacDonald of Glenaladale's case, he emigrated to Prince Edward Island in 1772, with two hundred Roman Catholics from the Clanranald estates in mainland west Inverness-shire and the islands of South Uist and Eigg plus nearby Barra.

Disquiet was also being felt in many of the Highland estates that had been seized by the Crown in Culloden's aftermath.[27] The high rents being charged by the Board of Forfeited Estates, which managed the estates, acted as yet another stimulus to emigration. Objecting to the excessive rents, contingents from the Coigach peninsula near Loch Broom in Wester Ross and from the Lovat estates in east Inverness-shire signed up with the Philadelphia Land Company in 1773 to go to Pictou, Nova Scotia.[28] While they were undoubtedly welcome additions to Nova Scotia's population, Governor Francis Legge felt it necessary to express his concern over the loss of 190 of "the King's subjects" to emigration.[29] Hardly a warm welcome! Legge reflected the dilemma facing the British government at the time. Its anti-emigration policy required it to lament the loss of people, and yet it needed loyal British emigrants for its North American colonies. It would have to face up to this quandary eventually, but in 1773 its principal

Artistic representation of the *Hector* landing at Pictou Harbour
in 1773, from John Murray, *Scots in Canada* (London: 1911).
Courtesy of Library and Archives Canada NLC 22627.

aim was to contain the emigration crisis, which appeared to be spiralling out of control.

Thus the forces driving the exodus from the Highlands and Islands were powerful and diverse. Writing in 1772, a commentator from the Island of Harris declared that "a spirit of emigration," which had "got in among the people," was set to "carry the entire inhabitants of the Highlands and Islands of Scotland to North America.[30] That same year "a gentleman of very considerable property in the Western Isles" claimed that "the people who have emigrated from this poor corner of Scotland since the year 1768 have carried with them £10,000 in specie."[31] As the political climate became more frenzied, the *Scots Magazine* expressed the hope, late in 1773, that "the emigrations will come under the consideration of parliament next session," but no action was taken.[32] Instead, the British government decided to collect more data in order to identify the scale and causes of the exodus.

In his April 1774 report, Thomas Miller, the Lord Justice Clerk, expressed concern that "this spirit of emigration" was spreading "to the Low Country and in the manufacturing towns and villages of Scotland and what is most alarming, it seems to affect not only the lower classes of people but some of the better sort of farmers and mechanics, who are in good circumstances and can live very comfortably at home." He feared that people would soon leave "not from the motive of getting bread, but from the motive of attaining a better situation in America than they can attain in their own country."[33]

Even more details came to light when customs officials were ordered by the government to produce detailed passenger lists for emigrant crossings from Scotland to North America in 1774–75.[34] Nearly 3,000 Scots gave high rents as their main reason for leaving. Large family groups were quitting the Highlands, while emigrants from the Lowlands were mainly young men with artisan skills, many of them travelling alone. As the government pondered a suggestion made in 1775 by Sir James Grant, an Inverness-shire landlord, to prevent the departure of emigrant ships, the American rebellion was under way, and, following the outbreak of war between Britain and what would have become the United States, the exodus was halted.[35]

With the ending of the American Revolution in 1783, the British government relocated a group of Inverness-shire Loyalists from New York state to an important defensive position close to the American border. Having been moved there to guard the area against a feared invasion from the United States, they created the remarkable Glengarry communities, named after the

Glen Garry estate in Scotland, from which they first originated. Following the division of the old province of Quebec into Upper and Lower Canada in 1791, these settlements would fall within the eastern extremity of Upper Canada.[36]

As far as the government was concerned this was to be a one-off exercise. Moving Highland families from the United States to Upper Canada was all that had been intended. But Inverness-shire emigrants came in droves to join the first settlers. Subsequent emigration brought many more people from Knoydart, Glen Garry, Glen Moriston, and Urquhart parishes – the very areas that had lost emigrants to New York before the war. A report written in the early 1800s revealed that many ships were taking emigrants from Arisaig, Glenelg, and Fort William to Quebec.[37] They were undoubtedly heading for Upper Canada. The "emigration fever," which so concerned the opponents of emigration, soon took hold in the neighbouring areas of Moidart, Glenelg, Loch Eil, Kilmorack, and Kiltarlity. By 1806, it was difficult to find a single parish in west Inverness-shire that had not experienced relatively high levels of emigration.[38]

An anonymous commentator believed that 4,000 people, mostly Roman Catholics, had left the lands "belonging to MacDonnel of Glengarry" between 1773 and 1803, all having emigrated to Upper Canada.[39] Judging from the number of transatlantic passengers reported in newspaper shipping reports, passenger lists, and Scottish customs records, it would seem that this figure has a ring of truth (Appendix I).[40] And yet, when considered in the context of the overall population of Upper Canada, which reached 71,000 by 1806, their numbers were miniscule.[41] Nevertheless Highlanders were present in substantial numbers during Upper Canada's formative years. The follow-on emigration from Inverness-shire was a most unwelcome development for the British government, which did everything in its power to stop it but failed. Meanwhile Glengarry residents prospered. Their culture and Gaelic language set them apart from the rest of the local population, and, being fiercely loyal to the British Crown, they played an invaluable role in safeguarding Upper Canada as British-held territory.

Emigration had great appeal because it offered people an escape from poverty and oppression. It held out the prospect of land ownership and a better standard of living.[42] And it had another advantage as well. Highlanders could have opted for work in the manufacturing industries of the Lowlands, but this would come at a price. They would lose their cultural identity once

Present-day ruins of St. Raphaels Roman Catholic Church, Glen-
garry, Ontario. The first St. Raphaels Church had been built in 1789.
This later church, built in the 1820s, was destroyed by fire in 1970.
Photograph by Geoff Campey.

they became absorbed within the melting pot of an urban society. However,
by emigrating to British America, they could transplant their communities
intact and continue with their traditional way of life. Faced with these two
alternatives, it is little wonder that so many Highlanders chose to emigrate.
Those who fretted about the harm being done to Scotland by the loss of so
many people could not halt the exodus, try as they did.

Report after report provided evidence of the growing loss of people from
the Highlands and Islands. George Dempster, who had "made a little excur-
sion to the counties where the spirit of emigration seems the strongest ...
from Fort William to Tain by Inverness," reported that 3,000 people had left
during the summer of 1784.[43] And emigrants had firm views on where they
wished to settle. In 1790, when the *British Queen* of Greenock arrived in
Quebec with eighty-seven destitute Inverness-shire emigrants, they insisted
on being taken to Glengarry despite an offer made by a Mr. P.L. Panet to
accommodate them in his Argenteuil seigneury "without any assistance
from the government excepting the loan of six bateaux ... to transport them
from Quebec to his estate."[44] Quebec's executive council agreed reluctantly
to finance the more expensive option of taking them to Glengarry.[45] The
imminent departure of the *Ajax* for North Carolina with five hundred souls
from Skye and Lewis may have influenced the council's decision. After all,
the 1790 arrivals were "a valuable acquisition" who might be lost to the
United States if they did not get their own way.[46]

So it went on. Writing in 1791, the secretary of the Society for Propagating Christian Knowledge reported that since 1772 "no less than sixteen vessels full of emigrants have sailed from the western parts of the counties of Inverness and Ross alone ... carrying with them, in specie, at least £38,400 sterling."[47] And further north, clergymen in the Orkney Islands were complaining about the loss of Orcadian men to the Hudson's Bay Company fur-trading operations in Rupert's Land:

> Nothing however contributes so much to the hurt of this place as the resort of the Hudson's Bay Company's ships to Stromness [in Orkney] and their engaging lads from this country. A few lads returning with money make excellent recruits for the Company's service ... Young men who have learned any of the trades needed there have good wages and often come home with considerable sums of money.[48]

While such workers, being on fixed contracts, would have had their passages to North America paid by the company, most emigrants had to finance their own crossings. As the Highlands and Islands seethed with talk of emigration, entrepreneurially inclined men, such as Major Simon Fraser, stepped forward to offer ship crossings. When the writer Patrick Campbell met Fraser at Fort William in 1792, he learned that Fraser had six hundred people "on his list, ready to embark for America," and that eight hundred more were preparing to follow the next year:

> which I knew was not owing to wantonness or desire of change of situation on their part, but principally to the inhumanity and oppression of their landlords, who either distressed them, or screwed up the rents to a pitch they could not possibly pay. Of this I could not be mistaken as I knew many of the people in this predicament, and some of them I has seen wringing their hands, crying most bitterly, deploring their miserable families and the state they were reduced to.[49]

Fraser was accused of cynically profiting from the zeal to emigrate, but he was responding to a real demand for affordable crossings. His success in finding passengers for his ships owed much to the good contacts that he had with tacksmen on Highland estates. This told him where the enthusiasm to emigrate was greatest, and, having lived near Pictou since his childhood days, he also knew about pioneer life. His ships ran so frequently to Pictou that he soon acquired the nickname of "Nova Scotia." To ram this point home, Edward Fraser of Reelig, one of his growing band of critics, claimed that Simon Fraser single-handedly "peopled" Nova Scotia with the Scots who had sailed on his ships.[50]

Reported to have "made a trade of the business since 1790," Simon Fraser first rose to prominence a year later when he took a group of Roman Catholics from the Western Isles to Pictou.[51] A total of 650 people were taken in two ships, one of them the *Dunkenfield* (or *Dunkeld*). But they arrived "in a wretched condition – the greatest part at this time are in want of sustenance and that number will daily increase."[52] Fearing that they might move on to South Carolina, Nova Scotia's lieutenant-governor, John Parr, took them under his wing and paid for their provisions himself. "My heart bleeds for the poor wretches and I am distressed to know what to do with them. If they are not assisted they must inevitably perish upon the beach where they [are] now hutted; humanity says that cannot be the case in a Christian country."[53]

Predictably, anti-emigration campaigners in Scotland seized on news of their suffering to highlight the perils and misfortunes of pioneer life. According to the *Caledonian Mercury*, the emigrants had been inveigled. "None have been enriched but the agents, and at the expense of the public."[54] But the newspaper failed to report all of the facts. The emigrants had actually arrived safely and in good health. Parr gave them food to survive their first winter, and when Father Angus MacEachern (later bishop), who was based in Prince Edward Island, learned of their plight, he hurried across to Pictou to provide them with spiritual as well as practical help.[55] A decade after their arrival, a visiting priest found that most of them had settled in the Antigonish area, where they were living "comfortably if they have been in any ways industrious."[56]

Even though Fraser's contacts with local tacksmen had given him some respectability, he was an easy target for Scottish establishment figures who continually vilified him, claiming that he preyed on vulnerable people for economic gain. And the emigrants themselves were castigated for their alleged foolishness and avarice in wishing to emigrate. Yet, despite the vitriolic

criticisms that both emigrants and ship contractors had to endure, the loss of
people to the so-called evil of emigration continued to gather pace. Having
reached new peaks in 1790–91, it rose again a decade later. The war between
Britain and France, which began in 1793, curtailed the exodus temporarily,
but with the resumption of a brief peace in 1801 yet another great surge in
emigration began, and a year later Scotland was in a general state of panic.

By 1802, the Highlands and Islands were buzzing with reports of emigrants who had left or were about to leave.[57] Advertisements were being
"publicly stuck up on the Church doors of some parishes and some of the
Catholic chapels" tempting emigrants "by the payment of a reduced
demand for their passage."[58] All of the Islands "from the butt of the Lewis
to Barra Head" were reported to be "in a ferment" despite measures taken
"to avert the spirit of emigration ... but it appears to have too deep a root."[59]
Sir James Grant learned from his factor that "the spirit of emigration to
America" was "creeping in amongst the lower classes of people" on his
Urquhart estate in southwest Inverness-shire.[60] And the urge was also
claiming recruits in Argyll, especially in North Knapdale.[61] In the midst of
this pandemonium, customs officials were ordered to provide the Lord
Advocate with full details of all emigrant-ship departures.[62]

It soon became clear that four ships were due to sail in June 1802 from
Greenock and Port Glasgow with 1,032 Highlanders and that a further
three were being fitted with passenger berths at Saltcoats before going on
to Fort William to collect even more people.[63] In addition, eleven vessels
were preparing to take out 3,300 emigrants in the spring of 1803, and
20,000 more people were due to leave that summer. And to make matters
worse, considerable capital was leaving the country. People were said to be
taking out £10 on average and some "a good deal beyond £1,000."[64]
Edward Fraser of Reelig, the customs collector at Greenock, confirmed
everyone's worst fears about who was leaving: "The most spirited – and
those who are in good circumstances," and "some very opulent people
go."[65] Faced with this evidence, the Highland Society proclaimed that "emigration is fast approaching to the point of complete depopulation of a large
district of the Kingdom."[66]

It was time to act. The Highland Society quickly seized upon the idea
of calling on the government to regulate passenger-ship crossings as the
best means of ending emigration. By carefully monitoring shipping data, the
society could prove that some emigrant ships had sailed under extreme

conditions of overcrowding. The Pictou-based shipping agent Hugh Dunoon provided them with one of the worst examples ever to be reported. He had supplied a large Inverness-shire group with three ships for their crossings to Pictou in 1801. The *Hope* of Lossie sailed from Ullapool in Loch Broom with one hundred passengers, while the *Dove* of Aberdeen and the *Sarah* of Liverpool sailed from Fort William with a combined total of 569 passengers: "but there is reason to believe that several people followed the vessels after their clearance and went on board on the passage to the Sound of Mull. It is suggested that no fewer than 700 people were conveyed in two vessels from Fort William."[67] Not only was this a very large loss of people from one part of the Highlands, but passengers had been packed like sardines in the ships that left from Fort William.

There were certainly other examples. Three hundred and forty people had been packed into the hold of the 240-ton *Northern Friends* of Clyde when she sailed from Moidart to Sydney, Cape Breton, in 1801, and six hundred people had sailed on the 308-ton *Neptune* of Greenock from Loch Nevis to Quebec in the following year, in what must have been extremely cramped conditions (Appendix I).

But all eyes were on Dunoon. Apparently he had agreed on a formula with customs officials that determined how passenger numbers for children under the age of sixten were to be counted. The formula, which allowed him to compute each child as a fraction of an adult, meant that legally he could pack more people in his ships. Thus, although the *Dove* (186 tons) actually sailed with 219 souls, Dunoon's formula reduced their number to 180.5 full passengers. Similarly, the *Sarah* (372 tons) sailed with 350 souls, but was cleared through customs as carrying 258 full passengers.[68] However, further intelligence revealed many more people came on board the two ships after customs clearance. This was irrefutable evidence that Dunoon's ships had greatly exceeded their passenger limits. The Highland Society now had the ammunition it needed to convince the government of the need for tighter regulation. Faced with this evidence, in April 1803, the House of Commons appointed a Select Committee on Emigration that was to consider what action to take. [69]

Arming itself with ship tonnage statistics and passenger numbers, the Highland Society had produced a devastating critique of extreme overcrowding, which it likened to conditions on board slave ships. The society's findings, together with concerns over the loss of men who might otherwise fight in the impending war with France, persuaded the Select Committee of the need to intervene. Acting with great speed, the House accepted the committee's advice and approved the Passenger Act, 1803, only a month after it formed the committee. The new legislation specified a minimum space requirement of one person for every two tons' burthen (ship's tonnage), an allocation that far exceeded earlier limits, and it stipulated the daily minimum of beef, bread, biscuit or oatmeal, molasses, and water for each passenger.[70] Predictably, Highland landlords heralded the act as a great humanitarian triumph.

Defining a minimum standard of comfort and provisioning on ships was indeed a laudable aim. But this was actually a disingenuous reform. Travelling by sailing vessels was a rough-and-ready business. Temporary decking and sleeping berths were simply hammered into the holds of ships. The unit cost of a fare was kept low by packing more people into the hold. It was a fact of life that poor people endured cramped and uncomfortable conditions for the sake of an affordable fare.[71] Later that summer, Edward Fraser of Reelig confirmed that the new law "has checked emigration and irritated numbers of the disappointed"[72] – exactly what it was intended to do. By greatly reducing the numbers who could sail on a ship of a given tonnage, the act caused fares to double, which in turn reduced the numbers who could afford to emigrate. Whereas before 1802 passages could be obtained for under £5 per person, now they would cost as much as £12,[73] thereby achieving the intended aim of pricing transatlantic travel beyond the reach of ordinary people.

Although a cost barrier was introduced, the underlying factors that drove emigration were still bubbling under the surface. And yet Highland landlords continued to uphold their rigid anti-emigration stance. They saw no inconsistency in making their tenants redundant, while at the same time hampering their attempts to emigrate. Alexander Irvine, a clergyman from Rannoch in Perthshire, summed up their position in *An Inquiry into the Causes and Effects of Emigration from the Highlands and Western Isles of Scotland, with Observations on the Means to be Employed for Preventing It* (1802). He asserted that poor Highlanders were not suffering from "the oppression, exactions or harsh treatment of superiors;" for any discontent they felt arose "from the perturbation of their own mind." It was their "avarice, or the love of money," that drove them to emigrate, and because they were motivated by self-interest they were susceptible to the false promises of shipping agents "who promote the ferment of the people and go about recruiting."

Once "their exaggerations and fictions" were used on people, they worked "like a talisman's wand or an electric shock."[74] However ridiculous such sentiments appear to us today, this condescending diatribe accurately reflected the views of the Scottish establishment.

Like most of his contemporaries, Irvine had the mistaken impression that emigration could be halted by negative propaganda and bluster. Great hopes were also pinned on the public-works schemes being recommended by Thomas Telford, the renowned civil engineer. The belief was that by creating new jobs through such schemes, Highlanders would lose the desire to emigrate and remain at home. One measure which was being promoted through the British Fisheries Society, provided fishing jobs in new villages that were being established. Dr William Porter, who supervised the society's fishing village at Lochbay in Skye,[75] thought that Highlanders should come to his village, rather than adding "strength to other nations by leaving this kingdom."[76] Feeling this to be a "matter of great national importance," he was certain that emigrants were being duped:

> The nation may not feel it, but the people themselves, they who emigrate know not when or where they are going. America is not now what it was, when best known to Highlanders. I mean before the Civil War [*sic*] of 1774 – they found it then a paradise where they had nought to do but pluck and eat; now they shall find it as the land of Egypt in the days of the plagues of Pharaoh.[77]

As far as Porter was concerned, emigrants had to be saved from the scurrilous men who would entice them abroad through forged letters from emigrants and whisk them away with a little "beating up with a bag-pipe and flag," mixed with "vast quantities of spirits," to the detriment of themselves and Scotland.[78]

Men such as Irvine and Porter believed that landlords had a God-given right to manage their estates solely for their own benefit. Fearing depletion of their workforce, landlords opposed emigration, even when their tenants were surplus to their requirements. The ruling classes thought that unemployed Highlanders should simply accept, without complaint, whatever job was offered in some public works scheme somewhere in the Highlands. They were to be fishermen, road or bridge builders, or canal diggers, and that was that. The elite never asked whether the people concerned actually

Photograph of a portrait of Thomas Douglas, Fifth Earl of Selkirk, believed to be by Sir Henry Raeburn. *Courtesy of Toronto Reference Library, J. Ross Robertson Collection.*

wanted to do these jobs. Nor did they inquire whether emigration offered them a better alternative.

But one very prominent man did ask these questions. Thomas Douglas, the 5th Earl of Selkirk, was the first eminent Scot to consider colonization from the common man's point of view. No one else of his class came close to understanding the issues involved. His liberal views placed him well ahead of his time, and in many respects he would have been far better suited to our present era. Shocked by what he had seen of the poor and destitute during his travels in the Highlands and in Ireland, he advanced arguments in favour of emigration. He believed that emigration enabled poor people to achieve a far better life and that, by moving to British North America, they actually strengthened British interests overseas. Here was a wealthy aristocrat who transcended and challenged the world of the rich and powerful. He had grasped the new concepts of social justice and liberty, which flowed from the Scottish Enlightenment,[79] and sided with the people over the landlords.

A "hands-on" aristocrat with liberal views and a passion to establish successful pioneer communities, Selkirk was completely out of step with the political and social climate of his day. Even people who sympathized with his aims were puzzled by his desire to devote his life and family inheritance to colonization schemes. But he had correctly anticipated the zeal for emigration from the Highlands and Islands. He could see that it was "an unavoidable result of the state of the country arising from causes above all control," and he offered people a way out.[80] He held out the prospect of a new life in British North America. Failing to win government backing for his ventures, he financed their relocation costs entirely from his own resources.

Selkirk made it his life's work to assist poor Highlanders in emigrating. In 1803, he and the eight hundred Highlanders he recruited, mainly from Skye, founded the important Belfast settlements in Prince Edward Island. A year later a much smaller Highland community was established through his efforts at Baldoon (later Wallaceburg) in western Upper Canada. His third venture took him to Rupert's Land, where recruits from Sutherland founded settlements at Red River (later Winnipeg), in the heart of this fur-trading region. This last project would have far-reaching consequences for Canada's development. Yet, while Selkirk quickly won the support of some of Edinburgh's intellectuals, his views and methods were fiercely opposed by Highland landlords, who thought him foolhardy and obstinate and fought him every inch of the way.

Selkirk was accused of exploiting the weak and vulnerable for his own selfish ends – allegations that did his reputation considerable harm. Yet, however much he was reviled by the landlords, public attitudes began to shift slowly in his favour. A lone voice at the beginning, he reached a turning point when his *Observations on the Present State of the Highlands* (1805) began to influence opinion formers. Robert Brown, the Clanranald factor, immediately countered with *Strictures and Remarks on the Earl of Selkirk's Observations on the Present State of the Highlands*, which sought to discredit Selkirk's arguments, but he failed to impress anyone.[81] Brown simply had no answers to the weighty intellectual arguments in Selkirk's book, despite attempting a point-by-point refutation. Nor was he able to discredit the very visible colonizing successes being achieved by Selkirk's settlers in Belfast, Prince Edward Island.[82] Arriving in 1803 with eight hundred frightened and sceptical Highlanders, Selkirk broke through much confusion and conflict and within a month had the new arrivals building houses and clearing land.[83] His great wealth enabled him to turn his intellectual theories into practice, although the staggering sums involved left his wife wondering whether their son would ever live to see his inheritance.[84]

Selkirk succeeded in signing up the eight hundred Highland Scots for his Belfast venture in 1803 because he had correctly read the mood of the people. Exaggerating the numbers somewhat, Edward Fraser of Reelig reported that "the four ships with 1,200 passengers" sent by Selkirk to Prince Edward Island "will elude the [Passenger] Act."[85] Thanks to Selkirk's careful planning, they certainly did evade the Act. Working frantically

Memorial to the Scottish emigrants who arrived with Lord Selkirk in Belfast, Prince Edward Island in 1803. *Photograph by Geoff Campey.*

behind the scenes to speed up the necessary paperwork, Selkirk managed to get his recruits to Prince Edward Island before the higher fares came into effect, and this no doubt contributed to the large response. In fact, it probably saved his venture. The original intention was that his Highlanders would go to Upper Canada, but wishing to contain the rising tide of emigration, the government, panicked and withdrew its support at the last minute. The persistent Selkirk salvaged his venture by persuading the government to let him purchase land in Prince Edward Island instead. So, having sold his recruits on Upper Canada, he then had somehow to convince them at the eleventh hour that Prince Edward Island was an even better place. In spite of much resistance over the sudden change in plan, Selkirk's promise that he would not increase the price of their fares mattered more than the change in destination, and in the end most of his recruits agreed to go with him to the Island.

Having come to terms with the loss of eight hundred people, Highland landlords had to face ever more worrying developments. As the good news from Belfast percolated back to Scotland, growing numbers of followers left the Highlands and Islands for Prince Edward Island. And many of them sailed on ships that had been supplied by James Robertson, one of Selkirk's agents. With his involvement in the Island's timber trade and his wide-ranging contacts in the Highlands, Robertson was ideally placed to organize their departures. Like Selkirk, he was an articulate man who understood Highlander grievances. When the *Inverness Journal* claimed that he caused impressionable Highlanders to imagine "a lairdship and an air-built castle of his own in Prince Edward Island," he countered by saying that he took particular pleasure in alleviating the suffering of so many people "from that abject servility in which they were maintained on several Highland estates":

> I have the pleasing reflection of ... having prevented their going to the American States and of having furnished them with the means of getting to a British settlement, where, if they are industrious, for idleness meets with no reward, they shall become their own masters, and not be considered slaves of other men, not born to toil under humiliating and rigorous privations.[86]

As the war of words continued, more and more people sailed away on Robertson's ships. By 1808, his activities were causing considerable consternation at Blair Athol, where it was claimed that he "has lately carried off about 700 whom he agrees to transport to Prince Edward Island at a rate of £9 a piece, upon which he will make a profit of £5 a head, independent of the profit on the sale of land or by the bondage to which some of them engage themselves."[87] Gilbert, second Earl of Minto, did not think that Selkirk had "been directly implicated in this system of kidnapping," clearly not appreciating that Robertson was acting for him. Yet, while his critics railed against him, Robertson maintained that he had offered reasonable terms and blamed the high fares on the new legislation that required him to stock more food and provide more spacious accommodation.

Despite the best efforts of the anti-emigration propagandists, high fares, and the wars raging between Britain and France, Highlanders made their way to Prince Edward Island in ever-increasing numbers.[88] At least six hundred of them reached the Island in 1806, and as they did their departures attracted far more interest than was normal. Seeking to monitor the crossings more carefully, the authorities produced passenger lists for the 1806 crossings of the *Rambler* of Leith, the *Humphreys* of London, the *Isle of Skye* of Aberdeen, the *Spencer* of Newcastle, and the *Elizabeth and Ann* of Newcastle and for the 1808 crossing of the *Clarendon* of Hull (Appendix I).[89] When the *Rambler* of Leith was wrecked in 1807 near Newfoundland, during a crossing from Thurso to Pictou, 138 emigrants and crew members were lost.[90] And yet the influx continued. The *Catherine* of Leith and *Phoenix* arrived in 1810 with three hundred more Highlanders seeking a new life in Prince Edward Island.[91]

However, with the ending of the Napoleonic Wars in 1815, public opinion became more favourably inclined towards emigration. With the deepening economic recession in Scotland, even the landlords began to be won over. The growing crisis transformed the political climate and created conditions that favoured emigration as a vehicle for solving Britain's social ills. The very landlords who had earlier sought to discredit Selkirk were now grasping at his ideas with great eagerness. Amazingly, John Campbell, who as law agent for Lord Macdonald had been closely associated with the Highland Society's anti-emigration campaigns, also changed sides.[92] And, by 1815, he was singing Selkirk's praises, "Lord Selkirk's book upon the subject of emigration and of the population in the Highlands contains many principles and remarks which are well-founded and which have been evinced since that publication ... His book was received at the time with some prejudice and excited considerable opposition. But it has been found that it contains much of truth in it."[93] When he prepared this tribute, Campbell was in charge of a major government-sponsored scheme that took hundreds of Scots to Upper Canada. Times were changing.

The scheme being managed by Campbell arose from the American invasion of 1812–14, which, though repulsed, had demonstrated the need for stronger defensive measures. Having nearly lost its North American colonies to the United States, the British government was desperate to minimize the continuing threat from the south. In a remarkable about-turn it shed its anti-emigration policies and instead actively promoted emigration from Scotland to Canada with public funds. It introduced a subsidized emigration scheme in 1815, which was targeted at both Highlanders and Lowlanders. Seven hundred Scots received free transport, free provisions, and free land in a scheme that relocated them to key defensive locations in eastern Upper Canada.[94] Defensive concerns had caused the government to do what would have been regarded as unthinkable in earlier years. Predictably, the scheme sparked off a huge demand throughout Scotland for further publicly aided emigration, but this was not forthcoming.

Therefore, 1815 marked the beginning of a new era. Emigration was seen to have its uses, and its appeal was spreading rapidly throughout Scotland. Before then, most emigrants had originated from the northwest Highlands and Western Isles, but now Lowlanders began arriving in great numbers. With the opening up of North America's timber trade, transatlantic shipping services were becoming more regular and fares were decreasing. The doubling of already high duties on European timber in 1811 priced it out of the market and paved the way for the North American timber trade. Timber exports to Scotland soared, and as they did more ships left Scotland for Charlottetown, Pictou, Halifax, Saint John, and Quebec. By 1816, all major Scottish ports were trading with British North America, and shippers were offering space on their vessels to emigrants wishing to cross the Atlantic.

Three

PUSH, PULL, AND
OPPORTUNITY

*I intend to emigrate from this country for America, the state of
this country being deplorable bad so that scarcely a
livelihood can be procured.*[1]

IKE MANY OTHER SCOTS OF the time, William Brodie of Lochwin-
nock (Renfrewshire) was planning to emigrate to British America.
Because of a downturn in his work prospects, he was facing a grim
future. He lived in the very heart of Scotland's cotton industry, centred in
the west Lowland counties of Lanarkshire, Renfrewshire, and north Ayrshire.[2] Greater mechanization was squeezing out many traditional handloom weavers like him. Although new forms of employment were available
in Scotland's growing manufacturing sectors, they were largely dreary,
badly paid factory jobs. William Brodie was one of many people who found
the anticipation of some day owning a farm in British North America far
more attractive than remaining at home. However, before the dream of a
better life could be realized, he had first to overcome the major stumbling
block of raising the money to relocate.

Rapid expansion of the cotton industry beginning in the late eighteenth
century, particularly in and around Glasgow, had initially created a huge
demand for handloom weavers. But with growing use of power looms from
1813 on and the influx of poorly paid Irish workers to the Clyde region,
weavers faced catastrophic conditions.[3] Their status and self-esteem as self-
employed artisans had once been considerable.[4] Over the previous fifteen
years their wage rates had fallen from twenty-five shillings a week to five.

Now they were working night and day for a pittance, and their families were starving.[5]

As the economic situation worsened, Lord Bathurst, secretary of state for the colonies, was hatching a plan that would offer a lifeline to the distressed weavers, but his primary motivation was not humanitarian. There was remarkably little sympathy for the poor at the time. Bathurst was being driven solely by colonial interests. The view in Whitehall was that Upper Canada would be lost to the Americans unless some action was taken to bolster its defensive capability. After the lessons of the War of 1812–14, when Britain came perilously close to losing its North American colonies, the government knew that it could not depend on the loyalty of the settlers of American origin who formed much of Upper Canada's population. So it became a case of discouraging Americans and encouraging British immigrants. The Rideau Valley, just west of Glengarry County, was identified as being of particular strategic importance, and this is where future immigrants were to be concentrated. And in addition to financing these new settlements, the government also funded an internal waterway, later the Rideau Canal, to act as an extra defensive measure (Figure 4).

Entrance of the Rideau Canal, Bytown, Upper Canada, 1839, watercolour by Henry Francis Ainslie (1803–79). The canal, which linked Kingston with Bytown (later renamed Ottawa), provided a secure route between Upper and Lower Canada. It was completed in 1832. *Courtesy of Library and Archives Canada C-000518.*

As a consequence, emigration was no longer regarded as the great evil that had to be eradicated. The intense hostility to emigration had gone, and the government was now about to endorse a limited amount of assisted emigration. None the less it would not encourage emigration for its own sake; instead it would divert those people to Upper Canada who would otherwise be lost to the United States. In other words, the policy was to redirect existing emigrant streams, not to expand them. Moreover Bathurst's 1815 scheme was only ever intended to be a once-only operation. Predictably, there was constant clamouring for further assisted emigration schemes but the government ignored all special pleading, believing that the country's interests were best served by restraining emigration. It certainly was not in the business of promoting it.

Given the long-standing enthusiasm for emigration in the Highlands, and the more recent but fast-growing interest in the southwest Lowlands, it was inevitable that Bathurst would look first to Scotland to provide the necessary recruits for his Upper Canada scheme. Using public funds as an inducement, he attracted seven hundred people – nearly all of them Scots, half Lowlanders and half Highlanders.[6] The large response from Knoydart and Glenelg in Inverness-shire and from Callander and Killin in Perthshire reflected the actual or threatened upheavals being caused by the spread of sheep farming.[7] Although the Lowland participants were far more widely dispersed, the majority were concentrated in the depressed textile districts of the southwest, particularly in Lanarkshire and Ayrshire.

To qualify, families had to provide certificates of good character and make a refundable £16 deposit for each male of sixteen years and over and two guineas for a married woman.[8] If they could pay their deposits, emigrants would receive free transport, one hundred acres of land, food rations, and farm implements. Thus the government's aim was to attract people who could have afforded to pay their relocation costs in the first place. The deposits ensured that no paupers would be selected and provided a strong incentive for settlers to stay in Upper Canada. Anyone drifting across the border to the United States in search of better opportunities would forfeit the deposit.[9] But settlers who remained in Upper Canada would have their money returned.

The seven hundred people who went to Upper Canada in 1815 represented only a tiny fraction of the total number of Scots who wished to emigrate.[10] Hoping to tap this large reservoir of potential emigrants, New

Brunswick's house of assembly offered an assisted emigration scheme of its own that same year. It agreed to pay £1,000 for the purpose of "encouraging immigrants from Great Britain and Ireland by paying passages."[11] In the end, 133 Scots signed up – nearly half of them originating from the two parishes of Kenmore and Callander in Perthshire, with most of the rest coming from the cotton districts in the Clyde region. When they arrived at Saint John that December on the *Favourite* of Saint John, the *Royal Gazette* reported that they had left Scotland "for want of employment and the providence of New Brunswick."[12]

Three passengers paid their own fares, while the others travelled "passage free." Although they were not required to pay deposits, stringent selection criteria favoured families with plenty of

Henry Bathurst, 3rd Earl, who was secretary of state for the Colonies, 1812 to 1827. *Courtesy of Library and Archives Canada C–100707.*

teenage sons and excluded those with infants. The priority was to encourage families that could handle the back-breaking labour that lay ahead.[13] Once again the havoc being caused by advancing sheep farms in the Highlands and greater mechanization in the Lowlands lay behind the enthusiastic response to this scheme.

Soon after the 1815 group reached Upper Canada, the British government was inundated by inquiries from people who wanted to know "whether the government intend to hold out the same encouragement for 1816."[14] The pressure for assisted emigration developed such a head of steam by the spring of 1816 that Bathurst had to instruct his officials to issue public notices stressing that it was no longer government policy "to provide for the conveyance of any further numbers of Scots to North America."[15] Having high hopes of going to Upper Canada in 1816, William Brodie learned from his minister, who "read a paper in the church," that the government was not offering free passages. "Those that wished to go upon their own expenses" would be entitled to some help once they arrived, but this was little comfort to Brodie who simply could not afford the fare.[16] The government was adamant that all future emigrants had to use the "ships in the timber trade."[17] That summer saw the beginning of a two-way trade in timber and emigrants between Quebec and Scotland's major ports that was to last over many decades. The slackening of the space-and-provision requirements of the Passengers Act of 1803, which came into force in 1817, brought fares down to more affordable levels, although they remained a barrier to many people.[18]

Departing from its original intention of restricting aid to the one Rideau Valley scheme, the government was persuaded in 1818 also to offer assistance to the Earl of Breadalbane's tenants in Perthshire. John Campbell, who had supervised the 1815 plan, was the earl's business manager, which probably helps to explain the government's sudden change of mind. The Breadalbane tenants were unhappy. Major clearances had occurred on their estate to make way for sheep farms, and high rents were also a bone of contention.[19] When he visited the area, John McDermid found many tenants "reduced to such an extreme state of poverty as to be unable to procure but one scanty meal per day."[20] Their minds were made up to emigrate. Campbell dismissed them as malcontents who were simply being lured "by news of the good treatment of a few neighbours who went to America under the encouragement of government in 1815."[21] But the earl had to resign himself to the loss of 442 tenants. They did not wish to remain and were desperate to find a better life overseas.

The government came forward with an assistance scheme, while the emigrants raised the required deposit money of £1,234.[22] The plan was not advertised generally and was targeted specifically at this one large group from the Breadalbane estate. In line with government policy of directing emigrants to the new military settlements in the Rideau Valley, they were required to go to Upper Canada, although not everyone agreed.[23] A small group that had intended to settle in Cape Breton ended up in Prince Edward Island, landing there "in a deplorable state of poverty."[24]

While the Breadalbane tenants secured aid, probably along with some behind-the-scenes help from their landlord, the tenantry on the Sutherland estate was not so fortunate. These people too were being displaced to make way for sheep, but their situation was far worse. Evictions had begun from the early 1800s in what was the most extensive of the clearances ever to be carried out in Scotland. Cleared first, in 1807, were the parishes of Lairg and

Farr, followed by Rogart in 1809; the Assynt, Kildonan, and Clyne clearances began in 1812, and these were followed, in 1814–15, by removals in Strathnaver, in the northern part of the estate.[25] Rioting broke out during the Kildonan evictions in 1813, thus bringing particular notoriety upon the factor, Patrick Sellar, who was accused of using excessive brutality.[26] Ninety-seven of the Kildonan people voted with their feet that year by accepting Selkirk's offer of a new life in his Red River Colony, with even more following in 1815.[27] The final stage of the clearance (1819–21) involved the southern parishes of Golspie, Loth, and Dornoch. According to Hugh Miller, by 1823 some 15,000 individuals had been removed "from the interior of Sutherland to its sea coasts or had emigrated to America."[28] Those who remained endured increasing economic distress. "When the fishing and the crops are comparatively abundant they live on the bleak edge of want, while failure in either plunges them into a state of intense suffering."[29]

The Countess of Sutherland's intention in evicting her tenants was simply to reposition them on her estate; she certainly did not want them to emigrate. It was a case of moving people to villages being created along the coast, where they could work in fishing or in industrial jobs. But her tenants saw things differently. William Young could not "account for the emigration from Rogart – there is not a man has been dislocated but with a view to make him better and that in place of having his land in run ridge it may now be in a lot on a nineteen year lease."[30] A great many people quite simply preferred the prospect of joining their fellow countrymen in Nova Scotia to the grinding poverty, uncertainty, and subservience that the Sutherland estate had to offer. News of Nova Scotia's opportunities had drifted back from the first group, which had sailed on the *Hector* in 1773, and from the many other Sutherland people who had followed them during the late eighteenth and early nineteenth centuries.[31]

The growing interest in emigration on the Sutherland estate caught Francis Suther's attention in 1817. One of the estate managers, he had "no doubt [that] many of the inhabitants, who are to be removed from the interior of this part of the [Strath]naver district of the estate, will, rather than settle on the lots to be offered them on the coast, buy a trip to America if they can possibly raise funds to pay for their passages." To his dismay, the dreaded Simon Fraser was supplying the ships: "There is a person at present by the name of Fraser ... I heard yesterday had gone to Strathnaver to endeavour to induce the people to go to America with him. This Fraser is from America and has come to this country for the sole purpose of taking out people."[32]

Suther disapproved of Fraser's search for paying passengers on his estate, but he was even more scathing of a certain Mr. Dudgeon, who appeared to be organizing the exodus. According to Suther, Thomas Dudgeon, a Ross-shire farmer, was forming an association to help people raise funds to emigrate. But "he cares less for the people than any man in Scotland... his forwardness in this business was merely to satisfy an old grudge he has to the family."[33] Being unmoved by the plight of the people and their longing for a better life overseas, Suther initiated a campaign to stop what he viewed as a threatening development.

Dudgeon called a meeting at the Meickle Ferry Inn, in Dornoch, in June 1819, just as the Golspie, Loth, and Dornoch tenants were about to be evicted. The Sutherland and Transatlantic Friendly Association was duly formed. It was a people's movement with the potential to cause great embarrassment. Estate managers had feared that a parliamentary inquiry might be in the offing as a result of mounting criticism of the Sutherland removals. Now Dudgeon was using his group to inflame the situation even more. His views on the injustices of the evictions, which were reported in the *Scotsman*, gave added negative publicity. And when Dudgeon asked that his association be consulted in the allocation of coastal lots that were being offered to tenants who remained on the estate, this was seen as open rebellion. It was a "most impertinent attempt to interfere in the management of private property."[34] Dudgeon had to be stopped.

Estate managers issued orders for notices, signed by a sheriff and two justices of the peace, to be displayed on the doors of parish churches. Tenants were ordered to stay away from Dudgeon's meetings, and if they ignored the notices they were to be intercepted and stopped.[35] People were told that Dudgeon had villainous and subversive aims and that his meetings were illegal. Predictably, these tactics worked. The Transatlantic Friendly Society was disbanded a few months later, and Dudgeon's reputation was in tatters.[36] But the people had the last word. In 1821–22, an unnamed "association at Edinburgh" and unknown sources in Bengal helped 360 Sutherland people to emigrate to Nova Scotia.[37] With this assistance, they purchased hatchets, spades, pick axes, saws, nails, Gaelic bibles, yards of tartan, and barrels of pork to see them through their first winter. The first group left on the *Ossian* of Leith in 1821, while the rest sailed on the *Harmony* of Aberdeen and the *Ruby* of Aberdeen in the following year.[38] The departure of the 1822 group from Cromarty harbour was witnessed by many people: "A vast assemblage of the relatives of these poor emigrants, supposed some thousands, attended to take leave of their friends; and the parting scene was of the most affecting nature, such as to draw tears from the eyes of some of the spectators unconnected with the parties."[39]

It was a tearful departure, but the ending was sweet in the sense that the emigrants acquired large tracts of good farmland in Nova Scotia and soon established thriving Sutherland communities there.

Meanwhile, as the economic situation in Glasgow and Paisley continued to deteriorate, pressure mounted on the government to provide more assisted emigration schemes. Despite the prevailing belief that the exodus should be restrained, Kirkman Finlay, who controlled much of Scotland's cotton industry, suddenly swung his weight in favour of public subsidies in 1820. He argued that unless something was done immediately to relieve the pressure there was a real danger of rioting on the streets of Glasgow. Before he came to this realization, people had hoped that government might be willing to help, but, when they wrote to the Colonial Office seeking financial aid, their requests had always been rejected.

Following the success of the people who had resettled in Upper Canada as a result of the 1815 scheme, weavers had been forming themselves into "Emigration" societies that were modelled on their so-called Friendly Societies.[40] By paying subscriptions into a common fund, Friendly Society members had been able to give themselves a financial cushion to rely on when they fell ill or were injured or when funeral expenses had to be paid. The emigration societies were an extension of this co-operative principle, although the funds needed to finance their emigration costs were considerably greater than the few shillings a year raised by their Friendly Societies. Being unable to finance their relocation themselves, the weavers turned to the government for help. Heart-wrenching petitions poured into the Colonial Office, but to no avail. So the weavers turned to more high-profile measures.

In June 1819, a public meeting on Glasgow Green attracted thousands of unemployed weavers. There they demonstrated their strength of feeling and begged the authorities to provide "the necessary means of transporting all those of the trade who may be disposed to emigrate to the British settlements

in North America."[41] The government responded by offering assisted emigration – not to Upper Canada but to the Cape of Good Hope in Africa.
Through their families and friends who had already emigrated, the weavers
knew what to expect in Upper Canada, but Africa was an unknown quantity.
"When we ask for bread you give us stone the poor weavers may well say,"
said a sympathetic *Inverness Courier* journalist.[42] Africa was firmly rejected.

By this time the depression was stimulating a rising tide of political agitation. People believed that their misery stemmed from bad government
and campaigned for parliamentary reform – especially universal suffrage
and annual parliaments. Those who supported the growing radical movement disapproved of emigration, believing that living conditions could be
improved by better government. But there were many who simply wanted
out, and they were the ones who campaigned for the funds to emigrate.[43]
And soon the situation began to turn very nasty.

In September 1819, a public meeting in Paisley and attracting between
12,000 and 18,000 people ended in a riot. In April of the following year,
posters inciting people to revolt appeared suddenly in Glasgow and Paisley,
as well as in neighbouring towns and villages. At the height of the distur-
bances, a relative of William Brodie reported to a family member in Montreal that "there is a vast number of what they call radicals rising up against
things."[44] Troops were called out to deal with the insurgents in what turned
out to be an abortive uprising.[45]

It was against this background of shared fear of imminent insurrection
that the government acquiesced. That same month local businessmen and
landowners formed the Glasgow Committee on Emigration. Government
backing for assistance was obtained a month later when Lord Archibald
Hamilton, Whig MP for Lanarkshire, and Kirkman Finlay, the Tory MP for
Malmesbury who led the committee, presented the weavers' case before the
House of Commons. A package was established, entitling emigration-
society members to free transportation from Quebec to Upper Canada, a
100-acre grant of land, and loans that had to be cleared within ten years.
However, society members would have to pay for their sea crossings.
Crucial to their success in doing this were the private donations, which
were being chanelled through the Glasgow Committee on Emigration.[46]
Robert Brown, the Duke of Hamilton's factor, acted as the conduit between

the Glasgow committee and the emigration societies, and once funding was available Robert Lamond, the committee's secretary, took charge of shipping arrangements.

A total of 1,100 people from five Lanarkshire emigration societies presented a joint petition to the Colonial Office.[47] However, because the total funds raised in 1820 provided for only eight hundred places, each society had to prune its lists, which it did by requiring members to draw lots. Because the government's terms were initially available just to petitioners from Lanarkshire, only their societies had proliferated. By 1821 Lanarkshire had thirty-one such groups, Renfrewshire three, and Clackmannanshire, Stirlingshire, West Lothian, and Dunbartonshire one each (Table 2). But faced with a petition from Paisley weavers presented by John Maxwell, MP for Renfrewshire, the government relented in the spring of 1821 and extended its scheme to other areas of southwest Scotland. By 1830 there were over one hundred societies, seventeen of them in Renfrewshire.[48] Just over half were in Glasgow, taking their names from the parish, street, or neighbourhood where their members lived.

Table 2

The Scottish Emigration Societies, 1820–21

Glasgow Emigration Societies
  Abercrombie (Friendly), Calton
  Abercrombie Street
  Barrowfield and Anderston (near Bridgeton)
  Barrowfield Road, Calton
  Bridgeton Canadian
  Bridgeton Transatlantic Social Union
  Brownfield and Anderston
  Camlachie
  Glasgow Canadian Emigration (Mutual Cooperation Society) Mile End
  Glasgow Junior Wrights Society for Emigration
  Glasgow Loyal Agricultural Society
  Glasgow Trongate
  Glasgow Union
  Glasgow Union, Hutchison Street
  Glasgow Wright's Society for Emigration
  Highland and Lowland (Gorbals)
  Kirkman Finlay

Muslin Street Society, Bridgeton
North Albion
Spring Bank (two)
St. John's Parish, Calton

Other Lanarkshire Emigration Societies
Anderston and Rutherglen
Cambuslang Canadian
Govan
Hamilton
Kirkfield Bank (Bothwell Parish)
Lanark
Lesmahagow Canadian
Rutherglen Union
Strathhaven and Kilbride (East Kilbride Parish)
Wishawton (Dalserf Parish)

Renfrewshire Emigration Societies
Cathcart
Paisley Townhead
Parkhead (Paisley)

Other Emigration Societies
Alloa (Clackmannanshire)
Balfron (Stirlingshire)
Hopetown Bathgate (West Lothian)
Milton (Dumbartonshire)

Those 2,700 people from Lanarkshire and Renfrewshire who did receive public funds to emigrate to the Rideau Valley settlements in 1820–21 made the transition from skilled artisan to farmer with surprising ease.[49] And the favourable reports that filtered back to Scotland encouraged many more to follow, despite the lack of further government subsidies. William Gourley was "very uneasy to know how all the poor people" back in Scotland "got through the winter [of 1821]. I wish that many of them were here, for they would be able to make themselves comfortable in a short time. Let our friends know that they would do well by taking land."[50] William Miller told his father that he "never thought such a country was here and I wish that I had been some years sooner. You may tell my friends that they need not come here but for farming; no tradesman is hardly wanted at all."[51]

Many weavers had a rural background, having had parents or grandparents who had been raised in the country.[52] As was noted by the Emigration Select Committee, which sat in 1826–27, a "great proportion of the hand

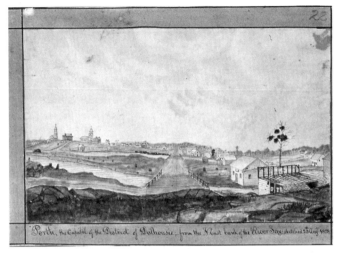

Perth, on the River Tay, 1828. The artist was Thomas Burrowes. The town became the principal administrative centre of the Perth military settlement, which was spread across Bathurst, Drummond and Beckwith townships in Lanark County. *Courtesy of Archives of Ontario C 1-0-0-0-22.*

weavers in Scotland in harvest and hay time work in the field."[53] Therefore, despite the government's initial fears that their seeming unfamiliarity with farming would cause them to fail, they proved highly successful colonizers. After visiting their settlements, John MacTaggart, a Scottish engineer working on the Rideau Canal, concluded that "a Glasgow weaver, although not bred to spade and pick axe ..., makes a much better settler, can build a neat little house for his family and learn to chop with great celerity, so that in a short time nobody should suppose that he had been bred amongst bobbins and shuttles."[54] Far from deploring the loss of their trades, they welcomed the opportunity to become farmers:

> I never was so happy in my life. We have no desire to return to Glasgow to stop there, for we would have to pay a heavy rent and here we have none: in Glasgow I had to labour sixteen or eighteen hours a day and could only earn about six or seven shillings a week – here, I can, by labouring about half that time, earn more than I need. There I was confined to a damp shop – but here I enjoy fresh air.[55]

Another weaver was "very well pleased to handle the axe instead of the shuttle and would not for a good deal give up my present for my past employment. I had to struggle here for a year or two. I had to do so always at home."[56] Glowing accounts of their success abounded. The *Glasgow Courier* thought that it "would be endless to enumerate all the examples that occur."[57] Yet it was careful to point out the scale of the adjustment that weavers had to make. They were exchanging sedentary manual jobs in town or city for hard physical labour in a wilderness:

> The native of this country goes upon new lands without emotion; but to the emigrant it is at first terrific to place himself in the midst of a wood – the trees heavy; not a ray of sunshine able to penetrate; no neighbours, perhaps within several miles, and only an axe in his hand – he is ready to despair. But he has only to persevere a very short time, and apply his strength judiciously and in a few months he will equal a native in felling trees and clearing lands.[58]

In managing the 1820–21 schemes, Robert Lamond had observed that "such is the desire to emigrate, that ... double the number of persons would have embarked, if the means of transportation had been afforded.[59] Public subsidies had raised hopes across Scotland, not just in the west Lowlands. Henceforth the government was never going to be able to satisfy the overall demand. In the following year, one hundred Argyll families requested "a small grant of land and small pecuniary help from H.M. Government similar to what is given to families in Lanarkshire and Renfrewshire, only they would be satisfied with a smaller sum."[60] The Duke of Montrose wrote to the Colonial Office on behalf of his Stirlingshire tenants who wished to emigrate to Upper Canada. And pressure for aid was also intensifying in the north-west Highlands and Western Isles. Archibald MacNiven, principal emigration agent for that region, petitioned on behalf of "many distressed families" after "hearing that your Lordship [Lord Bathurst] encouraged lists to be made and signed by poor people in certain districts of the Highlands."[61] However, there were no lists, and all such requests were rejected.

The shutters came down firmly in 1822 when the threat of civil unrest in Glasgow had receded. The Glasgow Committee saw no justification in continuing with its local scheme and advised the government that it had served its purpose, despite a petition that year from some 1,800 "mechanics, labour-

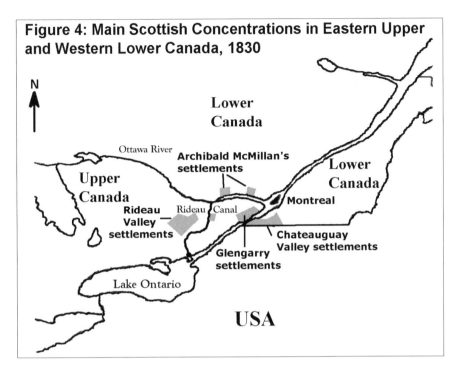

Figure 4: Main Scottish Concentrations in Eastern Upper and Western Lower Canada, 1830

ers and others residing in Glasgow and its vicinity," who wished to settle close to their friends and relatives in eastern Upper Canada, and countless other similar requests from many other parts of Scotland.[62] People continued for decades to complain about miserable conditions and prospects, but the authorities never relented. After 1822, people seeking to emigrate had to find the funds for their relocation costs themselves or from charitable bodies.

Overall, just over 4,000 Scots received financial aid to emigrate to British America between 1815 and 1821. Although this is a significant number, it represents less than a quarter of the total number of Scots who emigrated during this period.[63] Despite the difficulties they faced in raising money to emigrate, most Scots emigrants were self-funded. They purchased passages on the growing number of timber ships that were leaving Scotland, initially from Greenock, for British North America. As the timber trade grew and extended its geographical base, more Scottish ports became involved in the trade, and, by 1816, the east-coast ports of Aberdeen and Leith and the port of Dumfries in the southwest Borders were also providing ships that regularly crossed the Atlantic.

In 1820, a group from Glasgow and Paisley managed to reach the Chateauguay Valley in Lower Canada completely unaided (Figure 4). By not having to travel the greater distance west to Upper Canada they had reduced costs, but they faced major problems in acquiring land. Unlike their fellow countrymen in the Rideau Valley, who could rely on the organizational skills of the army officers to allocate land and manage settlement, they were left to their own devices. As new arrivals, they had to contend with numerous bureaucratic hurdles and a shortage of good land, owing to the acquisitive habits of property speculators. When faced with such problems, they took the only realistic option open to them — they squatted illegally on the land of their choosing.

Selecting a place in Godmanchester Township (Huntingdon County), they founded the Dalhousie settlement named after Lord Dalhousie, governor-in-chief of British North America.[64] However, to their dismay they soon discovered that most of the township was owned by Edward Ellice, the formidable merchant banker, landowner, and politician.[65] Unable to pay him for their holdings, the settlers were forced to leave.[66] With Dalhousie's help, they acquired new lots further south in what would later become Elgin Township.[67] "Thus ended in disaster the Dalhousie settlement,[68] whose early days were so promising ... furnishing an early warning ... of allowing Crown lands to pass into the hands of other than actual settlers."[69] Elgin soon acquired Clyde's Corners (William Clyde had settled in 1826); a number of other Scottish hamlets, including Beith (the name of an Ayrshire parish); and Kelvingrove (an area of Glasgow). Such place names bear witness to the steady influx of former handloom weavers to this area of Lower Canada.[70]

Another group of former weavers from Glasgow and Paisley who emigrated in 1820 also headed for Lower Canada. They took the unusual step of renting land in the Terrebonne seigneury, located just northwest of Montreal. Wishing to save the expense of a long journey after landing in Quebec, they were tempted by the availability of unoccupied land in the northern part of the seigneury. The Scottish seigneur Roderick Mackenzie, a former fur trader, was probably happy to have Scots who would rent his farmland and work in his flour mills, but they would have had to relinquish any hope of becoming land owners. They could only ever rent his land.[71] Nevertheless they at least had a secure base and better living conditions than would be available in most isolated locations. By 1824, some sixty-seven householders had settled on both sides of the rivière l'Achigan, over a distance of six miles. Three years later their New Glasgow and the two Paisley concessions southwest of it had about two hundred family heads, most of them Scottish.[72]

Once again, local place names attest to the influx of former weavers.[73]

Meanwhile, in the wool- and cotton-producing areas of the south-west Borders, handloom weavers were being squeezed out of their jobs by the introduction of power looms.[74] Proximity to Ireland exacerbated an already bad situation, since the region was being flooded with immigrant workers who were willing to accept low wages. However, this was also a region of small farms and as a consequence it was better able to adapt to the traumas associated with mechanization than was the case in the cotton districts of Lanarkshire and Renfrewshire. People from Dumfriesshire emigrated in the greatest numbers and funded their relocation themselves, rarely seeking help from the government.

George, 9th Earl of Dalhousie (1770–1838), governor-in-chief of British North America, 1819–28. Painting (circa 1830) by Sir John Watson Gordon, engraved by Thomas Lupton. *Courtesy of Library and Archives Canada C–005958.*

Despite the high cost of reaching Upper Canada, a Dumfriesshire group relocated to Edwardsburgh Township (Grenville County) soon after 1817. According to an anonymous letter writer of that year, "no fewer than 547 persons have ... emigrated from this port of Dumfries alone and we believe considerably more than 100 have sailed from Annan."[76] Attributing the "spirit of emigration" to Upper Canada's assisted-emigration scheme of 1815 and the favourable reports that were sent back to Scotland, he firmly believed that the group had gone to a place "where misery is already at its height."[77] Their undoubted success in building thriving communities would prove him wrong.

Two years later the *Dumfries and Galloway Courier* was fretting over the continuing loss of people, this time to New Brunswick: "The great majority are believed to come from Cumberland [England], Annandale, Dumfries, Wigtownshire and ... Kirkcudbright. They all describe themselves as labourers or small farmers." Although they included people of limited means, the newspaper claimed that "no less than £18,000 will be carried out on this

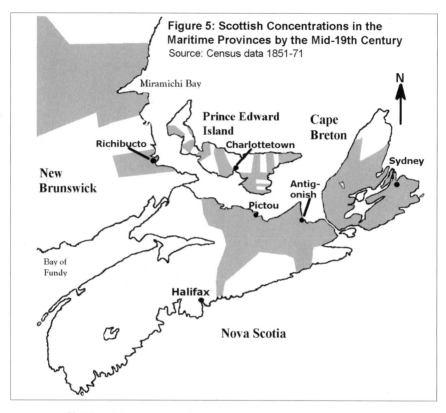

Figure 5: Scottish Concentrations in the Maritime Provinces by the Mid-19th Century
Source: Census data 1851-71

occasion."[78] The *Glasgow Herald* voiced similar concerns in 1821 over the departure from Dumfries of three ships carrying 340 people, some of them quite well-to-do. "Not a few of the emigrants, we are assured, possess capital of a few hundred pounds with which they propose to use to purchase land in New Brunswick and Prince Edward Island."[79] And they took with them "between two and three tons weight of furniture and provision." Most passengers were labourers and tradesmen, but clearly there were affluent farmers as well.

While some Dumfriesshire emigrants opted for Upper Canada, the majority sought destinations in the eastern Maritimes that were closer and therefore cheaper to reach. Initially, most of Dumfries's timber imports came from the New Brunswick ports of Miramichi and Richibucto, thereby ensuring a regular supply of sea crossings to these destinations. This one factor helps to explain the striking predominance of Dumfriesshire settlers in New Brunswick, with most being concentrated in the Richibucto area of Kent County and just to the north along the Napan River in the Miramichi

region (Figure 5).[80] The new community of Napan acquired many of its settlers from Annan, a centre of handloom weaving just east of Dumfries. "This
has arisen from the circumstances that a traffic in timber has long existed
between the Miramichi River and the town of Annan, the ships engaged in
which afford an easy passage to intending emigrants. Their sons are noted
as the best ploughmen and themselves they are among the best farmers in
the province."[81]

Though not present in such large numbers, Dumfriesshire immigrants
also went to eastern Nova Scotia from 1818, where they "were distinguished
by steady industry"[82] and to the southwestern side of Prince Edward Island
from 1820, where they were known for their "agricultural knowledge, domestic economy," as well as for their "steady industrious habits."[83] In Nova Scotia
they established a Dalhousie settlement (Pictou County) as well as a New
Annan (Colchester County).[84] When the Reverend Mitchell came from Tatamagouche to see them, he found "not the semblance of a road about New
Annan or even Tatamagouche. He had to travel from the seashore through
"blazed paths through the woods."[85] Yet "from their sturdy Scotch industry
and frugality these settlers soon attained comparative comfort." Writing in
1877, George Patterson observed "many of their descendants" to be "in good

View of Dalhousie, just to the east of Campbellton in Restigouche
County, New Brunswick. Attracting its first Scots sometime before
1810, it too was probably named after the Earl of Dalhousie. *Courtesy of
Provincial Archives of New Brunswick P 20/326, Nicholas Denys Historical
Society Collection.*

circumstances."[86] And Prince Edward Island also acquired its New Annan
during the 1830s — a lasting reminder of the Island's Dumfriesshire roots.[87]

Each year there were many thousands of other self-financing Scots who,
like the Dumfriesshire emigrants, slipped away quietly for British America,
leaving behind little or no documentation, apart from adding to the official
departure statistics, which were kept at the major ports from 1825. Because
of its landlocked location, Upper Canada had to await good roads and
canals before Scots would venture in any numbers beyond the major Glengarry and Rideau settlements in the east of the province. But being much
more accessible, Prince Edward Island, eastern Nova Scotia, and Cape
Breton readily attracted great numbers of Scottish settlers from the late
eighteenth century. The Scottish takeover of the eastern Maritimes became
even more extensive after 1815 when, with the growing importance of the
timber trade in the region, New Brunswick experienced a substantial influx
of Scots. Official statistics reveal that between 1825 and 1830 some 15,600
Scots sailed to ports in British North America. After 1830 the numbers
soared as the cost of sea passages declined sharply and improved communications made Upper Canada more accessible. Between 1831 and 1855
roughly 108,000 people left Scotland for British North America, and all but
16,500 sailed to the port of Quebec. Although a good many were heading
for the Eastern Townships in Lower Canada, those who intended remaining in British America would settle in Upper Canada.[88]

While reasonably affluent people could finance their own removal, the
poor had to rely on begging and pleading. Innumerable petitions reached
the Colonial Office during the early 1820s, and, as this happened, their plight
became more widely known to the general public. Thousands of paupers
from the Clyde textile districts sought help to emigrate. "It is too painful to
enter into minute details of all their sufferings," wrote a group from
Glasgow, while some Glasgow tradesmen hoped "that their deep distress
may be taken into favourable consideration – that they are starving and will
be ejected from their dwellings in a few days."[89] Aid continued to be refused,
but, with the growing unease being felt over their dreadful poverty and
sense of frustration, the government was forced to act. Once again it looked
at the question of assisted emigration. A Parliamentary Select Committee sat in 1826–27 to consider whether to offer state-aided emigration as a
means of relieving poverty. After sifting through a great pile of petitions

from all parts of Britain and hearing evidence principally from high-ranking officials, businessmen, and clergymen with personal knowledge of British America, the committee concluded that some public money should be given to aid poor people to emigrate, provided that it was repaid.

The committee's thinking appears to have been reflected in the petition of thirty-six unemployed heads of family from Kilmarnock in Ayrshire who wished to emigrate to Chaleur Bay in New Brunswick. In their 1827 petition they were careful to state that they would repay any money advanced to them. Moreover, their costs "would be no more to the government ... than if their expenses had been paid merely from Quebec to Upper Canada, to which place a great number [from Lanarkshire and Renfrewshire] formerly were taken."[90] However, because of concerns over the high costs of such schemes, the government rejected the committee's advice.[91] The outcome was a devastating blow to the 12,000 Scots who, having sought aid, now had to rely on their own fund-raising abilities (Appendix II).[92]

Contrary to what had been intended, the Select Committee's very existence had actually boosted the emigration frenzy within Scotland. The desperation people felt in west Inverness-shire is typical. They were suffering great distress "ever since the introduction of the sheep system" and sought a way out:

> That your lordship's petitioners, having learned the intention of government to give facilities to the surplus population ... to pass over into British Colonies in North America, humbly pray for aid to enable them to join many of their friends who preceded them and are comfortably settled in the province of Nova Scotia and islands of Cape Breton and Prince Edward Island ...
>
> That your lordship's petitioners ... declare that without some assistance they are utterly unable to defray the expense of passage for themselves and families across the Atlantic and if they do not get away this season, they must become a burden upon the public ... they pray for an advance of from £10 to £20 to each family according to their number which money ... shall be faithfully repaid within a reasonable time.[93]

A month earlier some anxious Knoydart people had waited for two days at the Arisaig Post Office to meet someone who could give them details of "government relief to enable them to transport themselves and families to Canada," but the person never appeared.[94]

There were even more agonizing developments in the Western Isles following the catastrophic decline of kelp manufacture. Foreign imports had virtually wiped it out by the mid-1820s, making thousands of people surplus to requirements. Inevitably large numbers of job losses take time to absorb, even in a vibrant manufacturing area, but in a weak and narrowly based economy prospects were bleak or non-existent. Predictably many people in North and South Uist, Benbecula, Barra, Lewis, Skye, Tiree, and Mull – the main centres of kelp production – sought an escape through emigration. In 1826, four hundred to five hundred Uist and Barra inhabitants asked the government for the "means to join their friends who were assisted to emigrate to Cape Breton in 1817."[95] Three hundred other Hebridean inhabitants sought "assistance to emigrate to Cape Breton" that year, and a year later 1,600 people from Mull, Benbecula, Barra, and North Uist wanted "to know if they will receive any aid from the Government to go to British America this season as they are in great distress."[96]

Duncan Shaw, the Benbecula factor, hoped that tenants on his estate might qualify for government-assisted emigration, but if they did he wanted to have a say in "selecting the emigrants" – otherwise "the most wealthy and industrious of our population will emigrate and we will be left with the dregs."[97] Shaw wanted to clear two parts of the estate "where the greater part of our inferior kelp is manufactured." The people cleared "will all go to Cape Breton and no where else if they can help it. They are accustomed to live almost exclusively on meal, milk and potatoes." If during a sea crossing "you substitute molasses for the milk" and "lay in a sufficient quantity of good meal and salt ... all will be well."[98] This arrangement would certainly lower provisioning costs. It was all very persuasive, but the government declined, just as it had all other applications for help.

Conditions were also very grim in Rum. The landlord, MacNeil of Canna, having decided that he could not maintain his tenantry, had gone to Rum in 1826 with a plan: He told his tenants that he would write off any outstanding arrears, give them their cattle, and add "£600 over and above, to enable you to remove to America, for I cannot afford the present system." It is doubtful that all of his tenants "very cheerfully accepted," as was claimed, but the exodus was apparently "conducted under the very best superintendence," and later reports indicated that his former tenants were "most comfortable."[99] About two hudred people sailed in 1828 to Ship Harbour, Cape Breton, where they dispersed into various parts of the island, while many others from Rum probably moved to Prince Edward Island.[100]

MacNeil of Canna was one of very few Highland landlords at this time who was prepared to spend his own money in helping his tenants to emigrate. Doing so made some observers and later commentators suspect that he had probably forced them to go.[101] But the great number of Hebridean petitioners seeking government aid speaks for itself, and a reasonable presumption is that the majority of Rum people actually wished to leave.[102] So landlord and tenant had a joint interest in backing the emigration scheme. These tenants were certainly far better off than the many poor crofters who sailed off to Cape Breton with little or no help, having scraped together resources as best they could:

> Their whole property consists of black cattle and small horses all of which are made over to the emigration agent at his own risk and which he sends to the southern markets at his own risk... the roof of their huts, their boats, in short everything they have must be converted into money by him before the necessary sum for defraying the freight can be realised.[103]

Some emigrants obtained help from family and friends, who were already settled, but others took the more desperate step of borrowing their passage money, which amounted to about £3 per person:

> Many of our people left their country without the means of paying their passage, the Captain accepting their note of hand for payments when they could; when they have been here a few years round comes the Captain's agent for principal and interest. Money they cannot have – their cow is taken and perhaps their land ... and the unhappy family must begin a new lot in the forest. At this moment a majority of settlers have not paid for their grants, which may sink them in ruin again.[104]

As economic conditions in the Highlands and Islands deteriorated, land-lords became increasingly desperate to rid themselves of their surplus tenants. With the approach of a compulsory Poor Law by 1845, which, for the first time, made Scottish landlords legally responsible for destitute people on their estates, their apprehensions increased. Forced evictions soon become a fact of life, and with them came the belief that landlord-assisted emigration, which often followed evictions, had also been forced on unwilling tenants. Despite the brutality of the clearances, it does not neces-sarily follow that people were coerced onto emigrant ships and sent to some unrecognizable place on the other side of the Atlantic. There were undoubtedly some instances of forced evictions, linked with emigration, but these were exceptional. As will become clear in the following chapter, Scots, whatever their circumstances, were highly selective in their choice of destinations: emigration was not a random leap into the dark. Whatever pressures people might have been under to leave, a particular place was chosen because of the attractions that it was believed to offer. Right from the beginning both push and pull factors were at work. The various forces operating in Scotland that influenced people to emigrate are well-known, but Canada's pulling power is not so well-documented and warrants closer examination.

Four

SETTLEMENT GROWTH IN EASTERN CANADA

*From pretty close observation over the past eight years, I have
come to the conclusion that the Scots are the best and most
successful of all emigrants. Come they with or without
money, come they with great working sons or with only
useless girls, it is all the same. The Scotchman is sure
to better his condition and this very silently
and almost without complaint.*[1]

D<small>R. R</small>OBERT A<small>LLING, THE EMIGRATION</small> agent in Guelph, Ontario, was
full of praise for Scottish settlers – particularly surprising, since he
was an Englishman. The adaptability of Scots to the trying conditions of pioneer life and their early successes were legendary. Spotting
the marketing potential of Alling's commendation, the Canada Company
inserted his comments in its promotional literature in the hope of attracting more Scots to its vast acreages in western Upper Canada. And the
Emigration Select Committee, which sat in 1841, was also made aware of
Alling's views by Dr. Thomas Rolph, a former Upper Canada emigration
agent, who quoted extensively from a letter that Alling had written to the
Canada Company: "The industry, frugality, and sobriety of the Scotch
mainly contribute to their success ... I have carefully watched the progress
and result of the Scotch, Irish and English emigrants in the race of the goal
desired by all, viz. to obtain a deed for their land and find that ... the
Scotchman is generally first in the winning post."[2]

Scots had been emigrating to British North America since the late eighteenth century. They were attracted by its huge economic potential, the prospect of land ownership, and the more egalitarian societies that were emerging. By 1815, they dominated large stretches of peninsular Nova Scotia, Cape Breton Island, and Prince Edward Island and were well concentrated in parts of New Brunswick, eastern Upper Canada, and western Lower Canada. Because of their relative accessibility from Scotland, the Maritime provinces had been favoured initially, but Scots increasingly opted for Upper Canada from 1830 on, as inland routes improved and the cost of travel decreased. With its better land, climate, and employment opportunities, Upper Canada had far more to offer.

The Highlands and Islands were the first regions of Scotland to lose their people to British America. Experiencing the disruptive effects of the advancing sheep farms, and feeling aggrieved by high rents and oppressive landlords, they began emigrating in substantial numbers in the 1770s. By 1803, they had colonized large swaths of the Maritimes but still confined most of their settlements in Upper Canada to a handful of tightly clustered townships in and around Glengarry County. However, the situation changed drastically in 1815, when the Napoleonic Wars ended and a severe depression gripped the whole of Scotland. This was also the time when the North American timber trade began its explosive growth, bringing with it affordable and regular sea crossings for emigrants. This development, together with three government-sponsored emigration schemes, which were introduced to promote the Rideau Valley settlements in Upper Canada, set the scene for the rising outflow of both Lowlanders and Highlanders that followed. Having been the main beneficiaries of the Rideau Valley schemes, Lowlanders headed in great numbers for eastern Upper Canada, although they soon extended their territory to Lower Canada and the Maritime provinces. Meanwhile, Highlanders maintained their long-standing allegiance to the Maritime region well into the 1850s, although they too were attracted by Upper Canada's advantages and formed many distinctive communities there.

A decisive factor in the settlement decision of many Scots was the pull of family and community ties. Once early footholds were established, they often attracted followers from the part of Scotland from which the first colonizers had originated. The co-operative spirit, which concentrated people from one part of Scotland in a particular area of Canada, produced

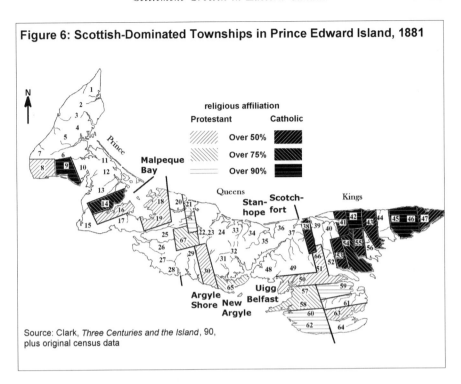

Figure 6: Scottish-Dominated Townships in Prince Edward Island, 1881

Source: Clark, *Three Centuries and the Island*, 90, plus original census data

distinctive communities that could take strength from shared culture and social values. When they emigrated, Highlanders generally transplanted themselves as whole communities. Their Gaelic language and Highland traditions set them apart, consequently making them far more visible than Lowlanders, who generally arrived in small groups and assimilated themselves into a number of different communities. Although they were latecomers when compared to Highlanders, Lowlanders actually dominated the influx to British America after 1815. Between 1825 and 1855, departures from Highland ports only accounted for about one quarter of the total.[3] This may seem surprising, given the emotive connotations that Highland emigration evoked, especially during the large-scale clearances of the late 1840s and early 1850s. Highland emigrants always had the higher profile, but Lowland emigrants were present in far greater numbers.

Emigration was never an easy option. People had to plot and scheme for years to obtain the funds and knowledge to transform themselves into New World farmers. Before the start of the Napoleonic Wars, when colonization was still in its infancy, potential emigrants were limited in what they could do for themselves. They required help in obtaining land and ideally in getting through the first phases of settlement. To meet this demand were the various proprietors who had acquired large acreages of wilderness land in British North America, for which they were seeking colonizers. What followed was the successful matching of peoples' desire to emigrate with the availability of land in a particular province.

First to attract settlers was Prince Edward Island. The sudden interest in it was due entirely to the fact that it was the first colony to be sold off to proprietors. In a single day in 1767, the entire Island was granted to a number of high-ranking people.[4] Most of them hoped to benefit by selling their land to speculators, having little interest in recruiting settlers or in the Island's development. However, there were three Scottish proprietors who did seek to found settlements.[5] The first to do so was Sir James Montgomery, Lord Advocate of Scotland, who recruited sixty Perthshire men to work in the flax plantation that he would establish at Stanhope (lot 34). Sailing on the *Falmouth* from Greenock in April 1770, the group was well-provisioned and arrived in good health.[6] Montgomery employed David Lawson, an experienced flax farmer from Callander (Perthshire), to recruit suitable emigrants and later to act as his plantation's manager. Because Lawson did his recruiting locally, most emigrants shared his Perthshire origins. Montgomery financed the venture and employed the emigrants as indentured servants, using their labour for four years in return for free passage and leaseholds at the end of the period.

As a pillar of the Scottish establishment, Montgomery could not be seen to be promoting emigration for its own sake. He instructed Lawson to recruit men only, and not families. He was to manage his "white negroes" and run the plantation "in such a manner as to incur as little observation as possible."[7] The Reverend William Drummond, who travelled with the original *Falmouth* group, reported them to be in a "mutinous" state soon after their arrival, having experienced incredible hardships.[8] Although many of Montgomery's men left the Stanhope area when their indentures expired, some remained and took up their land grant entitlements.[9] And in spite of their initial difficulties, more Perthshire emigrants followed in the early 1800s, with most settling at either Stanhope or Beaton Point (lot 47). As confidence in the Island's benefits grew still further, a new batch of settlers from Blair Atholl (Perthshire) arrived in 1808. They founded New Perth (lot 52) in the following year.[10]

The second group arrived on the Island in July 1770. They were Argyll settlers, who were led and partially financed by Lieutenant-Colonel Robert Stewart. Originating from Campbeltown (Argyll), he drew most of his recruits locally and helped them to relocate to his newly acquired land in Malpeque Bay (lot 18).[11] As with the Stanhope venture, the early years brought dreadful problems and misfortune, but eventually the community prospered. Even more Argyll emigrants arrived in Prince Edward Island in the early 1800s, this time from the islands of Mull and Colonsay, but instead of heading for Malpeque Bay they chose a site closer to the Island's economic heartland, just to the west of Charlottetown. There they founded Argyle Shore (lot 30) and New Argyle (lot 65).[12] Once again the initial settlers had attracted followers from their homeland, thereby becoming the initial catalyst that would give the Island its enduring links with Argyll.[13]

This process was repeated yet again following the arrival in 1772 of the third group – two hundred Roman Catholic Highlanders from the Clanranald estates in South Uist, Eigg, and mainland west Inverness-shire.[14] Wishing to escape religious persecution, these people sought a new life at Scotchfort (lot 36) under the leadership of John MacDonald of Glenaladale. However, the township was hardly a religious haven. Catholics were barred from holding land until 1780, and officials were instructed to exclude them from their statistical reports, since they were not considered to be bona fide settlers. Yet religious discrimination was the least of their worries as they faced the appalling privations that the first winter brought. A year later they were said to be "in great misery," and the local priest who travelled with them was doing all he could to "get them conveyed out of the Island."[15] But by the next year Bishop John MacDonald received reports back in Scotland stating that even "the malcontents" felt positive. He believed that there was now "sufficient room to hope that this undertaking will thrive well enough."[16] He was right. By 1790–91, the area was fast becoming a considerable Catholic enclave, particularly after MacDonald of Glenaladale acquired the township adjoining Scotchfort. Those nine hundred or so settlers who came in this second wave also originated from the Clanranald estates, principally from mainland west Inverness-shire and the islands of South Uist and Eigg.[17]

Conditions were extremely tough, and, because of their late arrival in September, the newly arrived emigrants had to seek assistance to tide them over the winter. Early reports spoke of half-starved, freezing, disillusioned people who were desperately unhappy with their plight: "This province is terrible cold, we have seven months of snow and frost and sometimes eight ... we came here we thought ourselves to make money but we came to freeze instead."[18]

Back in Scotland, the bleak reports of struggling emigrants were seized upon with great relish by anti-emigration campaigners, who gave them as wide a circulation as possible. One South Uist man's account of his tribulations and distress was obtained by the Highland Society of Edinburgh and given particular prominence: "You may tell [Colin MacDonald of] Boisdale about the people who left Uist, that they are crying every day, saying if Boisdale knew their conditions he would send for them again but, if you hear of any of them talking of emigration to this, for God's sake advise them to stay where they are else they will regret it."[19]

Any yet the reality was quite different. Catholic Highlanders had overcome their initial problems and were making good headway. This was in spite of being denied freeholds by MacDonald of Glenaladale, who insisted on exercising what he saw as his feudal rights in Prince Edward Island. This meant that his people were expected to content themselves with being mere tenants. This situation was not acceptable to independently minded, land-hungry immigrants. Showing remarkable initiative, they voted with their feet. Moving out of Scotchfort, they helped themselves to choice locations on the Island or in nearby Cape Breton, often taking their land by squatting. Scotchfort soon developed into a general distribution centre for Catholic Highlanders. It was a place where new arrivals found their bearings, not where people settled permanently.[20] Nevertheless, those who remained on the Island settled together, thus creating very large Catholic concentrations in Kings County on the east side of the Island. By 1848, some 61 per cent of the population in this one county claimed Scottish ancestry.[21]

Meanwhile, in 1791, another group of 650 Western Isle Catholics from the Clanranald estate were establishing themselves in Antigonish County, Nova Scotia, just opposite Prince Edward Island.[22] Father Angus MacEachern (later bishop), who was based on Prince Edward Island, had persuaded the newcomers to settle in Arisaig and other parts of Antigonish County in order to keep them separate from the many Highland communities with Presbyterian affiliations that had already formed in the Pictou area. As was the case in Prince Edward Island, Scottish settlement in Nova Scotia became segregated by religion from the outset. New arrivals would choose between particular

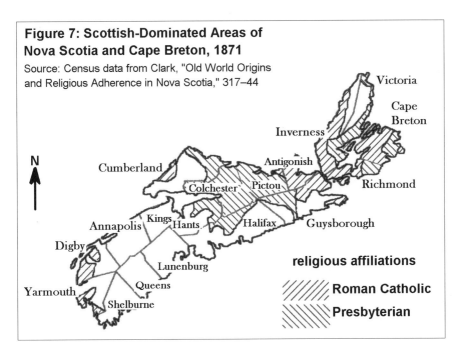

Figure 7: Scottish-Dominated Areas of Nova Scotia and Cape Breton, 1871

Source: Census data from Clark, "Old World Origins and Religious Adherence in Nova Scotia," 317–44

Presbyterian or Catholic territories, thereby creating the clear religious divisions that are revealed in later census data (Figures 6 and 7). Thanks largely to Father MacEachern's efforts, Scottish Catholics were effectively concentrated in one single part of the Maritimes. When he eventually took over this sprawling parish in 1807 from Father James MacDonald, Father MacEachern was able to oversee a thriving Catholic population lying within a compact triangle, taking in the east side of Prince Edward Island, the eastern end of mainland Nova Scotia, and large areas of Cape Breton (Figure 5).[23]

Unlike the three groups of Highlanders who first came to Prince Edward Island, the 190 or so people who sailed in the *Hector* in 1773 to found the Pictou communities did not have a well-heeled proprietor to lead them. They were the recruits of the Philadelphia Land Company, which had extensive acreages to colonize in Pictou.[24] They had been signed up by John Pagan, a Glasgow merchant, and the Reverend Dr. John Witherspoon, a Presbyterian minister from Paisley, who had the controlling shares in the company. Employing a Highland agent, Pagan and Witherspoon found willing recruits in Sutherland, east Inverness-shire, and Wester Ross.[25] A president of Princeton College, New Jersey, and later a signatory of the Declaration of Independence, Witherspoon was probably driven more by humanitarian motives

---

Reverend Angus Bernard MacEachern, first Bishop of Charlottetown, artist unknown. *Courtesy of Diocese of Charlottetown, PEI Public Archives and Records Office, 2320/70-3.*

than by financial gain. This was a man who believed in giving power to the common people. A venture that enabled poor Scots to throw off their feudal shackles would have appealed to his libertarian instincts. But to Pagan the emigrants were just another money-making cargo. To keep his costs to a minimum, he supplied a ship that was so decrepit that "the passengers could pick the wood out of her sides with their fingers."[26]

Having been subjected to an appalling sea crossing, the new arrivals discovered that they had been duped into believing that their land would be on coastal and river frontages when it was actually miles inland. An added blow was the realization that the promised houses and provisions were not waiting for them. Once again Highland resourcefulness won through. The settlers quickly realized that their best option was to "inhabit the rich lands bordering the three rivers," where they could fish and use the rivers as "the primary means of transportation."[27] An added benefit of being close to river frontages was the "large tracts of intervale" land that were available in the floodplains. Once the rivers subsided after the spring floods, these naturally occurring water meadows provided settlers with abundant quantities of good farmland.[28] The emigrants had uncovered the ideal colonization site.[29]

The *Hector* arrivals sent their first cargo of cut timber from Pictou in 1775, "the first of a trade very profitably and extensively carried on ever since."[30] Thus did they lay the foundations of Pictou's valuable timber trade, which would eventually come to dominate eastern Nova Scotia's economy. A decade later, ex-soldiers from two disbanded Scottish regiments – the Duke of Hamilton's (the 82nd) and the Royal Highland Emigrants (the 84th) – acquired land in the area, thereby giving the colonization efforts of

the original *Hector* settlers an enormous boost. What was particularly significant about the former soldiers was that most of them originated from east
Inverness-shire — one of the Highland areas from which the *Hector* settlers
had been recruited. However, it was the Sutherland people in the original
Hector group who would eventually draw the most followers.

From across the Northumberland Strait in Prince Edward Island, disgruntled Catholic Highlanders were relocating themselves to some of the
best river and coastal locations in Cape Breton. Not only were they dis-
pleased with MacDonald of Glenaladale's feudal tendencies, but they also
had to contend with Prince Edward Island's chaotic land-granting system
and the fact that its best sites were already occupied.[31] So in 1790 they began
moving to Cape Breton as pioneer squatters in spite of government regulations that were meant to keep them
out. Wishing to protect its coal-mining
interests on the Island, the British government had made Cape Breton as inac-
cessible as it possibly could to settlers.
Legally binding restraining orders, which
restricted freehold grants to Loyalists
and fish merchants, had been issued,
but Highland colonizers took no
notice of them.

At the end of the eighteenth century
Cape Breton was a sparsely settled and
largely undeveloped British colony.
Only about 2,000 people lived on the
Island, of whom half were French-
speaking Acadians; most of the rest
were Loyalist refugees from the
United States. There were no proprietors on hand to provide capital,
organization, and leadership. The cod
fishery supported most of the Island's
economy. Farming operated at a subsistence level only; agricultural communities consisted of a scattering of

A larger-than-life bronze statue of a
Highlander in full regimental dress,
which overlooks the Pictou waterfront.
The inscription reads "In proud com-
memoration of the courage, faith and
endurance of the gallant pioneer passengers in the ship *Hector*." *Photograph by
Geoff Campey.*

farms that were spread over very large areas. The Island had no roads, no churches, and no effective local government.[32] Nevertheless Scots came in their hundreds. Quickly establishing successful communities, they would attract many others to follow them, transforming Cape Breton into a major Scottish enclave.[33] By 1814, some 315 Scottish heads of households would be illegally occupying more than 62,000 acres of Crown land on the Island.

By 1803, when Lord Selkirk led eight hundred Highlanders to what would become the Belfast settlements in Prince Edward Island, the eastern Maritimes already had large concentrations of both Catholic and Presbyterian Highlanders. His settlers reinforced both religious groups. The largest contingent consisted of Presbyterians from Lord MacDonald's estate, on the east side of Skye, while Catholics from the Clanranald estates in South Uist also came in substantial numbers. Skye people maintained a long association with the Island, but this was not so with the South Uist emigrants, who soon changed their allegiance to Nova Scotia and Cape Breton.[34]

Skye had a long record of losing people to North America. Before Prince Edward Island became a popular destination, its emigrants had shown a marked preference for North Carolina.[35] Outraged over sudden and large increases in their rents introduced in 1769, some 370 people, including "people of property who intend making purchases of land in America," went from Skye to North Carolina, two years later, followed by a further seven hundred in the following year. [36] Apparently Skye was "a district which had so decided a connection with North Carolina that no emigrants had ever gone from it to any other quarter."[37] Indeed, Selkirk claimed that he had chosen people for his venture who would otherwise be lost to the United States. In relocating his settlers, Selkirk changed the direction of the clannish pull away from North Carolina to Prince Edward Island.[38] The success of the Belfast venture made it a powerful magnet for Skye settlers, and no other part of British America attracted them in such large numbers.

It was not just the eastern Maritimes that was proving to be popular with Highlanders. In spite of its greater distance and higher cost to reach, Glengarry in eastern Upper Canada had been attracting wave after wave of Highlanders in the late eighteenth and early nineteenth centuries.[39] According to Archibald McMillan of Murlaggan, a prominent Lochaber tacksman, who led 552 followers to the region in 1802, Highlanders "were pouring down every day in most astonishing numbers" and heading for Glengarry

County.[40] Because most of the available land was already occupied, newly arrived groups were unable to settle in large, compact groups as their predecessors had done. Although Crown land in other districts was available on easy terms, it was rejected. Refusing to be separated from friends and family in Glengarry, the 1802 arrivals acquired small, scattered tracts of unclaimed land in the immediate area, while some rented land on the Crown and Clergy reserves.[41]

In the continuing search for land, Highland communities had been spreading westward into Stormont County (Upper Canada) and eastward into Soulanges County (Lower Canada).[42] Archibald McMillan quickly realized the potential for even more outward spread from Glengarry. Being a Montreal resident, he was barred from obtaining land in Upper Canada, but he could acquire land in Lower Canada. By 1807, he had secured parcels of land along the north side of the Ottawa River just opposite Glengarry (Figure 4). His grant consisted of the Township of Suffolk (later Lochaber) and a quarter of Templeton Township (both in Papineau County), as well as much of Grenville Township (in Argenteuil County).[43]

But in spite of claiming to have the backing of seventy-five people who had travelled with him to Quebec, McMillan had difficulty in attracting settlers.[44] Even if it meant renting land, most people favoured Glengarry, because it enabled them to remain close to their relatives and friends. Nevertheless he eventually enticed appreciable numbers of Highlanders, both from Glengarry and from Scotland, to join him on the other side of the Ottawa River. McMillan's decision to move to Grenville Township ensured that it would attract most of his settlers.

Having acquired large forested areas, veined with river and streams and through which cut timber "may be floated down to the Ottawa River," McMillan pursued his lumbering interests with great energy.[45] As his profits from lumbering far exceeded what he could earn from farming, he became negligent in attracting sufficient emigrants to comply with the settlement conditions of his grant. The government lost patience with him by 1825 and confiscated his land. However, his intervention had stimulated the great spread of Scottish communities that developed along the Ottawa River. Eventually Scottish colonizers would be found as far west as Eardley Township, just beyond Hull, and would continue a northward progression along either side of the Gatineau River.[46]

"Chemin Scotch" in Grenville Township, in Quebec province. This road name provides a visual reminder of the large numbers of Scottish settlers who once lived in this township.
Photograph by Geoff Campey.

Sailing a year before the Passenger Act of 1803 came into effect, McMillan's group had paid fares of £5.5s each for their places on the *Helen* of Irvine, *Jean* of Irvine, and the *Friends of John Saltcoats*.[47] Had they sailed a year later, the new legislation would have required them to pay double that amount. But as a result of pressure from emigrants and shipowners, the government repealed the 1803 act and introduced new legislation in 1817 that allowed shipowners to supply less food and take on more passengers.[48] The *Dumfriesshire Weekly Journal* thought this to be a great step forward for emigrants, since owners were now promising to reduce their fares:

> We are anxious to state what we believe is not generally known, that the Bill which has recently had the Royal assent gives great facilities to persons who are desirous of proceeding as settlers to ... North America, in as much as, by reducing the tonnage to be allowed to each individual during the passage, it enables the masters of vessels ... to take passengers at a much lower rate than has been hitherto demanded.[49]

However, of even greater significance in achieving cheap fares was the emergence of the timber trade. It had huge implications for emigrant travel. The sudden and large increase in tariffs on Baltic timber, first introduced during the Napoleonic Wars, gave Canadian timber a considerable cost advantage over traditional supplies from the Baltic. As the volume of shipping between Scotland and Canada increased dramatically, emigrants were provided with affordable and regular sea crossings. From 1815 onwards they could simply purchase places in the holds of the many timber ships that were regularly crossing the Atlantic. Shipowners who sought the extra revenues of a passenger trade had to compete for the business, both on cost and quality, thereby creating a greatly improved service for emigrants.

The *Hector* settlers had exported timber to Britain just two years after their arrival in Pictou, Nova Scotia, in 1773. By 1803, "about twenty vessels at four hundred tons on average"[50] were loading up each year at Pictou Harbour, and, by 1805, the number had rocketed to fifty ships a year. The timber trade was also developing rapidly in Prince Edward Island and New Brunswick and fast becoming the bedrock of their economies as well. Enterprising Scots came over in their thousands to benefit from the region's burgeoning trade.[51] Scottish colonizers followed the path of the timber-clearance operations, clearing their land as a combined farming and lumbering operation. The trade brought untold economic advantages to local economies, providing diverse employment opportunities and contributing greatly to the livelihood of the early settlers.

Scottish financiers and merchants played a predominant role in the early development of British North America's timber trade.[52] Men such as Alan Gilmour and Alexander Rankin were in the forefront, becoming the great timber barons of their day. Earliest on the scene was the Morayshire-born William Davidson who, in 1765, founded the Miramichi region's important timber industry in New Brunswick.[53] Remaining under Scottish control, it became part of the Pollock, Gilmour and Company empire in 1812. The Glasgow-based enterprise, the earliest of the great timber firms, had branches throughout British North America. By 1832, it owned the largest shipping fleet in Britain, many of its vessels being built at shipyards along the Miramichi River. It was the largest operator in the North American timber market. Meanwhile, the Keith-born Edward Mortimer rose to the top of the Pictou timber trade. His wealth and influence earned him the title of "King of Pictou," and, because he gave settlers large amounts of credit, he became the linchpin of Pictou's economy.[54] The Caledonian influence was enormous. Timber-felling and transport activities were bankrolled by a cartel of Scottish merchants, sawmillers, and storekeepers.[55] Scottish cliques proliferated, and clannish favouritism meant that they would favour Scottish settlers in their dealings.

During its early stages the trade grew so quickly that settlers and ship masters were often caught trying to barter timber and goods with each other privately, in flagrant breach of customs regulations. In Cape Breton, where Scots were illegally occupying land, there would have been no checks at all. Settlers could have made informal arrangements with ship captains to have their timber collected from countless locations along the coastline. In Prince Edward Island there were regular complaints about a certain Donald MacDonald of Three Rivers, who kept evading customs procedures whenever he shipped his timber cargoes out.[56] The reality was that until enforceable regulations came into effect, settlers, ship masters, and speculative merchants were more or less free to make informal deals over timber when it suited them.

Apart from its financial benefits, the timber trade also acted as a conduit for settlement, channelling communities into specific areas. Settlers would clear forests along a river or coastal frontage up to a certain distance from the inlet or cove from which timber could readily be collected. They would then repeat the process along a neighbouring river, thereby creating distinct settlement pockets. The extensive land-grant records for Cape Breton, which were produced retrospectively from 1817 on once the legal restraints were removed, indicate that the earliest arrivals were concentrated on the western and southern shores.[57] They were the Catholic Highlanders from Prince Edward Island who had been steadily migrating to Cape Breton since 1790. Their choice of location is highly significant. Their settlements were close to the major timber export centre at Pictou and were situated along the route taken by the overseas ships that came to the region to collect timber (Figure 5). Situated on these stretches of coastline, they were highly accessible to passing timber ships and could therefore find a ready market for their timber.

During his visit to Glengarry in 1803, Lord Selkirk had noticed that "the young men, who have come over as children," were "as expert as any at the axe."[58] Because of the "advanced prices of lumber and potash," most of Glengarry's adult men were dividing their time between forest clearing and farming.[59] Their priest, Father Alexander Macdonell, had little time for axe skills and admonished his parishioners for neglecting their "agriculture and the raising of grain."[60] But they were simply following their entrepreneurial instincts. When Dr Thomas Rolph, who later became the official emigration agent for Upper and Lower Canada, visited Glengarry in the 1830s he too was critical of its inhabitants for "allowing their lands to be neglected," having been "induced by the greater wages to engage in lumbering."[61] But he also had to admit that this activity had contributed to their "considerable wealth and independence."[62]

The great pulling power of both the Glengarry and Rideau Valley settlements eventually created an enormous Scottish enclave on the south side of the Ottawa River. Archibald McMillan's Highland communities had stretched Glengarry's reach to the north side of the river, and yet other groups would extend Scottish colonization eastward into Lower Canada's Chateauguay Valley. They came in small groups from the early 1800s on, settling in the broad belts of land along which lumbering operations could be carried out, establishing their "Petite Écosse."[63] Here they would be won over by "the general goodness of the land, the variety of timber of every description, among which oak, elm, pine and beech are in great quantities," the extensive waterways through which felled timber could be taken to the St. Lawrence River, and "the easy access by main roads" to the United States.[64] Felled timber would "find a ready sale ... provided it is on the borders of a stream," and a settler could expect "a better price for his potash and pearl ash than in the upper country."[65]

Becoming concentrated in large stretches of Huntingdon County and the Beauharnois seigneury lying to the southwest of Montreal, Scottish colonizers settled primarily along the banks of the Trout, Chateauguay, and St. Louis rivers and along the major tributaries that flowed into them (Figure 4). Having to travel to many preaching stations, their Presbyterian minister, the Reverend Walter Roach, had a good appreciation of the extent of the Scottish influx:

No part of the Lower Province is more thickly populated with the Scotch than the Chateauguay [River], which taking its rise in the State of New York, winds its course through upwards of 60 miles of the most rich and fertile lands of Lower Canada, till it falls into the waters of the Saint Lawrence, a little above Montreal ... Georgetown, Ormstown, Huntingdon, Hinchinbrook and Trout River are following one another in regular succession ... all of them wholly peopled with Scotch with a few exceptions of Americans ...

Within six miles of Huntingdon alone there are not fewer than two hundred families who at present have not suitable instruction ... in Hemingford, according to the Census of 1831 there were 1,557 souls, of whom the great majority are Presbyterians ... in Beechridge and places adjoining there are not fewer than 150 families firmly attached to the Scottish Kirk, for whom the majority being Highlanders, a Gaelic preacher is prerequisite. In Ormstown there are not fewer than one hundred and twenty families, Presbyterians who have commenced building a church. All this I have from observation, that whole tract of country, comprising not less than one thousand square miles, having been mostly travelled over by myself.[66]

With its burgeoning timber trade, New Brunswick also attracted its fair share of Scots, but not until after 1815. Its massive forests and land-locked position were drawbacks, yet, however gloomy the forests were, New Brunswick's timber trade eventually drew large numbers of Scots to its major centres. Early-nineteenth-century colonizers carved out scattered farms and timber-felling centres along great stretches of the Miramichi River and its branches in Northumberland County. Richibucto, in Kent County, had particular appeal to emigrants from Dumfriesshire and the southwest Borders, who could obtain cheap fares on the timber ships that regularly left from Dumfries. Richibucto's first Presbyterian minister, the Reverend James Hannay, who arrived in 1833, presided over highly receptive communities:

I experience much kindness and attention from my people who are principally natives of Dumfriesshire and Galloway and know how to value our Presbyterian institutions. The accession of emigrants from Scotland during the last summer was considerable, and I had the pleasure of hearing some of them express their gratitude to the father of mercies for his goodness in directing them to a place of habitation, which but for the scenery around them, they could readily regard as some favoured spot in their native land.[67]

When, in the mid-1820s, the trade moved northward to the Chaleurs Bay area, the phenomenon was repeated once again.[68] In 1829–30, four hundred Arran settlers began transforming huge tracts of its wilderness into well-settled communities. The Reverend James Steven, their Presbyterian minister for nearly thirty-three years, had as ever to cope with a dispersed congregation:

The settlements on the River Restigouche under my care extend some distance below Dalhousie at the mouth to the Upsalquitch [River], a branch of it [the Restigouche River] – that is to say, 40 miles more or less, comprehending a scattered population of Protestants, exceeding a thousand souls, rapidly increasing by emigration and natural causes. Many, indeed most of them, are of the Church of Scotland and attend worship as regularly as the yet imperfect state of communication and the country for want of roads and bridges permits. My attendance at Dalhousie, a distance of 16 miles from Campbellton, where I now reside every third Sunday, affords the inhabitants between and in the immediate neighbourhood of these two places, the means of attending worship every other Sunday at either one or the other church ... The population on this river [Restigouche] principally depends on the lumber trade, agriculture being in its infancy among them.[69]

By 1851, Scots represented a staggering 60 per cent of all new arrivals in the Restigouche region.[70] All the while, the influx had been driven entirely by the progress of the timber trade.

In a visit to the Restigouche region in the mid-nineteenth century, J.F.W. Johnston, a British agricultural scientist, wondered "who had induced all these men and women to leave remote corners of Scotland to settle in this remote corner. The whole line of country is *terra incognito* at Quebec and Fredericton ... and yet humble Scotchmen and their families had made choice of it and already fixed upon it their future homes."[71] He concluded

Loading Timber at Beaubears Island in 1826, Showing the Former Fraser and Thom Shipyards. Evidence of the shipbuilding that took place on the island can still be seen on this National Historic Site. *Courtesy of Provincial Archives of New Brunswick P4-3-4.*

that the region's many advantages were being communicated through "an undercurrent of knowledge flowing among the masses, chiefly through the literary communication of far distant blood relations, of which public literature knows nothing and even governments are unaware."[72] The Scottish grapevine told of the great economic benefits to be had from the region's booming timber trade and fuelled the great influx of Scots to Restigouche.

The Arran settlers were fortunate in having their landlord's help in acquiring a site that was sufficiently large to accommodate their entire community. Left to their own devices, they would probably have been dispersed over wide areas of the province. The government may have hoped that new arrivals would establish compact settlements, but its policies actually conspired against this laudable aim. Its land policies, such as they were, promoted everything under the sun except effective colonization. Land speculators thrived, but ordinary colonists found it extremely difficult to cope.[73]

Settlers had low priority. From the late eighteenth century, the government had been granting huge quantities of land as rewards to favoured individuals. Most recipients sold their land on to speculators, who amassed huge holdings but did nothing to further colonization. The official policy of allocating Crown and Clergy reserves meant that millions of acres of land were beyond the reach of ordinary settlers. As a consequence, they had the residue, which was often inferior, and what holdings they could obtain were relatively small and scattered over huge distances. It was a bureaucratic muddle that favoured the rich and privileged while hindering the growth of well-organized settlements. However, people with a yen to emigrate could overcome such problems by planning ahead.

In 1813, the year when Sutherland people were being removed from their holdings in Assynt, Kildonan, and Clyne to make way for sheep farms, two Sutherland men, Donald MacIntosh and Angus Sutherland, who had already emigrated to Nova Scotia, acquired some land just to the west of Pictou. It was, in fact, the last portion of the Philadelphia Land Company's grant that remained available for colonization.[74] After seven years of clearing the forests, the site was declared open. Emigrants from Sutherland flocked to it and created the Earltown community in Colchester County. The province's deputy surveyor probably had these people in mind when he described emigrant Scots as "the most useful description of settlers that come here [Colchester] ... with a determination to settle immediately."[75] By 1836, Earltown had nearly two hundred families, families who were said to be "remarkable for their attachment to the [Presbyterian] Church and their knowledge of the Bible."[76] But by then Sutherland people had another destination in their sights.[77]

Just as the first settlers were heading for Earltown in 1820, two Sutherland brothers, Angus and William MacKay, began preparing yet another site, this time in western Upper Canada. Ten years later, in the midst of continuing clearances and a growing economic depression in Scotland, Zorra (in Oxford County) was ready to receive its first Sutherland colonizers.[78] Judging from the *Inverness Courier*'s account of events, those who left in 1830 were positively motivated about their future, having been "influenced by favourable reports from friends already settled." There were many who "possessed property," and some were "young and eager for adventure."[79] The emergence of a second major Sutherland settlement in western Upper Canada was almost certainly a factor in the "unprecedented" rise in emigration in the following year.[80] Five ships sailed from Cromarty to Pictou and Quebec by July, and two more were expected within days, "taking with them, in all, a population of 1,500 souls, and not a little of the metallic currency of the country."[81] And such was the demand for gold coins that emigrants had to pay an extra shilling to purchase them.[82] By 1833, Zorra had 110 Sutherland families, although some of them were migrants from Pictou.[83]

However, the Assynt settlers from Sutherland who emigrated to Nova Scotia in 1817–18 were less well-organized. Having been led to Pictou by the Reverend Norman MacLeod, a group of just over two hundred people scattered to a number of places, because no one site was large enough to accommodate them. To pay for his passage and other costs, MacLeod had taken up a job at the fishing station in Wick. But, although he had carefully planned his and the group's departure, he had not appreciated the difficulties there would be in acquiring suitable land. Nevertheless, his timing was impeccable. He and his group reached Cape Breton just as the Island's restrictive policies on land grants were being withdrawn. The early arrivals, who were mainly Roman Catholic Highlanders, had simply ignored the regulations and squatted illegally on Crown land, but from 1817 on settlers were welcome. Those already on the Island could now acquire documentation to legitimize their holdings, while newcomers could obtain land grants on the remaining available sites.

Thus, the Assynt emigrants were able to choose a good location on the northeast shore of the Island.[84] Two years later they founded their St. Anns community, which attracted many followers.[85] MacLeod assumed total control, making himself the minister, schoolmaster, and magistrate. A man of dour outlook and uncompromising views, he subjected his people to harangues from the pulpit that could last two to three hours at a time. With good reason the residents were widely known as "the most sober, industrious and orderly" settlers on the Island.[86] Becoming dissatisfied with Cape Breton, MacLeod led a large group to Australia in 1851, although enough remained behind for St. Anns to retain its Scottish identity. Because of MacLeod's disapproval of the gold rush, Australia was declared unsuitable, and so two years later the group moved on to New Zealand, where they settled permanently.[87]

The lifting in 1817 of the restraining order on the granting of freeholds in Cape Breton stimulated an immediate influx from the Highlands and Islands. People came in search of the prime locations around Bras d'Or Lake and the long stretches of coastline that remained unclaimed. Ten years later, when the collapse of the Hebridean kelp industry created terrible destitution, the influx accelerated even further.[88] In spite of their desperate poverty, these Western Isle emigrants managed to pay their passages themselves:

> As soon as it was known in Scotland that there was an allotment of land made on the Island of Cape Breton, a number of poor people in the North of Scotland where the customs-house regulations are not so strictly enforced, found the way to embark three or four vessels; and there were in the years 1824 and 1825, upon a moderate calculation at least, 300 settlers [who] came from the North of Scotland, whose passage did not cost them more than 50 s. or £3; for those people provided for themselves; all that the master of the vessel looks to is to see that they have a pound of oatmeal for every day he calculates the passage to run, from four to five weeks; and every man brings a pound of oatmeal for every day, and half that quantity for a child with perhaps about half a pint of molasses, a little butter and a few eggs; and he provides then with water in the passage, they paying about thirty to thirty five shillings. Those settlers come out there upon their own expense; there was not a mouthful of provisions or anything given to them by government; they settled themselves upon the land that Sir James Kempt [lieutenant- governor of Nova Scotia] allotted to them: and I doubt whether there is in Scotland so happy a set of people as those.[89]

When R.J. Uniacke, a North Sydney merchant, gave this evidence to the Emigration Select Committee of 1826, Cape Breton had already become a refuge for poverty-stricken Scots. As a Presbyterian minister ruefully observed, "There is not a place in the whole world professing Christianity where there are so many families so near to each other and so utterly destitute as our poor countrymen in this Island are."[90]

And yet they kept coming in ever greater numbers, even after Cape Breton's land regulations were changed in 1827. Free grants were abolished, and in their place was created a regime of land sales by public auction. Realizing that they could grab their land by squatting, Western Isle emigrants proceeded as normal.[91] By 1837, more than half of Cape Breton's population was thought to be squatting on Crown land, but by then settlers were finding it exceedingly difficult to acquire land.[92] Some Catholic Highlanders headed for the Codroy Valley in southwest Newfoundland during the 1840s, where they created enduring communities for themselves.[93] However, a more positive development for Cape Breton Island was the large capital investment made by the British-based General Mining Association in Sydney's coalfield.[94] The Sydney mines were greatly expanded beginning in 1827, and production rose sharply. Jobs in the coal-mining industry were snapped up by local people and were clearly drawing newcomers from the Western Isles. For instance, nearly half of all the South Uist emigrants who arrived in the 1840s settled in the Sydney area.[95] Similar employment benefits came to the New Glasgow area in mainland Nova Scotia when the same company developed the Albion mines.[96]

Meanwhile, as a result of the demise of kelp production in Skye and the evictions that followed in 1829–30, Lord MacDonald's tenants were heading for Prince Edward Island. By this time, Skye people had acquired a new township in the Island – named Uigg (lot 50), after Uig in Skye. It was adjacent to the already established Skye communities in Belfast, which had been founded in 1803. This was a major coup. Skye people now had two adjoining townships in which to expand their settlements. Their organizational abilities were very much on display when the first group of eighty-four families arrived in 1829. "With prudent foresight characteristic of their race they came provided with 12 months provisions and an ample stock of warm clothing. They have all relatives already settled in the Island chiefly about Belfast, and with the exception of one family it is, we understand, their intention to locate in that thriving settlement."[97]

Many more Skye groups followed over the next three years. Ten years later, following continuing economic devastation and further clearances, even more Skye settlers arrived on the Island. These later groups received financial assistance from their landlord to emigrate.[98] A group of 229, who came in 1840, were described as being "in robust health" and were expected to "prove themselves to be a hardy industrious class of settlers"[99] A second group of 315, who arrived shortly afterwards, were said to have "property and are likely to be good settlers."[100] The overwhelming impression is of positively motivated people who sought a better life in Prince Edward Island's Skye communities. Many of Lord MacDonald's North Uist tenants had also gone to Cape Breton at this time to join the extensive communities that had been formed there decades earlier.[101] As was the case with the Skye people, he had provided the funds for their transport, but the emigrants had chosen the destinations and planned their relocation with great care.

This pattern was repeated once again in Sutherland. With the passing of the Poor Law Amendment Act in 1845, landlords became legally responsible for the poor tenants on their estates, and in this changed situation they felt an urgent need to rid themselves of unwanted people. The solution was emigration, and by offering help with removal costs they hoped to achieve a result that suited their own pockets and the future interests of their tenantry. During the dark days of the Highland Famine, from 1846 to 1856, roughly 11,000 Highlanders and Islanders emigrated to British America.

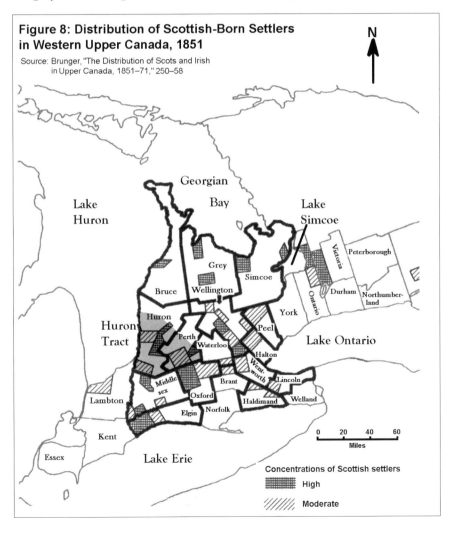

Figure 8: Distribution of Scottish-Born Settlers in Western Upper Canada, 1851

Source: Brunger, "The Distribution of Scots and Irish in Upper Canada, 1851–71," 250–58

While some left unassisted, most were given financial help by landlords and various philanthropic societies. The fallout from these harrowing times continues to evoke strong passions on both sides of the Atlantic. Nevertheless what followed was not a crude banishment of people to some unknown fate and place. When the Duke of Sutherland cleared about 1,000 people from Assynt and Scourie in 1847–48 and assisted them to emigrate, they ended up in various parts of Nova Scotia and in Zorra, Upper Canada.[102] These were the very places where earlier compatriots had established footholds. Similarly, when 663 people from Glenelg and Knoydart (west Inverness-shire) were assisted to emigrate by their landlords in 1849–53, they went to their bolt-holes in Glengarry.[103] Had either group been able to finance its own fares, these are the destinations that they would have chosen.

Having been the early birds of the Maritime provinces, Highlanders also predominated among western Upper Canada's earliest settlers. Settlement promoters, such as Thomas Talbot, acted as facilitators by acquiring grants of Crown land on the basis that they would encourage its colonization. An aristocrat of Anglo-Irish descent, Talbot was Upper Canada's foremost colonizer. Although he was a particularly unlovable character, his supervisory skills were outstanding. Beginning with a field officer's grant of 5,000 acres in Elgin County, he extended his control over twenty-nine townships that were situated along Lake Erie and in the Thames Valley (Figure 8). Together they totalled just over half a million acres.[104] His first settlers, who arrived in 1816, were Highlanders.

Originating from Sutherland, they had been recruited the previous year

Colonel Thomas Talbot (1771–1853) army officer and settlement promoter. He lived at his house in Port Talbot, called Malahide Castle after his ancestral home in Ireland, for fifty years. Talbot died at the age of 81, and was buried in the Anglican cemetery at Tyrconnell near Port Talbot. *Courtesy of Archives of Ontario, Ref: S1362.*

by Lord Selkirk for his Red River Colony in Rupert's Land. Now they were fleeing from the campaign of intimidation and violence that had been waged against them by the North West Company.[105] Upon reaching Upper Canada, some went to West Gwillimbury at the southern end of Lake Simcoe, while others chose to make a fresh start in Talbot's townships. The latter were joined in 1816 by more Highlanders from New York State.[106] Two years later thirty-six Argyll families, mainly Baptists who originated from Knapdale and mid-Argyll, followed them, and a year after that came many more Highlanders.[107] The favourable report sent by the Breadalbane arrivals of 1819 to the *Perthshire Courier* would have encouraged even more followers:

> We have had no trouble getting our lands. When we made choice of them, we applied to Col. Talbot and we have 2 years to perform the settlement duties, which is all to our own advantage. Several of our friends are now here and every new settler who has money, or is industrious, can buy provisions from our neighbours on Talbot Road and in Westminster, on the opposite side of the River Thames, to last until they can grow them from their farms.[108]

By the 1830s, large Scottish concentrations had formed in eleven townships spread across Elgin and Middlesex counties. The influx was being driven both by the adverse economic conditions in Scotland and by the excellent regime that Talbot could offer. Strict land-clearance and road-building goals were set, and, if they were not met, settlers had to vacate their land. Although this was Talbot at his most dictatorial, he achieved excellent results. Highlanders despised him as a person, but they flocked to his townships in great numbers. They did so in spite of the much higher costs involved in travelling this far west. Talbot offered good land, a well-managed regime, and sufficient space for Highlanders to settle together. They could uphold Highland culture while improving their material well-being. This meant that they had the best of both worlds.

Operating on a much smaller scale was William Dickson, a Dumfries-shire-born lawyer and merchant. In 1816, he obtained an entire township just to the east of Zorra, and ten years later his first recruits, from his native Dumfriesshire and nearby Roxburghshire and Selkirkshire, were heading

Site of the "Auld Kirk" in West Gwillimbury (Simcoe County), which
had attracted Highlanders who had fled from Red River. A timber-
framed church built in 1827 replaced a log church built four years
earlier. *Photograph by Geoff Campey.*

for Dumfries Township.[109] His success in attracting settlers was mainly due
to the generous financial terms he offered. By allowing people credit facilities to purchase stock, implements, and provisions and exemptions from
down payments, he essentially bankrolled their settlements. The Scottish
communities at Fergus and Bon Accord, in Nichol Township (Wellington
County), were established by prominent Scots who, having purchased their
sites, led families to them from their homeland. Fergus, which was founded
in 1833 by the Perthshire-born landowner Adam Fergusson and James
Webster, a lawyer from Angus, attracted mainly Perthshire people. A year
later Bon Accord was formed by Aberdeenshire people who had chosen
George Elmslie, an Aberdeen merchant, to select and purchase their site.[110]
As both settlements continued to draw followers, distinctive colonies were
formed by people with shared geographical origins and traditions.

Having acquired the newly surveyed townships of Thorah (Ontario
County) and Eldon (Victoria County), just to the east of Lake Simcoe, in
1825, Donald Cameron hoped to use his Highland contacts to locate settlers, but his colonizing career ended in failure (Figure 8).[111] Cameron had
little capital behind him and struggled to find people who could finance
their travel costs. To make his site seem more appealing, he claimed that his

land lay along the St. Lawrence River, and, to avoid being investigated by the government, he claimed to have far more settlers than he actually had. Once the government uncovered this deception, he ended up in jail, and legal battles dragged on for years. And yet in the midst of this shambles came large numbers of settlers from the Argyll islands, especially from Islay. When a Presbyterian minister from the Glasgow Colonial Society visited Thorah and Eldon in 1833, he found feisty Highlanders who were clearly enjoying their new-found freedoms:

> The generality of the people of Thorah and Eldon seemed to me to be rugged as the rocks they had left in Scotland and wild as the forests they possess in Canada. They seemed much given to drink, and if I judge from what I witnessed, a few of them are given to fight. Free from the restraints of religion and education they are growing up like wild beasts.[112]

The Lake Simcoe region together with the areas to the north and west of York (Toronto) attracted wave after wave of Argyll settles over many decades.

Emigration from Scotland to Upper Canada reached new heights beginning in 1830 when inland communications improved and the Canada Company became operational.[113] John Galt, the well-known Scottish novelist, gave the enterprise added appeal to Scots when he became its first commissioner. The company provided settlers with an overall framework within which colonization could proceed.[114] It offered land on reasonable terms, employment opportunities,

John Galt in 1824, artist Edward Hastings. Galt was the first secretary and superintendent of the Canada Company. The son of a sea captain, he was born in Ayrshire and was educated at a Greenock grammar school. In later life he became an internationally renowned novelist. Picture engraved by T. A. Woolnoth. *Courtesy Library and Archives Canada C–007940.*

credit facilities, and an infrastructure of roads, churches, and schools.[115] Nearly half of its two-and-a-half million acres fell within the Huron Tract, a vast triangle of a little over a million acres fronting on Lake Huron (Figure 8).[116]

In his *Caen-Iuil an Fhir-Imrich do dh'America Mu-Thuath* (*The Emigrant's Guide to North America*), written in Gaelic and published in 1841, Robert MacDougall warned fellow Highlanders of the voluminous quantities of literature being written about the Huron Tract. "When the Company began selling their own land in the Huron Tract, they filled not only America, but nearly the whole world with papers concerning it."[117] He cautioned them against being taken in by the company's exaggerated claims that "everything would be wonderful" when the reality was so very different.[118] And yet, in spite of this over-zealous marketing, the Canada Company attracted large numbers of Scots to its holdings. With the threat posed by advancing sheep farms in the Breadalbane (Perthshire) estate during the early 1830s, tenants headed for the townships of North and South Easthope in the Huron Tract, where they found conditions very much to their liking:

> The land here is good and well-watered, the terms of the Upper Canada Land Company are liberal, requiring the settler only to pay a fifth of the purchase money when the land is applied for, and the remainder in five yearly instalments with interest at six per cent ... There are grist mills and saw mills within a few miles of us east and west, also a store where goods of all kinds are sold. This settlement is mostly Scotch, almost wholly so where we are settled, and the utmost goodwill and unanimity prevails. We enjoy, though obtained at present by hard labour and perseverance, all the necessary worldly comforts and with the prospect, if we and our families are spared, of seeing them and us all independent and comfortable farmers, farming our own land.[119]

The first group came unaided, but those who followed in the 1840s received funds from the second Marquis of Breadalbane.[120]

The great distress experienced in Tiree, Mull, and Iona following crop failures brought around 2,100 Hebridean settlers to western Upper Canada between 1847 and 1851.[121] Although they arrived in a destitute state, they had firm views on where they would settle. Some took up holdings in the Highland-dominated community at Fergus, but the majority settled in the untamed wildernesses of Bruce and Grey counties, to the north of the Huron Tract, which were just being opened up to colonizers.[122] Most of them received some financial help from their landlord, the 8th Duke of Argyll, but they also had to rely on the charitable "Emigrant Fund," administered by the Upper Canada authorities, to get to their final destinations.[123] A considerable number petitioned the duke for assistance to emigrate, although there were some who preferred to remain on "the patches on which they are annually half-starved."[124]

East Williams Township in the Huron Tract was the eventual destination of the many hundreds of people who were cleared from Colonel John Gordon of Cluny's estates in South Uist, Barra, and Benbecula and from Lord Macdonald's estate in North Uist. About 3,000 of Colonel Gordon's former tenants sailed to Quebec in ten ships between 1848 and 1851, while, on a much smaller scale, three hundred people left from Lord Macdonald's North Uist estate in 1849 in two ships.[125] All of the emigrants were financially assisted by their landlords. Lord Macdonald's evictions at Sollas, at the northern end of North Uist, attracted great controversy, while Colonel Gordon's brutal clearance methods caused a national outcry.[126] Colonel Gordon's "people go away quietly and are most anxious to leave, offering to sell their clothes and do anything to get away."[127] While this was one of the most infamous of all the clearances, the fact remains that Gordon's tenants could now look forward to a better life. As Adam Hope, a wheat merchant in St. Thomas, Upper Canada, noted, "These poor emigrants will no doubt endure a good many privations during the coming winter, but I predict they will get more to eat in the township of Williams [Middlesex County] than they would have got in Uist had they remained there. Provisions are abundant and of course cheap and labour dear. The land is of the very finest quality and much of it is in the hands of the Canada Company."[128]

The same was true of the Lewis tenants who transplanted their communities to remote stretches of the Eastern Townships in Lower Canada. Having begun the process of establishing sheep farms on the island in 1838, Stewart MacKenzie of Seaforth assisted fifteen families to emigrate to an area of the Eastern Townships under the control of the British American

The Tolsta Pioneer Cemetery in Winslow Township (Frontenac County).
Tolsta is named after Tolsta in Lewis. *Photograph by Geoff Campey.*

Land Company.[129] There were no previously formed Lewis communities
for them to go to, and so it had been a case of choosing a new site. In spite
of the huge difficulties that they faced in adapting to their strange and for-
bidding surroundings, the initial Lewis settlers were optimistic about their
prospects and wrote favourable reports back home. Thus began one of the
largest, sustained influxes from a Hebridean island to a single area of British
North America. Successive groups came over a period of forty years and
colonized a huge area stretching across six townships and three counties.[130]

The influx was particularly large in 1851, when the island's owner, Sir
James Matheson, assisted roughly 1,500 people to emigrate.[131] Matheson's
funding was very generous. When he met the Lewis settlers at Quebec,
Archibald Buchanan, the Quebec immigration agent, could not help but
contrast their fit and healthy condition with the miserable state of Gordon
of Cluny's Barra and South Uist tenants, who kept arriving with insufficient
provisions.[132] All in all, Matheson spent over £10,000 on the removal costs
of some 2,337 Lewis people who emigrated between 1851 and 1855.[133]

Matheson provided his Lewis tenants with an escape route to a better
life. Another Highland landlord went one step further by seeing for himself
what the New World had to offer. Having assisted four hundred of his Islay
tenants to emigrate in 1862–63, John Ramsay went to visit them in the
wilds of Lake Simcoe eight years later.[134] There he met men such as James

Jamieson, who could speak "of the advantages which working men have in Canada in strong terms, as compared with Islay." People "spoke cheerfully of the abundance of all the necessaries of life, which they possessed, in contrast with their straitened means at home."[135] His visit convinced him of the merits of emigration, not because it had relieved him of unwanted paupers, but because of the better life it gave to the people who had left: "I went ... to visit the residents from Islay who are located on the bank of Lake Simcoe, Georgian Bay and Lake Huron ... and what I saw there fully satisfied me that whatever people thought of the fact of people emigrating to Western Canada, I came home with the solid conviction that it was certainly the people who had occasion to be benefited by their removal from the Western Isles. I know I am subjecting myself to the criticism of those who deprecate the removal of a single soul from the Hebrides."[136]

About the time when Ramsay was visiting his former Islay tenants, a Kincardineshire sea captain, by the name of William Brown, was attracting

Stonehaven Railway Station, where many of William Brown's recruits began their journey to New Brunswick. The platforms are the same today as they would have been in 1873 when the first group boarded their train to Glasgow. Just over five hundred people, who originated mainly from Kincardineshire, travelled that year on the steamship *Castalia* to Saint John. A further group of two hundred arrived in the following year. *Photograph by Geoff Campey.*

a huge following in the northeast of Scotland simply by selling the notion
of family emigration. In all, he persuaded some seven hundred emigrants to
follow him to Victoria County, New Brunswick, where they founded
New Kincardineshire, named after their home county.[137] It was one of the
largest groups ever to reach New Brunswick.

The factors that pulled Scots to British America were every bit as important as those that caused them to leave. Most emigration, whether by Lowlanders or by Highlanders, was voluntary, self-financed, and carefully planned.
Undoubtedly, some Highlanders were pressed to emigrate, but, even in these
circumstances, the positive benefits of the New World played their part in
determining where they would settle. Location preferences changed as new
areas were opened up for colonization. The Maritime provinces had lost out
to Upper Canada by the 1830s, and, later in the century, it would be Upper
Canada's turn to lose out to the prairie provinces. Ontario Scots suddenly
rushed into the prairies during the 1870s and 1880s to take advantage of the
region's fertile land, and, shortly after this, fresh waves of emigrants began
arriving from Scotland.

Five

SETTLEMENT GROWTH IN WESTERN CANADA

I have met a Canadian on his way to Barrie,
[Upper] Canada ... he told me that a man would be better off
in one year in the Red River territory than he would be in
[Upper] Canada in ten.[1]

B Y 1870, THE GOOD FARMLAND IN the Red River region of the new Province of Manitoba was attracting Scots who had previously emigrated to Ontario. Alexander Campbell, who lived near Winnipeg, wanted his friends in Ontario and those back in Scotland to know what a "good country" it was. "A man don't have to work the life out of himself working as there are no stones or stumps to contend with."[2] He had heard that a large number of people had come to Riding Mountain, 150 miles to the northwest of Winnipeg, in the spring of the previous year and was now recommending it to his friends. And yet, although the region had obvious agricultural potential, its merits were only just beginning to become widely known.

Fur traders had been careful to keep silent about the fertile lands in the Red River region. Having visited the area in 1814, Lord Selkirk's agent, Miles MacDonell, raved about "the fertility of the soil in the highest terms" and thought that there was little doubt "of the practicability of raising good crops."[3] Selkirk appreciated even then that the region would one day yield far greater riches in crops than it ever would from the fur trade. He actually predicted that it would become one of the great bread baskets of the world: "It is a very moderate calculation to say that if these regions [Assiniboia] were occupied by an industrious population, they might afford ample means of subsistence for thirty millions of British subjects."[4] So he decided to found an agricultural community, but in the process he had to contend with the mighty fur-trade barons who resisted his every move. Because the region had traditionally been dedicated solely to the needs of the fur trade, Selkirk's intervention was viewed with great alarm. Spending vast sums of money and putting his settlers in grave peril, Selkirk saw his venture through to the bitter end, but his battles left him with a tarnished reputation and sent him to an early grave.

Selkirk became a shareholder of the Hudson's Bay Company through marriage, and, after investing £35,000 in it, acquired overall control by 1811.[5] He obtained over 116,000 square miles in the Assiniboia District from the company that same year on condition that he recruit two hundred men annually to work for it. The company, which had earlier experienced difficulties in finding recruits, believed that Selkirk with his contacts and influence in the Highlands of Scotland and Ireland would be the ideal person to command the operation. In taking on this recruitment task, Selkirk was more than happy to be "bound in a penalty of £10 for each man deficient," arguing that he could "buy his way out of the commitment if need be."[6] He kept silent about the fact that his real motive in acquiring the land was to launch an agricultural settlement. He loathed the fur trade but recognized that he had to work within it rather than around it.

Selkirk scoured all parts of the Highlands and Islands but rapidly came to the conclusion that the men needed "are of a description that can be found only in Orkney."[7] Orcadian men had been recruited for the firm on a regular basis since 1722, and by the end of the century they represented nearly 80 per cent of the company's workforce.[8] Selkirk believed that these men, "though less alert and animated than the natives of some other parts of the Kingdom, make up that defect by other qualifications of at least equal importance and in particular are remarkably careful, steady and sober."[9] They were also known to be particularly good at adapting to a harsh climate, while Stromness, being the last port of call before leaving Britain, was an ideal place to load provisions on company ships.

Having joined in 1801, Joshua Halcro, "a respectable, well-informed and excellent clerk and trader," worked in the area east of Lake Winnipeg for twenty-one years and then returned to Orkney.[10] Andrew Wilson signed on

Plaque in Stromness com-
memorating the place where
Orkney men were recruited by
Hudson's Bay Company
agents. *Photograph by Geoff
Campey.*

in 1806, returned home again in 1818, and two years later resumed his service. Renowned for his boating skills, he was particularly "useful in going to Indian tents to fetch furs and provisions."[11] And Thomas Isbister, who began work in 1812 as a labourer, "deficient in education," proved to be "a tolerable trader" and ended up as a company postmaster by 1830.[12] Often three or four brothers would work for the company. James, the eldest son of the Tait family, joined in 1778 and was followed in the next six years by John, William, and one other younger brother.[13] James, John, and William later settled at Red River.

However, finding recruits was the least of Selkirk's worries. His real difficulties began when he selected the Red River site. He reasoned that, with the proximity of the Hudson's Bay Company headquarters, his colonists would have a ready-made market for their farm produce. He also intended that his colony would increase its population by attracting retired company workers who would otherwise be returning home. But to Simon MacGillivray, the London agent for the North West Company, the Hudson's Bay Company's principal rival, Selkirk's decision to plant a colony in this fur-trade heartland was a declaration of war. Fearing that the North West Company's supply routes would be put in jeopardy, he declared that Selkirk "must be driven to abandon" his venture, since "his success would strike at the very existence of our trade."[14] Caught in the bitter feuding, which eventually became a battle for overall control of the North American fur trade, Selkirk's settlers were opposed every inch of the way.

In spite of the spoiling tactics of the North West Company, Selkirk's agents made good progress initially. In 1811, they enlisted 125 men as company workers, the majority originating from the Orkney Islands.[15] An advance party from this group laid the foundations of the Red River settlement in the following year, and in that same year a second group arrived, which included ten families from Mull and Islay. They were "well-selected families" with "scarcely any children below eight years old and the numbers of lads and lassies fully or nearly grown and without the parents not super annuated."[16] Then, in 1813, "a most interesting body of emigrants from a quarter not hitherto in our contemplation but extremely promising in every respect," came to Selkirk's attention. They were Sutherland Highlanders from Kildonan, "where one great sheep farm had led to the displacing of more than 100 families."[17] In fact, more Sutherland people came forward in 1813 than could be accommodated in the available Hudson's Bay Company ships. Having been told that they were "at a loss how to proceed," Selkirk persuaded ninety of them to board the *Prince of Wales* at Stromness, bound for Churchill in June 1813:

> If they [Sutherland emigrants] do well and are satisfied with the situation, they will be the means of attracting a great body of their friends and others from the same County, who must emigrate in the course of a few years. People of a superior description than any we have yet had to do with. The Sutherland men seem to me, both in person and moral character a fine race of men. There are great numbers among them who have prosperity enough to pay their passage and settle themselves with very little assistance and many capable of paying in cash for their land.[18]

After suffering a typhus epidemic during the crossing and a bleak winter at Fort Churchill, the group reached Red River in June of the following year. They soon faced a further ordeal. Miles MacDonell, the colony's first superintendent, had enraged the North West Company by suddenly banning the export of preserved buffalo meat (pemmican) from the region. The staple food of local Natives, it was essential to the North West Company's fur-trade brigades.[19] So the company took its revenge. Rumours were spread that the Highlanders were in imminent danger of being attacked, and, while this

Painting by Peter Rindisbacher, 1821, of ships meeting in the North Atlantic. The *Prince of Wales* and the *Eddystone*, two Hudson's Bay Company ships, are shown in the foreground. *Courtesy of Library and Archives Canada C–001908.*

was being done, a company spokesman dangled an offer of an all-expenses-paid transfer to the safety of Upper Canada.[20] These tactics worked. In the summer of 1815 most of the Sutherland colonists were taken to Upper Canada, after which their settlement was razed to the ground. However, some brave stalwarts remained nearby and later returned.[21] And, despite the negative publicity that his venture must have generated back in Scotland, Selkirk managed to persuade a second Sutherland contingent of 118 people to emigrate to Red River that same year.[22] Their unhappy situation at home, coupled with Selkirk's offer of credit to finance their travel and other relocation costs, proved sufficiently compelling to cause them to risk everything on a better life abroad.[23]

Realizing just how determined Selkirk was to found his settlement, the North West Company intensified its counterattack and employed even more brutal methods. Soon after the arrival of the second Sutherland group, the colony was attacked by men in the employment of the firm. Twenty-one settlers and Robert Semple, the governor of the Hudson's Bay Company territories, were slaughtered in the infamous Seven Oaks Massacre of July 29, 1816.[24] Fleeing to nearby Jack River, the remaining one hundred or so settlers survived the winter with the help of Peguis, the Saulteaux chief, and his kinsmen, who hunted for them and dragged food supplies to them on sleds over great distances. Selkirk's arrival in the following year, with his Swiss mercenaries from disbanded de Meuron and de Watteville regiments, brought the settlers their first glimmer of hope.[25] The military muscle that he brought with him, his wealth, and his mere presence brought immediate order and calm, and soon the colony was back on its feet again.[26] Nevertheless Selkirk misjudged the political climate, and in the propaganda war that followed the North West Company turned public opinion against him. He was portrayed as the aggressive enemy of the fur trade who had put his people in grave danger for his own selfish motives.

Permanent peace came to Red River through the merger of the two warring fur-trade companies in 1821, the year after Selkirk's death.[27] The two enterprises united under the name of the Hudson's Bay Company, and the settlement prospered thereafter. The sudden influx of workers who were made redundant following the merger enlarged its population, while another factor in its eventual success was the continuing support given to the colony by Selkirk's family. In all, some 1,300 redundant trappers, traders, clerks, labourers, and voyageurs[28] took up residence. The new arrivals were

Edward "Bear" Ellice, M.P., fur trade baron, merchant banker and property speculator. Being the most influential of the North West Company partners, he was one of Selkirk's deadliest enemies. Ellice was a key figure in the merger of the two fur trade companies and he was also a founding director and deputy governor of the Canada Company. *Courtesy of Library and Archives Canada C-104372.*

mainly of Orkney, French-Canadian, Native,[29] and mixed-race extraction, the last group being the so-called Métis, who were the offspring of Orkney and French-Canadian company workers and their First Nation wives.[30] The Orkney Métis families, who were English-speaking, settled separately from the French Métis community, but together they formed the largest ethnic group in Red River. Meanwhile, the Orkney Métis soon attracted the evangelical efforts of the Church Missionary Society, an Anglican organization, which promoted the Christian faith in remote corners of the world. Because it extolled the ideals of a self-sufficient and agriculturally based society, Selkirk's vision came closer to realization, although it would take many decades before Red River's farming potential was fully developed.

For understandable reasons, the Kildonan settlers had failed to attract any followers. But, although their numbers were small, Orkney men continued to trickle into the colony once their employment contracts were completed, with some arriving even before the merger of 1821.[31] A group of "Orkneymen came with their wives, white and brown," in 1818, together with their children, and settled along the Assiniboine River. There they laid the foundations of "Orkney Town," in what would become St. James Parish.[32] But none the less, before 1821 Red River's population grew very slowly. Survival depended on acquired hunting skills. The Kildonan settlers had learned to "kill buffalo, walk on snow-shoes, had trains of dogs trimmed with ribbons, bells and feathers in true Indian style; and in other respects were making rapid steps in the arts of savage life."[33] Plagues of locusts in 1818–19 added to their difficulties, and, but for food aid supplied by Lord Selkirk, they probably would have perished.

The 1821 company merger was a major turning point. Having foreseen that different ethnic groups would need to be accommodated, Selkirk had directed Miles MacDonell nine years earlier to keep the English-speaking and French Métis families "a little distance apart so as to avoid the occasion of quarrels and disturbance."[34] Accordingly, the Orkney Scots and other English-speaking Métis were concentrated mainly at the northern end of the colony, while the French Métis lived at the southern end (Figure 9).[35] The various communities lived side by side, although they were very different.[36] The Métis had hunting and fur-trapping traditions, while most of the Kildonan settlers were farmers.[37] The French Métis were Roman Catholic, while the Orkney Métis were Anglican. The Reverend John West, the colony's first

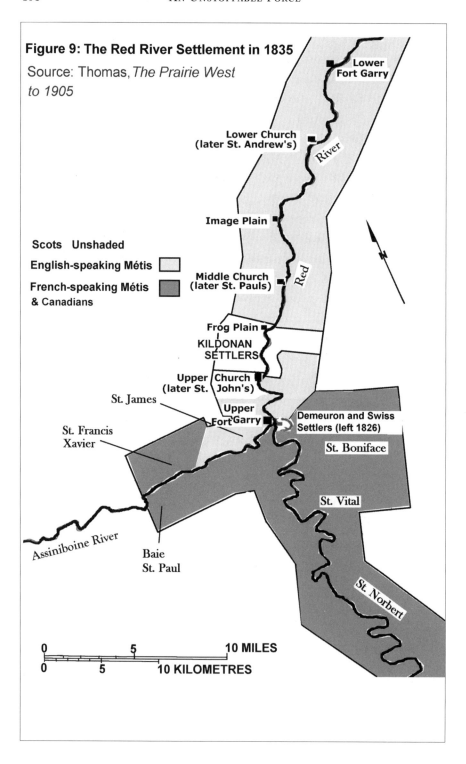

Figure 9: The Red River Settlement in 1835

Source: Thomas, *The Prairie West to 1905*

Lower Fort Garry

Lower Church (later St. Andrew's)

River

Image Plain

Scots   Unshaded

English-speaking Métis

French-speaking Métis & Canadians

Middle Church (later St. Pauls)

Red

Frog Plain

KILDONAN SETTLERS

Upper Church (later St. John's)

St. James

St. Francis Xavier

Upper Fort Garry

Demeuron and Swiss Settlers (left 1826)

St. Boniface

St. Vital

Assiniboine River

Baie St. Paul

St. Norbert

0   5   10 MILES

0   5   10 KILOMETRES

Kildonan Church, which was completed in 1853. *Photograph by Geoff Campey.*

Anglican missionary, who arrived in 1820, made the building of a log church his top priority, and three years later it was completed.[38] But nothing was done for the Gaelic-speaking Presbyterians of Kildonan. Numbering "upwards of fifty heads of family," they desperately wanted "a minister of their own tenets" who could preach in "their own language."[39] Despite constant pleading, they had to wait nearly thirty-five years for a minister. In deperation, they attended the Anglican church, but they "never became reconciled to the Prayer Book and would take no part in the response."[40]

Among the new arrivals of 1823 were people who needed to be assisted through their first winter, but there were also "several who have saved considerable sums and will become useful and respectable colonists."[41] They included retired Orkney men such as William Flett and his brother George, who were long-serving company workers. The Morayshire-born Alexander Ross, who arrived two years later with his Native wife, Sally, and four children, had led expeditions for the Hudson's Bay Company's Northern Department after the merger.[42] James Sutherland, another Orcadian, worked first as a trader and later as a chief factor in charge of a district.[43] Retiring to the Rapids (St. Andrew's Parish) with his Native wife in 1827, he liked what he saw and a year later wrote to his brother back in Orkney extolling its virtues: "Here I have everything that a man requires for the good of both soul and body. Religion in its purity, the best of climates, a soil that produces all the productions of the earth in perfection with very little labour; the society is not extensive but agreeable."[44]

In just four years he acquired "800 acres, of the best land," and had a farm that was "well-stocked with cattle, horses and pigs."[45] James Sutherland was unusual in having so much farmland. Most people in the Métis communities lived almost "entirely by the chase," relying on buffalo hunts and fishing to support themselves, although they also had small farms.[46]

Red River's French Métis population rose substantially in 1824, when a large number of families moved to the colony from Pembina, an area to the south of the settlement.[47] By 1826, Red River's population of roughly 1,500 included former fur-trade workers from many corners of the world. In order to meet their needs the Reverend John West had to distribute copies of the Bible in English, Gaelic, German, Danish, Italian, and French, which "were all gratefully received in this polyglot community."[48] Then five years later thirty-six Orcadian, four English, and twenty Métis families arrived in Red River from James Bay.[49] Shortly after this, in 1831, came a change in the Hudson's Bay Company's recruitment policy, which suddenly brought Lewis men to the region.

Having experienced difficulties in recruiting Orcadian men for the Hudson's Bay Company's Northern Department, Governor George Simpson recommended that men from Lewis should be sought. No doubt the dire poverty being experienced on Stewart MacKenzie of Seaforth's Lewis estate had stimulated interest in company jobs. His factor, Alexander Stewart, was on hand when the Hudson's Bay Company ship departed in 1832 with what would be the first of many Lewis contingents:

The Hudson's Bay squadron have been in the harbour [at Stornoway] for the last four days – they have taken on board forty young men and sailed last evening ... I have taken upon myself as a present, from you, to have sent on board the ships a small supply of vegetables from the Lodge garden ... they are to touch here next year and will probably continue to do so; they have not touched here before now since the year 1810.[50]

The arrival of Lewis men became a regular event, making them the second-largest labour source after the Orkney Islands.[51] But, unlike the Orcadian men, very few Lewis men remained at Red River. They rarely sought a lifelong career in the fur trade or the farming opportunities to be had in the colony after retirement.[52]

By 1835, Red River was principally a Métis society of some 3,000 people who derived their livelihood from the combined pursuits of fishing, hunting, and farming.[53] Each settler was cultivating, on average, about five to six acres annually, which was roughly half the amount being farmed by the Kildonan settlers.[54] The Kildonan settlers were its main farmers, but in numerical terms they were a diminishing element. Of 533 adult males, only sixty were classed as Scottish and seventy as Orcadians.[55] They were a tiny minority. People such as Thomas Anderson, Margaret Garrioch, Mary Tait, and George Spence, who might be mistaken for Orcadians, had become assimilated within the Métis community.[56] More than anything the colony was a very cosmopolitan place, having attracted retired fur traders from many countries – men such as Ferdinando Sebeller from Italy, Andre Jankasky from Poland, Joseph Gugoretz from Switzerland, Peter Ezasmus from Denmark, and Henry HicKenberger from Guernsey.[57]

In 1871 W.L. Morton described the still-visible "farmsteads of the half-breeds and the Orkney and Kildonan Scottish settlers, which presented an

St. Andrew's Anglican Church in Red River, Manitoba. It is the oldest stone church in western Canada. Built from 1844–49, it replaced an earlier log church that had been founded in 1831 by the Reverend William Cockran. *Photograph by Geoff Campey.*

almost unbroken line along the west bank" of the Red River.[58] The Kildonan settlers occupied a small area known as Frog Plain, just to the north of
the forks of the Red and Assiniboine rivers, while the Orkney and other
English-speaking Métis communities were concentrated to the north of
Frog Plain in the parish of St. Andrews. Meanwhile, the French-speaking
Métis families were to be found along the southern stretch of the Red River
and on both sides of the Assiniboine River (Figure 9). Selkirk's policy of
granting the various groups their own separate lands ensured that each
would expand within distinct boundaries. However, these harmonious
arrangements became increasingly unstable as pressure mounted in the late
1850s to hasten the end of Hudson's Bay Company rule in the region and
to transfer Red River to Canada.

John Gunn wrote to his brother James Ross in Toronto to tell him that
Red River was "in a regular ferment about getting joined to Canada ... We are
determined never to relax our efforts until their [the Hudson's Bay
Company's] despotic power is laid in the dust, and we are protected by the
noble fabric of the British constitution which has been reared by wisdom and
cemented by the blood of our forefathers."[59] Gunn was certain that a petition
requesting "the protection of the Canadian government's laws and institutions" would be "a numerously signed one."[60] Its organizer, Captain William
Kennedy, a Métis of Orcadian and Cree descent, made sure that it was.
Feeling bitter towards his ex-employer, the Hudson's Bay Company,
he spoke forcefully against the company's trade monopoly in Rupert's Land
and rallied support for the cause of Canadian annexation. Having attracted
whole-hearted support from Red River's Kildonan Scots and the Orkney
Métis, the petition was presented to the Parliamentary Select Committee,
which sat in 1857 to consider the British territories under the administration
of the Hudson's Bay Company.[61] The committee, having heard testimonies
from company, church, and settler representatives, concluded that the firm's
record in preventing settlement was damaging to Canadian interests, and it
also warned of the dangers of American encroachment. Nevertheless, twelve
years elapsed before the government took any action.

Plans to transfer the Northwest to Canada, which began in earnest in
1868, aroused strong feelings from the French Métis, who were understandably outraged at not being consulted in the matter. Concerned that their
status, land rights, and way of life would be threatened by Canada's

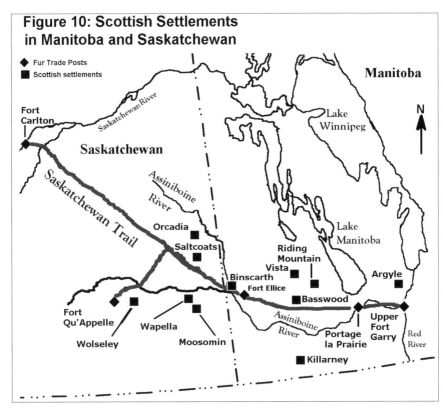

Figure 10: Scottish Settlements in Manitoba and Saskatchewan

takeover of their region, they mounted a campaign of resistance, which was led by Louis Riel.[62] With their support concentrated almost entirely among French-speaking Métis, the Resistance of 1869–70 ultimately failed. A military expedition sent to Red River in 1870 by Canada's new government secured its authority over the new province of Manitoba, but the resentment and bitter feelings lived on.[63]

Selkirk's Red River colonists focused the attention of both the British and Canadian governments at a particularly crucial time. Their protestations – that they were British subjects and wanted "the same liberty and freedom of commerce, as well as security of property," as was enjoyed by people "in all other possessions of the British Crown" – put down an important marker.[64] In 1869, just a year before Manitoba joined the Dominion, the Hudson's Bay Company governor had been predicting that annexation of Rupert's Land to the United States was unavoidable. The nation to the south had been hankering after the region's fertile lands for some thirty years. But for the existence of the Red River colony, this vast territory would almost certainly have been lost to the United States. Selkirk had foreseen these dangers decades before anyone else. His colonists had presided over the region until Britain and Canada woke up to its potential and sought to include it in the Confederation of Canada.[65]

Although people from Kildonan and St. Andrew's had campaigned as one on the annexation to Canada issue, they did not benefit equally from the outcome. The prospects of the Orkney Métis of St. Andrew's plummeted with the sudden influx to the region of English-speaking settlers from Ontario, which began in 1871. As political power passed into the hands of these newcomers, their own influence waned. The bigotry and intolerance shown to the so-called half-breeds blocked their integration into the Red River Society and caused many Orkney Métis to leave the area.[66] Meanwhile, as Red River became Winnipeg, colonization soon progressed beyond its original boundaries.

With their early domination of the fur trade, and extensive investment in the railways and land companies, Scots were well placed to take advantage of the new opportunities that were opening up in the prairies.[67] Predictably, they were well-represented in the waves of Ontario migrants coming into the area during the 1870s and 1880s. They had heard "of the new frontier, with its prairie land, which held neither stone nor stump to check the plough."[68] Scots from Ontario's Lanark, Bruce, Huron, and Grey counties had already moved to the fertile prairie lands of the mid-western United States, and now hundreds of them were heading for the Canadian

Reconstructed Red River cart at Lower Fort Garry in the province of Manitoba. The ox- or horse-drawn carts were used initially by fur-trade brigades and later by immigrants. The carts were constructed entirely of wood and leather. With the building of the Canadian Pacific Railway, the overland brigades came to an end. *Photograph by Geoff Campey.*

prairies.[69] As they arrived before the railways were built, their initial settlements were threaded together by the old Saskatchewan Trail – a wagon trail – which ran from Upper Fort Garry at the forks of the Red and Assiniboine rivers to Fort Carleton, a distance of over five hundred miles (Figure 10).[70] Scottish communities gradually formed along this route or on the north side of the Assiniboine River. Although they made significant inroads into Manitoba and Saskatchewan, Scottish colonizers would not penetrate further west to any great extent until the twentieth century.

Iona settlers, who had previously settled in Grey and Bruce counties in Upper Canada, began arriving in the Vista and Basswood areas of Manitoba during the 1870s and 1880s.[71] And a decade later Islay settlers from Simcoe County were founding a community to the north of Winnipeg which they called Argyle.[72] Ontario settlers who had originated from Ayrshire, Perthshire, Aberdeenshire, and the Lothians ventured much further west to Moffat (near Wolseley) in present-day Saskatchewan.[73] Arriving in 1883, they attracted many followers, with almost half coming from one district in Aberdeenshire, demonstrating the pulling power of family ties.[74] In all, their communities were spread over four townships. That same year seventy Scottish families from Ontario founded Binscarth, naming it after William Bain Scarth, a descendant of the Binscarths of the Orkney Islands, who was a director of the Ontario and Manitoba Land Company.[75]

Meanwhile, the Reverend George Corbett of St. Andrews, Ontario, was complaining bitterly about the steady loss of his congregation to Manitoba. The westward drift of Catholic Highlanders from Glengarry and Stormont counties was due in his opinion to "exaggerated rumours." At first hoping that people would return to Ontario once they realized their mistake, Father Corbett later had to accept the fact that this movement of people was irreversible. In desperation he wrote to Bishop Angus MacDonald in Oban to ask for replacements: "I should prefer some of the Highland Class to fill up vacancies and help to keep up the old Gaelic language among us."[76]

A group from the Isle of Eday (in Orkney) that arrived in 1882 was one of the earliest to reach the region directly from Scotland. Having purchased land from the York Farmers' Colonization Company, they founded Orcadia, north of what is now Yorkton (Figure 10). Many more Orkney families joined them in the years that followed.[77] Impoverished Scots were emigrating in search of better prospects just as others had done decades earlier, only now people came as settlers rather than fur traders. Alexander Begg, who had helped the group to relocate to its "Orkney settlement," found the people "in a very prosperous condition" while maintaining themselves "under the old flag."[78]

As economic conditions deteriorated yet again in the Hebridean islands during the 1880s, some landlords sought to remedy the extreme poverty and distress their tenants were experiencing by offering emigration schemes. However, large-scale clearances were no longer politically acceptable. By this time crofters were making vociferous claims for land rights, and they were resisting enforced removals. It was against this background of crofter discontent and radical agitation that Lady Emily Gordon Cathcart decided in 1883 to offer financial aid to twelve families from her Benbecula and South Uist estate to emigrate to the prairies. Ten families accepted.[79] They, and the forty-five additional families who arrived in the following year, founded Moosomin and Wapella (now in Saskatchewan).[80] Through her philanthropy Lady Cathcart hoped to demonstrate that emigration could help to alleviate the plight of impoverished crofters. "We only tried this experiment as a *test* to see how it would work, hoping that when the government came to legislate they would take into consideration emigration, among other measures, for the relief of crofters."[81]

Lady Cathcart believed that the home secretary had been wrong to "denounce emigration as a 'poor remedy,' as I believe it to be the most beneficial relief that can be given to the poor people if they are willing to avail themselves of it." She had tried to divide the available land on her estate into manageable parcels but was defeated by "the utter impossibility of accommodating all the people." With its isolated location, poor soil, and harsh climate, her estate could not support "the immense population of crofters and squatters." So she concluded that emigration was part of the solution, in spite of the vehement opposition of local activists:

> Since my accession to this property six years ago, I may tell you that I have thrown myself heart and soul into the cause of ameliorating the condition of the crofter population, and I have spared neither interest, money or anxious consideration in the hope of being able to accomplish this end. The result has, however, ended (owing to the mischievous acts of outside agitators) in bitter disappointment to me,

and has put a complete stop to the plans for improvements which I was carrying on, and which were beginning to bear fruit ...[82]

Although Lady Cathcart's crofters would have had limited axe and farming skills, they transformed themselves into prairie homesteaders remarkably well. Giving her impressions four years later, an unnamed Inverness woman who lived a short distance from Moosomin found the Scottish homesteaders to be "in most comfortable circumstances."[83] Being Roman Catholic, they were under the charge of the Reverend David Gillies, a Gaelic-speaking priest from Nova Scotia, who was receiving an annual salary of $350 from the government. "They have built a small place of 16 [feet] by 24 [feet], which serves as a Presbytery, chapel and schoolroom."[84] Donald MacDonald, one of the settlers, liked the fact that in Moosomin "the land is my own." People "would not come back [to Scotland] for love nor money."[85]

The next subsidized emigration scheme, launched in 1888, took thirty families from Lewis, Harris, and North Uist to Killarney (Manitoba). Under this venture, financed by the British government, each family was advanced a loan of £120 and given 160 acres of farmland.[86] Then, in the following year, another forty-nine families from these same islands took up homesteads near Saltcoats (now in Saskatchewan) under an identical scheme.[87] Both schemes had been hotly opposed by local commentators who felt that the money would have been better spent in promoting economic improvements in the Highlands. The schemes had also been hastily implemented and were beset by administrative and financial difficulties.[88] While the Killarney homesteaders thrived, being in a well-settled area, those in the remotely situated Saltcoats had a more difficult time. Even so, Charles Docherty claimed in 1891 that he would not leave Saltcoats "unless I am dragged from it by ropes." And Alexander McDonald thought it "the best place in the world for a man with a family," while another Saltcoats resident, who had worked for the Hudson's Bay Company, said that he "would not return home on any condition."[89] Being mainly fishermen, with little experience of farming, most of the homesteaders gradually left Saltcoats, and, by 1900, it had collapsed as a settlement. Nevertheless the underlying objective of providing an escape from poverty was realized. While they failed to establish their own farms, the Saltcoats settlers found well-paid employment in neighbouring towns or in more prosperous farming districts.

As a result of these resettlement efforts, several hundred poor Hebridean Scots were brought to the prairies. However, they were but a fraction of the total number of Scots who emigrated at this time. Most of the arrivals were self-financing and dispersed themselves widely as they sought the most favourable locations available to them. Completion of the Canadian Pacific Railway across the prairies by 1885, growing awareness of the west's farming potential, and the onset of a severe agricultural depression in Britain stimulated a growing influx that would reach flood proportions by the early twentieth century.

There is no doubt that Scots were well represented. In 1904, when some 12,267 Scots left Glasgow for Canada, 3,391 were bound for Manitoba, 1,005 for the Northwest Territories, and 445 for British Columbia. And five years later, when there were 11,810 arrivals from Scotland, 1,886 were destined for Manitoba, 1,776 for Saskatchewan and Alberta, and 1,495 for British Columbia.[90] Scots increasingly shunned the Atlantic provinces and Quebec in favour of Ontario and the West. A great number of Canadian immigration agents, who operated throughout Britain, assisted prospective emigrants in choosing where they would settle.

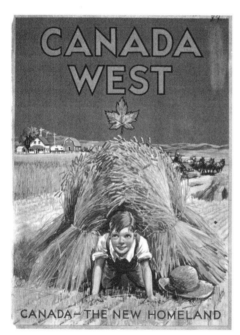

Front cover of the 1927 edition of *Canada West.* The magazine promoted the Prairies, in the hope of attracting British and American immigrants. *Courtesy of Library and Archives Canada E-008224121.*

One such agent was John McLennan. A Canadian of Highland descent, he worked from his office in Aberdeen, from which vantage point he covered the whole of the north of Scotland. He was inundated with inquiries, generally receiving twenty-five to thirty visitors daily.[91] In just one week in March 1907, he carried out 214 interviews, and in the following year he spoke to packed lecture halls all over the area, clocking up 5,500 interviews at one Highland gathering.[92] Interest in the prairies was intense. Thirty Scottish families and several single men were prepared even to settle as farm tenants in an area north of Brooks, Alberta, having been recruited by agents of the Duke of Sutherland in 1913.[93] The duke had purchased 9,000 acres of land with the intention of creating a tenant-farmed estate. However, the scheme flopped. Once the duke's land was offered for sale his former tenants were able to purchase the lots they had been renting, and so it was a positive outcome for them.

Some years earlier the Earl and Countess of Aberdeen had devised a scheme to attract immigrants as far west as the Okanagan Valley of southern British Columbia. Hoping to establish fruit farming in this region, they purchased a 480-acre ranch in the Kelowna area in 1889 from George Grant MacKay, an engineer who had previously built roads at Lady Aberdeen's father's Inverness-shire estate. Naming their property Guisachan, the name given to the Highland estate, they purchased even more land and sold off plots to fruit growers. Although the scheme attracted affluent Scottish and English families to the region, it ended in failure for Lord Aberdeen. He ended up with heavy financial losses on his investment. Nevertheless he was instrumental in establishing the Okanagan Valley as one of Canada's major fruit-growing regions.[94]

As economic conditions in the Hebridean islands plummeted even further during the 1920s, state-aided emigration schemes were introduced once again. The failure of forestry, fishing, and hydro projects to produce substantial improvements in living conditions increased public support for emigration, which by now was regarded in a very positive light. Nearly six hundred Hebridean settlers came to Canada in 1923 under resettlement schemes that were funded jointly by the British and Canadian governments.[95] Roughly three hundred Lewis people, mainly young men, sailed from Stornoway on the *Metagama*,[96] while just under three hundred people travelled as families from the Catholic islands of South Uist, Benbecula, and Barra, sailing on the *Marloch* from Lochboisdale.[97] The Lewis emigrants had farming jobs to go to in Ontario, while the latter were hoping to become homesteaders in Red Deer, Alberta. The jubilant scenes as the *Metagama* sailed away reflected the optimism of everyone concerned:

Great crowds saw them off, the Territorial Pipe Band played them aboard; the Canadian Pacific Company gave a lunch for town councillors and harbour commissioners. The crofters saw them off in their own way: On the north shore the heather was burning and the fire smell came drifting across on a quiet wind to the *Metagama*. Beacons were lit on the coast. Hector MacInnes of North Tolsta told his friends to set fire to the thatch as the ship sailed past the Traigh Mhor. Donald MacLeod of Ness saw a light flashing from the Butt, which he knew to be the torch of a boyhood friend with whom he had often played at signalling. 'What ship,' the flashlight asked, 'this time?' Later his friend told him the ship had signalled a reply: "S.S *Metagama* and *Goodbye*.[98]

Both Hebridean groups attracted very favourable press coverage as they entered Canada. The Lewis group, having been met by Manning Doherty, an Ontario government minister, when it arrived at Saint John, received "a hearty reception" in Toronto. On their arrival, the *People's Journal* of Scotland stated, the "lads and lassies" from Lewis had "achieved a temporary

Scottish immigrants on a train heading west, c. 1911. After 1900 the fastest-growing cities were in the prairie provinces. *Courtesy of Library and Archives Canada, William James Topley, PA-010391.*

The village of Clandonald, Alberta, in 1928, showing grain elevators at the right. *Courtesy of Library and Archives Canada C–028455.*

greatness in the public eye of Canada.”[99] But they were regarded less favourably after many of them broke their work contracts and took up more attractive jobs in the building trade, which were available in big cities such as Toronto and Detroit. Although there were calls for them to be sent back to Scotland, the Ontario government was content for them to remain, as long as they repaid the money lent to them to cover their passages.[100]

The South Uist, Benbecula, and Barra group also received a warm welcome at Saint John. “A new Uist will be born in Alberta,” declared the *People's Journal* soon after the *Marloch* docked. “On all sides were expressions of approval at the appearance of the immigrants.”[101] The Hebridean settlers were welcomed on the quayside by S.R. Jack, president of the St. Andrew's Society, Fred Fisher, mayor of Saint John, and Father Andrew MacDonell, a former Benedictine monk who helped them to find farming jobs or farms of their own in the area. Having founded the Scottish Immigrant Aid Society, MacDonell used the money raised to assist two further contingents of Hebridean Catholics to emigrate to northern Alberta in 1926. By 1928, some 1,315 colonists had been recruited, although not all came from the Western Isles.[102] In northern Alberta they founded the Clanranald Colony on a 30,000-acre tract of land, but it suffered many setbacks. Poor planning, inadequate administration, and recurring crop failures caused debts to accumulate, and as this happened some people left to take up employment in more populated areas.[103] Nevertheless MacDonell's Hebridean Catholics largely succeeded in establishing their colony. In 1954 one-third of the original settlers were still living in Clandonald, and by then its future was secure.[104]

The unfavourable publicity that percolated back to Scotland from Clandonald strengthened the hand of anti-emigration commentators who criticized MacDonell for encouraging the depopulation of the Hebrides. What was needed, they argued, was more public investment in job creation schemes, but as such efforts invariably failed to deliver their promised aims public support for emigration revived once again. Such debates always kept the political spotlight firmly on the Highlands and Islands, thereby placing undue emphasis on this one region.

Although they slipped away virtually unnoticed, Lowlanders actually dominated the overall exodus to Canada. It should also be remembered that extreme poverty was not the sole preserve of Highlanders. Many Lowlanders were also escaping from dire happenings in Scotland. But in addition to these negative factors was the positive desire for self-betterment. Canada's vast acreages, excellent job opportunities, and more liberal social climate were compelling factors in the decision to emigrate.

Six

DID THEY GO,
OR WERE THEY SENT?

Imagine nearly 200 carriages, four-wheeled, scattered all about
outside the church. It was such a sight as I never saw and
never could have seen in the Highlands; yet here there is
hardly a family which does not drive to church and market in
a nice light wagon or carriage; but in spite of all this, mistaken
people at home will advise the poor crofter not to emigrate to a
country where such things are possible to those who came out a
few years ago in a state of penury and want.[1]

DURING HIS 1880 VISIT TO PICTOU, NOVA Scotia, Alexander Mackenzie gazed with disbelief at the two hundred carriages that were
lined up outside the Presbyterian church. As he joined the congregation of seven hundred people, he reflected on the financial rewards that
the New World could offer. Being a crofter's son, he identified with the
many people around him who were of Highland extraction. They had left
"in impoverished circumstances but are now in comfort and even affluence,
possessing lands and means of their own."[2] He went on. "The beauty on all
sides is simply indescribable. The pretty, clean-looking white-painted
wooden houses surrounded by fine arable land, in its turn enclosed within
a thick and beautifully variegated forest, each appearing in miniature like
one of our lordly mansions at home." He was completely mesmerized. "I
cannot see for the life of me why, nor can I conscientiously advocate that,
my brother Highlanders should continue to remain at home in a servile and

often starving position on the grounds of mere sentiment and love of their native soil when such a country as this is open to receive them."[3]

Flushed with the memory of his Canadian visit, Mackenzie argued that "instead of encouraging Mennonites and Icelanders to the North West, we should encourage British immigrants and especially poor Highlanders to emigrate to Canada." But when he reached Inverness-shire, this man with the purple prose began recommending the exact opposite.[4] Now as the champion of the local crofters, who were trying to regain their lost lands and stop any further removals of people, he railed against all state-aided emigration. Public opinion had become far more disapproving of such schemes. People argued that instead of using public money to relocate poor Hebridean crofters to the prairies, it should instead be employed in rejuvenating the Highland economy. If that happened, they claimed, the problems of a congested and desperately poor population would be resolved and there would then be no justification for encouraging people to leave to better their conditions. County Councillor Alexander Mackenzie took up their cause with great fervour and went into battle.

Through his writings he evoked the dreadful memories of forced removals earlier in the nineteenth century and used these tales to justify the anti-emigration stance being taken by local crofters. Events typifying the suffering of the common people and the alleged cruelty and greed of their landlords were described in vivid detail in his popular *History of the Highland Clearances*. As he fulminated against the clearances, he planted the notion that all Highland emigration had been forced on reluctant victims. Furthermore, Mackenzie's literary efforts were given an unintended boost when the government, alarmed at the growing agitation in the Highlands, appointed the so-called Napier Commission in 1883 to investigate the conditions of crofters. By way of gathering evidence, it invited local people to recall the days of the hated clearers and generally to voice their grievances about the past. Mackenzie himself was a principal witness. However, as the commissioners noted, the "allegations of oppression and suffering," which were "painfully loaded" in the pages of evidence received, "would not bear a searching analysis."[5] What had been offered was the vitriolic outpourings of the people who had stayed behind in Scotland. The voices of the people who had emigrated and the positive reasons why emigration might have attracted them were not on the agenda. Relying mainly on recycled stories of alleged atrocities, Mackenzie gave emigration its many monstrous demons and sorry victims, but his published works have little to do with historical accuracy.

The reality of Highland poverty was inescapable. Commentators regularly expressed the vain hope that the Highland economy might somehow be rendered more viable by state-funded improvements schemes, but such schemes always flopped. Successive famines always exposed the vulnerability of the population and its reliance on food aid and charitable support. On every occasion the relief measures failed to provide long-term solutions. As the resources of the landlords became more stretched, even they faced indebtedness and insolvency. Meanwhile their tenants lived in a wretched state of poverty and endured prolonged periods of suffering and near-starvation. It was an unsustainable situation all round.

Confronted with this dilemma, it is little wonder that emigration attracted so many people. Good reports about the better life that could be had in Canada helped to fuel the great influx from both the Highlands and the rest of Scotland. However, with few exceptions, people who emigrated were simply the ones who could afford to finance their own crossings. The vast number of begging petitions and letters in the Colonial Office's correspondence files speak volumes about the deep longing felt by poor Scots, as

An empty strath—a view from Dunrobin Glen, Sutherland, seen from near Backies. People emigrated to Canada from the early 1800s, leaving the emptiness that we see today. *Photograph by Geoff Campey.*

they sought to find an escape from their misery. Highlanders were no exception. And yet, after the devastation caused by the Highland Famine,[6] which struck in the mid-1840s when more and more people obtained the financial backing of either their landlords or the government to emigrate, anti-emigration campaigners like Mackenzie claimed that they must have been coerced. If the landlord paid out his money, they argued, it can only have been to benefit himself and not his tenants. While some people refused on principle to leave their native land, most would have grabbed the money with both hands. This was their one and only chance to escape misery and poverty.

The great amount of publicity that has been given to the Highland Clearances has left the mistaken impression that emigration was simply the final stage after an eviction and that it was concerned solely with dispossessed Highlanders. Scottish emigration is in fact mainly a Lowland story. Only about 25 per cent of the Scottish exodus to Canada between 1825 and 1855 involved Highlanders. Far more Lowlanders emigrated to Canada than Highlanders. They moved out quietly, either as individuals or in small family groups, and became assimilated in scattered settlements across Canada. Meanwhile, Highlanders attracted much more notice. Travelling in large groups, they transplanted themselves as whole communities. Their departures were regularly reported in local newspapers, and, once their Gaelic-speaking settlements were founded, they became distinctive features within Canada's evolving society.

Although Mackenzie had seen with his own eyes the attractions of the New World, he kept very quiet about them when he returned to Scotland. The prospect of becoming a land-owning farmer had enormous appeal, and this had been a decisive factor in stimulating the exodus to Canada, whether from the Lowlands or from the Highlands. Canada had provided Scottish emigrants with an environment in which they could excel. Highlanders were singled out for special acclaim by commentators such as Abraham Gesner, who witnessed their pioneering achievements at first hand:

> Perhaps there are no race of people more adapted to the climate of North America than that of the Highlands of Scotland. The habits, employments and customs of the Highlander seem to fit him for the American forest, which he penetrates without feeling the gloom and melancholy, experienced by those who have been brought up in

towns and amidst the fertile fields of highly cultivated districts. Scottish emigrants are hardy, industrious and cheerful – and experience has fully proved that no people meet the first difficulties of settling wild lands with greater patience and fortitude.[7]

Having been in correspondence with clergymen in Upper Canada, the Reverend Norman MacLeod, a Glaswegian Presbyterian minister, told the Emigration Select Committee that sat at Westminster in 1841 about "the peculiar adaptation of the Highland population for Canada." It was, he said, "greater than any other people that can be sent out. They can turn their hands (to use a common expression) to anything; they can make carts ... boats ... their women can weave cloth."[8] The Honorable Christopher Hagerman went on to describe the "excellent farms" and "considerable wealth" that had been acquired by the Glengarry settlers – benefits that were "within reach of all of them."[9] John Bowie, who was involved in the management of several Highland estates, spoke of the many pioneers who "have sent home letters strongly recommending their friends to follow them."[10] It was a virtuous circle of success reinforcing success. Set free from the constraints of a feudal society, Highlanders grasped the opportunities to be had in Canada and prospered.

Their encouraging reports back to their family and friends ensured that followers would join them. But their success was hardly a foregone conclusion. These people originated from areas of Scotland with few trees and limited agriculture – hardly the best credentials for clearing a forested wilderness in North America. Highlanders did succeed not due to any practical skills they brought with them but because of their toughness and ability to cope with isolation and extreme hardships. When it came to harsh conditions and remoteness, there was no better training ground than the Highlands and Islands of Scotland.

Before 1840, emigration from the Highlands was almost entirely self-financed, but afterwards it relied increasingly on government or landlord assistance. People scrimped and saved for the chance of owning a farm in Canada.[11] When they could join already-established Highland communities they had a double incentive to emigrate. Hugh McEwen, who emigrated to Glengarry from Perthshire in 1819, was typical. Having acquired two hundred acres of land for himself, he obtained another two hundred acres "beside my place" for his brother, still in Perthshire. He told his brother that he was "satisfied and content in this place ... I have taken my land in the 17th Concession where Malcolm Fisher and Donald McDougall are living. Donald is living on one side of me and a man from the north on the other."[12] In this way, a network of Perthshire people was slowly forming, all of them self-financed emigrants who had been attracted by the glowing reports emanating from Glengarry. It was a similar story for the many other Highland groups that had family and friends in the area, but their besetting difficulty was raising sufficient money to emigrate.

Donald MacCrummer, a Skye merchant, knew of "several hundred people in Glenelg in Inverness-shire and in Glenshiel, Kintail, Lochalsh and Loch Carron in Ross-shire who, "deploring of being able any longer to live in comfort in the land which has produced the kilted heroes of Waterloo," planned to emigrate and join "their relatives comfortably settled in America."[13] He wanted to arrange ships to Quebec for them, but they could not afford their fares, which were about £6 to £7. Similarly, John McRa of Lochalsh, a shipowner, had dealings with a "few hundred poor people" from Wester Ross who longed to emigrate but because of "their extreme poverty" could not afford to pay for their passages.[14] John McMillan from Kintail pleaded with the Colonial Office for help to be given to the twenty or thirty families from Wester Ross who wanted to join friends who had settled in Upper Canada,[15] but to no avail. Countless numbers wanted to emigrate, but it was an option open only to people who could afford to finance their own transport.

Even so, enough emigrants had left Glenelg by 1841 to prompt the local minister to claim ruefully "that America rejoices in a Glenelg, with a population at least equal to that which the parent parish still possesses." Those who departed initially had "the means of procuring a comfortable home beyond the Atlantic," but those remaining were simply "too poor to follow" or preferred to remain; but the latter group, when "induced by the flattering tidings which reached them from the western continent," also found the funds to emigrate.[16] By the late 1840s, as the famine took its toll and landlords coped with mounting debts, Glengarry in Canada once again found its Highland population being replenished. Having become a major focal point of Highland settlement in Canada, it was an obvious destination. However, most of those who arrived had their Atlantic crossings paid, at least in part, by their landlords.

The emigration stone at Cromarty, designed and carved by Richard Kindersley, 2002. Most of the names of the thirty-nine ships, which had collected Highlanders from the port of Cromarty between 1814 and 1851 to take them to Canada, are carved around the edges. *Photograph by Geoff Campey.*

With the help of finance from the Highland Destitution Committee, James Baillie, a wealthy Bristol merchant and banker, assisted 341 of his Glenelg tenants to emigrate to Glengarry in 1849. They had requested financial aid from him and pledged themselves "to remove at whatever time of the ensuing season we may receive notice."[17] His tenants were "not only provided with a free passage to this port [Quebec] but furnished, in addition, with full means for their inland transport to their respective destinations."[18] Next to leave were MacDonald of Lochshiel's Moidart tenants. The eighty-two who emigrated in 1850 had their passages to Quebec paid by their landlord, but he left the Canadian authorities to finance their inland travel.[19] Father Ronald Rankin, their priest, had been campaigning for greater emigration, believing it to be "the only probable means of preserving human life threatened by famine." This stance no doubt suited the landlord, but, as Father Rankin observed, many Moidart people "would cheerfully emigrate if there were anyone to lead them in whom they had confidence."[20] Putting himself forward as their leader, he emigrated with a group probably in 1851, although its final destination is unclear.[21] Glengarry's Highland population increased further that year, when one hundred people from Mr. Lothian's

Glen Garry estate were assisted to emigrate."[22] However, when Mrs. Josephine Macdonell cleared the last remnants of her Knoydart estate in 1853, she attracted the full blaze of publicity.

Borrowing £1,700 under the terms of the Emigration Advances Act, Mrs. Macdonell provided 322 of her tenants with generous removal terms.[23] As they appeared to be "a fine healthy body of emigrants" when they arrived, the immigration agent at Quebec felt certain that "the increasing demand for labourers of all descriptions throughout the province" would enable them "to do well."[24] But, thanks to the literary efforts of Donald Ross, attention soon focused on the sixty uncooperative tenants who remained behind.[25] A Glasgow lawyer and fiery critic of the clearances, Ross wrote that Mrs. Macdonell's tenants had been "packed off to North America like so many African slaves to the Cuban market," and those who defied her order were now camping in outdoor shelters.[26] Understandably, Mrs. Macdonell's harsh treatment of her tenants had attracted a public outcry.[27] But Ross's allegation that all of her tenants had been forced to emigrate is laughable. Reports from Knoydart people, who had arrived in Canada a few months earlier, described the unbelievably good circumstances that awaited then. "Tell all the young men about Inverie that they are in the dark stopping there when they can get such good pay here and all ready cash."[28] Thus, regardless of what the few who remained behind might have wanted, the majority were relocated at Mrs. Macdonell's expense to a part of Canada where they had family and friends living in increasing affluence.[29]

Donald Ross probably did not realize just how attractive Canada had become. From his vantage point in the Talbot settlements in Aldborough Township (Elgin County), Duncan McDermid was well placed to inform his Perthshire friends about its prospects:

> The early settlers suffered great hardships and privations. Now, we have our stone, plank and railroads etc. etc. Uncleared lands are now worth £1 to £3 per acre, improved land can be purchased at from £4 to £6 per acre with good houses and barns erected thereon ... People coming here must expect (unless they have money) hard work for a few years but in the course of time by industry and perseverance they became owners of land of their own, which is a privilege and advantage not easily obtained in Scotland.[30]

The offer of assisted emigration to destinations about which a good report such as this was being circulated back home would have been a great enticement to most people. This is why the Belfast communities in Prince Edward Island, founded in 1803 by Skye people, continued to attract followers. The large groups that arrived in 1830–31 paid their own way, but the group of just over 1,600 who came in 1840–42 were assisted by their landlord, Lord Thomson, and the Edinburgh and Glasgow Relief Fund Committees.[31] Nevertheless probably some of them had to fund part of their relocation costs themselves. The Emigration Select Committee of 1841 was informed that only the very poorest had their expenses paid in full. In many instances the people "came forward with more than one-half, in some instances, two-thirds of the amount; and some have emigrated without receiving any assistance whatever from the proprietor."[32] As the merchant Adam Hope, from St. Thomas, Upper Canada, observed, in such circumstances Highlanders tended to exaggerate their poverty:

> One trait in the character of the Highlander struck me as caused in great measure by poverty, and that is that they are not *ashamed* to let you know that they are *paupers* and to make themselves out poorer than they are. In changing some one pound Scotch Bank Notes in our stores they let us understand they durst not allow their notes to be seen in Scotland or they would not have got their passage paid!!! In less than five years you will find that their Highland pride won't allow them to acknowledge that they got their passage paid. By that time they will own a cow and oxen, etc., etc.[33]

There was little mystery behind the Skye group's choice of destination. As a Skye landowner explained to the Emigration Select Committee in 1841, Skye people "are very much inclined... to emigrate to Prince Edward Island ..." because "they have a great many friends there before them and another [reason] is that the mode of living by cultivation and fishing is like what they are used to at home."[34] Another group of three hundred emigrants from Skye and Raasay arrived in the Belfast area of Prince Edward Island in 1858, and even more in 1861–63, but their sources of funding are unknown. A Raasay arrival summed up his situation to a friend back home in fairly basic terms: "There's not a lot of money, but there's plenty to eat."[35] A more eloquent summary came in a letter written by an unnamed emigrant Scot, which was published by John Lawson in 1851 in his *Letters on Prince Edward Island*:

> He little dreamed, as he often told me that, when he was carrying on his back 15 or 20 miles a single bushel of potatoes around the margin of the shore, he should live to see the day when he would be able to drive in his carriage from one end of the Island to the other.[36]

That was an ordinary person's dream come true, and such letters would have resonated around Scotland.

Although the relocation of many hundreds of Lord Thomson's tenants on Skye had progressed peacefully, the removals in 1849 of three hundred of his Sollas tenants, in North Uist, provoked great indignation and hostile headlines in the Scottish press.[37] The total failure of the potato crop in 1846–47 had brought a desperate situation to breaking point. Patrick Cooper, Lord MacDonald's agent, had persuaded the Sollas tenants that they should emigrate. Being three years in arrears with their rents, they would be freed of their outstanding debts and be given free passages to Canada. They accepted initially but later changed their minds. According to the local minister, "a feeling had got up amongst themselves that they were singled out from the whole district of the country, not with a very amiable disposition and they resisted and hence the evictions."[38] Another explanation for their reluctance to emigrate may have been the inaccessibility of Cape Breton, the destination of choice of earlier North Uist people.[39] Having been flooded with pauper immigrants, the province announced in 1847 that it could not cope with any more arrivals. The situation in Sollas became very nasty:

> A force of thirty picked men of the Inverness-shire Constabulary, accompanied by the Sheriff and Procurator-Fiscal of Inverness was at once sent to the island ... The police force provided by the government went to the Sollas district, where they found a mob of more than two thousand waiting for them ... the mob after a time attacked the party with stones. The authorities ... captured four of the ringleaders, but were compelled to retire ... without having effected their

main purpose ... it was resolved to proceed to extreme measures and bring up the troops.[40]

At this point a compromise was reached whereby the Sollas people were allowed to remain until spring on condition that they accept Lord Mac-Donald's emigration scheme. What followed was unexpected. About three hundred North Uist tenants "in equally poor circumstances, amongst whom were a few from the Sollas district, volunteered to emigrate at once."[41] Sailing on the *Waterhen* of London (167 of them) and the *Cashmere* of Glasgow (115) to Quebec in 1849, they settled mostly in East Williams Township (Middlesex County) in Upper Canada.[42]

However, few of the Sollas people actually emigrated in 1849–50. Instead, they were relocated to other North Uist townships, using funds provided by the Perthshire Destitution Committee. But their attempts at forming a financially viable community failed, and, by 1852, most of them were on their way to Australia. Giving Patrick Cooper the last word: he asked, "who has been their best friend ... the nobleman who took them from a state of starvation at home and at his own charge placed them in comfort and comparative affluence among their countrymen abroad, or those advisors who dissuaded them from leaving home to continue at best an existence there so precarious as to be frequently dependent on the charity of their more fortunate country-men?"[43] Once they were comfortably settled in Upper Canada, most people probably gave the nobleman a hearty cheer.

By the early 1840s, Highland landlords were coming forward increasingly with emigration schemes to assist their poorest tenants. In some instances the tenants took a leap into the unknown by settling in places that had not been tried and tested by earlier compatriots. Evander McIver explained to the Emigration Select Committee of 1841 how he, as factor of the Loch Broom estate, had "sent out some families" who were in arrears with their rent and very destitute. "The proprietor very kindly came forward and paid their passage to ... the Eastern Townships of Lower Canada ... in the year 1837 or 1838; I have a near relation living close to them who corresponds with me; through him they sent me many thanks for having assisted in sending them to Canada. I have a letter from my relation very lately saying they are very comfortable and that they never were so well off in Loch Broom."[44]

Three hundred and fifty Harris tenants "of the poorest class," from the Dunmore estate, were also offered an assistance package at this time, but they declined it.[45] They were told in 1838 that "those able to emigrate" would have "their whole arrears passed from, and that they and their families would be landed free of expense ... either at Cape Breton, where their friends and countrymen were already settled, or in Canada at their choice."[46] But "not one of them went to America." The result was a major confrontation between the tenants, with troops being summoned to quell the ensuing disturbance. These strong-arm measures left many people living as squatters on the Dunmore estate, and journalists had a field day reporting their wretched conditions. By 1841, the factor stated that they were ready to emigrate:

> They [Harris tenantry] have seen the consequences of the bad advice they have received and their folly in supposing the law would not be enforced; I have received a great many letters from them offering to go and Lord Dunmore has agreed to give £500 to assist them to go ... there was an extensive emigration from that country about 13 years ago, since then there has been no emigration; but the people who then went are doing well at Cape Breton and I believe a great many Harris people are now willing to join them.[47]

In such circumstances the question of their willingness to emigrate is a moot point.

There was no doubt that Neil Malcolm of Poltalloch's Argyll tenants wished to emigrate. Three hundred and twenty-seven people from Glassary and north Knapdale went willingly to Upper Canada in the early 1840s, having been given generous terms, which included onward fares to final destinations.[48] Mr. James of Sandside "liberally assisted" his Reay tenants in Caithness at a time when other Reay people "were under the necessity of soliciting subscriptions throughout the county," while the Marquis of Breadalbane helped some of his poorer Perthshire tenants to emigrate.[49] However, this is by no means the whole story.[50] Customs data reveal that a steady flow of Highlanders had been emigrating to Canada for decades without any financial help.[51] The Inverness newspapers ran a regular stream of advertisements of ship crossings, some a page in length, that were targeted at fare-paying emigrants. This was the quiet movement of people from the Highlands, which until the mid-1840s actually represented the majority of those who emigrated.[52]

NOTICE TO INTENDING EMIGRANTS
TO THE
British Settlements of North America.

TO SUCCEED THE " OSPRAY,"

THE First Class British built Brig, BRITISH KING, Register 243 Tons, 400 Tons Burthen, A. BROWN, Commander, is on the Berth at Cromarty, and to Sail about 5th JUNE direct for QUEBEC.

The Subscribers pledge themselves to have this vessel fitted up in a manner that will give satisfaction to intending Emigrants, and as a great proportion of the Passengers are already engaged, they would earnestly request that those who have the intention of availing themselves of this conveyance, make immediate application to the Agents in their locality.

Messrs M'L. and S. having made arrangements to keep up a regular succession of first-rate Ships for the conveyance of Emigrants to these Colonies, beg leave to state that nothing shall be wanting on their part to make Passengers as comfortable as circumstances will admit; and from the experience D. M'L. has had in the trade, and the universal satisfaction his arrangements have always given, they have no doubt of being able to meet the wishes of all parties; and that they will continue to afford every facility and information to those who may require it.

DUNCAN MACLENNAN,
Emigrant Agent, Inverness ;
JOHN SUTHERLAND,
of Nova Scotia, Wick.

AGENTS.—Messrs T. Clark, Woollen Factory, 40, High Street, Inverness ; W. Munro, clothier and grocer, Cromarty ; A. Ross, ironmonger, Dingwall ; D. Macgregor, schoolmaster, Evanton ; R. Douglas, bookseller, Tain ; J. Mackenzie, merchant, Nairn ; J. Hamilton, Glasgow Warehouse, Forres ; L. Macbean, merchant tailor, Kingussie ; W. Kinloch, Fort-William ; William Innes, innkeeper, Reay ; William Munro, merchant, Dornoch ; John Ross, innkeeper, Bonar Bridge ; Thomas Mackay, innkeeper, Lairg ; Wm. Sutherland, post-master, Brora ; Peter Reid, bookseller, Wick.

N.B. Intending Passengers from Caithness for the British King, will have a Boat in waiting on the morning of the 4th June next, at Wick, to convey them and their luggage to the Ship's side at Cromarty.

Advertisement in the *Inverness Journal*, May 29, 1840, for the *British King* of Dundee's departure to Pictou and Quebec from Cromarty.

Also assisting his tenants to emigrate in the early 1840s was the second Duke of Sutherland. No landlord has attracted more revulsion in the Highlands than this man's predecessor, the first duke. Being regarded as the person responsible for the extensive Sutherland clearances between 1807 and 1821, his immense statue atop Ben Braggie continues to conjure up anguished feelings of lost people and empty straths. Patrick Sellar, the Countess of Sutherland's factor during the time of the great clearances, is the loathsome scoundrel who actually masterminded the evictions. The estate was to be given a radical overhaul. Sheep farming was to be introduced, and crofters were to be removed from their inland locations to new villages on the Sutherland coast where they would be provided with fishing and industrial employment. However, the people resisted. In his determination to remove them, Sellar was said to have burned houses and used violence, but, although he was charged with "culpable homicide," he was acquitted by an Inverness court in 1816. Nevertheless his infamy lives on to the present day.[53]

Sellar may well have believed that the Sutherland Highlanders were going to be better off in their new homes. But he made no attempt to win their co-operation or to understand their feelings. After all, he was asking them to abandon a way of life that had been practised from ancient times. But this incident certainly demonstrated to the outside world that Highlanders knew how to attract widespread publicity. The lessons to be learned were clearly taken on board by the second duke, who became particularly cautious in later years in the way that he handled removals. He even sided with his tenantry in 1841 when James Anderson, a substantial entrepreneur in Durness who had previously been engaged primarily in cod fishing, began "embracing the alternative of sheep farming." To proceed, Anderson needed to get rid of the people on his land. In spite of appealing to the second duke "for shelter against the threatening and soon expected storm of tyranny," his tenants had to accept their fate. Anderson was within his legal rights, and not even a mighty nobleman could stop these evictions.[54]

The unfavourable publicity of the past probably explains the duke's subdued approach when dealing with the fallout from the great famine in the 1840s, which made emigration inevitable. In the spring of 1847 Evander McIver, the estate factor, offered assisted emigration to people in Assynt parish in west Sutherland, but "he did not press them – they were left to the freedom of their own will."[55] He had to tread carefully. As the Reverend

William Findlater, the Durness minister, observed, emigration was often more appealing to the better off on the estate. According to him, "the almost indomitable love of country" that caused people to resist emigration "generally increases in proportion to their ignorance and poverty."[56]

Nearly four hudred people agreed to emigrate that year, each family being promised £2, a pair of shoes and cotton shirts for the children, and "as much meal as their voyage may require." The local Free Church ministers "who depend on the people for their sustenance" were unhappy with this outcome, but that was to be expected.[57] The people themselves had a merciful release from their poverty. News of their safe arrival soon reached the merchant Adam Hope:

> I observe from an account in one of the Montreal papers that the Duke of Sutherland has chartered the *Panama* of Liverpool, and given a free passage to 287 persons, tenants and their wives and children residing on his estates in Sutherlandshire to Quebec, besides furnishing the whole with 10 weeks wholesome provisions for the voyage. The consequence was that they all reached Canada in good health, without a case of sickness or death occurring on board and last week the whole party I am informed have safely reached the township of Zorra [Oxford County] in good health.[58]

Six hundred Sutherland people followed without incident in 1848, all receiving financial help from the Duke of Sutherland [59] They too settled in the long-standing Sutherland bolt-holes in Zorra, although some of them joined the Sutherland communities near Pictou, Nova Scotia.

Meanwhile the sixth Duke of Argyll was also wrestling with the combined problems of extreme poverty and congestion in Mull and Tiree. According to the Reverend Norman MacLeod, the duke had "shed tears over the distress of the Island of Tiree" during the famine in 1836–37. He remembered the duke saying, "These people wish to remain, they are devotedly attached to that Island and I cannot think of removing them; they were my fencible men and I love them."[60] Taking a personal interest in those of his tenants who wished to emigrate, he was careful to point out, when requesting Crown land on their behalf, that they wanted to go "to [Upper] Canada where many of their countrymen are happily settled."[61] But

Dunrobin Castle, Sutherlandshire. The magnificent baronial palace of the Earls of Suther-
land was built on a clifftop near Golspie in Sutherland. This was the centre of the vast
Sutherland estate. From William Daniell, *Voyage Round Great Britain,* Volume V (1821).
Courtesy of Birmingham Central Library, United Kingdom.

the duke was certainly not in the business of paying his tenants' removal
costs himself.

In 1841, when the sixth duke was considering large-scale emigration
schemes, he turned to the government for aid, but his requests were
rejected.[62] In the following year he threw his weight behind the unsuccess-
ful and short-lived British American Association for Emigration and Colonization, becoming its president.[63] Formed by the Upper Canada
emigration agent, Dr. Thomas Rolph, this commercial body sought to raise
government funds to finance the removal costs of poor Highlanders to
British North America. But, once it was realized that Rolph was lining his
pockets through land purchases in Canada, the association closed down
and the Duke of Argyll promptly withdrew his support.[64]

By the late 1840s, when the eighth duke was in charge, squalor and
poverty had overtaken both islands. Failing to obtain government funds to
assist his tenants to emigrate, the duke financed his own schemes in 1847,
which involved about 1,100 people. But two years later, when about six
hundred Mull and Tiree people were assisted to emigrate, many of them

"had not the shirts on their backs" when they arrived in Quebec.[65] They were "suffering from sickness and disease" and lacked the funds to go on to their final destinations in Fergus, Hamilton, and Owen Sound.[66] Incensed by their wretched state, the *Inverness Advertiser* told its readers that, while it had been exposing "the sufferings and privations to which the victims of the clearing system were exposed," this incident plumbed new depths.[67] People were dying from cholera, and, because "emigration-sheds" were already full with miserable Irish," the arrivals from Mull and Tiree were having to huddle together on "a wharf without shelter." The Duke of Argyll had "the fearful guilt of blood lying at his door."[68]

Having earned himself such negative publicity, the eighth duke might have been expected to show a more kindly regard for his later tenants, but his parsimony was also evident in 1851 when four hundred Mull and Tiree emigrants had to rely on Canadian provincial authorities to finance their onward travel.[69] But the duke's attitude had changed by this time. He was now sensitive to the charge that emigration benefited only the landlord and was therefore holding back, hoping that his tenants would come to him on their own initiative.[70] This volte-face caused consternation to 136 Tiree families, who suddenly found that their landlord was reluctant to give them funds to emigrate. So they petitioned Sir John McNeill, chairman of the Scottish Poor Law Board, to use his influence to persuade him to change his mind. They explained how overly optimistic misrepresentations of the island's capabilities were causing the duke to withhold "his bounty and depriving us of the power of participating in the enjoyments and comforts, they are from day to day informed, their friends in Canada enjoy to such an extent."[71] In all, the eighth duke assisted 2,500 of his tenants to emigrate between 1847 and 1851 at a total cost of £6,500.[72]

When it came to acts of inhumanity, Colonel John Gordon of Cluny had no equal. Combining evictions with emigration, he relocated nearly 3,000 of his South Uist, Barra, and Benbecula tenants to Upper Canada, Cape Breton, and Prince Edward Island between 1848 and 1851. But he did so at minimum cost to himself and maximum suffering to his tenants. Generally arriving in Canada as half-starved paupers dressed in rags, they aroused great pity from the authorities and attracted many column inches in newspapers on both sides of the Atlantic. The 167 people from South Uist who arrived at Pictou on the *Lulan* in 1848 could not have had a worse beginning. Gordon of Cluny had not made suitable arrangements for them. Having been told to go to the Clyde, they boarded a vessel that was bound for Boston. Someone in the group "who understood a little of the English language" discovered this "deliberate deception" in time for the others to disembark at Glasgow and wait for a ship that would take them to Pictou, but none came and:

> the poor creatures were obliged to find shelter where they best could, and while some got tolerably well housed, a large number, including women and children, several of the latter being ill with whooping-cough and measles, were obliged for want of funds to bivouack [camp] under the sheds of the Broomielaw [Glasgow]. This homeless group attracted the notice of the authorities and one portion was sheltered and fed in the Anderston Police-Office and the other in the Night Asylum.[73]

When they finally reached Pictou they could not pay their "head tax;"[74] so the Nova Scotian authorities had to find the required £470 as well as additional money to cover their onward travel costs.[75] Smallpox was raging below decks, and Board of Health officials found the passengers to be "very scantily clad," most of them being "in extreme poverty."[76]

Of all the sad incidents involving emigrant ship crossings none sticks in the mind more than the plight of the 1,700 South Uist emigrants who came to Quebec in 1851. There was no loss of life, nor even any disease, but their suffering defies belief. They were the former tenants of Colonel Gordon of Cluny, who sailed in five ships from ports in the Outer Hebrides. Speaking only Gaelic, they arrived in a destitute state. Archibald Buchanan, the immigration agent, had seen nothing like it before:

> I never during my long experience at the station saw a body of emigrants so destitute of clothing and bedding; many children of 8 and 9 years old had not a rag to cover them. Mrs. Crisp, the wife of the master of the *Admiral*, (which vessel brought 413 of their number), was busily employed all the voyage in converting empty bread-bags, old canvas and blankets into coverings for them. One fully grown man passed my inspection with no other garment than a woman's petticoat.[77]

Table 3

Vessels Used by Emigrants Who Relied on Some Form of Assistance, 1815–53

[PRO CO 385/2, CO 384/6, *Inverness Journal, Paisley Advertiser,* Parliamentary Papers, Lamond, *Progress of Emigration from the Counties of Lanark and Renfrew,* 8, 15, 59, 61, 63; MacLaren, *The Pictou* Book, 108–110, 122, Devine, *Highland Famine,* 219, 323–6, *Lloyd's Shipping Register.*]

(# denotes crossings where passengers received funds from provincial government agencies, upon arrival in British North America, to pay for onwards travel to their final destinations.)

Vessel	Year sailed	Psgr Nos.	Source of funds	Departed	Arrived	Built	Tons	Lloyd's Code
Atlas	1815	242	Gov't	Glasgow	Quebec	Shields, 1801	435	E1
Baltic Merchant	1815	140	Gov't	Glasgow	Quebec	n/k	n/k	n/k
Dorothy	1815	194	Gov't	Glasgow	Quebec	Prize	530	E1
Eliza	1815	123	Gov't	Glasgow	Quebec	n/k	n/k	n/k
Broke	1820	176	Emig. Socs.	Greenock	Quebec	Salem, 1812	252	A1
Commerce of Greenock	1820	402	Emig. Soc. Glasgow	Greenock	Quebec	Quebec, 1813	425	A1
Prompt of Bo'ness	1820	370	Emig. Soc. Lesmahagow	Greenock	Quebec	Montreal, 1816	353	A1
Commerce of Greenock	1821	422	Emig. Socs.	Greenock	Quebec	Quebec, 1813	425	A1
David of London	1821	364	Emig. Socs.	Greenock	Quebec	Pictou, 1812	390	E1
Earl of Buckinghamshire	1821	607	Emigration Societies	Greenock	Quebec	Quebec, 1814	n/k	n/k
George Canning	1821	490	Emigration Societies	Greenock	Quebec	Montreal, 1812	482	A1
Margaret	1821	180	Emig. Soc. Anderston & Rutherglen	Grange-mouth	Halifax	Kirkaldy, 1820	218	A1
Ossian of Leith (Sutherland emigrants)	1821	108	private subscription	Cromarty	Pictou	Leith, 1813	194	A1
Harmony of Aberdeen (Sutherland emigrants)	1822	125	Association at Edinburgh	Cromarty	Pictou	Aberdeen, 1801	161	E1

Vessel	Year sailed	Psgr Nos.	Source of funds	Departed	Arrived	Built	Tons	Lloyd's Code
Ruby of Aberdeen (Sutherland emigrants)	1822	125	Association at Edinburgh	Cromarty	Pictou	Aberdeen, 1805	128	E1
Mary	1828	206	Emig. Soc, Paisley	Greenock	Quebec	n/k	n/k	n/k
Cornelia of Greenock	1841	98	Emig. Soc. Glasgow	Glasgow	Quebec	N. B., 1840	260	A1
Mary Ann of London	1841	220	Emig. Soc. Glasgow	Greenock	Quebec	n/k	275	AE1
Rosebank	1841	160	Emig. Soc. North Quarter Glasgow	Belfast	Quebec	n/k	308	n/k
Stirling	1841	154	Emig. Soc. Glasgow	Glasgow	Quebec	n/k	203	n/k
Wanderer (Argyll emigrants)	1841	141	Neill Malcolm	Glasgow	Quebec	N. B., 1839	280	A1
Bowlin of Glasgow	1842	157	Emig. Socs.	Glasgow	Quebec	Glasgow, 1842	242	A1
Carleton	1842	70	Emig. Socs. North Quarter Glasgow	Glasgow	Quebec	n/k	n/k	n/k
Harper	1842	235	Emig. Socs.	Glasgow	Quebec	n/k	n/k	n/k
Joseph Green of Peterhead	1842	239	n/k	Cromarty, Thurso & Lochinver	Quebec	Sunderland, 1819	353	AE1
Pactolus	1842	182	public & private	Glasgow	Quebec	n/k	n/k	n/k
Renfrewshire	1842	568	Emig. Socs.	Glasgow	Quebec	n/k	n/k	n/k
Wexford of Wexford	1842	200	Emig. Socs.	Greenock	Quebec	Quebec, 1829	254	AE1
Wingrove of Newcastle	1842	160	Emig. Socs.	Glasgow	Quebec	Sunderland, 1829	261	A1
#*Bona Dea*	1843	446	Emig. Socs. Societies	Glasgow	Quebec	n/k	n/k	n/k
Brilliant of Aberdeen	1843	191	Landlords from Johnson (near Glasgow)	Glasgow	Quebec	Aberdeen, 1814	332	AE1

Vessel	Year sailed	Psgr Nos.	Source of funds	Departed	Arrived	Built	Tons	Lloyd's Code
Eleutheria of South Shields	1843	160	Emig. Socs.	Glasgow	Quebec	Shields, 1835	340	A1
#*George* of Dundee	1843	215	public & private	Loch Laxford	Quebec	Quebec, 1829	n/k	n/k
#*Jane Duffus* of Irvine	1843	257	Emig. Socs.	Glasgow	Quebec	Pictou, 1840	352	A1
Romulus of Greenock	1843	165	Emig. Socs.	Greenock	Quebec	N. B., 1831	467	AE1
Tay of Glasgow (Argyll emigrants)	1843	327	Neil Malcolm	Greenock	Quebec	N. B., 1840	470	AE1
Charlotte Harrison of Greenock (Mull and Tiree emigrants)	1847	305	parish & private	Greenock	Quebec 1847	Quebec, 1841	557	AE1
Eliza of Cardiff (Mull and Tiree emigrants)	1847	269	Duke of Argyll	Glasgow	Quebec	Quebec, 1846	384	AE1
Jamaica of Glasgow (Mull and Tiree emigrants)	1847	212	Duke of Argyll	Greenock	Quebec	Grnk, 1796	334	AE1
Panama of Liverpool (Sutherland emigrants)	1847	279	Duke of Sutherland	Loch Laxford	Quebec	n/k	n/k	n/k
Serius (Sutherland emigrants)	1847	117	Duke of Sutherland	Thurso	Pictou	n/k	n/k	n/k
#*Canada* of Greenock (Barra, S. Uist & Benbecula emigrants)	1848	98	Col. John Gordon	Glasgow	Quebec	Grnk, 1831	330	A1
Ellen of Liverpool (Sutherland emigrants)	1848	154	Duke of Sutherland	Loch Laxford	Pictou	N. B., 1834	398	AE1
#*Erromango* of Greenock (Barra, S. Uist & Benbecula emigrants)	1848	99	Col. John Gordon	Glasgow	Quebec	Grnk, 1845	351	A1
Greenock (Sutherland emigrants)	1848	399	Duke of Sutherland	Loch Laxford	Quebec	n/k	n/k	n/k
#*Lulan* of Pictou (South Uist emigrants)	1848	167	Col. John Gordon	Glasgow	Pictou	N. Scotia, 1848	473	A1

Vessel	Year sailed	Psgr Nos.	Source of funds	Departed	Arrived	Built	Tons	Lloyd's Code
Scotia of Belfast (Sutherland emigrants)	1848	196	Duke of Sutherland	Loch Eribol	Quebec	n/k	n/k	n/k
#*Atlantic* (Barra, S. Uist and Benbecula emigrants)	1849	366	Col. John Gordon	Ardrossan	Quebec	n/k	n/k	n/k
#*Barlow* (Mull and Tiree emigrants)	1849	246	Duke of Argyll	Greenock	Quebec	N. B., 1834	436	AE1
#*Cashmere* of Glasgow (North Uist emigrants)	1849	115	Lord Macdonald	Glasgow	Quebec	N. Scotia, 1841	347	AE1
#*Charlotte* (Mull and Tiree emigrants)	1849	333	Duke of Argyll	Glasgow	Quebec	n/k	n/k	n/k
Liskeard of Liverpool (Glenelg emigrants)	1849	341	James Baillie M.P.	Inverness	Quebec	N. Scotia, 1847	648	AE1
#*Mount Stewart Elphinstone* of Glasgow (Barra, S. Uist and Benbecula emigrants)	1849	250	Col. John Gordon	Loch Boisdale	Quebec	Grnk, 1826	387	AE1
#*Tuskar* of Liverpool (Barra, S. Uist and Benbecula emigrants)	1849	496	Col. John Gordon	Stornoway	Quebec	N. B., 1845	900	AE1
#*Waterhen* of London (N. Uist emigrants)	1849	167	Lord Macdonald	Glasgow	Quebec	Hull, 1825	355	A1
Argo (Sutherland emigrants)	1850	50	Duke of Sutherland	Thurso	Quebec	n/k	n/k	n/k
Conrad of Greenock (Mull and Tiree emigrants)	1850	200	Duke of Argyll	Glasgow	Quebec	Quebec, 1847	759	A1
#*George* of Dundee (Moidart emigrants)	1850	82	Mr. McDonald	Oban	Quebec	Pictou, 1839	676	n/k
#*Admiral* of Glasgow (Barra, S. Uist and Benbecula emigrants)	1851	413	Col. John Gordon	Stornoway	Quebec	n/k	707	A1
Barlow (Lewis emigrants)	1851	287	Sir James Matheson	Stornoway	Quebec 1834	N. B.,	436	AE1

Vessel	Year sailed	Psgr Nos.	Source of funds	Departed	Arrived	Built	Tons	Lloyd's Code
#*Birman* of Greenock (Mull and Tiree & emigrants)	1851	270	Duke of Argyll (130) Sir James Matheson (50)	Greenock	Quebec	Grnk, 1840	448	A1
#*Brooksby* of Glasgow (Barra, S. Uist and Benbecula emigrants)	1851	285	Col. John Gordon	Loch Boisdale	Quebec	Grnk, 1843	423	A1
Canmore of Saint John	1851	104	landlords	Glasgow	Quebec	N. B., 1843	264	AE1
#*Conrad* of Greenock (Mull and Tiree emigrants)	1851	388	Duke of Argyll	Greenock	Quebec	Quebec, 1847	759	A1
Ellen of Liverpool (Glen Garry emigrants)	1851	100	Mr. Lothian	Liverpool	Quebec	N. B., 1834	397	AE1
Islay (Lewis emigrants)	1851	68	Sir James Matheson & Glasgow	Stornoway	Quebec	n/k	n/k	n/k
Jamaica of Glasgow	1851	179	landlords	Greenock	Quebec	Grnk, 1796	334	AE1
#*Liskeard* of Liverpool (Barra, S. Uist and Benbecula emigrants)	1851	104	Col. John Gordon	Stornoway	Quebec	N. Scotia, 1847	648	AE1
Marquis of Stafford (Lewis emigrants)	1851	500	Sir James Matheson	Stornoway & Troon	Quebec	n/k	n/k	n/k
#*Montezuma* of Liverpool (Barra, S. Uist and Benbecula emigrants)	1851	440	Col. John Gordon	Loch Boisdale	Quebec	Quebec, 1846	462	A1
#*Perthshire* of Greenock (Barra, S. Uist and Benbecula emigrants)	1851	437	Col. John Gordon	Stornoway	Quebec	n/k	459	A1
Prince George of Alloa (Lewis emigrants)	1851	203	Sir James Matheson	Stornoway	Quebec	London, 1789	312	AE1
#*Sesostris* of Glasgow (Lewis emigrants)	1851	302	Stranorlar Union & Sir James Matheson	Glasgow	Quebec	N. Scotia, 1840	632	AE1
Susan of Glasgow (Inverness-shire emigrants)	1851	69	Mr. Orme	Glasgow	Quebec	PEI, 1847	321	A1

Vessel	Year sailed	Psgr Nos.	Source of funds	Departed	Arrived	Built	Tons	Lloyd's Code
Urgent of Belfast (Lewis emigrants)	1851	370	Sir James Matheson	Stornoway	Quebec	n/k	592	AE1
#*Vesper* (Sutherland emigrants)	1851	52	Duke of Sutherland	Thurso	Quebec	n/k	n/k	n/k
Wolfville of Ardrossan (Lewis emigrants)	1851	161	Sir James Matheson	Glasgow	Quebec	N. Scotia, 1841	415	AE1
Blanche of Liverpool (Lewis emigrants)	1852	453	Sir James Matheson	Stornoway	Quebec	N. B., 1850	966	A1
Allan Kerr (Mull and Tiree emigrants)	1853	18	Duke of Argyll	Glasgow	Quebec	n/k	n/k	n/k
Sillery of Liverpool (Knoydart emigrants)	1853	332	Mrs. Josephine Macdonell	Skye	Quebec	Quebec, 1853	994	A1

In addition to the distress of having been cleared out of their homes, they were packed off to Quebec "without the means of leaving the ship or of procuring a day's subsistence for their helpless families." With Buchanan's help and government funding, the South Uist emigrants reached their final destinations in western Upper Canada.[78] The colonial authorities later wrote to Colonel Gordon asking him to reimburse them for their costs, but he refused. As many people on both sides of the Atlantic would come to realize, Gordon was a tight-fisted, contemptible brute who lacked compassion or any feelings of remorse.[79] When the dust settled, the new arrivals, who were all Roman Catholic, wrote home stating that they now needed a priest.[80]

Gordon of Cluny attracted even more bad headlines in 1851 when some of his Barra tenants refused at the last minute to board ship. Allegations that some of the breakaway group had been brought on board after being collared and handcuffed turned the incident into the highest form of melodrama. Predictably, Alexander Mackenzie magnified the tale with great relish some forty years later. However, the people concerned tell a different story. On their arrival, the *Quebec Times* printed a statement on behalf of Hector Lamont and seventy other passengers who had sailed on the *Admiral* of Glasgow.[81] They stated that they and most of the 450 people on board had embarked voluntarily on the understanding that their fares to Quebec would be paid by

Colonel Gordon. According to Lamont and his group, only twenty or so people had "absconded from their homes to avoid the embarkation," and they were later captured and forced back to the ship.[82] Moreover, in spite of their beggarly appearance, Gordon of Cluny's tenants had actually crossed the Atlantic on first-class sailing ships. This is a surprising revelation, since one assumes that his cheapskate tendencies would have extended to shipping. But in all cases where Lloyd's of London shipping classifications can be found, they show the consistent use of "A1" and "AE1" ships – vessels of the very highest quality (Table 3).[83] Possibly this had been part of the negotiation between tenant and landlord, or it may simply signify Gordon of Cluny's desire to avoid damaging headlines from mishaps at sea.

It was not only poor Highlanders who attracted attention at Canadian ports. Destitute handloom weavers all too frequently arrived at Quebec in a penniless state. In 1843 James Forrest, the lord provost of Edinburgh, wrote of the "great suffering" of the more than 3,000 "operatives in the city's manufacturing districts."[84] They were desperate to emigrate but lacked funds. Several thousand workers in Aberdeen were also facing unemployment and severe distress. George Thompson, the city's lord provost, hoped that the government would help cover their travel costs, but the Colonial Office always refused such requests.[85] Nevertheless nearly 4,000 former weavers from Lanarkshire and Renfrewshire managed to raise their removal expenses during the 1840s. They generally headed for the Rideau Valley, where they could join communities that had been founded by their own people some twenty years earlier.

Nearly all of the former weavers who emigrated at this time had insufficient funds for their onward travel. As a result, many were dependent on finding immediate work.[86] Archibald Buchanan, the immigration agent at Quebec, occasionally grumbled about the arrivals from Glasgow who seemed unwilling to work for their onward fares, expecting the provincial government to look after them. In May 1843, Mr. J.W. Campbell, co-ordinator of the fundraising activities of the various Glasgow emigration societies, warned the Colonial Office that "between 800 and 900 souls" were on their way to Quebec from Glasgow "without the means to carry themselves further." The people knew the difficulties that they faced, but "they had a strong desire to better their conditions in Canada."[87] However, his honesty prompted a stern rebuke from Lord Stanley to the lord provost of Glasgow.

It was, he stated, unfair to place "special burdens" on the provinces, [of Canada], which were growing weary of having to subsidize the growing numbers of poverty-stricken immigrants who were flooding to their ports.[88] These were difficult times.

Yet some Scottish arrivals had good reason to be thankful for the generous backing they received with their emigration expenses. Having taken possession of the Isle of Lewis in 1844, Sir James Matheson went on to spend large sums in improving conditions on the estate. But, by 1851, he reluctantly came to the conclusion that the estate could not support its population and that assisted emigration was the only effective remedy. He cancelled all his tenants' debts, provided free transport to wherever they wanted to settle, gave them suitable clothing and other provisions and paid the £50 per annum salary of the Reverend Ewen McLean, who accompanied them.[89] The island's previous owner, Stewart MacKenzie of Seaforth, had funded the emigration costs of fifteen Lewis families in 1838, and they had been followed in 1841–42 by just over 350 Lewis people who had almost certainly paid their own expenses.[90] Their chosen destinations were the British American Land Company holdings in the Eastern Townships of Lower Canada. With the arrival of Matheson's tenants in 1851, much of Compton, Frontenac, and Wolfe counties would become a transplanted Lewis, having place names such as Tolsta, Stornoway, Galson, Gisla, and Dell, all of which told the world of the Hebridean origins of its people.[91]

Matheson had used a gradual approach. William MacKay, a later factor on the Lewis estate, explained to the Napier Commission how the tenants were given plenty of time to decide whether to accept their landlord's terms. Those who remained simply "settled in other townships, in vacant lots from which the people went to America."[92] Although the Reverend Angus MacIver, the Established Church minister, later painted a picture of forced removals to the Napier Commission, on further questioning he admitted that he was actually objecting to the loss of people.[93] Of course, the minister was bemoaning his declining congregation. While organizing the 1851 departures, John Mackenzie, Sir James's factor, had also to deal with the disgruntled Reverend McLean, a Free Church minister. Learning that he "had been preaching against emigration," Mackenzie "had a long argument with him on that subject and told him my opinion very plainly, I hope he will be more careful of what he says in future."[94]

The feedback from the 1851 arrivals was highly positive, thus ensuring that the stream of emigrants from Lewis to the Eastern Townships would continue for many decades. As Maurice Macfarlane explained to a relative back in Lewis, "They give better victuals to their swine here than what most gentlemen give to their servants at home. Don't you think I am telling lies – no, I am before God!"[95] Letters were winging home describing the excellent job opportunities on the railways and the comfortable living standards. Shortly after her arrival, Peggy MacIver pleaded with her family and friends to join her: "I would advise all my friends to come here, fully aware that it would be for their benefit. I hope you will all be preparing to come here. It is in my power to assist you even now." In 1863, people from North Galson actually petitioned Matheson "to be sent to America." And yet, in spite of these large-scale removals, the population of Lewis continued to rise in the following decades. The policy of assisted emigration could only ever bring temporary relief to the demographic pressures within the Highlands and Islands.[96]

One hundred and twenty of John Ramsay of Kildalton's Islay tenants emigrated with obvious willingness in 1862.[97] In their petition of May 6, 1862, they stated that they had "no opposition" to their landlord's decision to dispossess them of their lands. Having learned that "there were no openings" on the estate, they requested assistance to emigrate to Canada West. According to Ramsay, his tenants' "drive to get to Canada" in the following year was unprecedented, and "they wish to get away at all hazards while the facilities are afforded them."[98] Ramsay of Kildalton was one of the few Highland landlords to empathize with the ordinary person's dilemma. He financed emigration for people when they were ready to leave and later took the unusual step of visiting them to see how they were getting on in Canada. His was a rational and humane approach, born of understanding and compassion.

Also leaving Scotland in 1862 were the 139 people from Fair Isle (Shetland). Having been evicted from their crofts, they ended up in the Miramichi region of New Brunswick.[99] Although they arrived at Saint John in a healthy state, they were completely destitute. The Board of Supervision for the Relief of the Poor in Scotland, which had stepped in to finance and organize their crossing, provided them with £52 10 s. on landing, a payment that had to be shared among them.[100] Being housed initially in Saint John's old Poor House, "they were given food and other necessaries" from funds placed by the government with Lauchland Donaldson, president of the St. Andrew's Society, and Robert Shives, the provincial emigration officer.[101] "The charitably disposed of the City furnished the women and children with a large quantity of clothing and many things of which they stood greatly in need." The families were then separated into small groups and "were forwarded by rail and steamer" to various parts of the Miramichi, where "they were comfortably housed free of rent by the people there."[102] Although this was a shameful outcome for the Scottish Poor Board, Sir John McNeill, its chairman, provided highly favourable reports of the crossing in the Scottish press. Readers were spared details of the impoverished state of the emigrants when they arrived at Saint John.[103]

Had the Fair Isle crofters been brought reluctantly to New Brunswick, or were they willing emigrants? Their story was scarcely recorded at the time. However, the infamous evictions carried out in Glencalvie (Ross-shire) in 1845 represent the other side of the coin. They attracted widespread publicity and continue to evoke great anger to this day. The removal process had begun peacefully at nearby Croick. In 1840, the tenants had "been urged to go to Cape Breton, where the people are so happy to have them, as to have promised to make provision for their reception." Dr Norman MacLeod, the energetic clergyman who campaigned so forcefully through his *Gaelic Magazine* in support of Highland emigration to British America, had taken up their cause:

> The whole parish of Croick, in the north, are ready to go – to a man; and their clergyman has resigned his living, stipend, glebe and manse and will set off as soon as the necessary arrangements are entered into to provide a place for their reception and location. Thus the pastor and his whole flock will secure a home where they will not be exposed to a removal in the summary manner in which they have been warned to leave their present possessions ... Out of 350 ready to start, not more than twenty have sufficient means to ensure their own passage. Our [Glasgow] Destitution Committee voted them £250 last Tuesday to aid them in their outfit.[104]

There seemed little dissension, but five years later, when Major Robertson of Kindeace was threatening to evict eighteen families from their homes

Croick Parish Church, built 1825–27, in accordance with a plan drawn up by the famous engineer, Thomas Telford, and supported with government grants. *Photograph by Geoff Campey.*

The east window of Croick Parish Church, with its scratched messages, provides a poignant reminder of the Glencalvie evictions in 1845. *Photograph by Geoff Campey.*

in Glencalvie, the people took the extraordinary step of tipping off the national newspapers. Because he was in Australia at the time with his regiment, Robertson would have been unaware of the journalistic campaign that was slowly gaining ground. So the evictions proceeded under the watchful gaze of a *Times* reporter. The "wretched spectacle" of poor people being "marched out of the glen in a body with two or three carts filled with children, many of them mere infants," provided vivid imagery, as did their subsequent attempts to find shelter. The only refuge they could find was a little enclosure in the churchyard at Croick. While camping there, some of them scratched their names and messages such as "Glen Calvie – the wicked generation" on the east window of the church. Robertson's clearance of his tenants at Greenyards in Strathcarron (Easter Ross) in 1854 was equally traumatic. Becoming known as "the massacre of the Rosses," the evicted people added their message to the church window.[105]

The Glencalvie episode came to symbolize all that was terrible about forced removals. Later in the century, Alexander Mackenzie used it and other emotional horrors to denounce all Highland emigration to the New World. This interpretation of history suited his political agenda. Other writers, who held a romantic vision in their minds of a prosperous Highlands that could support its inhabitants, also decried the loss of people. Although rational arguments in favour of emigration were being advanced, they became submerged by the passionate rhetoric of the Highland sympathizers. As will become evident in the chapter that follows, truth and reason struggled to be heard.

Seven

EMIGRATION MYTHS
AND REALITIES

*Some adventurous individuals greedy of change ... may
recklessly transfer themselves to other lands; but to suppose that
numerous families would, as a matter of choice, sever
themselves from their loved native soil ... is an
hypothesis too unnatural to be encouraged
by any sober, well-regulated mind.*[1]

WRITING IN 1850, THOMAS MULOCK, the impassioned editor of the *Inverness Advertiser*, denounced Highland emigration as reckless and unnatural. Feudal serfs were destined to live the rest of their days in the Highlands, and that was that. The thought that people might aspire to a better life through emigration was alien to his way of thinking. But for nearly a century Highlanders had been fleeing Scotland in search of the better economic opportunities and personal liberties that Canada could offer. It was a perfectly natural and rational response. Such was the zeal to emigrate that no amount of criticism or interference could dampen its appeal. The unstoppable force, having been unleashed, acted like a magnet to more and more Highlanders, but, as ever, the high cost of Atlantic crossings set a limitation on the numbers who could actually emigrate. And yet Mulock and other anti-emigration commentators would have us believe that most emigrants left the Highlands unwillingly.

Although the Highland exodus was being driven in part by disastrous economic conditions, Mulock preferred to lay the entire blame for it at the feet of wicked landlords. An anti-landlord bandwagon had first begun to

roll when Hugh Miller, the eminent geologist, rebuked the Countess of
Sutherland and Lord Stafford, her English husband, for having introduced
major changes on their Sutherland estate. In relocating their tenantry from
inland sites to the coast, they had dismantled an ancient agricultural regime.
Miller's blood boiled at the loss of a system that, according to him, had
given people an idyllic life of pleasure and abundance. So he began a verbal
assault with his pen. He likened what was happening to "an interesting
experiment ... on dissecting a dog alive for the benefit of science. The
agonies of the dog might have their softening influence on the dissector,"
but the duke was apparently immune to such influences. "He merely issues
orders to his footman that the dissection should be completed, remaining
himself out of sight and out of hearing."[2]

Miller's disturbing prose would firmly establish the first Duke of Sutherland and his factor, Patrick Sellar, as the arch demons of emigration folklore, a remarkable achievement given that the Sutherland removals had
nothing whatever to do with emigration. They were concerned solely with
the repositioning of crofters to new locations. It was always their intention
that the people would remain on the Sutherland estate. The last thing that
estate managers wanted to see was the loss of tenantry to Canada; nevertheless this is what happened. Having been ordered to discard their way of
life and take up jobs as fishermen or canal diggers, many crofters left for
Nova Scotia to join previously established Sutherland communities. They
left despite the obstacles put in their way by estate managers who wanted
them to remain.[3] Yet many commentators, both then and now, would have
us believe that they had been forced to emigrate.

Miller's denunciation of the crofter relocations in Sutherland laid the
foundations of a victim culture that eventually enveloped the entire Highland exodus. Donald MacLeod, a stonemason from Strathnaver, contributed to the fast-developing mythology through his highly theatrical
recollections of eviction horrors that he claimed to have witnessed. A
typical episode was his description of Patrick Sellar's words to a bedridden
elderly woman in Strathnaver, who was too ill to be removed:

> Damn her, the old witch; she has lived too long. Let her burn! Fire
> was immediately set to the house and the blankets in which she was
> carried were in flames before she could be got out. She was placed

in a little shed and it was with great difficulty that they were prevented from firing it also. The old woman's daughter arrived while the house was on fire and assisted the neighbours in removing her mother out of the flames and smoke, presenting a picture of horror which I shall never forget.[4]

MacLeod could tell a masterly horror story, but, given that Sellar was acquitted of all charges against him, one wonders whether the melodrama that he described actually happened.

Miller always took the broader position, attacking the reasoning behind the removals and claiming that they had been unnecessary. Using his great literary gifts, he turned the Highland dilemma on its head by harking back to a Golden Age that had never existed. He perpetuated the myth that the old agricultural regime had provided plentiful food when it had not. The region was barely capable of supporting its people. It only ever gave them a subsistence living, and that was why landowners were converting it to large sheep farms. They were far more efficient than the small feudal holdings of

The statue of Hugh Miller (1802–56), which was erected in the churchyard of the Gaelic Chapel in Cromarty two years after his death. The sculptor was said to have transferred Miller's stalwart form and facial expression to the stone. *Photograph by Geoff Campey.*

the past. The change to pastoral farming may have been introduced too quickly and in some cases too harshly, but the need for change was irrefutable. It was not the recklessness and greed of landlords that caused it, but the region's fundamental inability to support its people under the old regime. The Napier Commission could have been describing Hugh Miller when it observed that "the tendency to paint the past in attractive colors will not easily be abandoned ... Those who hold emigration to be unnecessary have not given sufficient attention to the statistics bearing on the subject."[5] However, firebrand writers of later years continued to ignore harsh realities as they perpetuated the villainy of landlords as the sole explanation for the Highlander exodus to the New World.

Of course, Miller's fiery condemnation of the suddenness of the Sutherland relocations was understandable. The vision of an empty glen where once had lived Highland communities still evokes great sadness. When Beriah Botsfield observed the remains of burned-out houses on his 1829 visit through Sutherland, he described feelings that still carry great resonance:

> In this secluded valley all was silent and dead; no token of its once peaceful and happy inhabitants remained, save the blackened ruins of their humble dwellings ... When we reflect that all this desolation has taken place under the abused name of improvement, we must deeply regret that the change, which the progress of time may have rendered necessary, was not effected with a gentler hand and a kindlier spirit; and that more humane measures were not pursued respecting an ancient and attached tenantry, whose irreproachable moral conduct and tried fidelity, ought to have entitled them to some consideration from their natural guardians and feudal superiors.[6]

Yet, had he visited the empty dwellings in Abercrombie Street in Glasgow, Botsfield might have reflected on the distress and anguish that had been experienced by redundant handloom weavers. Their destitution was as awful as that of the Highlanders, but no one noticed them. And although they left in their thousands for a new life in Canada, no one mourned their loss to the country.

Thus public sympathy has always been firmly fixed on the Highlands,

The colossal monument to the first Duke of Sutherland, built in 1836. This statue, erected at the Marquess of Stafford's Trentham home in Staffordshire, is a copy of the larger statue on Ben Bhragaidh, which overlooks Golspie, Sutherland. *Photograph by Geoff Campey.*

particularly on the controversial removals in Sutherland. The 100-foot statue of the first Duke of Sutherland, which towers over Golspie, remains a highly visible reminder of the turmoil and suffering of earlier times:

> His red sandstone effigy, in a red sandstone toga, rears thirty feet from a pedestal seventy-six feet high at the top of Ben Bhraggie, which is itself thirteen hundred feet above the green water of the Dornoch Firth. Its back is to the glens he emptied, it faces the sea to which his policies committed five thousand people as emigrants or herring-fishers."[7]

With the large-scale evictions of the late 1840s and early 1850s, anti-emigration campaigning intensified. Prominent commentators such as Donald Macleod and Donald Ross, who could give first-hand accounts of alleged landlord atrocities at the drop of a hat, were not interested in a reasoned debate. They did not concern themselves with Canada's attractiveness to the hungry, long-suffering Highlander but instead focused on alleged landlord villainy. Ross claimed that landlords had simply not "done their duty." If they had, "there would be room enough, soil enough, and resources enough in the Highlands of Scotland for double the population which they at present contain."[8] Yet the awful handicaps of poor soil and extreme climate were far greater limiting factors than the actions of wayward landlords.

Donald MacLeod believed that Highland landlords had been determined to "drain the nation of its best blood and to banish the Highlanders across the Atlantic, there to die by famine among strangers in the frozen regions of Canada."[9] Ramming home what he claimed were the damaging consequences of emigration, he gave his own rendition of the founding of Lord Selkirk's Red River Colony:

The [Kildonan settlers] found themselves deceived and deserted by the Earl, left to their unhappy fate in an inclement wilderness. They were without any protection from the hordes of Red Indian savages by whom the district was infested and who plundered them of their all on their arrival and finally massacred them. A small remnant who managed to escape travelled through immense difficulties across trackless forests to Upper Canada.[10]

In fact the colonists survived all of their tribulations, relying on the help they received from Chief Peguis and the Saulteaux people!

Meanwhile Free Church ministers, such as the Reverend Thomas McLauchlan, offered more restrained comment. They were concerned that emigration was robbing them of people to fill their churches. Typically, the Reverend McLauchlan questioned the perceived benefits of emigration. He wondered why anyone would want to leave places such as North and South Uist. Better known for their rocky terrain, peaty moorland, and abundant seaweed, McLauchlan argued, they were islands of plenty. These "fine, fertile islands ... having hills clothed with a rich covering of the most nutritious pasture ... and a continuous succession of the most beautiful downs" were a proper paradise. "What gives the forests of Canada the advantage over the heaths of Uist but different management?" he asked.[11] He might have pointed out that the Uists had some of the worst agricultural land in the whole of Britain. And with the collapse of the kelp industry, their landlords faced bankruptcy and their tenants were starving. As Rowland Hill MacDonald observed, "the Free Church, undoubtedly, claims the Highland crofters as her children." Many of them "admit that they are opposed to emigration on the grounds that the support of the Christian ministry, ... their own means of livelihood – depends on the people remaining on their native soil."[12]

Thomas Mulock simply could not grasp the notion that anyone should want to emigrate. Even when shown a petition in 1849 listing the names of 115 Glenelg families asking their landlord James Baillie "for assistance to enable us to remove ourselves and our families to the Colonies," he was unconvinced that they had left willingly.[13] Because the families told him that their decision to emigrate stemmed from the hopeless state of Glenelg, he pronounced them to be unwilling exiles. His feudal mindset prevented him from seeing Highlanders as free-thinking individuals, who would choose to better themselves when an opportunity to do so came their way. Their remarkably independent spirit made them highly successful Canadian pioneers, yet in the Highlands it was a trait that had always to be suppressed by the all-powerful feudal system.

There is no doubt that some evictions were carried out brutally and that, on occasion, violence was used.[14] But in general Highland landlords certainly do not deserve the verbal abuse that has been hurled at them over the years. They, like their tenants, were completely overwhelmed by the growing economic and demographic crises that gripped the Highlands and Islands. Most landlords accepted some moral responsibility for their tenants and made changes opportunistically. A desire to escape the attention of the press made them more cautious than they otherwise might have been when planning removal and emigration schemes. They normally acted with restraint and gave their tenants plenty of time to consider where they would settle. Suitable sites had to be located, and ideally they needed to be close to already established kinsfolk. Landlords frequently negotiated for land with the Colonial Office on behalf of their tenants. For instance, the tenth Duke of Hamilton, who assisted his Arran tenants to emigrate to the Chaleur Bay area of New Brunswick in 1829–30, hoped that Colonial Office officials would allocate his tenants land that was close to water so that followers would be able to settle with "their kindred islanders."[15] Although the Marquis of Breadalbane had evicted hundreds of families from his estate, he was the one person whom his former tenants, once they were settled in Upper Canada, turned to for help when they wanted funds to build churches.[16]

Colonel Gordon earned venomous criticism in 1851 following the eviction of 1,700 people from his South Uist, Barra, and Benbecula estates. While his failure to adequately fund their departures to Quebec provoked outrage, it cannot be assumed that his tenants left for Canada unwillingly. People in the remotest areas of the Highlands had clung on the longest to the old feudal regime, but as their precarious existence became unsustainable, both tenant and landlord faced a humanitarian crisis. Once the famine struck, people had to rely on external aid to avoid starvation. Landlords were subsidizing a regime that left them with mounting debts and gave their tenants a miserable existence. Although people would have left for Canada with a heavy heart and some bitterness, the chance of being rescued from extreme destitution through emigration must have been a strongly positive motivation.

Large-scale clearances ended after 1855, and, with the rise of the crofter land-reform movement in the 1880s, interest in emigration declined. After the passing of the Crofters' Act of 1886, which gave crofters security of tenure and effectively prevented their being cleared by a landlord, people had more hopeful prospects. Nevertheless, because their holdings remained small, the intractable problems of chronic poverty and overpopulation remained. But in this new political climate public opinion became more sceptical of the benefits of emigration, particularly when, as was the case with the prairie schemes, it was subsidized with public funds. Such money, they argued, would be much better spent on development in the Highlands and Islands.

Alexander Mackenzie, the leading spokesman of land reform, was desperate to contain the Highland exodus. Like Hugh Miller before him, he held a passionate belief in the Highlanders' ancient attachments to the land. As a result of the new legislation, they could hold their land more securely and be self-sustaining. But, as various crofter plans came and went, the age-old problems remained insuperable, and, by the early 1900s, Highland emigration once again resumed its steep upward climb.

Mackenzie's contribution to the emigration debate was immense. While Miller gave emigration its demons, Mackenzie gave it its dark associations with forced exile. His desire to keep emigration at bay caused him to stigmatize it in every way he could. Being a prolific writer and holding political office in local government, he knew how to attract attention. Quoting widely from stories provided by Donald MacLeod and Donald Ross in his *History of the Highland Clearances*, he treated the events as a great act of genocide. Similar evidence that was submitted to the Napier Commission at the time reinforced the notion of cruel evictions and forced exile. John MacKay of South Uist saw a man seized and tied on the pier at Lochboisdale, "and it was by means of giving him a kick that that he was put into the boat and knocked down."[17] Angus McKinnon, a crofter from Benbecula, heard that arrivals in Canada "were so poor after landing, without food or clothing, that they died upon the roadside and were buried into holes where they died."[18] Of course, such lurid accounts came from the people who had remained behind. Although real atrocities did occur, one suspects that those who emigrated may have had less colourful recollections.

In support of his land-reform objectives, Mackenzie also pressed ahead with a campaign to discredit ongoing emigration to the prairie provinces of Canada. This he achieved through the *Scottish Highlander,* a weekly newspaper that he launched specifically to attack landlords' and government's involvement in emigration schemes. And, given that he was a member of Inverness-shire County Council and Inverness Town Council and editor of the *Celtic Magazine,* Mackenzie was not short of other platforms from which to promulgate his views!

Of course, Mackenzie's thinking had changed diametrically from his earlier expressed views. This was the same man who had drooled over Canada's high standard of living during a visit in 1880. Now the crofter's son was exerting his considerable influence against emigration.[19] The man who said that he couldn't "recall a single instance in which of any of them [Highlanders] who have settled down here [Nova Scotia] on their own lands would wish to go back and live in the Highlands,"[20] now scorned crofters who accepted "inducements" from their landlords to emigrate. Now they "ought to be held up before public opinion as a cowardly set."[21]

Mackenzie's account of the Sollas affair was typical of the unprincipled way in which he reported events. He claimed that the Sollas district "was completely and mercilessly cleared of its inhabitants numbering 603 souls" in 1850, when in fact almost no one had left the area.[22] Using funds raised by the Perthshire Destitution Committee, the people had tried to establish themselves in two of the Sollas townships, but their attempts ended in failure. In 1852 "a deputation from the people" asked Charles Shaw, the principal law officer, "to apply to Sir John McNeill to have them carried away along with the Skye people" to Australia. The Sollas people did leave for Australia, but imagine their surprise when the redoubtable Donald Ross turned up on their

Skye crofters planting potatoes in the late nineteenth century. Growing crops relied on the intensive use of fertilizers. Only a meagre agricultural subsistence was possible at the best of times. *Courtesy of Aberdeen University, Special Libraries and Archives, George Washington Wilson C2724.*

ship as they were leaving the Clyde. Distributing leaflets in Gaelic "denouncing emigration as only a milder type of penal servitude for life, concocted by rapacious landlords, with the approval of the government," he advised everyone to return home at once.[23] He is unlikely to have won any converts. A few years later some of the Sollas emigrants wrote to Shaw from Australia, enclosing money for him to give to their friends back in Scotland. "They put a sum of money together and remitted it to me with a request that I would purchase my wife a ring with it, as a token of their gratitude to me, for all the trouble I had from first to last taken in their matters."[24]

It was in his reporting of the developing Hebridean communities in the prairies that Mackenzie was at his most deceitful. He lambasted "the landlords of the old country" for turning Hebridean crofters over "to the land and railway schemes of Canada so that they may in turn rob them of the fruits of their labour on virgin soil."[25] Favourable reports had been received from Wapella, but despite this, Mackenzie printed "a warning from North West Canada" in his *Scottish Highlander* newspaper advising crofters "not to accept inducements to emigrate."[26] Irritated that his settlement was being unfairly pilloried, Lauchlan McPherson, one of the Wapella settlers, fought back:

> Everything bad that we were hearing before we left was all lies. You haven't heard a single true word about it ... I haven't seen better looking corn and potatoes in my life ... You won't believe the crop and grass that is here, when you don't see it, but you may believe that I am telling the truth ... I haven't seen the least thing to frighten me, not even so much as an Indian. There is no wild beast here. The mosquitoes was pretty bad last month but not much worse than the midges when they are bad at home. When we came there was not a single house to be seen far or near, and I could scarcely count them today. They are coming up from Ontario ... I am sorry that my brothers hath not come with me ... They would do better here in one year than three at home.[27]

Yet earlier that year Alexander Mackenzie had claimed that the Wapella crofters faced ruin. Their plight should "be a sufficient warning to those at home to stay and face the ills they know, rather than come here and face those they know not."[28]

However, it was the Saltcoats settlement that received the full benefit of Mackenzie's campaigning invective. Under the headline of "Starving Crofters in Canada," an 1890 article in the *Scottish Highlander*, gave details of the "acute destitution" among the Lewis, Harris, and North Uist crofters who had settled near Saltcoats.[29] It claimed that the Saltcoats scheme had been "a complete failure" and warned its readers not to offer themselves "to these new experiments in starvation."[30] Three months later the newspaper repeated its earlier warning "that all intending emigrants should keep clear of Saltcoats."[31] The first clue that the crofters had of this negative reporting was the sudden arrival of clothing bundles, which included "overcoats with collars and cuffs."[32] The mystery was solved when they realized that a petition, sent in their names and printed in the *Scottish Highlander*, had complained of terrible experiences en route to the settlement and of inadequate food, clothing, and accommodation. So bad was the news of their plight that the good people of

Winnipeg had collected items of clothing for them. Once the Saltcoats crofters realized what was happening they issued a firm rebuttal:

> There are no cases of destitution among crofters as reported and so well off are some of them that they have money, earned since they came here, on deposit in the savings bank ... There are few better fed people out here and their clothing is warm and suitable to the climate ... It is a piece of misplaced charity to forward clothing ... While people here appreciate their kindly feelings, there never was ground or excuse for any appeal for assistance and the supplies sent were, when we left Saltcoats, still in the shed and likely to remain there.[33]

Having spoken to the crofters, Joseph Colmer, secretary of the Imperial Colonization Board, discovered that the petition complaining of their circumstances was not quite what it seemed:

> A few of those, whose names appear, say they never signed the document; others protest that they did so under the impression that they were signing a school petition; others that they did not know what they were signing. One and all express great sorrow for having signed statements which they admit to be untrue. From the time they arrived they have known no real need of either food or clothing ... Their rations have always been of sufficient quantity and good quality. When the crofters arrived at the end of their journey they expressed general satisfaction ... there was not one complaint ... At different times the greater number of the crofters have distinctly told me that they would not return to Scotland under any circumstances as they are convinced that in a few years ... they will be independent men with a good farm and stock around them.[34]

Mackenzie's allegations, when investigated that year by the Select Committee on Colonization, were found to be untrue.[35]

The passion and outrage felt by Mackenzie and his followers have intensified over the years. In his *Butcher's Broom* (1934), Neil Gunn claimed that the Countess of Sutherland's actions would apparently have "revolted the

The emptiness of the strath near Rogart, looking west from Miltonbank. *Photograph by Geoff Campey.*

stomach of an African slave-dealer." In betraying the people, she made for herself a name "that stinks of the unforgivable sin of treachery ... as surely as if she were Judas, she has crucified the Gael."[36] In her *And the Cock Crew* (1945), Fionna Maccolla compares the clergy's deceit in helping a villainous factor to St. Peter's denial of Christ.[37] In more modern times Ian Gimble's *Trial of Patrick Sellar* seeks a comparison of the Sutherland clearances with the unspeakable atrocities committed against Jews in the Second World War.[38]

David Craig also likened the Highland clearances to the extermination of Jews in the Holocaust but went one step further by also drawing a parallel with Stalin's "ethnic cleansing" of the old Soviet Union.[39] Yet while searching Canada high and low for the descendants of the "survivors" of the Highland clearances, he encountered people "who were proud to have been part of the migration rather than troubled that it had ever been necessary."[40] The thought that Highlanders may have actually wanted to emigrate seemed to take him by surprise. John MacLeod believed that Colonel Gordon's agents, who pursued the small breakaway group in Barra and forced them onto a ship, had behaved like slave hunters on the African coast.[41] And so it went on. Meanwhile John Prebble has drawn heavily on

The Emigrants sculpture by Gerald Laing, located at Helmsdale in Sutherland. It commemorates the people from the Highlands and Islands who emigrated to the far corners of the world. *Photograph by Geoff Campey*

Mackenzie's work, providing a modern platform for his flawed anthology of wretched happenings.

The evidence from petitions, emigrants' letters, and Highlanders' highly selective choice of settlement locations all points to the conclusion that the voluntary exodus was far greater than the emigration that was forced by landlords. Crofters were not the down-trodden victims of landlord cruelty as portrayed by Mackenzie and Prebble. They understandably sought an escape from their suffering and poverty. Canada provided this. Ironically, Mackenzie's anti-emigration campaigning was similar in method to that used by landlords a century earlier. Both were concerned with keeping crofters in the Highlands to serve what they perceived to be the common good. Mackenzie believed that crofters banding together could advance the agricultural development of the Highlands, while earlier landlords had believed that the viability of their estates required crofter labour to remain where it was. Neither saw crofters as individuals. They were just permanent fixtures.

Lord Selkirk was well ahead of his time in his ability to empathize with the plight of Highlanders. What is so remarkable about him was his capacity to understand the wishes and motivations of ordinary people. He cut through the landlord self-interest of his day and, using his immense personal wealth, helped hundreds of Highlanders to emigrate to Canada. While Selkirk's colonization achievement won him little acclaim, Hugh Miller continues to evoke warm feelings for his chastisement of emigration. Selkirk lost the propaganda battle but had a major impact on the outcome of the emigration saga. Miller and his fellow romantics had none.

The Highland clearances continue to cast a long shadow over Scotland. Just recently the Scottish Parliament has seen fit to officially repent of them. Long-standing campaigns to topple the Duke of Sutherland's statue at Golspie have failed, but a new bronze sculpture has now been erected at nearby Helmsdale to commemorate the people who were cleared.[42] While retribution is sought, few people remember the actual story. Highland emigration was a victory of the little people over an oppressive system. They had to defy public opinion that, in the early days, was strongly opposed to emigration. Later many of them had to beg for help to finance their crossings. When they reached Canada they had to use their initiative and spunk to obtain land. Their ability to function well in groups and their strong self-belief saw them through the long periods of isolation and privation. The avalanche of followers who joined them later spoke volumes for their success. It may suit some commentators to portray such people solely as victims, but to do so is a travesty of what actually happened.

Eight

WHAT ABOUT THE "COFFIN" SHIPS?

I was awakened this morning by one of the sailors
telling us to rise and see Quebec and going on deck we got a
view of it by moonlight. In about an hour the sun began to rise
and his first rays struck upon the house tops and spires covered
with zinc. They all shone like burnished silver.
It was well worth rising to see. The river is
covered as far as the eye can reach with
ships and steamboats ...
I never saw so many vessels together.[1]

HAVING ENDURED VIOLENT STORMS IN the North Atlantic on board the *Jane Boyd* of Aberdeen, John Rhind's joy at reaching Quebec safely in October 1854 was understandable. By the time the doctor came on board to check the health of the passengers, music could be heard. The passengers were "dancing reels on deck, looking as healthy and happy as if they had only come on board the day before." Earlier that week they had collected money "for the purpose of presenting a testimonial of our respect to the Captain, as a mark of our appreciation of his gentlemanly conduct and kind treatment."[2] Yet this happy picture is light years away from popular depictions of emigrant sea crossings, which concentrate on squalor, disease, and high death rates.

The so-called coffin ships regrettably did claim the lives of many Irish immigrants during the famine years of 1846–51, when unprecedented numbers came to North America. In 1847 about 17,500 immigrants, most of them Irish, died from dreadful typhus and dysentery epidemics, either on board ship or shortly after landing at Quebec.[3] Between 1847 and 1851, forty British ships were wrecked at sea with a loss of 1,043 lives, but almost all of the people who died were Irish.[4] Never before or since have so many fatalities or so much suffering been endured at sea. But although this was essentially an Irish horror story, its impact has been allowed to envelop the whole history of emigrant sea travel. By burying the comparatively minis-cule Scottish immigrant numbers in with the Irish figures, some later com-mentators have given the deeply erroneous impression that high death rates occurred on Scottish crossings – when they did not.

In his history of the Highland clearances, John Prebble refers to the death of over 1,000 emigrants from cholera in November 1853, failing to point out that these were nearly all Irish deaths. Fourteen thousand emi-grants, most of them Irish, had sailed in that one month – three times the Scottish total for the entire year. John MacLeod's dubious and unsubstanti-ated account of the forty-nine emigrant ships "laden with miserable people" that sank without trace between 1847 and 1853 is intended to shock readers. Moreover, it fails to point out that it was primarily the poor Irish who were offered inferior shipping.[5] In his account of Highland clearance victims, John Craig mentions the 11,200 deaths during sea crossings "in a single year in the late 1840s," neglecting to point out that most of the deceased were Irish. According to Craig, Cape North "is strewn with human bones and other memorials of the frequent wrecks. Heedless captains were more concerned to offload the human cargo and take in payload for the return trip than to deliver families to the port named in the contract with the agent."[6] By confusing death rates in this way and taking isolated worst-case examples of dreadful crossings, such authors greatly exaggerated the miseries and risks of sea travel.

Emigrant accommodation in a ship's steerage was certainly very basic. Temporary wooden planking was hammered over crossbeams, and tempo-rary sleeping berths were constructed along each side of a hold. There were no portholes nor any means of ventilation beyond the hatches. And in stormy seas the hatches had to be kept battened down to stop water from pouring into the hold – sometimes for days at a time. The stench and squalor would have been unbearable. However, it was not that shipowners and captains were being deliberately cruel or irresponsible; this was how shipping services operated at the time. While affluent emigrants could afford the privacy and comparative comfort of a cabin, anyone else had to put up with the primitive accommodation offered in the hold of a ship. They had no other means of crossing the Atlantic.

In 1847, the worst year on record for Irish deaths, Stephen E. De Vere booked himself a place in an Irish ship bound for Quebec so that he could experience what it was like being a steerage passenger. It was an appalling crossing. "Hundreds of people – men, women and children of all ages, were packed together like sardines in a tin without light, without air, wallowing in filth," with inadequate water, food, or medicine.[7] Although this was an extreme example, authors such as John Prebble have since perpetuated the myth that such conditions were typical throughout each crossing. To Prebble, all sleeping berths were "noisome dungeons, airless and lightless," and the hold was always "a reeking den" because no one ever made any attempt "to purify" the "pestilential atmosphere." To complete this sordid picture he imagines that "the groans and screams of a patient in the last agonies of the plague" were frequently heard.[8]

Prebble was a masterful dramatist, but his description of life in a ship's hold is not one that John Rhind would have recognized. Yes, there were perils and discomforts, but they should not be made to sound more harrowing than they actually were. Disease could spread more rapidly when people were crowded together in the hold, but major outbreaks were rare on Scottish ships. The captain and crew followed a strict routine for cleaning the ship and provided assistance to anyone who fell ill. However, there was little they could do to alleviate seasickness. According to Rhind, "there is no one [who] can have any idea" of such miseries.[9] He was dreadfully sick initially, and, when at last he was able to face food, he then had to master the peculiar delights of cooking over an open fire. This required him "to be continually holding on to something to keep himself from falling into the fire while, to vary the amusement, he gets himself every now and again drenched to the skin by shipping and sea."[10] There was the added problem of coping with smelly and foul-tasting drinking water. Because it was stored for the duration of a journey in crude wooden casks, water soon became contaminated. People tried to offset the offensive taste by adding vinegar, but often this proved ineffective.

Many travellers had to endure awful periods of sickness, but, mindful of this, the captain and crew did what they could to cheer them up. After a week out at sea John Rhind found himself being ordered out onto the deck by Captain Ganson with all of the other passengers. They were all told to go "upon deck whether they were sick or not ..." then the ships' sailors appeared "with a female passenger on each arm" and walked about trying "to laugh" the passengers "out of their sickness."[11] Rhind found that "there is no end to the civility and kindness of the sailors." In bad weather, crewmen "hauled up water from the sea to enable the women to wash their dishes." And in high winds, when standing up was a problem, they would assist the passengers "backwards or forwards to any part of the ship." In one particularly severe storm, a sailor cooked Rhind's potatoes for him and in the morning brought coffee to him and his brother George "before we were out of bed."[12] When a baby died during the crossing, Captain Ganson ordered the ship's carpenter "to make a box and the poor little thing was put into it ... stones were put in and it was nailed shut." The coffin was then taken to the side of the ship "and placed upon one of the hatches." As it was committed to the deep, "Mr. Duff said an appropriate prayer."[13] Hardly the actions of a brutish man. There were plenty of exemplary captains who left a trail of grateful passengers over their long and successful careers at sea.

Although a well-organized and caring crew could make a huge difference to the comfort and well-being of steerage passengers, this was nevertheless a time when shipping services paid little heed to the needs of passengers. Paramount were the requirements of the timber trade. Ships were selected primarily for their good stowage capabilities and ability to survive heavy seas, with accommodation for people being a mere afterthought. So travelling in the hold was always going to be a rough and ready experience. When Lord Selkirk sought a vessel to take four hundred Skye emigrants to Belfast in Prince Edward Island in 1803, he specified that the sleeping berths should be "6 ft by 18 inches, with the allowance of 56 gallons water and 2 barrels bulk of stowage for each person besides sufficient room to be left in the hold for provisions."[14] Incredibly cramped accommodation and the most basic of provisions by modern-day standards, yet this was the norm at the time. There was no reported loss of life, and in later years people remembered with particular pride and affection those who had "sailed on the *Polly.*"[15]

With the introduction of duties on Baltic timber during the Napoleonic Wars, making North American timber the cheaper alternative, Scottish

Short Stay among the Orkney Islands, June 3, 1821, a painting by the Swiss
artist Peter Rindisbacher. It depicts passengers boarding a ship anchored in
the harbour off one of the Orkney Islands. Having been taken out in a
small boat, they are climbing onto the ship using a rope ladder. *Courtesy of
Library and Archives Canada C–001902.*

ships crossed the Atlantic in ever greater numbers to collect timber cargoes.
As they did, more and more shipowners sought emigrants to take out on
their vessels' westward crossings. Because there was a huge shipping capacity seeking a relatively small number of people, competition was fierce.
Shippers had to compete with each other, both on the price they charged
and on the quality of the service they offered. The service may have been
haphazardly run and very basic by today's standards, but it was affordable
and regular. Moreover, because emigrants consulted each other over available choices, they could make or break a shipper's trade through their recommendations and thus had some leverage over unscrupulous people who
broke their promises. Contented passengers gave a shipper his repeat business. This simple fact kept shipowners and their captains in check far more
than passenger legislation, which was largely unenforceable.[16]

Emigrants with easy access to major Scottish ports, such as Glasgow,
Aberdeen, and Leith, could simply arrange their crossings through local shipping offices. But people who were scattered across large distances in the

Highlands and Islands had to rely on emigration agents to convey them to their destinations. Agents were the linchpins in a well-co-ordinated process that took emigrants to ports in the Highlands, where they could be collected by passing timber ships. Situated midway between the Dornoch and Moray firths and having an excellent harbour, Cromarty became the main departure port for the northeast Highlands, while Tobermory played a similar role for the Hebridean islands.[17] Later Thurso in the extreme north became another major collecting point for emigrants. The agents agreed terms and conditions with individual shipowners, notified emigrants of departure times, and arranged for steamers to take them to the embarkation ports. The ships on offer looked like a purpose-built fleet, but of course the vessels had different owners and rarely did the same journey more than once. Nevertheless agents sought a consistently good standard of shipping, knowing full well that their future business depended on a good "word of mouth recommendation"

And yet anti-emigration campaigners always depicted agents as ogres who preyed on vulnerable and misguided emigrants. They foolishly hoped that by doing so they would diminish the zeal to emigrate, but their smear tactics never worked. The sad image of the emigrant suffering at the hands of unscrupulous agents continues to find a place in later writing. In her study of malpractices on emigrant vessels, Miss M.A. Walpole failed to appreciate that the verbal attacks made against agents in the early nineteenth century were part of a hard-fought propaganda campaign to thwart the exodus from Scotland. She wrongly assumed that all of the criticism was justified.[18] In his colourful portrayals of sea crossings, John Prebble places emigration agents on a par with typhus, cholera, and dysentery.[19] But the major agents were not fly-by-night scoundrels; they remained in business over long periods and could have done so only by providing reliable service.

The much-maligned Simon Fraser, who ran a successful emigration agency in the Highlands and Islands for at least twenty-five years, was followed by Archibald MacNiven, who arranged ships for people in the Hebridean islands over a twenty-year period.[20] William Allan, a Leith-based shipping agent, established Cromarty's role as a major embarkation port during the 1830s, a time when Scotland was in a deep depression and transatlantic fares had reached an all-time low (Appendix IV).[21] Duncan MacLennan and John Sutherland, who followed Allan in the 1830s, had the most important agency ever to operate in the Highlands.

Duncan MacLennan, an Inverness lawyer, and John Sutherland, a former agent of the British Fisheries Society in Wick, were a formidable combination.[22] They each accompanied emigrants on crossings and had detailed knowledge of the land and job opportunities that were available in British America.[23] Having lived for twenty years in Nova Scotia, the Gaelic-speaking Sutherland could talk to Highlanders with some authority on its many advantages.[24] In fact, he claimed that it was sight of the "wretched state of the poor tenantry" in Sutherland and Caithness, during a visit in 1839, that prompted him to return to Scotland.[25] MacLennan and Sutherland arranged transport for 3,000 emigrants between 1840 and 1845 – the busiest period of their agency – although they handled greater numbers than this.[26]

Although Maclennan and Sutherland's crossings were generally incident-free, there were two instances when disease afflicted their passengers. Their reputation took a severe knock in 1841 when many of the 240 passengers on board the *Lady Grey* of North Shields fell ill on their way to Pictou and Quebec. Both the sick and the healthy were removed from the ship at Pictou in order that it could be cleaned and fumigated before passengers could be taken on to Quebec. Thanks to an immigrant tax of five shillings payable by all immigrants that had been introduced at all major ports by 1832, quarantine and other medical facilities were already in place to treat sick passengers.[27] As was revealed by the emigrants themselves, the cause of the problem was Captain Grey's refusal to concern himself with the cleanliness of the ship. Because of the wet and filthy decks, disease had spread rapidly. The passengers gave a full account of the captain's atrocious behaviour in the *Mechanic and Farmer* magazine and advised "intending emigrants ... to enquire into the character and disposition of the masters of vessels they intend sailing in, upon whom in a great measure depend the lives of themselves and families, whilst under their charge."[28]

Two years later, disease was also rampant in another of the partners' ships. When the 307 passengers who sailed on the *George* of Dundee arrived at Pictou, health officials found conditions below deck "almost intolerable." The *Halifax Times* attributed all of the blame for the outbreak on the unscrupulous men "who call themselves agents," although the emigrants themselves claimed that the real cause of their distress was the exceptionally long delay they experienced before leaving Scotland, which caused them to run short of provisions.[29] General slurs against agents are easy to make, but, in assessing MacLennan and Sutherland's performance, the truth is in the detail.

Table 4

Vessels Chartered by Duncan MacLennan and John Sutherland, 1832–51

[*Elgin Courant, Inverness Courier, Inverness Journal, John O'Groat Journal, Lloyd's Shipping Register*, British Parliamentary Papers, *Quebec Mercury*]

Vessel (Tonnage)	Built	Lloyd's Code	Dep. Year & Port	Arr	Psgrs
Canada (269)	1811, Montreal	E1	1832 Cromarty	Pictou & Quebec	241
Robert & Margaret (420)	n/k	n/k	1833 Cromarty	Pictou & Quebec	66
Swift of Sunderland (280)	1837 Sunderland	A1	1837 Cromarty	Quebec	215
Osprey of Leith (382)	1819 Greenock	AE1	1840 Cromarty & Thurso	Pictou & Quebec	150
British King of Dundee (239)	1825 Sunderland	AE1	1840 Cromarty	Pictou & Quebec	157
Quebec Packet of Aberdeen (196)	1822 Aberdeen	A1	1840 Cromarty	Quebec	60
Fairy of Dundee (248)	1801 York	E1	1841 Cromarty & Thurso	Quebec	123
Lady Grey of North Shields (285)	1841 Sunderland	A1	1841 Cromarty & Thurso	Pictou & Quebec	240
Margaret Bogle of Leith (321)	1804 Ayr	E1	1841 Thurso & Loch Laxford	Pictou & Quebec	117
Saphiras of Whitby (277)	1838 Sunderland	A1	1841 Loch Laxford	Quebec	202
Superior of Peterhead (306)	1813 Shields	AE1	1842 Cromarty & Thurso	Pictou & Quebec	191
Joseph Green of Peterhead (353)	1819 Sunderland	AE1	1842 Cromarty, Thurso & Lochinver	Quebec	239
Lady Emily of Sunderland (285)	1840 Sunderland	A1	1842 Cromarty, Thurso & Loch Laxford	Pictou & Quebec	150

Vessel (Tonnage)	Built	Lloyd's Code	Dep. Year & Port	Arr	Psgrs
Pacific of Aberdeen (402)	1826 Aberdeen	AE1	1844 Cromarty & Thurso	Quebec	n/k
Harriet (n/k)	n/k	n/k	1844 Cromarty & Thurso	Quebec	n/k
Lord Seaton of Aberdeen (440)	1840 Quebec	A1	1845 Cromarty & Thurso from Aberdeen	Quebec	64
Joseph Harrison (380)	n/k	n/k	1845 Cromarty & Thurso	Quebec	n/k
Sovereign of Kirkwall (476)	1814 Hull	AE1	1845 Stromness & Lochmaddy	Pictou, Sydney, C.B. & Quebec	n/k
Lord Seaton of Aberdeen (440)	1840 Quebec	A1	1846 Cromarty & Thurso from Aberdeen	Quebec	18
Kate of Newcastle (478)	1846 Sunderland	A1	1846 Cromarty & Thurso	Quebec	43
Prince Albert of Arbroath (257)	1842 Arbroath	AE1	1849 Cromarty & Thurso	Quebec	125
Argo (500)	n/k	n/k	1850 Thurso from Leith	Quebec	50
George of Dundee (676)	1839 Pictou	n/k	1850 Cromarty, Thurso & Loch Laxford	Pictou, Quebec & Montreal	82
Empress of Banff (359)	1845 Nova Scotia	AE1	1851 Thurso from Banff	Quebec	n/k
Vesper (n/k)	n/k	n/k	1851 Thurso	Quebec & Montreal	52

When John Sutherland accompanied the 150 passengers during the 1842 crossing of the *Lady Emily* of Sunderland, he won praise for "his uniform kindness and attention." The emigrants hoped that he might "be successful in inducing thousands of our fellow countrymen to follow us."[30] He saw to their "health and comfort during a voyage unusually protracted by calms and contrary winds." They also commended Captain Stove, "who at the sacrifice of his personal comforts, supplied some of us with the means of subsistence out of his own stores for a period of twenty days, and if he should continue in future to bring out passengers for Mr. Sutherland, we shall have great pleasure in recommending such of our friends as may be disposed to follow us to this, the land of our adoption, to take passage with Captain Stove."[31]

Meanwhile, the *John O'Groat Journal* added its tribute to John Sutherland that same year:

> Nearly 2,000 emigrants have been sent out by him within two years in vessels of the first class. So far as we know Mr. Sutherland has left behind him a character for uprightness and integrity. His conduct to the poorer classes of emigrants has been very praiseworthy – he very frequently granting free passages to many members of a family where the head of it could not command sufficient means to carry them all out.[32]

The newspaper also felt that people in northern Scotland were "peculiarly indebted to Mr. Sutherland for laying on his vessels in this part of the country – for before he established himself, those desirous of emigrating had to bear the expense of removal to Greenock, which equalled if not exceeded the whole sum now charged for the passage to America."[33]

The favourable press coverage continued. When the *Superior* of Peterhead, another of the partners' ships, arrived in Pictou that same year, the *Pictou Observer* commented that it had "never seen a healthier or more respectable set of immigrants arrive at our port." The passengers "speak of Captain Donald Manson's urbanity and kindness in the highest terms" during a tedious passage of some fifty days. His conduct "was such as will accrue for him a place in our remembrance while we live, in whatever corner of the globe providence may order our lot."[34] The partners also did well when they selected the *Lord Seaton* in 1845, captained by William Talbot. All of the passengers signed this glowing tribute, sent a copy of it to their friends and family back home, and then forwarded it to the *Quebec Gazette* for publication:

> The whole passengers on board the *Lord Seaton* having experienced the greatest kindness and attention from Captain Talbot, during their passage from Aberdeen, feel it their duty to make this public acknowledgement of the

same, by recommending him to their friends and countrymen, who may be intending to emigrate to America, as a
person of much kindness and every way qualified to render
all on board comfortable. The *Lord Seaton* is a commodi-
ous, fast-sailing and seaworthy barque, Quebec, 9th September, 1845.[35]

And when the *Prince Albert* of Arbroath left Thurso for Quebec with 125
passengers in 1849, the *John O'Groat Journal* once again lavished praise on
John Sutherland. Having gone on deck to see the accommodation for themselves, the reporters concluded that "the arrangements were such as to give
entire satisfaction." And the emigrants, " 'ere the *Prince Albert* sailed, gave
expression to this feeling and to the sense of the honourable and gentlemanly
conduct of Mr. Sutherland."[36] The accommodation was light and airy, and
the "height between decks ... was such that we could safely promenade
amongst this veritable colony."[37] Sutherland insisted on some last-minute
improvements "to secure the greater comfort to the passengers," and "the
owner, thereupon, ... complained that Mr. Sutherland was much more particular as to the fitting out of vessels than was customary with others in his line."[38]
   However, the really convincing proof that MacLennan and Sutherland
offered a first-class service is to be found in the *Lloyd's Shipping Register.* This
documentary source, dating back to the late eighteenth century, records the
overall quality of each of the ships listed.[39] As a major insurer, Lloyd's of
London needed reliable shipping intelligence, which it procured through
the use of paid agents in the main ports in Britain and abroad. Vessels were
inspected by Lloyd's surveyors and assigned a code according to the quality
of their construction and maintenance.[40] These codes were then used by
insurers to determine levels of risk and freight rates. Shipowners actually
complained that the codes were too stringent, particularly in the way a
ship's age and place of construction could affect its classification.[41] The
Lloyd's Shipping Register entries for MacLennan and Sutherland's vessels
reveal that they generally offered the very best of ships (Table 4). Shipping
codes have been identified for nineteen of the twenty-five vessels that they
are known to have used between 1832 and 1851 (Table 4). Eighty-four per
cent of these vessels were rated at "A1" or "AE1" – signifying first-class construction and condition and the highest state of repair.

Factual data such as these are at odds with the highly negative reports on emigrant ships that often appear in the secondary literature. Edward Guillet claimed that "the worst [vessels] only were generally used in the emigrant trade ... very old, very ill-manned, very ill-found," basing his assertions on remarks made by a solitary Gross Île physician and an unnamed "contemporary newspaper."[42] Then there is Arthur Lower's claim that "the Canadian timber trade became the last refuge of all battered hulks on the Atlantic."[43] Since emigrants generally travelled on timber ships, the inference is that they were offered only "battered hulks." However, the *Lloyd's Shipping Register* provides abundant evidence that good-quality timber ships were used to carry passengers, and so such claims are factually incorrect. The truth is that MacLennan and Sutherland's *Swift* of Sunderland, *Lady Grey* of North Shields, *Saphiras* of Whitby, *Lady Emily* of Sunderland, *Lord*

**TO SAIL FROM SCRABSTER ROADS,
FOR QUEBEC & MONTREAL,**

The well-known, fast sailing, newly Coppered Ship, MARGARET BOGLE of Leith, 320 Tons Register, 500 Tons Burthen, WALTER SMITH, Commander, will be on the Berth at SCRABSTER ROADS about 30th May, where she will remain two days for the embarkation of Passengers.

This conveyance is equal, if not superior, to any hitherto offered to the emigrating population in the north. Captain Smith has had great experience in the transport of Passengers. As a proof of the Ship's speed, she left Cromarty in 1837 for Quebec, and crossed the Atlantic in the incredible short space of 21 days. Intending Passengers, from Caithness and Sutherlandshire, would do well to avail themselves of the above conveyance, and, in order to enable the Subscribers to despatch the Ship on the day advertised, intending emigrants would do well to engage their passage forthwith.

Newspaper advertisement from the June 4, 1841, edition of the *Inverness Journal*, announcing the sailing of *Margaret Bogle* from Scrabster Roads (Thurso) to Quebec and Montreal.

Seaton of Aberdeen, *Kate* of Newcastle, *Prince Albert* of Arbroath, and *Empress* of Banff were not only "A1" or "AE1" ships, but they were also newly built at the time that they sailed.

Another of the partners' objectives was to provide spacious accommodation. The *Robert and Margaret,* sailing in 1833, could offer six feet between decks, nine years before the legal limit was raised to that height. Before 1842 the only stipulation was that "ships are not allowed to carry passengers to the Colonies unless they be of the height of five and a half feet between decks."[44] The *Fairy,* a former whaling ship, was chosen for the same reason.[45] So too was the *Superior* of Peterhead, which also had "a great height between decks." Given its relatively roomy proportions (102' x 26' 2" x 18' 7"), the *Pacific* of Aberdeen would have offered far more space than was average. And the *Margaret Bogle*'s similarly large dimensions (104' 2" x 27' x 18' 11"), together with her highly experienced captain, Walter Smith, explains why she was chartered so frequently for the Atlantic passenger trade.[46]

Emigrants also had access to high-quality shipping from the Clyde. So-called regular traders plied between Glasgow or Greenock and ports in British North America twice or even three times a year, usually under the same captain.[47] By offering A1 ships and experienced captains, Alexander Allan, founder of the Allan Line, quickly came to dominate the Clyde passenger trade to Quebec and Montreal.[48] It was a modest beginning. After acquiring eight shares in the *Jean* in 1819, Allan went on in 1825 to acquire the *Favourite,* which boasted "six feet between decks ... ample room for steerage passengers and ... good accommodation in the cabin. "[49] His third ship, the *Canada* of Greenock, purchased in 1831, was also built to a high standard. Having put his son Hugh in charge of a branch office in Montreal, Alexander continued to expand his fleet and was soon able to offer several crossings a year between the Clyde and Montreal.

By the 1840s the firm had six additional ships – the *Arabian* of Greenock, *Brilliant* of Glasgow, *Favourite* of Greenock, *Blonde* of Montreal, *Caledonia* of Greenock, and *Albion* of Greenock – each of which attracted large numbers of steerage passengers (Table 5). The needs of the timber trade were still paramount, but passengers were now being offered more spacious accommodation in ships that were capable of greater speeds.[50] Later, when services became more specialized, ships such as the *Glencairn, Marion, Ottawa,* and *Harlequin,* built in the 1850s and registered in Glasgow, would carry as many emigrants in one crossing as the earlier Allan Line ships had taken in several.[51] To ensure that the Allan Line could always offer its newest vessels, each ship in the fleet saw service for an average of only five years before being withdrawn. Between 1830 and 1855, the Allan Line carried roughly 10,000 emigrants from the Clyde to Quebec, primarily as steerage passengers. Large though this figure is, it represents only about one quarter of the total passenger trade from the Clyde (Table 7).[52] The remaining 36,000 people, who left from Greenock and Glasgow, travelled on one of the many other regular traders operating from the Clyde,[53] which were not owned by the Allan firm.

Table 5

The Allan Line Passenger Trade from the Clyde to Quebec, 1819–51
[Thomas Appleton, *Ravenscrag, The Royal Mail Line*, 194–7; British Parliamentary Papers, *Quebec Mercury, Lloyd's Shipping Register, Clyde Bill of Entry*.]

Vessel	Year Built	Ton-nage	Lloyd's Code	Master(s)	Year Psgrs first carried	No. Psgrs
Jean	1819	170	A1	Allan, Alexr.	1819	28
Favourite of Montreal	1825	296	A1	Allan, Bryce	1826	550
Canada of Greenock	1831	330	A1	McArthur	1834	999
Arabian of Greenock	1837	355	A1	Allan	1837	125
Favourite of Greenock	1839	355	A1	Greenhorn	1841	692
Blonde of Montreal	1841	604	A1	Crawford	1842	1865
Caledonia of Greenock	1841	383	A1	Greenhorn	1841	944
Albion of Greenock	1845	414	A1	Allan, Bryce	1846	392
Polly of Glasgow	1845	629	AE1	Allan	1852	409

Vessel	Year Built	Ton-nage	Lloyd's Code	Master(s)	Year Psgrs first carried	No. Psgrs
Marion of Glasgow	1848	670	A1	n/k	1852	297
Glencairn of Glasgow	1850	850	A1	Allan	1851	651
Harlequin of Glasgow	1851	702	A1	n/k	1852	835
Ottawa of Glasgow	1851	480	A1	McArthur	1851	125

But what about the overall quality of emigrant shipping? This can be judged by concentrating on the vessels that carried the majority of emigrants from Scotland to Canada (Appendix III). Some 270 vessels, between them, carried a grand total of 95,000 passengers. Lloyd's shipping codes have been located for 199 of these vessels: [54] One hundred and fifty-one of them with known codes, representing 76 per cent, were "A1" or "AE1" – in other words, of the highest quality.[55] Forty-seven were "E," or second class – seaworthy, but with minor defects. The *Hector,* which sailed to Pictou from Loch Broom in 1773, was the only vessel to be assigned an "I" classification, indicating that it was not seaworthy. And yet in a recent history of the Highlands and Islands, John MacLeod makes the ludicrous claim that "leaky old boats" were always "relegated to the transport of timber. When they were too battered, swollen and creaking even for that ... they ended their careers carrying emigrants from Scotland, Ireland and the poor north of England."[56] These ridiculous pronouncements are not borne out by the facts.

Basil Lubbock, the eminent British marine author, has asserted that the typical emigrant ship was "little better than a hermetically sealed box; as deep as it was long, with clumsy square bows and stern with ill-cut, ill-set sails ... and as for the crews, they were commonly composed of 'rum-soaked illiterate bear-like officers.'"[57] But here again, the truth is in the detail. By checking ship dimensions in port shipping registers, it can readily be shown that, before the mid-1830s, emigrants generally sailed in vessels whose hull length was roughly five times greater than their depth.[58] With the improvements in design that followed, when hulls became longer, shallower, and thinner, greater speeds were possible.[59] By the 1840s, the length of the average hull was generally six times its depth.[60] Also, as two-masted brigs and snows gave way to the larger three-masted vessels, rigged as barques or ships, emigrants had access to even speedier and roomier vessels. These were not hermetically sealed boxes! But what abot the rum-soaked crews!

At sea everything depended on the captain's navigational skills and cool head. This was a time when captains shouted out their latitude and longitude positions to each other, using "a speaking trumpet" when their ships passed at sea.[61] There were almost no technical aids, and everything came down to the captain's competence under pressure. Ice flows and heavy gales bedevilled the north Atlantic route, and so experience of such conditions was vital. The long stints of continuous service that various Aberdeen captains had, with either the same shipowner or sometimes the same vessel, provide irrefutable evidence of their knowledge of Atlantic conditions. James Oswald is a typical example. Having captained the *Cambria, Louisa,* and *Mary* on their crossings to Halifax with emigrants between 1813 and 1821, he then captained the *Aberdeenshire* of Aberdeen from 1827 to 1835 (Table 6). Taking about twenty passengers from Aberdeen in the spring and summer of most years, the *Aberdeenshire* offered a steady and reliable service to Halifax.

Thus the same captain often remained in charge of the same vessel over many years. He frequently owned shares in the vessel he commanded, thus giving him an added incentive to attract repeat business.[62] Having been captain of the *Aimwell* of Aberdeen intermittently from 1816 to 1832, John Morison became the *Pacific* of Aberdeen's principal captain from 1836 to 1844, in charge of nearly five hundred emigrants on six crossings. As captain of the *St. Lawrence* of Aberdeen, James Tulloch presided over twenty-two crossings involving nearly 2,000 passengers between 1842 and 1854. James Elliot had nearly twenty years' combined experience in charge of the *Brilliant,* a former whaling ship, and the *Berbice* – vessels that together carried 3,500 emigrants.[63] Then there was Alexander Leslie, who captained the *Albion* of Aberdeen for twenty-three years. Sailing with an average of twenty emigrants each time, Leslie was in charge of twenty-nine crossings between Aberdeen and Halifax. Forty passengers were relieved to have the benefit of his experience during a stormy crossing in 1836. "The unremitting assiduity with which Captain Leslie attended to our comfort during a tedious, stormy passage" was much admired. "We would strongly recommend to emigrants and others, crossing the Atlantic, to do so by the *Albion,* as from experience, we can assure them that under the command of

MIRAMICHI TIMBER.

There will be sold by public roup, upon an early day, to
be afterwards fixed,

THE Entire CARGO of the Brig
ALBION, Capt. LESLIE, just arrived from Miramichi consisting of
320 Loads YELLOW PINE.
12 Do. BIRCH.
1400 Superficial Feet FIR PLANK ; and
2550 ASH BILLET STAVES.

The above Cargo is of excellent quality, and of very
large scantling. It may be seen on the piece of ground
belonging to Messrs Duffus & Co. adjoining Footdee
Church Yard ; and farther particulars can be known, on
applying to   ROBERT DUTHIE
Quay, Nov. 7, 1826.

The *Albion*'s timber cargo offered for sale, followed by an announcement of its return journey to Quebec (*Aberdeen Herald*, March 5, 1836).

FOR HALIFAX, PICTOU, AND MIRAMICHI.

THE FINE NEW AND FAST SAILING
BRIG ALBION,
266 Tons per Register,

ALEX. LESLIE, Commander,

Will be ready to receive Goods on board for the above
ports in the course of a few days, and will positively be
dispatched on first March. The accommodation for
Cabin and Steerage Passengers is superior, having good
height between decks.

For Freight and Passage, apply to Captain Leslie
or to   ROBt. DUTHIE.

Who has for Sale, 15,000 feet Miramichi TIMBER
of fine quality, imported in November last, per the
Albion. Also, for Sale, 100 Barrels Belfast Prime
MESS PORK, newly cured.
(One concern.)
Quay, Jan. 15, 1828.

Captain Leslie the greatest care will be paid to their comfort and safety."[64]

Good captains were like magnets and attracted the bulk of Aberdeen's Atlantic passenger trade. William Shand, one of seventy-five passengers on board the *Hercules* of Aberdeen in 1834, greatly admired Captain Duncan Walker:

> It is but justice to Mr. Walker to say that in my opinion there is not a man better adapted for his business than he is – a very clever shrewd man with a good deal of experience and so completely sober that he tastes no drink of any kind no stronger than water and seems to have his thoughts on nothing but his business and the safety of his crew. He acted as surgeon to the whole of them when they were sick, visiting them each day, giving them medicine.[65]

John Rhind was full of praise for Captain Herman Ganson's navigational skills, which were tested to the full in violent storms. As the barque had to

Piano Forte

Baron MacKay van Ophemert in the Netherlands 1938.

Sir Donald James 11th baronet of Strathnaver was 13 Lord Reay

Clan Mackay Society is in Glasgow.

~~[illegible] Dad's birth~~

~~Flanders [illegible]~~

~~West Park~~

be steered through mountainous waves, the passengers were rocked from side to side, and "kettles, cans, pots and pans were chasing and knocking each other about the ship." Passengers could hear "the howling of the wind through the rigging and the roaring of the sea." Such was the ferocity of the storm that the man in the berth above Rhind complained that "the skin of his posterior" had been "rubbed off."[66] In another storm the same man had to cling on for dear life to "a post in the middle of the ship, having been pitched out of his bed. For some minutes the ship had rolled about from side to side like a cradle."[67] John Hart, one of four hundred steerage passengers sailing in the *Carleton* from Glasgow in 1842, experienced a storm "the like of it, we never saw, and the hatches all down but one, and the sea running down in among us; our bed was all wet. I have described the sea as running mountains high, but I knew nothing about it till now ... It was like Campsie Fells and the wind roaring, the like of it I never heard." Testing times for captains, sailors and passengers![68]

Table 6

Aberdeen Sea Captains, 1806–55
[ACA CE 87/11, Aberdeen Post Office directories]

Captain	Ship	Owner/Agent
George Allan	*Pilgrim* (1831, 1838)	Donaldson Rose
	Sarah (1840–42)	Donaldson Rose
Daniel Anderson	*Sir William Wallace* (1833–37)	Donaldson Rose
Alexander Anderson	*Emerald* (1806)	
	Patriot (1812–19)	Robert Catto
	Quebec Packet (1822–34)	Robert Catto
	Annandale (1831–32)	Robert Catto
James Clayton	*Cambria* (1814)	Peter Ritchie
	Mary (1816–17)	Peter Ritchie
Alexander Duncan	*Carolina* (1815–16)	William White
	Ploughman (1816)	Saunders & Mellis
Alexander Duthie	*City of Aberdeen* (1826–7)	William Allan
	Brilliant (1833–36)	William Duthie
James Elliot	*Brilliant* (1836–45)	William Duthie
	Berbice (1848–54)	Alexander Duthie

Captain	Ship	Owner/Agent
Alexander Leslie	*Albion* (1829–52)	Robert Duthie
(1829–38)	*Empress of Banff*	Alex. Stephen(1839–41)
	(1851–52)	Alex. Cooper (1842–53)
James Morrison	*Centurion* (1811)	Peter Ritchie
	Mary (1811–12)	Peter Ritchie
John Morison	*Aimwell* (1816–18)	Donaldson Rose
	Douglas (1817)	Geo. Thompson
	Pacific (1836–44)	Alexander Cooper

A captain's reputation and expertise were crucial to a shipowner's success in attracting emigrants. Countless accolades have appeared in newspapers and in emigrants' diaries. The 285 emigrants who sailed from Tobermory to Pictou in 1819, on the *Economy* of Aberdeen, praised Captain Frazier's "kind treatment" during a five-week passage.[69] Captain Murray's "humane treatment" when in charge of the *Glentanner* of Aberdeen, which sailed with 141 passengers from Tobermory to Sydney, Cape Breton, in the following year, won a warm commendation, as did Captain Alexander Watt who was at the helm of the *Emperor Alexander* of Aberdeen when she did the same voyage in 1823 with 160 passengers.[70] And Captain Jacobson was acclaimed by 330 of his grateful Skye passengers who sailed on the *Mary* of Newcastle in 1830 to Quebec and ports in the Maritimes.[71] The *Fairy* of Dundee's grateful passengers praised Captain D. Ritchie's "humane, caring and attentive manner" on their 1833 crossing from Dundee to Quebec.[72] And so it went on. These tributes are but a small sample of the total.

Though a minority, there certainly were some dreadful captains. Walter Riddell, one of 137 passengers sailing from Dumfries to Quebec on the *Lancaster* in 1833, realized to his horror that his ship had become trapped in the ice, and dealing with the situation was a drunken captain:

Last night about 10.00 o'clock got among a field of ice; it was that thick we could see no way through it; about 6 [a.m.] the Captain appeared to be drunk and the seamen would not obey his orders; at the same time, Edgar Mitchell, one of the seamen got his thigh bone broken between the yard and the mast; the Captain having hold of the helm, run the ship betwixt two pieces of ice and some of the seamen cried we are all gone! John Fairgrieve ran and took the Captain from the helm; they struggled together till some of the men interposed; the Captain threatened dreadfully what he would do when we reached Quebec; saw a vessel to the windward of us; about 10 a.m. the ice cleared away and we saw no more of it. We were scarcely out of the ice when the wind blew about a hurricane from the south-east ... the waves were higher than I have ever seen them.[73]

As was to be expected, Walter Riddell pretty well fell on his knees when he caught sight of Quebec. "What with the calmness of the day, what with being so long on the solitary ocean, and what with the largeness of the shipping and the grandness of the scene, I shall never forget that day."[74] It was with good reason that Thomas Fowler, who sailed from Aberdeen to Quebec on the *Brilliant* of Aberdeen in 1831, captained by the splendid Alexander Barclay, advised emigrants "to pay some attention to the selection of a sober, staid commander, as their comfort will in a great measure depend upon him whatever kind the weather may happen to be."[75]

Some captains failed to provide adequate food provisions and drinking water. The captain of the *Ann* of Banff, which sailed in 1819 with sixty passengers, actually faced criminal charges for his inadequate provisioning.[76] The 1803 Passenger Act, the first attempt at legislation, stipulated the daily minimums of beef, bread, biscuit or oatmeal, molasses, and water that were to be given to each passenger.[77] However, some shippers complained that, because the daily allowances applied equally to children, they had to pay for and stock food items that were never eaten. Predictably, the act was largely ignored. In any case, minimum daily food requirements had little relevance to the many steerage passengers, who actually supplied their own food. And sometimes providence would bring additional supplies. Spotting an emigrant ship in the distance, an opportunistic Mull farmer found a buyer for his "fine pig" by rowing out to it; twenty-one of the steerage passengers on the *Carleton*, who were on their way to Quebec from Glasgow, "joined together" and bought the squealing pig for 21 shillings. It would be slaughtered by three of them next morning.[78]

The passengers sailing in the *Canada* from Cromarty to Quebec in 1830 were not so fortunate. Six lives were lost because the captain failed to provide adequate drinking water. "A severe fever owing to bad water" broke out among the 244 emigrants. The ship's wooden casks, having previously contained palm oil, had been used to store water. Being badly contaminated, the water "could not be used for tea or coffee or anything else."[79] When the *Clansman* of Glasgow arrived at Sydney, Cape Breton, in 1836 with just over two hundred Hebridean passengers, several were "under the disease of small pox." Having failed to observe the quarantine regulations, the captain had allowed his passengers to disembark at the mouth of the harbour. "A military force was immediately applied for, and obtained, which accompanied by a magistrate, prevented any more persons being landed." It was soon discovered that most of the passengers "were entirely destitute of provisions," some having been without food for more than twenty-four hours.[80] It seems that the shipowner and captain had been highly negligent in failing to provide adequate provisions.

The twenty-nine Mull and Tiree emigrants who lost their lives through illness during the 1847 crossing of the *Eliza* of Cardiff were exceedingly badly provisioned, but the fault here appears to lie more with their landlord than with the captain.[81] But the loss of life on the *Circassian* of Aberdeen's miserable crossing from Glasgow to Quebec two years later certainly was the captain's fault. Their ship having been stuck in ice for a long period, the

View of the Quarantine Station at Grosse Île in 1850, oil painting by Henri Delattre (1801–76). *Courtesy of Library and Archives Canada C–120285.*

209 emigrants ran short of food, and as they did they succumbed to disease. Seventy people died, fifty-three from cholera and seventeen from typhus, with most of the deaths occurring at the quarantine station and hospital at Grosse Île.[82] Sufficient provisions had been put on board for only six weeks. When stocks ran out, the passengers had to purchase additional food from Captain G. Dixon. His shameful conduct, in charging for food under these circumstances, caused "the largest proportionate mortality" experienced on any ship that season.[83]

A good-quality ship does not in itself guarantee a comfortable crossing. Overcrowding was often excessive, particularly during late eighteenth and early nineteenth centuries, when large contingents of Highlanders left Scotland for North America. In fact, it was widespread concern over the suffering caused by extremely crowded emigrant ships that mobilized the Highland Society of Edinburgh to campaign for changes in legislation. The resulting Passenger Act of 1803, which specified a space allocation of one person for every two tons' burthen, caused fares to double, although it did curb extreme crowding for a limited period. Overcrowding was often a direct consequence of low fares, since shipowners only offered reduced prices when they could attract a reasonable volume of business.[84]

The Highland Society had been galvanized into action by discovering the extent of overcrowding on the *Dove* of Aberdeen and the *Sarah* of Liverpool, two ships that had sailed from Fort William to Pictou in 1801. However, these were by no means the only cases of extreme overcrowding. When she sailed that year from Moidart to Sydney with 340 Highlanders, the *Northern Friends* of Clyde was three times over the space limit defined in the 1803 legislation. The 1,100 Highlanders who went to Glengarry, Upper Canada, in 1802, also endured extremely cramped conditions on their ships – the *Neptune* of Greenock, *Helen* of Irvine, *Jean* of Irvine, and *Friends of John Saltcoats*. The *Neptune*'s passenger-to-tonnage ratio exceeded the legal limit by a factor of four.[85]

When emigration surged ahead again with the ending of the Napoleonic Wars, the government succumbed to pressure from shipowners to allow vessels to carry less food and more people by having legislation passed in 1817 that weakened the requirements of the 1803 act. Following the slackening of the space limits to one-and-one-half tons per person, overcrowding became more common. For instance, the 141-ton *Morning-*

field of Aberdeen, which sailed from Tobermory to Pictou in 1819 with 264 emigrants, was three times over her legal limit. Regulations were tightened up in 1823, but they were repealed once again in response to continuing commercial pressures, and, by 1828, the passenger-to-tonnage ratio was three passengers for every four tons.[86] But the space limits were made more generous again in 1835, when the ratio was increased to three passengers for every five tons.[87]

Excessive crowding tended to occur most frequently on the ships that carried Western Isle emigrants to Cape Breton. This no doubt reflects the desperate poverty of the Hebridean settlers who flocked there in great numbers. Such was the overcrowding in the *Universe* of Aberdeen when she sailed to Sydney in 1828 that six families "were obliged to live in the long boat during the whole voyage."[88] The *Two Sisters* of Pictou, sailing that same year, carried fifty-six more people than her legal limit allowed. When they arrived, the passengers were said to be "very much in want of provisions, having been on allowance all the voyage, owing as the master states, to deceptions which were practised with regard to the number of passengers and the stock of provisions put on board."[89] Clearly the emigrants had understated their numbers, presumably to keep their overall costs down. The *Malay,* sailing in 1830 from Tobermory, and the *Banffshire* of Dundee, sailing in 1841 from Lochmaddy in North Uist, had also exceeded their legal space limits. People had almost certainly consented to travelling in these cramped conditions for the sake of low fares.

Such problems evaporated with the arrival of steamships. With their introduction in the 1850s, sea transport entered a completely new phase. Crossings were much faster, schedules were far more reliable, and, for the first time, passengers were given custom-built accommodation. Sailing in April 1857, the SS *Clyde* offered the first-ever steamship crossing from Glasgow to Montreal.[90] Carrying three hundred passengers, she completed the journey in just twelve-and-a-half days. With "sumptuously furnished" cabins and a "well-lighted and ventilated" hold, she offered state-of-the-art accommodation.[91] Because of their great size and sophistication, steamships could sail only from major ports. This effectively meant that Scottish shipping services became increasingly centralized around Glasgow and Liverpool. And because they were no longer dependent on the vagaries of the weather and wind direction, steamships could depart at a predetermined time.[92] More and more emigrants opted for their greater speed, safety, reliability, and creature comforts, and, by 1870, steam had replaced sail.

The railways were another important development. They carried emigrants to the major ports of Glasgow and Liverpool and also took them inland through Canada. The Canadian Steam Navigation Company, established in 1853, ran regular services from Glasgow and Liverpool to Quebec and Montreal twice a month in summer and once a month in winter. Also linking its services with the railways, it offered emigrants an all-inclusive fare for both sea and land transport during winter months. Thus, when the St. Lawrence was frozen over in the winter, emigrants could disembark at Boston, then take a rail link from Portland, Maine, to Montreal.[93] And, with the opening of the Great Western Railway, they had no longer to dread the arduous and slow journeys west from Montreal, by river and lake, on boats and steamers. Now there were timetables, booking procedures, enforceable controls, interconnecting services, and comparatively few delays.

Irrefutable evidence of the overall high standard of shipping that was offered to emigrant Scots during the sailing ship era has been presented in

Scottish immigrants waiting to go ashore at Quebec, October, 1911. *Courtesy of William James Topley/Library and Archives Canada PA–010225.*

this section. There was one reported shipwreck and there were some wretched crossings, but these were exceptional events.[94] Clearly rapacious shipowners and battered, disease-ridden tubs have little place in the Scottish emigrants' story. To suggest otherwise flies in the face of the wide-ranging factual evidence.

Table 7

Emigrant Departures to Quebec from Scottish Ports, 1831–55
[PP, Annual Reports of the Immigration Agent at Quebec]

Scottish Port	Emigrant Totals
Glasgow	28238
Greenock	18008
Aberdeen	10409
Highlands & Islands*	10081
Misc. Small Ports#	5459
Leith	4411
Stornoway	3362
Dundee	2294
Dumfries	394
Children under 1 year	292
Cabin Passengers	1152

*Excludes Stornoway
#For example, Alloa, Annan, Ayr, Irvine, Montrose, Peterhead and Stranraer

Many commentators, both past and present, lament the loss of Scots to the New World. They find it hard to accept that any Scot would leave willingly in order to attain a better life in Canada. People able to influence events at the time even resorted to rumours and scare stories to thwart the exodus, but the unstoppable force was impervious to such tactics. Robert Kippen's experience is typical. When Robert sailed to Quebec in 1833 in the *Tamerlane* of Greenock, his brother John, back home in Perthshire, picked up a rumour, spread by "some evil persons," that his ship had been "totally lost." It was "very happy for us that Robert Thomson was in Greenock." He had seen the captain of the *Tamerlane* "and spoke personally to him," telling him that his brother arrived safely with all of the other passengers and that he "went off in the first steamboat." The relieved John Kippen relayed the tale to his brother, adding that had his brother remained in Breadalbane he would still be one of the "poor, miserable tenants."[95] No doubt, John was planning to join his brother in the thriving Breadalbane community being created in Glengarry, Upper Canada.

In 1831, the *Aberdeen Journal* reported that emigration from northern Scotland would have been far greater "but for a prevailing rumour that the government intend next year to give emigrants a free passage to America," but the newspaper doubted whether that expectation would ever be realized.[96] Of course it would not. This was just another deliberate lie, intended to reduce the numbers emigrating in that particular year. The reality was that people were desperate to emigrate. Yet in John Prebble's imaginings, most emigrants were so desperate to remain that "they flung themselves on the earth they were leaving, clinging to it so fiercely that sailors had to prise them free and carry them bodily on boats."[97] What nonsense!

During his 1829 visit to Sutherland, Beriah Botsfield witnessed "the melancholy spectacle of a flock of men, women and children of all ages, hasting in their holiday attire, to embark on board a brig from Brora to Upper Canada."[98] He may have been melancholy, but the emigrants were probably rejoicing. They had found the money for their crossings, and a more prosperous life awaited them.[99] Two years later, when Hugh Miller witnessed the departure of the *Cleopatra,* he could not resist adding a negative spin to the occasion. The large crowds lining the harbour cheered, as did the emigrants, but to him, and only him, their cheers sounded more "like a lamentation and wailing."[100]

Leaving Scotland brought sadness, but the emigrant's goal of a better future was cause for celebration. When the large contingent of Lowland Scots left for Lanark County in 1815, they were taken by steamer from Glasgow along the River Clyde to Greenock. Even though it was two o'clock in the morning, thousands of people "lined the shore bidding *Adieu* to their departing friends."[101] The Kincardineshire emigrants who left for New Brunswick in 1873 had a similar send-off. Large crowds gathered at Aberdeen railway station to say their goodbyes, and, as their train made its way to Glasgow, the emigrants could see "farewell signals" draped on the remote farmhouses as they sped along. "Field labourers paused in their work to telegraph their good speed to the wanderers."[102]

And when, in the grim days of the Highland Famine, reporters went on board the *Prince Albert* of Arbroath at Thurso, just before the ship departed, they were struck by the buzz and activity. They met Sutherland and Caithness people of all descriptions. Some were "sick and hearty," others, "lively and sad." They were "talking, singing, crying, laughing, joking, reading, sewing, packing, eating, sleeping, musing, washing etc."[103] The departure was the beginning of a long process. Life had to go on. Some people may have viewed the departure with resignation, but others were no doubt bubbling with excitement. Ewan Cameron, who was preparing to sail from Greenock for Quebec, certainly was:

> I merely write a few lines, as they intend sailing tomorrow and I may not have another opportunity. The passengers appear to be very agreeable, but especially the two brothers which you saw are unusually frank. There are three fiddlers aboard and I have already got the offer of a fiddle which is very agreeable. The Captain has got plenty of books but no kind of game ... I stood long waiting for the *Earl Grey* but never saw her go past ... You must excuse the rigmarole letter as they are singing all about.[104]

And the safe arrival was an even greater cause for celebration. As the four hundred passengers sailing on the *Carleton* neared "the long-looked-for Banks of Newfoundland" in May 1842, the band was summoned on deck and "we had some reels and ... some songs. It was a fine night and a fine wind. We all went to bed as happy as we would have been on a Saturday night in Glasgow."[105]

Although most people would have felt apprehensive about crossing the Atlantic, they expected to arrive safely. The vast majority did. On reaching their destinations they then faced the daunting task of clearing the vast wildernesses that lay around them.

Nine

CANADA'S
SCOTTISH HERITAGE

Farewell to the land of the hills and the heather,
the land of our ancestors, land of our love,
it is today firmly enslaved
with distress and cries of woe in every place.

The King of Glory will be our hope
and we will find land, freedom and sustenance
in the great wide forests
and every sorrow will disappear.

'The earth and all that it contains belongs to God'[1]

THE HIGHLANDERS WHO LANDED AT Orwell Bay and founded the Belfast communities in Prince Edward Island could never have imagined that their descendants would one day have these poignant lines inscribed in Gaelic on a large piece of stone. The carefully chosen words speak of their suffering in Scotland and of the better future they hoped to find in the New World. There was no mourning for a lost Highland homeland here!

Although Scots predominated in the early British influx to Canada, their relative position quickly declined. By the turn of the twentieth century, people of Scottish ancestry accounted for a mere 15 per cent of Canada's population.[2] And yet their impact on the country's development was huge.

Memorial, inscribed in Gaelic, to Belfast's Highland pioneers, who first arrived in 1803. *Photograph by Geoff Campey.*

Scots enjoyed a visibility out of all proportion to their numbers, dominating much of the country's business, professional, and political life. Pierre Berton attributed their astounding success to the Scottish work ethic:

> For the Scots it was work, save and study; study save and work. The Irish outnumbered them, as did the English, but the Scots ran the country ... they controlled the fur trade, the great banking and financial houses, the major educational institutions and, to a considerable degree, the government.[3]

The high profile enjoyed by Scots owes much to their early arrival, which enabled them to make full use of their obvious entrepreneurial talents. Their early dominance in the fur trade, combined with the commercial endeavours of the merchants of Scottish ancestry who moved to Montreal, Halifax, and Saint John from the United States after the American War of Independence, gave them an enormous head start. But there was more to their success than this. Highlanders had a particularly strong sense of identity and self-belief and proved to be remarkably good at coping with the privations and isolation of pioneer life:

> At political meetings, on St. Andrew's Day, in sermons, in homilies for the children at the Christmas concert and even in conversation, the intellectual and moral leaders reminded themselves and others of the fortitude of men and women who had left the Highlands to make their way in this strange land and of the legacy of strength and courage which they had left to their children and grandchildren.[4]

Arriving with an uncompromising desire to maintain their own separate identity, the early settlers gave Canada its well-rooted Scottish heritage, which continues to flourish.

Scots came with traditions and customs that were often centuries old. Highlanders committed their Gaelic poems and songs to memory and passed them down from generation to generation. The tradition of singing Gaelic songs in groups while performing communal tasks was one of many practices to be transferred to the New World. Settlers in the Codroy Valley of southwest Newfoundland had a repertoire of Gaelic milling songs that were sung during the final stages of processing woollen cloth.[5] Having initially emigrated to Cape Breton, they had come to the Codroy Valley during the mid-nineteenth century to take advantage of its better land opportunities. Using spinning wheels brought with them from Scotland, they produced their own cloth while perpetuating their musical traditions.[6] Gaelic songs also began to flourish in the Eastern Townships of Quebec in the early 1830s, when Arran settlers conveyed their traditions of spinning and "milling bees" to Megantic County.[7] Lewis settlers further to the south in this same region developed the tradition one stage further by singing the 23rd Psalm ("The Lord Is My Shepherd") in Gaelic as they marked out the boundaries of each family's plot of land. "They'd sing that [the psalm] over so many times, and they'd keep time walking through the woods."[8]

Although the Gaelic language lived on in many parts of Canada, and still does in some areas, it was in a general state of decline by the late nineteenth century. It has survived the longest in Antigonish County, Nova

Scotia, and in Cape Breton. When Alexander Mackenzie visited in 1880, he found that "hundreds" of Antigonish's inhabitants "cannot speak any but the Gaelic language," while nearly all of Cape Breton's residents could "still speak the Gaelic language." Gaelic was spoken more commonly when Highlanders gathered in Pictou than "you would find it now in any part of Sutherland or Ross-shire." According to Mackenzie, nine-tenths of Cape Bretoners were of Highland extraction, and Antigonish was quite simply "the most Highland in Canada."[9] Antigonish had even a Gaelic/English newspaper – the *Casket*, which was first published in 1852 – although the Gaelic content was short-lived and had all but disappeared by 1857.[10] Cape Breton still has the largest Gaelic-speaking population in the world outside Scotland.

When John Buchan (Lord Tweedsmuir) visited Cape Breton in 1937 as governor general of Canada, he found it to be "more Highland than the Highlands." He was welcomed by six pipers "all MacDonalds in faded tartans – long lean men from the [coal] mines whom one could easily picture leading a raid through the Lochaber passes." He was constantly addressed in Gaelic. "I wish to goodness I knew some Gaelic," he said, since "I can only look sheepish. The worst of it is I have a bogus reputation, for at first, when I received letters of welcome in Gaelic, with the help of Ian

Barn with a Gaelic name at Mount Auburn, east of Red Islands, Cape Breton. "Beinn Phadruig" is Gaelic for Patrick's Mountain. *Photograph by Geoff Campey.*

Mackenzie, my Minister of Defence, I answered in Gaelic. Oh, what a tangled web we weave when first we practice to deceive!"[11]

Vast stretches of the Eastern Townships of Quebec had nothing but Gaelic-speakers for much of the nineteenth century. However, as descendants of the old Hebridean communities left the area, the language slowly declined. In his "Guard the Gaelic" poem, written in 1894, Angus MacKay (Oscar Dhu) exhorted his fellow Highlanders to remain where they were, but he spoke in vain.[12] The prospect of the better economic opportunities that western Canada and the United States had to offer led to a steady decline of the Hebridean component of the overall population. Between 1881 and 1941 it plummeted from 20 per cent to 5 per cent.[13] Nevertheless, even as late as the 1920s, a Gaelic concert held at the Oddfellows' Hall in Scotstown could attract up to two hundred people.[14]

The Gaelic language was particularly resilient in those areas where large groups of Highlanders had once been concentrated. A Presbyterian minister who visited New Brunswick's Miramichi region in 1832 found two hundred to three hundred fellow Presbyterians at Tabusintac, Bay du Vin, and Black River, "of whom probably 140 speak the Gaelic language, with a few understanding no other language."[15] Having first arrived in the region in the early 1770s, they were desperate to have a resident minister who could speak Gaelic.[16] The many Arran settlers who came to the Eastern Townships in the early 1830s arrived with a plentiful stock of "bibles, both English and Gaelic, these having been brought out in considerable quantities, as they were under the impression that in the new country it would be almost impossible to get such books."[17]

Ontario also had its Gaelic strongholds. When he visited Kincardine in Bruce County in 1880, Alexander Mackenzie heard the Gaelic language spoken "almost universally and with great purity."[18] Contributing to this large Highland nucleus had been people of Highland ancestry who, having previously emigrated to Cape Breton, moved there in the 1850s. In Lochiel Township in Glengarry County, Ekfrid Township in Middlesex County, and Puslinch Township in Wellington County, Presbyterian services spoken in Gaelic attracted far greater numbers than those in English, and this was the case well into the late nineteenth century.[19] Its usage in Ontario was sufficiently widespread in 1841 to warrant a monthly Gaelic newspaper, which was produced in Kingston and distributed throughout the province.[20]

Scots also transferred their zeal for education and learning to their New World communities. William Rattray commented on the poor Scots who arrived in Canada with "a sound education," thus giving them an "an obvious advantage over their neighbours."[21] Since virtually every town in Scotland had a lending library, a good many of them also came with a healthy appetite for reading books. The former weavers, who came from the beleaguered textile districts in Lanarkshire and Renfrewshire during the first half of the nineteenth century, were especially well-known for their intellectual pursuits. Bringing their own books with them to the Rideau Valley region of Ontario, they immediately began building a lending library in Dalhousie Township. They formed the Dalhousie St. Andrew's Philanthropic Society to raise funds, although the group had the additional aims of providing "mutual assistance in case of sickness or misfortune" and maintaining "our Scotch feelings and customs amongst us." They completed their library by 1832, largely as a result of "very valuable donations" from the Earl of Dalhousie, governor-in-chief of British North America:

> He has become a patron to a Public Library which we have established ... and has sent us one hundred dollars and two boxes of books including a complete set of the Encyclopaedia Britannica as a foundation stone (to use His Lordship's own words) ... The books have not yet reached us, so that I cannot tell you what number of other volumes there may be. I need not tell you ... the desire for knowledge appears to be a particular inherent principle in Scotsmen. And though we have expatriated ourselves, and are now obscured in interminable forests in Canada, we are still anxious to keep the intellectual machinery in motion. [22]

Even Sir Walter Scott was asked to use "a little of your vast influence which you must possess with many of our generous countrymen" to help build and stock the library, but whether he did so is unclear.[23] Books could be borrowed six times a year and on such days the library "was crowded from morning till night."[24] It was certainly well-used. One man tramped through the woods in the hope of borrowing "the whole twenty volumes of the *Encyclopaedia Britannica*," only to be turned away "sorrowful," since this would have broken "the rules."[25]

The Pipes and Drums of the 42nd, Lanark & Renfrew Heritage Band, Perth and district, 1996. *Courtesy of Frank Roy, Brian Noonan and the 42nd, Lanark & Renfrew Heritage Pipe Band.*

At the other end of the social spectrum were the elite and successful Scots who founded Canada's many Scottish societies. Their function was usually to promote the greater glories of Scottish culture and to channel funds to needy Scots. The North British Society of Halifax, founded in 1768, was first to be formed, and it was followed thirty years later by the St. Andrew's Society of Saint John. The latter group gave its members a platform for declaring "the qualities that distinguish the Scotchman, and have put him in the front rank in every walk of life."[26] Fredericton's St. Andrew's Society, founded in 1825, had similar aims. It gave "pecuniary relief to such natives of Scotland and their descendants as may have fallen into distress," promoted "a taste for Scottish music and literature," and acted as a social club for local businessmen.[27] St. Andrew's societies grew rapidly in popularity, and by the late nineteenth century most major Canadian cities had one.

The Highland Society of Canada, formed in 1818, sought to celebrate and preserve "the language, martial spirit, dress, music and antiquities of the ancient Caledonians."[28] The Society, an offshoot of the earlier-formed Highland Society of London,[29] was composed of prominent Scots, having either Highland or Lowland connections.[30] Its leading lights were Bishop Alexander Macdonell of Glengarry and the Montreal-based North West Company partners.[31] Regular meetings were held in Glengarry, the St. Lawrence region's principal Highland stronghold. At a general meeting held each year "to celebrate the anniversary of the Battle of Waterloo," members would

appear "in the garb of Highlanders" and dispense provisions to needy Highlanders living in Ontario.[32] Some North West Company partners also left
their mark on the province's architectural heritage by contributing to the
building, during the 1820s, of the magnificent St. Raphaels Catholic Church
in Glengarry County.[33]

The Maritimes Highland societies also received their charters from the
Highland Society of London, and were similar in most respects to the Highland Society of Canada. Founded in the late 1830s, the Nova Scotia society
required its officers and members to wear "scarves of the Highland tartan"
on all public occasions. They were to extend "the blessings of education" and
by so doing "elevate the character of Scotchmen and their descendants. The
distinction between Highlander and Lowlander is forgotten in a generous
emulation to do good."[34] The Antigonish Branch of the Society concentrated more on artistic expressions of Highland culture. It wished to preserve
"the aesthetic in Scottish life and counter the impression that there was no
artistry in the songs and poems and music of the Scottish Highlands."[35] The
Miramichi Society in New Brunswick, founded in 1842, laid great stress on
education and in helping "distressed Highlanders," while Prince Edward
Island's High Society first appeared around this time as well.[36]

Two years after its founding in 1861, the Antigonish Highland Society
sponsored the first of what have since become annual Highland Games,
although such events were held on an informal basis long before this. The
Reverend Walter Johnstone clearly observed such a gathering in Belfast,
Prince Edward Island, in the early 1820s. To his dismay, men were engaged
in "feats of bodily strength," such as "running, wrestling and throwing the
stone," on the Sabbath![37] Interest in Highland traditions, encouraged in good
measure by Sir Walter Scott's writings, was rising, as Scotland was seeking a
more distinctive national identity. By adopting the cultural emblems of the
Highlands and Islands, the nation redefined its heritage and gave itself a rich
panoply of pipe bands and tartans. The same process also happened in
Canada.[38]

Highland Games commemorate the feats of strength that were once
practised in the Highlands, although the pageantry and tartans associated
with them are modern inventions. These gatherings first became formally
organized annual events in Scotland in the 1820s and were beginning in
Canada at mid-century. The Montreal Caledonian Society, set up in 1855,

The Antigonish Highland Society Memorial dedicated to "the Highland Pioneers who left the Isles and Highlands of Auld Scotland to settle in this part of New Scotland nearly two centuries ago." *Photograph by Geoff Campey.*

sponsored the first-ever Montreal Highland Games,[39] while the following year, 1856, saw the first of the Embro Highland Games, which were held in Zorra Township in Ontario.[40] The Caledonian Society of Glengarry held its first games in Williamstown in 1858, having been formed for the purpose of "establishing athletic games and plays as were customary in Scotland."[41] The more recent version of the Glengarry Highland Games and Tattoo, held each year at Maxville, Ontario, since 1948, attracts thousands of visitors.

A proliferation of similar events has followed across Canada, with most being quite recent. The Fergus Highland Games, established in 1945, regularly attracts large numbers of visitors from across the continent, making it one of the most successful festivals of its kind in Canada. In 2002, when Fergus hosted the coming together of the Clan Maxwell Societies of Canada and the United States, its Highland Games brought one hundred Maxwells together in a combined celebration of Scottish heritage.

Robbie Burns became yet another Scottish symbol, finding expression in annual Burns Suppers and in statues built in his honour in nine Canadian cities, the first being erected just over a hundred years ago in Victoria,

An advertisement for the annual Highland Games being held at
Embro in Zorra Township (Ontario). Six farmers from Embro won
the tug-of-war championship at the Chicago World Fair in 1893.
Photograph by Geoff Campey.

British Columbia. The St. Andrew's Society of Fredericton constructed its
statue partly to pay tribute to the great poet but also "to foster Scottish sentiment and strengthen the ties of Scottish brotherhood throughout the
province of New Brunswick."[42] Built in 1906 when the Society's member-
ship was in sharp decline, the bronze statue attracted some controversy from
members who believed that the money would have been better spent on the
relief of "poverty or distress."[43] The St. Andrew's Society of Montreal,
founded in 1835 by Scottish business leaders and fur traders, erected its
Burns statue on Dorchester Square in 1930, despite the stock-market crash
of 1929. Burns's associations with the everyday cares of ordinary people
probably explain his great popularity in Canada. Certainly people in Scotland believed he "came to this earth, sent of God, to help the humble man."[44]

Scots had their most stunning cultural success with curling. Being "essentially democratic and traditionally open to all classes," curling had immediate
appeal in the New World.[45] The Royal Montreal Curling Club, founded in
1807 by Scots "who were identified with the fur trade," was the earliest.[46]
Choosing Trois-Rivières (Three Rivers) as a half-way point, the Montreal
club played a match with the Quebec Curling club in 1835, with some

members arriving on their own sleighs.[47] Ontario's first curling club was formed in Kingston in 1820, with the Fergus club following soon after, but the sport did not reach the Maritime provinces until the 1850s and only arrived at Prince Edward Island in 1887.[48] In addition to their curling, Scots also imported shinty. Although shinty did not survive as a game in Canada, it contributed to the origins of ice hockey.[49]

Scottish culture continues to captivate people across Canada, as evidenced by the plethora of St. Andrew's societies, Burns suppers, pipe bands, and other Scottish groups that are enjoying increasing support in modern times.[50] Most Canadian provinces even have their own official tartans, which are registered in Scotland. Although many of the traditions brought by the early settlers have disappeared into the mists of

Statue of Robert Burns on Queen Street, Fredericton. Burns became a cult figure and is revered all over the world. *Photograph by Lucille Campey.*

times, various institutions are ensuring that their spirit and memory are kept alive. The Scottish Studies departments of the University of Guelph, the Simon Fraser University of Vancouver, and the Universty of Victoria, and the Gaelic Studies Department at St. Francis Xavier University in Antigonish are each dedicated to the nurturing of Scottish culture and history. Nova Scotia now has an Office of Gaelic Affairs, answerable to a government minister, which promotes Gaelic culture and language throughout the province. Highland traditions continue to be fostered at the Gaelic College of Celtic Arts and Crafts in St. Anns, Cape Breton, and at the College of Piping in Summerside, Prince Edward Island.

A particular strength of Scottish culture has been its ability to adapt and reflect modern tastes. Highland music remains a living tradition in many parts of Canada, crossing modern ethnic boundaries as it widens its appeal. With the transformation from rural to industrial communities in Nova Scotia and Cape Breton, fiddles and bagpipes began to be combined with

A Curling Match in Montreal, 1855, watercolour by W. S. Hatton. This watercolour is a copy of the woodcut *Curling Match, Montreal* by James Duncan reproduced in the *Illustrated London News,* February 17, 1855, 145. *Courtesy of Library and Archives Canada C–040148 W. H. Coverdale Collection of Canadiana.*

pianos and brass bands.[51] Glengarry and the Ottawa Valley have developed their own distinctive styles of fiddling, as have the Maritime provinces, where fiddling is heavily influenced by Irish music.[52]

But, although fiddles and bagpipes provided early settlers with much-needed entertainment, these pioneers kept their memories of homeland alive principally through their churches. Their faith offered spiritual support and continuity with the past. A Presbyterian minister would bring a part of Scotland with him whenever he visited. The Reverend James Souter, the Newcastle minister in the Miramichi region, observed that when his parishioners first arrived they felt "that they are indeed in a strange land, and lament the necessity which led them to leave a country endeared by so many tender ties and recollections: – but, give them their church, their minister, and their school, and they become, after a time, quite reconciled to the land of their adoption."[53] However, Presbyterian ministers sent out from Scotland faced stiff competition from Methodist and Baptist churches as well as from the new religious sects that were prospering throughout Canada.[54] The Reverend Samuel MacLeod attracted a good many Presbyterians to his highly successful Baptist ministry in Prince Edward Island by offering a version of the Gaelic Psalms that had been approved by the Established Church of Scotland.[55] He offered the best of both worlds – old-country links were preserved, but the religious needs of his New World congregation were also being addressed.

Highlanders had to be subservient in Scotland but not in Canada. They were not afraid to challenge the established order and had a healthy disregard for authority. When the Edinburgh lawyer John Howison met Highland settlers in western Ontario during the 1820s, he found people who had already grasped the egalitarian ways of their new country:

> The Scotch ... do not fail to acquire some of those ideas and principles that are indigenous to this side of the Atlantic. They soon begin to attain some conception of the advantages of equality, to consider themselves as gentlemen, and become independent; which in North America means to sit at meals with one's hat on; never to submit to be treated as an inferior; and to use the same kind of manners toward all men.[56]

As Howison discovered, these settlers certainly had no intention of deferring to him! Thomas Fowler, an Aberdeen businessman, had also noticed that "the very lowest" in Ontario "stand up briskly for equality and in general insist on being admitted to table with every master they serve."[57]

Set free from the stifling economic and social constraints that held them back in their homeland, Scots prospered in Canada. As they made the transition from Scottish immigrant to Canadian settler, they grasped the freedoms and opportunities of the egalitarian society that they helped to form. They could now "reach for the sky." Given their dogged determination and entrepreneurial talents, many achieved phenomenal success. Yet, strangely enough, Highlanders continue to be mourned as victims. But they were no different from the destitute industrial workers of the Lowlands, who sought an escape from their poverty through emigration. Emigration was the rational response of all free-thinking Scots who were caught up in dire economic circumstances. Combined with their knowledge of the better life that awaited them in Canada, this produced the cocktail of influences that became the unstoppable force.

Appendix I

SHIP CROSSINGS FROM SCOTLAND TO QUEBEC AND MARITIME PORTS, 1770–1815

Explanatory Notes

The table below lists the year, month of sailing and number of passengers carried by each vessel which left Scotland for British America between 1770 and 1815. The captain's name, where known, is given, as are the departure and arrival ports. All known recorded crossings are shown.

The passenger figures are approximations and some are ambiguous. Uncertainties arise as to whether passenger numbers include all adults (not just heads of households) and children and infants. The various documentary sources used in locating passengers are given. Where known, vessel details are provided showing the tonnage, vessel type, year built, place built and the Lloyd's Shipping Code. Occasionally, dimensions are provided as well. For a fuller explanation of the vessel types and Lloyd's Shipping Codes, see the introduction to Appendix III.

Year	Mth	Vessel	Master	Psgr. Nos.	Departure Port	Arrival Port
1770	04	*Falmouth*	McWhae, John	60	Grnk.	Charlotte-town

MacEwan, Andrew, B.W., "The *Falmouth* Passengers," *The Island Magazine*, vol. 10 (1981) 12–19; Adams and Somerville, *Cargoes of Despair and Hope*, 54–5; Malpeque Historical Society, *Malpeque and its People, 1700–1982* (Malpeque: 1982) 22–27.
     The group was taken to Lord Advocate James Montgomery's township at Stanhope in lot 34. He employed David Lawson, an experienced flax farmer to run his plantation, using emigrants as indentured servants. The *Falmouth* passengers were recruited by Lawson and many shared his Perthshire origins.

Year	Mth	Vessel	Master	Psgr. Nos.	Departure Port	Arrival Port
1770	07	*Annabella*	Stewart, Dugald	100	Campbel-town	Charlotte-town

Rev. James Lawson, "Early Scottish Settlement on Prince Edward Island: The Princetown Pioneers, 1769–1771," in *SG*, vol. xli (1994) 112–30; *SM*, vol. xxxiii (1771) 379.
     Lt. Col. Robert Stewart, who purchased half of lot 18, recruited many emigrants from his native Argyll. Another Robert Stewart (Robert's brother-in-law) travelled on the *Annabella* and organized the initial settlement. Some settlers later left Malpeque (lot 18) and moved to Low Point (lot 13) on the west side of Malpeque Bay, where there had been an Acadian settlement.

Year	Mth	Vessel	Master	Psgr. Nos.	Departure Port	Arrival Port
1771	07	*Edinburgh* of Campbeltown	McMichael, John	100	Campbeltown	Charlottetown

Passenger List (Partial): NAS SC 54/2/106.

Frank Bigwood, "Two Lists of Intending Passengers to the New World, 1770 and 1771" in *SG*, vol. xliii (1996) 17–22; Malpeque Historical Society, *Malpeque and its People*, 21, 319.

Sources differ, but it is likely that at least seventy emigrants from Argyll travelled on the *Edinburgh*; some families had their fares paid by Provost (Peter) Stewart, a Campbeltown merchant who became Chief Justice of P.E.I. in 1775. Given the Stewart's ownership of lot 18, it is probable that the group initially settled in the Malpeque Bay area.

Vessel Details: bg, 79 tns., built Leith, 1765.

Year	Mth	Vessel	Master	Psgr. Nos.	Departure Port	Arrival Port
1772	03	*Alexander*	Kirkwood, J.	214	Arisaig and Lochboisdale	Charlottetown

Rev. James Lawson, "Passengers on the *Alexander*, Arisaig to St. John's Island, April–June 1772" in *SG*, vol. xxxix (1992) 127–43; Bumsted, *The People's Clearance*, 57–61.

The group, all Roman Catholics, was led by John MacDonald of Glenaladale, a Clanranald tacksman. They settled at Scotchfort (lot 36) on land purchased from Lord Advocate James Montgomery. The emigrants came from South Uist, Barra and Eigg while many of the mainland emigrants originated from Moidart and Knoydart. John MacDonald chartered the brig *Alexander* from John Buchanan & Co. of Greenock.

Vessel Details: Foreign built, date n/k, E2, 82'9" x 22'8" x 12'6".

Year	Mth	Vessel	Master	Psgr. Nos.	Departure Port	Arrival Port
1773	06	*Hector*	Spiers, John	180	Loch Broom from Grnk.	Pictou

Passenger List: MacLaren, *Pictou Book*, 31–34

Patterson, *History of the County of Pictou*, 450–6; Adams & Somerville, *Cargoes of Despair and Hope*, 76; MacKay, *Scotland Farewell*, 89–105.

Most passengers originated from Wester Ross, Sutherland, and east Inverness-shire. Ship arrived Sept. 15. The emigrants were recruited by John Ross, an agent for the Philadelphia Land Company, which owned 200,000 acres of wilderness land in Pictou. The *Hector* was owned by John Pagan.

Vessel Details: s, 200tns, Dutch prize, I2, 83' x 24' x 10'.

Year	Mth	Vessel	Master	Psgr. Nos.	Departure Port	Arrival Port
1774		*Lovelly Nelly*	Sheridan, William	67	Whitehaven	Charlottetown

Passenger List: NAB T 47/12. The passenger list is undated but almost certainly refers to a 1774 crossing.

The passengers came from Kirkcudbrightshire & Dumfriesshire. Many of the emigrants later moved on to Pictou. The group included 4 masons, 1 blacksmith, 2 wheelwrights, 2 farmers, 3 joiners, 9 labourers and 1 sailor. The Captain's name is given as William Sherwin in the *Lloyds Shipping Register*. The *Lovelly Nelly* had been assigned an "I" shipping code, signifying that the brig's hull was in poor condition.

Vessel Details: bg, 150 tns., built Britain, 1731, I2.

Year	Mth	Vessel	Master	Psgr. Nos.	Departure Port	Arrival Port
1774	04	*John and Jean*	n/k	59	Aberdeen	Halifax & Quebec

Adams and Somerville, *Cargoes of Despair and Hope*, 124, 217; NSARM MG7 vol. 3A.
"Brought a number of settlers and some indented servants."

Year	Mth	Vessel	Master	Psgr. Nos.	Departure Port	Arrival Port
1775	03	*Friendship*	Smith, John	8	Port Glasgow	Quebec

NAB T 47/12
Ships carpenters going out to build vessels.
Vessel details: bg, 200tns., built Ayr, 1773, A1.

Year	Mth	Vessel	Master	Psgr. Nos.	Departure Port	Arrival Port
1775	04	*Lovelly Nelly*	Sheridan, William	82	Dumfries	Charlotte-town

Passenger List: NAB T 47/12
    The group, from Dumfriesshire, Kirkcudbrightshire and Peebleshire, included 2 joiners, 2 weavers, 12 labourers, 1 gardener, 1 chapman (pedlar), 1 blacksmith, 1 school master, 1 mariner, 1 clerk and 1 farmer. Some of the emigrants later moved to Pictou.
Vessel details: bg, 150 tns., built Britain, 1731, I2.

Year	Mth	Vessel	Master	Psgr. Nos.	Departure Port	Arrival Port
1775	06E	*John and Elizabeth*	n/k	52		Charlotte-town

PAPEI Acc 2779/1; Adams and Somerville, *Cargoes of Despair and Hope*, 61; Prince Edward Island Genealogical Society, *From Scotland to Prince Edward Island: Scottish emigrants to Prince Edward Island from Death and Obituary Notices in Prince Edward Island 1835-1910* (n.d.), 8.
    Seven families from Morayshire intended to settle at Orwell Bay (lot 57), acquired in 1767 by Samuel Smith, a merchant, but they left without trace. It is thought that the settlement failed because of inadequate provisioning and its remote location. The group included William Simpson, and his wife, Janet Winchester. Helen Simpson, from Morayshire, wife of William Clark is also likely to have sailed on the *John and Elizabeth*.

Year	Mth	Vessel	Master	Psgr. Nos.	Departure Port	Arrival Port
1775	08	*Elizabeth*	n/k	14	London	Charlotte-town

Orlo, J. and Fraser D., "Those Elusive Immigrants, Parts 1 to 3," *The Island Magazine*, no. 16 (1984) 36–44; no. 17 (1985) 32–7, no. 18 (1985) 29–35, (Part 3) 30; Adams and Somerville, *Cargoes of Despair and Hope*, 59–60.
    The passengers from Argyll boarded ship at Cork. They included Chief Justice Peter Stewart's family and servants (Peter was brother of Robert Stewart, proprietor of half of lot 18). Peter Stewart leased Stanhope, part of lot 34, from Sir James Montgomery. He had expected that a large number of single men would wish to go to P.E.I. with him, but alarming news of an impending war discouraged most from emigrating.

Year	Mth	Vessel	Master	Psgr. Nos.	Departure Port	Arrival Port
1783	n/k	*Mercury*	n/k	n/k	Aberdeen	Halifax

NSARM MG7 vol. 3A.

Year	Mth	Vessel	Master	Psgr. Nos.	Departure Port	Arrival Port
1784	n/k	*Glasgow*	n/k	n/k	Grnk	Halifax

James Lawson, *The Emigrant Scots* (Aberdeen: Aberdeen & North East Scotland FHS, 1988) 39; NSARM MG7 vol. 3A.
    Ship carried "indented passengers." The arrivals petitioned for land in Pictou.

Year	Mth	Vessel	Master	Psgr. Nos.	Departure Port	Arrival Port
1784	n/k	*John*	Allen, Robert	n/k	Aberdeen	Halifax,

Patterson, *History, Pictou County*, 122–23, 465; *AJ*, Feb. 23, May 17, 1784; George Patterson, *Memoir of the Rev. James MacGregor* (Philadelphia: Joseph M. Wilson, 1859) 81; MacKay, *Scotland Farewell*, 167.

In 1784, "a few families of Highlanders...arrived at Halifax, removed to Pictou, and settled on the East River." They probably sailed on the *John*. She was to call at Cromarty to collect passengers. The brig was "to be fitted up entirely for the reception and accommodation of passengers" and would be "supplied with plenty of the best provisions." The *John* was also due to call at Shelbourne, NS, and Philadelphia, USA.
Vessel Details: bg, 120 tns., built America, 1772, E1.

Year	Mth	Vessel	Master	Psgr. Nos.	Departure Port	Arrival Port
1785	n/k	n/k	n/k	n/k	Glasgow	Halifax

NSARM MG7 vol. 3A.

Year	Mth	Vessel	Master	Psgr. Nos.	Departure Port	Arrival Port
1785	06	*Philadelphia*	n/k	300	n/k	Quebec

McLean, *People of Glengarry*, 101–8.
Arrived Quebec in 1786.
Vessel details: s, 300 tns., built Hull, 1773; E1.

Year	Mth	Vessel	Master	Psgr. Nos.	Departure Port	Arrival Port
1786	07	*Macdonald*	Stevenson, R.	539	Knoydart	Quebec

McLean, *People of Glengarry*, 108–16.
Glengarry settlers.

Year	Mth	Vessel	Master	Psgr. Nos.	Departure Port	Arrival Port
1788	n/k	**Neptune**	n/k	60	n/k	Quebec

Adams and Somerville, *Cargoes of Despair and Hope*, 185.
Glengarry settlers.

Year	Mth	Vessel	Master	Psgr. Nos.	Departure Port	Arrival Port
1788	n/k	*Sally*	n/k	n/k	Aberdeen	Halifax

Bumsted, *The People's Clearance*, 72.
Thirty-nine people died on the crossing and others died soon after arriving.

Year	Mth	Vessel	Master	Psgr. Nos.	Departure Port	Arrival Port
1789	04	*Ann*(1)	Johnston	9	Port Glasgow	Quebec

QG July 2
Passengers: Col. John Nairn, George Cunningham, John Anderson and family, Thos. Hunter and Joseph Murdoch.
Vessel Details: bg, 160 tns., built Scotland, 1770, E1.

Year	Mth	Vessel	Master	Psgr. Nos.	Departure Port	Arrival Port
1789	04	*Flora*	Henry, Archibald	7	Port Glasgow	Quebec

QG, June 26
Passengers: Capt. Plenderluch and family; Messrs Graham and Parker.
Vessel Details: s, 230 tns., built Glasgow, 1782, A1.

Year	Mth	Vessel	Master	Psgr. Nos.	Departure Port	Arrival Port
1789	04	*Nancy*	Cochran	3	Grnk	Quebec

QG May 29
Passengers were three males.
Vessel Details: bg, 120 tns., built Grnk., 1786, A1.

Year	Mth	Vessel	Master	Psgr. Nos.	Departure Port	Arrival Port
1790	04	*Canada*	Harvey	6	Grnk.	Quebec

QG May 13
Passengers included: A merchant and his wife, two captains from the 26th Regiment and Thomas Blackwood.
Vessel Details: bg, 205 tns., built Wales, 1789, A1.

Year	Mth	Vessel	Master	Psgr. Nos.	Departure Port	Arrival Port
1790	04	*Nancy*	Cochran	3	Grnk	Quebec

QG May 13
Passengers: Mr. & Mrs. Simpson, Mr. Ourns.

Year	Mth	Vessel	Master	Psgr. Nos.	Departure Port	Arrival Port
1790	07	*Jane*	Fisher	186	Drimindarach	Charlotte-town

Passenger List: NSARM MS File and SCA (Oban Papers).

Rev. James Lawson, "*Lucy, Jane* and the 'Bishop', A Study in Extant Passenger Lists" in *SG,* vol. xlii (1995) 1–13; Adams and Somerville, *Cargoes of Despair and Hope,* 191–92. Daniel Cobb Harvey (ed.), *Journeys to the Island of Saint John or Prince Edward Island, 1775–1832* (Toronto: Macmillan Co. of Canada, 1955) 76, 77.

The *Jane* and *Lucy* sailed in convoy. The passengers, from North and South Morar, Moidart, Eigg and South Uist, were from the Clanranald estate. Most had Catholic affiliations. One hundred and eleven of the 186 passengers were adults. The *British Queen* sailed in the same convoy, but she took her passengers on to Quebec.

Year	Mth	Vessel	Master	Psgr. Nos.	Departure Port	Arrival Port
1790	07	*Lucy*	Robertson	142	Drimindarach	Charlotte-town

Passenger List: PANS MS File and SCA (Oban Papers).
See above.
Vessel Details: s, 133 tns., built Newbury, 1781, E1.

Year	Mth	Vessel	Master	Psgr. Nos.	Departure Port	Arrival Port
1790	08	*British Queen* of Greenock	Deniston	87	Arisaig	Quebec

Passenger List: [NAC] RG 4A1 vol. 48, 15874–75.
QG Oct. 21; McLean, *People of Glengarry,* 16–21.
Glengarry settlers.
Vessel Details: s, 191 tns., built Grnk., 1786, A1.

Year	Mth	Vessel	Master	Psgr. Nos.	Departure Port	Arrival Port
1791	n/k	*Dunkenfield* and another vessel	n/k	650	West Highland port	Pictou

MacLaren, *Pictou Book*, 118; Colin S. MacDonald, "Early Highland Emigration to Nova Scotia and Prince Edward Island from 1770 to 1853" in *Nova Scotia Historical Society (Collections)*, vol. xxiii (1936) 44; MacKay, *Scotland Farewell*, 182–83.

Vessel also known as the *Dunkeld*. Simon Fraser was the emigration agent. Mainly Roman Catholics from the Western Isles. Dispersed to P.E.I., Antigonish and Cape Breton. Vessel Details: s, 400 tns., built 1783, A1.

Year	Mth	Vessel	Master	Psgr. Nos.	Departure Port	Arrival Port
1791	04	*Canada*	Harvey	30	Grnk	Quebec

QG June 2

Passengers were military personnel and their families (mainly from the 26th Regiment); a surgeon's mate from the 60th regiment and one man from the 65th regiment.

Year	Mth	Vessel	Master	Psgr. Nos.	Departure Port	Arrival Port
1791	04	*Oughton*	Sime	4	Leith	Quebec

QG May 24

Passengers: Mr. & Miss Hope; Capt. Spears, Capt. Rankin of the 24th Regiment.

Year	Mth	Vessel	Master	Psgr. Nos.	Departure Port	Arrival Port
1791	06	*Mally* of Greenock	Maxwell, John	236	Grnk	Charlotte-town

NLS Adv.MS.73.2.13; PAPEI RG9 (Customs); NAS E504/15/59; *PEIRG* 9 Sept. 1791.

The *Mally* carried 174 "full passengers" (i.e. adults). She left Greenock with 30 passengers and the remainder were probably collected from Uist. According to *The Royal Gazette* the *Mally* "was without fuel part of passage and her water was so bad that it was scarcely possible to use it." The emigrants settled in lots 37 to 39. The *Mally* was due to sail on to North Carolina. Vessel Details: bg, 148 tns., built Grnk., 1784, A1.

Year	Mth	Vessel	Master	Psgr. Nos.	Departure Port	Arrival Port
1791	06	*Queen* of Greenock	Morison, William	300	Grnk	Charlotte-town

NLS Adv.MS.73.2.13; PAPEI RG9 (Customs); NAS E504/15/59; *PEIRG* 9 Sept. 1791.

The *Royal Gazette* stated that the *Queen* arrived with 300 passengers who spoke "handsomely of the kind treatment they received from Capt. Morison; his conduct is worthy of being followed by all masters of vessels and humanity should dictate a similar treatment." She carried 240 "full passengers." Forty passengers left from Greenock and the remainder were almost certainly collected from Uist. The emigrants settled in lots 37 to 39. The *Queen* was due to sail on to North Carolina. Vessel Details: bg, 200 tns., built Hull, 1782, A1.

Year	Mth	Vessel	Master	Psgr. Nos.	Departure Port	Arrival Port
1792	07	*Unity*	Service	200	Grnk	Quebec

QG Sept. 27; McLean, *People of Glengarry*, 123.
Glengarry settlers; 40 Highland families.
Vessel details: s, 219 tns., built Ayr, 1791, A1.

Year	Mth	Vessel	Master	Psgr. Nos.	Departure Port	Arrival Port
1793	n/k	*Argyle*	n/k	150 Grnk	Glenelg from town	Charlotte-town

Orlo and Fraser, "Those Elusive Immigrants" (Part 1), 37.
   This group from Glen Garry, Inverness-shire was en route to Glengarry County in Upper Canada. They were delayed by bad weather spending the winter of 1793 in P.E.I. They reached their final destination the following year.
Vessel Details: bg, 139 tns., built Nova Scotia, 1790, A1.

Year	Mth	Vessel	Master	Psgr. Nos.	Departure Port	Arrival Port
1793	06	*Argyle*	n/k	150	Glenelg	Quebec

McLean, *People of Glengarry*, 123–25.
Wintered in P.E.I., then went to Quebec in two schooners.

Year	Mth	Vessel	Master	Psgr. Nos.	Departure Port	Arrival Port
1794	05	*Joseph*	McLean, Alexander	7	Grnk	Quebec

QG July 3
Passengers: Messrs. Jas. Stewart, Jas. McKay, John Hamilton, John Dunn, Jas. Dunn, John McIntyre, Mrs. Dunn.
Vessel Details: sn, 101 tns., built Nova Scotia, 1792, A1.

Year	Mth	Vessel	Master	Psgr. Nos.	Departure Port	Arrival Port
1800	04	*Eliza*	n/k	43	Port Glasgow	Quebec

Bumsted, *The Peoples Clearance*, 224.

Year	Mth	Vessel	Master	Psgr. Nos.	Departure Port	Arrival Port
1801	n/k	*Alexander*	n/k	n/k	Fort William	Pictou

Angus Anthony Johnston, *A History of the Catholic Church in Eastern Nova Scotia,* (Antigonish: St. Francis Xavier University Press, 1960) 2 vols.,163.
   Many Catholics from the West Highlands and Western Isles.

Year	Mth	Vessel	Master	Psgr. Nos.	Departure Port	Arrival Port
1801	n/k	*Fame*	Forrest, F.	79	Grnk	Quebec

Bumsted, *The Peoples Clearance*, 225.
Vessel Details: bg, 144 tns., built Chester, 1790, E1.

Year	Mth	Vessel	Master	Psgr. Nos.	Departure Port	Arrival Port
1801	n/k	*Good Intent* of Aberdeen	Beverly, Robert	n/k	Fort William	Pictou

MacLaren, *Pictou Book*, 118; Johnston, *History of the Catholic Church in Eastern Nova Scotia*, 163.
Vessel incorrectly recorded as *Golden Text*. Passage of three months. Passengers mainly Roman Catholics from Glen Moriston.

Year	Mth	Vessel	Master	Psgr. Nos.	Departure Port	Arrival Port
1801	n/k	*Hope* of Lossie	n/k	100	Isle Martin (Ullapool)	Pictou

NLS MS9646.
A total of 122 souls from the estate of Struy (Strathglass) on board. They were calculated as being equivalent to 100 adults (children and infants totalled separately and recomputed as adult equivalents). George Dunoon was the shipping agent.
Vessel Details: sp, 74 tns., built Banff, 1796, A1.

Year	Mth	Vessel	Master	Psgr. Nos.	Departure Port	Arrival Port
1801	n/k	*Nora*	n/k	500	Fort William	Pictou

MacLaren, *Pictou Book*, 118; Johnston, *History of the Catholic Church in Eastern Nova Scotia*, 163; NAS RH4/188/2.

Smallpox broke out on the passage and 65 children under five died. Most arrivals moved to P.E.I., Truro, Antigonish and Cape Breton.

| 1801 | n/k | *Union*(1) | n/k | 55 | Grnk | Quebec |

Bumsted, *The Peoples Clearance*, 225.
Vessel Details: bg, 171 tns., built Ayr, 1799, A1.

| 1801 | 06 | *Dove* of Aberdeen | Crane | 219 | Fort William | Pictou |

Passenger List: NAS RH2/4/87
NLS MS9646; Adams and Somerville, *Cargoes of Despair and Hope*, 193; *PP* 1802–03; Johnston, *History of the Catholic Church in Eastern Nova Scotia*, 163; Bumsted, *The People's Clearance*, 91, 92.

There were 153 adults and 66 children under 16 years. Most of them originated from Inverness-shire. Hugh Dunoon, the emigration agent, was on board. George Dunoon from Pictou also named as an agent.

| 1801 | 06 | *Sarah* of Liverpool | Smith | 350 | Fort William | Pictou |

Passenger List: *NAS* RH2/4/87
NLS MS9646; Adams and Somerville, *Cargoes of Despair and Hope*, 193; *PP* 1802–03; Johnston, *History of the Catholic Church in Eastern Nova Scotia*, 163; Bumsted, *The People's Clearance*, 91–2.
Most passengers originated from Inverness-shire. Hugh and George Dunoon were agents. Ship arrived in August.

| 1802 | n/k | *Tweed* of Ullapool | n/k | 70 | Isle Martin (Ullapool) | Pictou |

NLS MS9646; Brown, *Strictures and Remarks*, Appendix, State of Emigrations, 1801, 1802 and 1803.

Settlers probably originated from Sutherland and Wester Ross. Agent was A. McMillan.
Vessel Details: sp, 75 tns., built Hull, 1763, I1.

| 1802 | n/k | Two unnamed vessels | n/k | 900 | Lochboisdale | Pictou |

NLS MS9646; Brown, *Strictures and Remarks*; Johnston, *History of the Catholic Church in Eastern Nova Scotia*, 197.

Emigration agent was J. Ure. Catholics from the Clanranald estate in South Uist and Barra who mainly settled in Antigonish and Cape Breton.

Year	Mth	Vessel	Master	Psgr. Nos.	Departure Port	Arrival Port
1802	05	*Northern Friends* of Clyde		340	Moidart from Grnk	Sydney

NLS MS9646; Brown, *Strictures and Remarks*; NAS RH4/188/2.
Emigration agent was Andrew McDonald. There were 340 souls, who were recalculated as 250 adult passengers (converting children and infants to adult equivalents). Mainly Catholics from Inverness-shire.

Year	Mth	Vessel	Master	Psgr. Nos.	Departure Port	Arrival Port
1802	06	*Eagle*	Conolly, N.	21	Grnk	Quebec

QG Sept. 11.
Vessel Details: s, 179 tns., built Whitehaven, 1791, A1.

1802	06	*Helen* of Irvine	Service, G.	166	Fort William	Quebec

Passenger List: LAC MG 24 I183 file 2, 7, 9–11; McLean, *People of Glengarry*, 142–44.
Glengarry settlers.
Vessel Details: sw, 157 tns., built Leith, 1775, A1.

1802	06	*Jean* of Irvine	Mac-Donald, J.	250	Fort William	Quebec

Passenger List: LAC MG 24 I183 file 2, 7, 9–11; *QG* Sept. 9; McLean, *People of Glengarry*, 142–44.
Glengarry settlers
Vessel Details: s, 167 tns., built Saltcoats, 1799, A1.

1802	06	*Mennie* of N. B.	McKellar, Daniel	274	Port Glasgow	Charlotte-

NAS RH 4/188/1 pp.531–35; Jones and Fraser, "Those Elusive Immigrants" (Part 1) 37.
After leaving Port Glasgow the *Mennie* almost certainly collected her passengers in Uist. Passenger baggage is recorded in the P.E.I. customs records but numbers are not given. The passenger total of 274 is taken from the *Highland Society of Scotland's* records, which show that the *Mennie* had been fitted out at Port Glasgow to take passengers from the Western Isles to America.
Vessel Details: s, 274 tns., built New Brunswick, 1802, A1.

1802	06	*Neptune* of Grnk	Boyd	600	Loch Nevis (Near Fort William)	Quebec

QG, Sept. 11; McLean, *People of Glengarry*, 136–39.
Glengarry settlers.
Vessel Details: s, 308 tns., built New Brunswick, 1802, A1.

1802	07	*Albion*	Service, G.	167	Fort William	Quebec

QG, Sept. 9.

Year	Mth	Vessel	Master	Psgr. Nos.	Departure Port	Arrival Port
1802	07	*Aurora* of Grnk	MacLean, Alan	128	Fort William from Grnk	Pictou

NLS MS9646; Brown, *Strictures and Remarks*; Johnston, *History of the Catholic Church in Eastern Nova Scotia*, 197; Patterson, *History, Pictou County*, 232–33.

Simon Fraser was emigration agent. There were 82 passengers above 16 years and 46 below. Mostly Catholics from Inverness-shire who settled in Antigonish, Nova Scotia. Vessel Details: s, 191 tns., prize, E1.

Year	Mth	Vessel	Master	Psgr. Nos.	Departure Port	Arrival Port
1802	07	*Friends of John Saltcoats*	Hen, John	136	Fort William	Quebec

Passenger List: LAC MG 24 I183 File 2 7, 9–11; *QG* Sept. 15; McLean, *People of Glengarry*, 142–4.
Glengarry settlers.

Year	Mth	Vessel	Master	Psgr. Nos.	Departure Port	Arrival Port
1803	n/k	n/k	n/k	116	n/k	Passama-quoddy Bay, N.B.

PANB MC 1672. Passengers from Sutherland, originally bound for Wilmington, North Carolina. They founded Scotch Ridge in Charlotte County, New Brunswick.

Year	Mth	Vessel	Master	Psgr. Nos.	Departure Port	Arrival Port
1803	n/k	*Alexander* & 2 other ships	n/k	600	Stornoway	Pictou

Brown, *Strictures and Remarks*; NAS GD 46/17 vol. 23.
Two vessels provided by R. Macever (who was probably Roderick MacIver of Stornoway) and the third by J. MacKenzie of Lochead.

Year	Mth	Vessel	Master	Psgr. Nos.	Departure Port	Arrival Port
1803	n/k	*Bess*	n/k	80	Tobermory	Charlotte-town

Thomas Telford, *A Survey and Report of the Coasts and Central Highlands of Scotland*: Second Appendix to the First Report (London, 1803).

The *Bess* was in a list of vessels with more than 30 passengers, which were preparing to clear out in 1803; her destination was P.E.I.

Year	Mth	Vessel	Master	Psgr. Nos.	Departure Port	Arrival Port
1803	n/k	Four unnamed vessels	n/k	480	Moray Firth	Pictou

Brown, *Strictures and Remarks*.
Settlers from Strathglass. Four vessels each carrying 120 passengers. Agents were D. Forbes and a Mr. Clark. One of the ship crossings was organized by "a club of Strathglass people."

Year	Mth	Vessel	Master	Psgr. Nos.	Departure Port	Arrival Port
1803	n/k	Two unnamed vessels	n/k	n/k	n/k	Pictou

Brown, *Strictures and Remarks*.
Vessels arranged "by Major Simon Fraser who has made a trade of the business since 1790."

Year	Mth	Vessel	Master	Psgr. Nos.	Departure Port	Arrival Port
1803	03	*Rosina*	Potter, James	70	Grnk	St. John

Passenger List (Partial): *PANB* MC1672.
RG May 11. The passengers, who were "chiefly mechanics and farmers," arrived in May. Seven families (40 people) had their passages paid by the New Brunswick legislature. Six families settled in Sussex Vale and one in Saint John.
Vessel Details: s, 467 tns., built New Brunswick, 1798, A1.

Year	Mth	Vessel	Master	Psgr. Nos.	Departure Port	Arrival Port
1803	04	*Ann*(2)	McKinley, John	4	Grnk	Quebec

QG 16 June.
Passengers: John Mann, J. Orkney, Capt. Hurst, Mrs. Alunn.

Year	Mth	Vessel	Master	Psgr. Nos.	Departure Port	Arrival Port
1803	04	*Aurora*	Boyd	2	Grnk	Quebec

QG May 19.
Passengers: Henry Black, John Hamilton.
Vessel Details: s, 217 tns., built Lancaster, 1792, E1.

Year	Mth	Vessel	Master	Psgr. Nos.	Departure Port	Arrival Port
1803	04	*Countess of Darlington*	n/k	4	Grnk	Quebec

QG May 26.
Passengers: Messrs. McNider, May, Young and White.
Vessel Details: bg, 155 tns., built Ayr, 1797, A1.

Year	Mth	Vessel	Master	Psgr. Nos.	Departure Port	Arrival Port
1803	04	*New Success*	Fraser, Wm.	6	Grnk	Quebec

QG 16 June.
Passengers: Hugh Auld, Alexr. Farlane, Mr. Wilson, Jas. Griffin, David Ferguson, Alexr. Smith.
Vessel Details: bg, 136 tns., prize, E1.

Year	Mth	Vessel	Master	Psgr. Nos.	Departure Port	Arrival Port
1803	05	*Nelly*	Manson	60	n/k	Pictou

Bumsted, *The People's Clearance*, 226.

Year	Mth	Vessel	Master	Psgr. Nos.	Departure Port	Arrival Port
1803	06	*Dykes* of Maryport	Thompson, John	200	Tobermory from Liverpool	Charlotte-town

NAS CS 96/1238; PAPEI RG9; *GC* 9 April, 1803, *GH* 24 June, 1803; White, *Lord Selkirk's Diary 1803–04*, 4, 6, 35; Adams and Somerville, *Cargoes of Despair and Hope*, 197, 222.

One of three ships (*Dykes*, *Oughton* and *Polly*), which took 800 people from Uist and Skye as well as from Wester Ross and Argyll to the Selkirk settlements at Belfast (lot 57). Selkirk himself sailed on the *Dykes*.
Vessel Details: sw, 235 tns., built Maryport, 1798, A1.

Year	Mth	Vessel	Master	Psgr. Nos.	Departure Port	Arrival Port
1803	06	*Favourite* of Kirkaldy	Ballan-tyne	500	Isle Martin (Ullapool)	Pictou

Brown, *Strictures and Remarks.*
The *Favourite* sailed with another vessel. Both were owned by Major Melville of Ullapool. The agent was D. Roy from America. Most passengers probably originated from Sutherland and Wester Ross.
Vessel Details: bg, 165 tns., built Kirkaldy, 1797, A1.

Year	Mth	Vessel	Master	Psgr. Nos.	Departure Port	Arrival Port
1803	06	*Hope* (1)	Jappie, George	8	Grnk	Quebec

QG Aug. 25.
Passengers: McClaren, Banter, Love, Cochran, McDonald, McKormac, Scott and Waddell.
Vessel details: s, 244 tns., built Belfast, 1801, A1.

Year	Mth	Vessel	Master	Psgr. Nos.	Departure Port	Arrival Port
1803	06	*Oughton*	Baird, J.	200	Uist from Grnk	Charlotte-town

NAS CS 96/1238; PAPEI RG9; *GC* 9 April, 1803; *GH* 24 June, 1803; White, *Lord Selkirk's Diary 1803–04*, 4, 6, 35; Adams and Somerville, *Cargoes of Despair and Hope*, 197, 222. One of three ships (*Dykes, Oughton* and *Polly*), which took 800 people from Uist and Skye as well as from Wester Ross and Argyll to the Selkirk settlements at Belfast (lot 57). The *Oughton* sailed on to Quebec to collect a cargo of wheat and timber before returning to Scotland.
Vessel Details: bg, 207 tns., built Leith, 1787, E2.

Year	Mth	Vessel	Master	Psgr. Nos.	Departure Port	Arrival Port
1803	06	*Polly*	Darby, Thomas	400	Skye from Grnk	Charlotte-town

NAS CS 96/1238; PAPEI RG9; *GC* 9 April, 1803; GH 24 June, 1803; White, *Lord Selkirk's Diary 1803–04*, 4, 6, 35; Adams and Somerville, *Cargoes of Despair and Hope*, 197, 222.
One of three ships (*Dykes, Oughton* and *Polly*), which took 800 people from Uist and Skye as well as from Wester Ross and Argyll to the Selkirk settlements at Belfast (lot 57). The *Polly*, owned by her captain, took 280 "full passengers" or 400 persons to Belfast. Selkirk apparently advertised for his ships. The *Glasgow Courier* stated that a ship was required to carry 400 passengers from Skye to P.E.I. or Pictou, Nova Scotia. The berths for each person were to be 6 feet by 18 inches and there was to be an allowance of 56 gallons of water and 2 barrels bulk of storage for each person besides sufficient room to be left in the hold for provisions.
Vessel Details: s, 284 tns., built Whitby, 1762, E1.

Year	Mth	Vessel	Master	Psgr. Nos.	Departure Port	Arrival Port
1803	08	*Commerce*	Galt, Robert	70	Port Glasgow	Pictou

Passenger List: NLS MSS 1053 (Appendix I).
Settlers from Perthshire. Most said they had emigrated because their farms "had been taken" from them, or their rents had been raised.
Vessel Details: s, 200 tns., built 1772, E1.

Year	Mth	Vessel	Master	Psgr. Nos.	Departure Port	Arrival Port
1803	08	*Rosamund*	Cuthel, William	16	Grnk	Quebec

QG Oct. 27.
Passengers: Mr. J. Lithgow and family, Benjamin Turnbull and family, John Russel and family, Wm. Sulough.
Vessel Details: s, 194 tns., built New York, 1770, E2.

Year	Mth	Vessel	Master	Psgr. Nos.	Departure Port	Arrival Port
1804	04	*Ann* (2)	McKinley, John	8	Grnk	Quebec

QG July 5.
Passengers: John Blackburn and family, Mr. Brady and wife, Mr. Kerr.

Year	Mth	Vessel	Master	Psgr. Nos.	Departure Port	Arrival Port
1804	04	*Countess of Darlington*	Thomson, Alexander	4	Grnk	Quebec

QG July 19.
Passengers: Charles Cameron, Alexander Gibson, John Watson, Alexander Rose.

Year	Mth	Vessel	Master	Psgr. Nos.	Departure Port	Arrival Port
1804	04	*Margaret* of Leith	Hardie, Duncan	12	Grnk	Quebec

QG June 7.
Passengers: John Auld, Robert Greig, Dougal Cameron, George Murray, John McDonald, Donald McDonald, Archibald Campbell, John MacLearan and family.
Vessel Details: bg, 125 tns., built Boness, 1803, A1.

Year	Mth	Vessel	Master	Psgr. Nos.	Departure Port	Arrival Port
1804	04	*Recovery*	Bogg, Robert	14	Grnk	Quebec

QG 19 July
Passengers: John Bettson and family, Alexander Johnson, Andrew Whyte, John Renwick and family, Margaret Hardie, Alexander Hardie.
Vessel Details: bg, 169 tns., built Irvine, 1792, E1.

Year	Mth	Vessel	Master	Psgr. Nos.	Departure Port	Arrival Port
1804	05	*Aurora*	n/k	14	Grnk	Quebec

QG 26 July.
Passengers: Alexander Burns, William Smith, Claudius Allan, James Todd, William Miller, Thomas Terrance, Alan Renwick, William Davidson and six seamen.

Year	Mth	Vessel	Master	Psgr. Nos.	Departure Port	Arrival Port
1804	05	*Caledonia* of Alloa	McFar-lane, William	3	Leith	Quebec

QG July 5.
Passengers: William Mason, Mr. & Mrs. Miller.
Vessel details: s, 279 tns., built Philadelphia, 1779, I2.

Year	Mth	Vessel	Master	Psgr. Nos.	Departure Port	Arrival Port
1804	05	*Oughton*	Baird, John	102	Kirkcudbright	Quebec

Passenger List: LAC MG 24 I8 vol. 4, 105–8; Campey, *The Silver Chief,* 51–76.
Lord Selkirk's Baldoon settlers.

| 1804 | 06 | *North Star* | n/k | n/k | Leith via Grnk (for repair) | Pictou |

NAS CS.96/3355; *GA* Apr 6.
The *North Star* set out with passengers bound for Pictou but had to return to Leith for repairs.

| 1804 | 06 | *Rosina* | Potter, James | n/k | Grnk | Saint John |

GA May 4.
Vessel "will sail by 1st June for Saint John, New Brunswick, and will land passengers at Digby [Nova Scotia] if a sufficient number offer."

| 1804 | 07 | *Emily* | Murphy, John | 16 | Port Glasgow | Quebec |

QG Aug. 30.
Vessel Details: bg, 157 tns., built Gateshead, 1802, A1.

| 1804 | 08 | *Commerce* | London | 42 | Oban | Quebec |

NAS GD202/70/12.

1805	n/k	*Polly*	n/k	n/k	n/k	Canso,
						Cape
						Breton

MacDonald, "Early Highland Emigration to Nova Scotia and P.E.I.," 44.

| 1805 | n/k | *Sir Sydney Smith* | n/k | n/k | Stornoway | Pictou |

MacLaren, *Pictou Book*, 119; MacKay, *Scotland Farewell*, 196.

| 1805 | 03 | *Margaret of Leith* | Hardie | 5 | Grnk | Quebec |

GA March 26; *QM* May 18.
Passengers: Mr. & Mrs. Auld and family (cargo to Messrs. Auld, Lang, Montreal).

| 1805 | 04 | *Betsey* | Snowdon | 3 | Grnk | Quebec |

GA April 5; *QM* May 18.
Passengers: Mr. Henderson, Alexander Moss and Agnes Kyle.
Vessel Details: s, 217 tns., built Hull, 1795, E1.

Year	Mth	Vessel	Master	Psgr. Nos.	Departure Port	Arrival Port
1805	04	*Caledonia* of Ayr	Wilson	10	Grnk	Quebec

GA April 5; *QM* May 18.
Passengers: Adam MacNider, James Wilson, James Rabton, Hames Youg, McNae, Col. & Mrs. Shanks, Jane Hancock, Miss MacNider, Jannet Rodman.
Vessel Details: bg, 177 tns., built Ayr, 1803, A1.

Year	Mth	Vessel	Master	Psgr. Nos.	Departure Port	Arrival Port
1805	04	*Canada*	Harvey	5	Grnk	Quebec

GA April 5; *QM* May 18.
Passengers: Messrs Service, Marshall, Waddle, Burnside and Biggar.

Year	Mth	Vessel	Master	Psgr. Nos.	Departure Port	Arrival Port
1805	04	*Jean* of Irvine	Wilson	24	Grnk	Quebec

QM May 18; *GA* April 5

Year	Mth	Vessel	Master	Psgr. Nos.	Departure Port	Arrival Port
1805	05	*Union* (2)	Tulloch	5	Leith	Quebec

QM June 8.
Passengers: Capt. Cameron and family.
Vessel Details: s, 289 tns., built America, repaired 1799 & 1805, I2.

Year	Mth	Vessel	Master	Psgr. Nos.	Departure Port	Arrival Port
1805	05	*Nancy*	Church, W.S.	32	Tobermory	Charlotte-town

PAPEI RG9; *GA* 12 March 1805; Harvey, *Journeys to the Island*, 76–77.
The *Greenock Advertiser* stated: "for freight or charter to Halifax, New Brunswick, Pictou or Newfoundland; The schooner *Nancy*...would engage to carry out a load of passengers. Alan Ker & Co." The passengers, from the west Highlands and Islands, were landed at Three Rivers.

Year	Mth	Vessel	Master	Psgr. Nos.	Departure Port	Arrival Port
1805	05	*Neptune* of Ayr	Neil	7	Ayr	Quebec

QM Sept. 7.
Passengers: James McTavish, Alexander McTavish, Dr. Robertson, M Crooks, John McClure, William Ure, Thomas Manson.
Vessel Details: bg, 167 tns., built Ayr, 1799, E1.

Year	Mth	Vessel	Master	Psgr. Nos.	Departure Port	Arrival Port
1805	06	*Countess of Darlington*	Thompson	2	Grnk	Quebec

QM Aug. 19.
Passengers: Mr. Dick, Charles Harrower.

Year	Mth	Vessel	Master	Psgr. Nos.	Departure Port	Arrival Port
1805	06	*Minerva* of Leith	Wildgoose	4	Ayr	Quebec

QM Oct. 2.
A voyage of 14 weeks. The fourteen passengers were "intended settlers on new land." Seven others were landed at Percee.
Vessel Details: bg, 162 tns., built Kirkaldy, 1801, A1.

Year	Mth	Vessel	Master	Psgr. Nos.	Departure Port	Arrival Port
1805	08	*Caledonia* of Ayr	Wilson	4	Ayr	Quebec

QM Oct. 10.
Steerage passengers: James Hendry, William McKay, Mrs. Smiley, Mrs. Bagnell.

1805	08	*Northern Friends of Clyde*	McPherson, Archibald	91	Stornoway	Charlotte-town

PAPEI RG9; Brehaut, Mary C., "Early Immigration (from the United Kingdom) to P.E.I., 1769–1878.

The ship carried a group of passengers from the Outer Hebrides & Wester Ross, led by Kenneth McKenzie of Ross-shire destined for Flat River (lot 60). She returned to the Clyde in Dec. 1805 with a cargo of timber.
Vessel Details: s, 245 tns., Prize, built Finland, 1790, E1.

1805	09	*Betsey*	Snowdon	3	Grnk	Quebec

QM Oct. 30.
Passengers: Margaret Lawson, Capt. J MacKenen, Mr. Whitelaw.

1806	04	*Betsey*	Snowdon	5	Grnk	Quebec

QM May 15.
Five passengers and a crew for a vessel.

1806	04	*Emerald*	Anderson	7	Aberdeen	Quebec

QM June 2.
Passengers: Joseph Lesfly, Mr. R. Blair, wife and family.
Vessel Details: bg, 200 tns., built Peterhead, 1800, A1.

1806	04	*Hope*(2)	Henry, Matthew	3	Grnk	Quebec

GA April 4; *QM* May 15.
Passengers: Mr. McQuarter, Capt. McKie, Capt. Service.
Vessel Details: bg, 180 tns., built Nova Scotia, 1803, A1.

1806	05	*Canada* of Irvine	Dow, Robert	9	Grnk	Montreal

NAS E504/15/79; *GA* Mar. to May; *QM* July 13.
Passengers: D. Nevin, D. Buchanan, S. Fraser, William Bryson, Alexander Harvey, Robert Jack, Robert Hunter, Mrs. Hendry, Agnes Little.
Vessel Details: sw, 183 tns., built Irvine, 1802, A1.

1806	05	*Europe* of Ayr	Steel, James	9	Ayr	Quebec

NAS E504/4/11; *QM* July 13.
Passengers: John Young, T. Hunter, James Miller, T. Brakwight, Robert Dunlop, S. Armour, Robert Patterson, McCauly.
Vessel Details: bg, 159 tns., built Ayr, 1804, A1.

Year	Mth	Vessel	Master	Psgr. Nos.	Departure Port	Arrival Port
1806	05	*Rambler* of Leith	Norris, James	130	Tobermory	Charlotte-town

Passenger List: PAPEI MSS 2702.
NAS E504/35/1; *Lloyds List.*
The *Rambler* carried passengers from the West Highlands and Islands, especially from Mull and Colonsay to P.E.I. where some settled in lots 62 and 65. Passenger baggage: 77 chests, 41 bushels, 24 bags, 10 bundles, 3 trunks, bed clothing and wearing apparel. The *Rambler* returned to Leith from Pictou with a timber cargo in October.
Vessel Details: bg, 296 tns., built Leith, 1800, A1.

Year	Mth	Vessel	Master	Psgr. Nos.	Departure Port	Arrival Port
1806	06	*Humphreys* of London	Young, John	97	Tobermory	Charlotte-town

Passenger List: PAPEI MSS 2702.
NAS E504/35/1.
The emigrants came from the western Highlands and Islands, especially Mull and Colonsay. Some settled on lots 62 and 65. Passenger baggage: 42 chests, 23 barrels, 10 bags, 2 bundles, 17 beds, 7 trunks, 4 bags of used wearing apparel, beds and bed clothing.
Vessels Details: s, 250 tns., built Stockton, 1785, E1.

Year	Mth	Vessel	Master	Psgr. Nos.	Departure Port	Arrival Port
1806	06	*Margaret* of Leith	Hardie	6	Grnk.	Montreal

NAS E504/15/79; *QM* Aug. 19.
Passengers: John Sims, Alexander, John and Margaret Rollo, James Barry, John Barry, Robert Brown.

Year	Mth	Vessel	Master	Psgr. Nos.	Departure Port	Arrival Port
1806	07	*Isle of Skye* of Aberdeen	Thom, John	37	Tobermory	Charlotte-town

Passenger List: PAPEI MSS 2702.
   NAS E504/35/1; PAPEI RG9.
The emigrants came from the western Highlands and Islands, especially Mull and Colonsay. Some settled on lots 62 and 65. Passenger baggage: 22 chests, 5 trunks, 7 parcels, 13 casks containing used wearing apparel and bed clothes.
Vessel Details: sw, 181 tns., built Aberdeen, 1806, A1.

Year	Mth	Vessel	Master	Psgr. Nos.	Departure Port	Arrival Port
1806	07	*Pallas*	Robinson	n/k	Grnk	Quebec

GA 11 June, 1806; *QM* 24 Sept., 1806.
The *Pallas* was bound for Quebec. The *Greenock Advertiser* stated, "If sufficient numbers of passengers offer, the Pallas will be able to call at a port in the Highlands to take them on board and will land them at the Island of Saint John (P.E.I.), Sydney, Pictou or any other convenient port in the Gulf of St. Lawrence as they may incline."
Vessel Details: s, 632 tns., built Prussia, 1802, A1.

Year	Mth	Vessel	Master	Psgr. Nos.	Departure Port	Arrival Port
1806	07	*Spencer* of Newcastle	Brown, Forster	114	Oban	Charlotte-town

Passenger List: PAPEI MSS 2702.
NAS E504/25/3.

The emigrants came from the western Highlands and Islands, especially Mull and Colonsay. Some settled on lot 65. Passenger Baggage: 72 chests, 4 trunks, 35 barrels, 8 boxes, 1 hogshead, 1 kettle, 40 parcels, wearing apparel/bedding.
Vessel Details: s, 330 tns., built Shields, 1778, E1.

Year	Mth	Vessel	Master	Psgr. Nos.	Departure Port	Arrival Port
1806	08	*Elizabeth and Ann* of North Shields	St. Girese, Thomas	107	Thurso	Charlotte-town

Passenger List: PAPEI MSS 2702.
GA 13 August 1806; *NAS* E504/7/5.

The emigrants came from the northeast Highlands, with some from Durness and Tongue in Sutherland. Some settled at New London (lot 20) and Granville (lot 21) in P.E.I. According to the *Greenock Advertiser*, the *Elizabeth and Ann* was destined for Pictou.
Vessels Details: s, 293 tns., built Whitby, 1782, I1, had four guns.

Year	Mth	Vessel	Master	Psgr. Nos.	Departure Port	Arrival Port
1806	08	*Hope*(2)	Henry, Matthew	47	Port Glasgow	Halifax & Quebec

QM Oct 30; *GA* Aug 20.
47 steerage passengers disembarked at Quebec. She was also to call at Halifax.

Year	Mth	Vessel	Master	Psgr. Nos.	Departure Port	Arrival Port
1806	09	*Rebecca and Sarah* of Leith	Condee, James	118	Tobermory	Charlotte-town

NAS E504/35/1.

The emigrants came from the western Highlands and Islands, especially Mull and Colonsay. Some settled on lots 62 and 65. Passenger baggage: 72 chests, 6 trunks, 36 barrels containing wearing apparel and clothing.
Vessel Details: 284 tns., built 1778, Dutch Prize, E1.

Year	Mth	Vessel	Master	Psgr. Nos.	Departure Port	Arrival Port
1807	06	*Active*	Stirling, J.	36	Fort William	Pictou

NAS E504/12/6.
The passengers on this crossing originated from Inverness-shire, the western Highlands and Islands.

Year	Mth	Vessel	Master	Psgr. Nos.	Departure Port	Arrival Port
1807	09	*Rambler* of Leith	Norris, J	130	Stromness from Thurso	Pictou

NAS E504/7/5; *IC* Oct. 9, 1807, Feb. 8, 1808.
Wrecked on October 29 near Newfoundland. A total of 138 people perished. The *Rambler* had taken emigrants in the previous year to P.E.I. The passengers on this crossing originated from Sutherland (Farr, Lairg and Rogart parishes) and Caithness.

Year	Mth	Vessel	Master	Psgr. Nos.	Departure Port	Arrival Port
1808	06	*Baltic*	Baird, Alexander	9	Dundee	Quebec

QG July 7.

1808	07	*Elizabeth*	Milne, William	96	Oban	Charlotte-town

PAPEI RG9.
The emigrants came from the western Highlands and Islands, especially Mull and Colonsay. Some settled at New Argyll, P.E.I., (lot 65) and at Wood Islands (lot 62).
Vessel Details: s, 214 tns., built Grnk, 1791, E1.

1808	07	*Mars*	Caithness, George	94	Oban	Charlotte-town

PAPEI RG9.
The emigrants came from the western Highlands and Islands, especially Mull and Colonsay. Some settled at New Argyll, P.E.I. and at Wood Islands (see *Elizabeth*, above).
Vessel Details: sw, 208 tns., built Sunderland, 1806, A1.

1808	08	*Clarendon* of Hull	Hines, James	208	Oban	Charlotte-town

Passenger List: NAB CO 226/23.
The emigrants came mainly from Perthshire (Fortingall, Rannoch and Atholl) and Argyll (especially Mull). Some settled in lots 47 and 52. The passengers consisted of 188 settlers and 20 crew. Some of the emigrants established New Perth (lot 52).
Vessel Details: s, 416 tns., built Bristol, 1783, E1.

1809	05	*Albion*	Kidd, R.	99	Dundee	Charlotte-town and Quebec

Orlo and Fraser, "Those Elusive Immigrants" (Part 1), 37; *QG* July 6,1809.
Thirty-nine passengers disembarked at Charlottetown. A further sixty passengers sailed on to Quebec on the *Albion* arriving in early July.
Vessel Details: bg, 152 tns., built Dysart, 1805, A1.

1810	n/k	*Catherine* of Leith	Lillie, Jas.	124	Oban	Charlotte-town

MacDonald, "Early Highland Emigration to Nova Scotia and P.E.I.," *Weekly Recorder of Charlottetown, P.E.I.*, no. 17 (Sept., 1810), 41–48. The emigrants came mainly from the west Highlands and Islands, especially Mull. They mainly settled in lots 30 and 65.

1810	n/k	*Ocean*	n/k	17	Grnk	Quebec

Bumsted, *The People's Clearance*, 227.

Year	Mth	Vessel	Master	Psgr. Nos.	Departure Port	Arrival Port
1810	n/k	*Phoenix*	Airey, Wm.	176	Tobermory	Charlotte-town

MacDonald, "Early Highland Emigration to Nova Scotia and P.E.I.", *Weekly Recorder of Charlottetown, P.E.I.* , no. 17 (Sept., 1810), 41–48.

The emigrants came mainly from the west Highlands and Islands, especially Mull. They mainly settled in lots 30 and 65.

Year	Mth	Vessel	Master	Psgr. Nos.	Departure Port	Arrival Port
1810	04	*Dunlop*	Stevenson, Allan	54	Glasgow	Quebec

QG June 14.
Vessel Details: bg, 331 tns., built Montreal, 1805, A1.

Year	Mth	Vessel	Master	Psgr. Nos.	Departure Port	Arrival Port
1810	04	*Johns*	Cochran, John	47	Grnk	Quebec

QG May 31.
Passengers: Mr. D. Munn, 45 seamen, carpenters etc. and their families.
Vessel Details: bk, 169 tns., built Saltcoats, 1802, A1.

Year	Mth	Vessel	Master	Psgr. Nos.	Departure Port	Arrival Port
1810	05	*Mary Anne* of Irvine	Lindsay, William	9	Grnk	Quebec

QG June 28.
Passengers: 9 men, women and children.
Vessel Details: bg, 94 tns., built Scotland, 1805, E1.

Year	Mth	Vessel	Master	Psgr. Nos.	Departure Port	Arrival Port
1810	06	*Fairfield* of Aberdeen	n/k	4	Aberdeen	Quebec

QG Aug. 16.

Year	Mth	Vessel	Master	Psgr. Nos.	Departure Port	Arrival Port
1810	06	*Hero*	McCaull	5	Grnk	Quebec

QG Aug. 16.
Passengers: 3 men and 1 woman.
Vessel Details: bg, 110 tns., built Scotland, 1800, E1.

Year	Mth	Vessel	Master	Psgr. Nos.	Departure Port	Arrival Port
1810	08	*Favourite* of Grangemouth	McDonald, Alexander	31	Oban	Pictou

NAS E504/25/3.
Journey time of 12 weeks.
Vessel Details: bg, 165 tns., built Kirkaldy, 1797, E1.

Year	Mth	Vessel	Master	Psgr. Nos.	Departure Port	Arrival Port
1810	09	*Active* of Peterhead	Souter, John	80	Oban	Charlotte-town

David Dobson, *Ships from Scotland to America 1628–1828*, 3 vols. (Baltimore: Gen. Pub. Co., 1998) vol. II.

Active was due to sail with emigrants but returned to Oban because of storm damage.

Year	Mth	Vessel	Master	Psgr. Nos.	Departure Port	Arrival Port
1811	03	*Ploughman* of Aberdeen	Yule, Alexander	28	Aberdeen	Pictou

NAS E504/1/24.

Year	Mth	Vessel	Master	Psgr. Nos.	Departure Port	Arrival Port
1811	04	*Betsey*	Gordon, J.	15	Grnk	Quebec

QG July 11
Vessel Details: bg, 148 tns.; prize; E1.

Year	Mth	Vessel	Master	Psgr. Nos.	Departure Port	Arrival Port
1811	04	*Diana* of Dundee	Patrick, James	3	Dundee	Quebec

NAS E504/11/18; *QG* June 12.
Passengers: William Cooper, James Currance, Alexander Hyde.
Vessel Details: bg, 196 tns., built Dundee, 1810, A1.

Year	Mth	Vessel	Master	Psgr. Nos.	Departure Port	Arrival Port
1811	04	*Malvina* of Aberdeen	Smith, John	12	Aberdeen	Quebec

NAS E504/1/24; *QG* June 12.
No record in *Quebec Gazette* of passenger arrivals. They may have disembarked at Nova Scotia.
Vessel Details: sw, 203 tns., built Aberdeen, 1806, A1.

Year	Mth	Vessel	Master	Psgr. Nos.	Departure Port	Arrival Port
1811	04	*Mary* of Aberdeen	Morrison, James	30	Aberdeen	Halifax

NAS E504/1/24.
Vessel Details: sw, 139 tns., built Aberdeen, 1810, Lloyd's code n/k, dimensions 73' 1" x 21' 6" x 12' 5".

Year	Mth	Vessel	Master	Psgr. Nos.	Departure Port	Arrival Port
1811	04	*Neptune* of Ayr	Neil, J	n/k	Grnk	Charlotte-town

NAS CS 96/4475; *QG* 6 June, 1811; Jones and Fraser, "Those Elusive Immigrants" (Part1), 37.
Major Drummond of the 104th Regiment left at Charlottetown.
Vessel Details: bg, 167 tns., built Ayr, 1799, E1.

Year	Mth	Vessel	Master	Psgr. Nos.	Departure Port	Arrival Port
1811	05	*Anne* of North Shields	Tod, James	26	Stornoway	Pictou

NAS E504/33/3.
A surgeon travelled.
Vessel Details: s, 284 tns., built Bristol, 1785, E1.

Year	Mth	Vessel	Master	Psgr. Nos.	Departure Port	Arrival Port
1811	05	*Elbe*	Johnson, J	9	Irvine	Quebec

QG June 12.

Year	Mth	Vessel	Master	Psgr. Nos.	Departure Port	Arrival Port
1811	06	*Aurora*	Craige, A.	15	Grnk	Quebec

QG Sept. 26.

Year	Mth	Vessel	Master	Psgr. Nos.	Departure Port	Arrival Port
1811	06	*Spring* of Aberdeen	Grant, Peter	15	Aberdeen	Quebec

NAS E504/1/24; *QG* Aug. 29.
Passengers: Included crew of 11 seamen and Captain Robson.
Vessel Details: bg, 109 tns., built Aberdeen, 1810, A1.

| 1811 | 07 | *Centurion* of Aberdeen | Morrison, James | 18 | Aberdeen | Halifax |

NAS E504/1/24.

| 1811 | 07 | *Eddystone* | Ramsay, Thomas | 27 | Stornoway | Hudson's Bay |

LAC MG19 E4 vol. 1, 145, 151; NAS E504/33/3.
Passengers: Hudson's Bay Company workers and early colonists for the Red River settlement.
Some men originated from Lewis, but most came from the Orkney Isles.
Vessel Details: s, 245 tns., built Hull, 1802, A1.

| 1811 | 07 | *Edward and Anne* | Gull, Thomas | 61 | Stornoway | Hudson's Bay |

LAC MG19 E4 vol. 1, 145, 151; NAS E504/33/3.
Passengers: See *Eddystone.*
Vessel Details: s, 238 tns., built 1805, Danish Prize, A1.

| 1811 | 07 | *Prince of Wales* | Hanswell | 27 | Stornoway | Hudson's Bay |

LAC MG19 E4 vol. 1, 145, 151; NAS E504/33/3.
Passengers: See *Eddystone.*
Vessel Details: s, 342 tns., built 1793, major repairs 1806, E1.

| 1812 | 03 | *Barbara* of London | Epsom, William | 4 | Aberdeen | Quebec |

NAS E504/1/24.
Vessel Details: bg, 162 tns., built 1812, E1.

| 1812 | 03 | *Ploughman* of Aberdeen | Main, James | 12 | Aberdeen | Pictou |

NAS E504/1/24.
Vessel Details: sw, 165 tns., built Berwick, 1804, A1.

| 1812 | 04 | *Alert* | Johnston, Andrew | 2 | Aberdeen | Quebec |

QG May 30.
Vessel Details: bg, 177 tns.; foreign built; E2; 82' 9" x 22' 8" x 12' 6".

Year	Mth	Vessel	Master	Psgr. Nos.	Departure Port	Arrival Port
1812	04	*Collingwood*	Gilchrist, James	25	Grnk	Quebec

QG 23 May.
Passengers: 25 seamen for shipbuilding.
Vessel Details: bg, 275 tns., built 1808, A1.

Year	Mth	Vessel	Master	Psgr. Nos.	Departure Port	Arrival Port
1812	04	*Elisa* of Dundee	Wrougham, William	4	Dundee	Quebec

NAS E504/11/18.
Vessel Details: bg, 163 tns., built Burntisland, 1811, A1.

Year	Mth	Vessel	Master	Psgr. Nos.	Departure Port	Arrival Port
1812	04	*Mary*	Harvey, Alexander	13	Grnk	Quebec

QG May 23.
Passengers: Alexander Parlane, Fisher, Brown, Davies, White, Captain Stevenson, Captain Livingston, Alexander Gibson, Buchannan, Edmonston, Whitfield, Reed. Plus 23 seamen.
Vessel Details: s, 270 tns., built Irvine, 1810, A1.

Year	Mth	Vessel	Master	Psgr. Nos.	Departure Port	Arrival Port
1812	04	*Mary* of Aberdeen	Morrison, James	20	Aberdeen	Halifax

NAS E504/1/24; *AJ* Jan. 29.

Year	Mth	Vessel	Master	Psgr. Nos.	Departure Port	Arrival Port
1812	04	*Neptune*	Neil	2	Grnk	Quebec

QG June 6.

Year	Mth	Vessel	Master	Psgr. Nos.	Departure Port	Arrival Port
1812	04	*Patriot* of Aberdeen	Anderson, Alexander	2	Aberdeen	Quebec

QG May 30.
Vessel Details: bg, 198 tns., built Aberdeen, 1811. A1.

Year	Mth	Vessel	Master	Psgr. Nos.	Departure Port	Arrival Port
1812	04	*Trader*	Dyet	8	Grnk	Quebec

QG June 6.
Passengers included one woman.

Year	Mth	Vessel	Master	Psgr. Nos.	Departure Port	Arrival Port
1812	05	*Cambria* of Aberdeen	Pirie, James	33	Aberdeen	Halifax & Quebec

NAS E504/1/24; *AJ* Jan. 29.
Some of the 33 passengers left at Halifax.
Vessel Details: bg, 120 tns., built Aberdeen, 1808, A1.

Year	Mth	Vessel	Master	Psgr. Nos.	Departure Port	Arrival Port
1812	05	*Diana* of Dundee	Patrick, J.	3	Dundee	Quebec

QG June 13.
Passengers: Wm. Cooper, James Currance, Alex'r Hyde.
Vessel Details: bg, 196 tns., built Dundee, 1810, A1.

Year	Mth	Vessel	Master	Psgr. Nos.	Departure Port	Arrival Port
1812 *QG* June 13.	05	*Elbe*	Johnson, J.	9	Irvine	Quebec
1812 *QG* Sept. 26.	06	*Aurora*	Craigie, A.	15	Grnk	Quebec
1812 *QG* July 11.	06	*Betsey*	Gordon, J.	15	Grnk	Quebec
1812	06	*Robert Taylor*	n/k	71	Sligo, Ireland	Hudson's Bay

Passenger List: LAC SP(C-1), 560-62.
Passengers: Hudson's Bay Company workers and settlers for Red River. Included ten families from Mull and Islay. The Company workers originated mainly from the Orkney Islands and Ireland.

Year	Mth	Vessel	Master	Psgr. Nos.	Departure Port	Arrival Port
1812 *QG* Oct. 31.	08	*Dunlop*	McKenzie, J.	5	Port Glasgow	Quebec

Passengers: McWerter, Anderson, McKay, Whitehead, Stewart.

Year	Mth	Vessel	Master	Psgr. Nos.	Departure Port	Arrival Port
1813	03	*Cambria* of Aberdeen	Oswald, James	25	Aberdeen	Halifax

NAS E504/1/24.

Year	Mth	Vessel	Master	Psgr. Nos.	Departure Port	Arrival Port
1813	03	*Ploughman* of Aberdeen	Main, James	7	Aberdeen	Halifax

NAS E504/1/24.

Year	Mth	Vessel	Master	Psgr. Nos.	Departure Port	Arrival Port
1813	04	*Venus* of Aberdeen	Begg, Alexander	3	Aberdeen	Quebec

NAS E504/1/24.
No record of passenger arrivals in *Quebec Gazette*.

Year	Mth	Vessel	Master	Psgr. Nos.	Departure Port	Arrival Port
1813	06	*Prince of Wales*	n/k	97	Stromness	Churchill

Passenger List: LAC MG19E4 vol. 1, 165–8.
Passengers: Red River settlers, who mainly originated from Sutherland. Some Irish included. The vessel was accompanied by the *Eddystone,* which carried workers for the Hudson's Bay Company. The *Prince of Wales* arrived in August. Passengers were mainly families but also included a blacksmith, a carpenter, a millwright and a surgeon. There were many deaths on board and shortly after arriving.

Year	Mth	Vessel	Master	Psgr. Nos.	Departure Port	Arrival Port
1814	03	*Mary* of Aberdeen	Oswald, James	30	Aberdeen	Halifax

NAS E504/1/25.

1814	04	*Ayrshire*	McDonald	4	Grnk via Cork	Quebec

QG June 4.
Passengers: G. Ross, Peddy, Porteous, Douglas plus Captain King and the crew for a new vessel.
Vessel Details: s, 337 tns.. built Quebec, 1813, A1.

1814	05	*Montreal*	Allen	18	Grnk	Quebec

QG July 14.
Vessel Details: s, 306 tns.; built Irvine, 1814; A1.

1814	07	*Perseverance* of Aberdeen	Moncur	n/k	Cromarty	Pictou

IJ May 27.
Agents were: Peter Ritchie, Aberdeen; Alex McKenzie, Cromarty; James Lyon, Inverness.
Vessel Details: bg, 116 tns., foreign built, 65' 4" x 20' 10" x 11' 6".

1814	08	*Cambria* of Aberdeen	Clayton, James	35	Aberdeen	Halifax

NAS E504/1/25.

1814	08	*Halifax Packet* of Sunderland	Hogg, John	7	Aberdeen	Halifax

NAS E504/1/25.
Vessel Details: sw, 185 tns., built Sunderland, 1814, A1, 76' 8" x 24' x 15'.

1814	08	*Sophia* of Ayr	Dunn	3	Grnk via Cork	Quebec

QG Sept. 29.
Passengers: Messrs Thompson, Campbell, Todd.
Vessel Details: bg, 230 tns., built Ayr, 1811, A1.

1815		*Prince William*	n/k	95	Cromarty or Thurso	Pictou

Passenger List: NSARM MG100 vol. 226 #30 (Appendix I).
Nineteen families from Sutherland who petitioned for land in West Pictou. Some of the petitioners had served in the Local Militia of Scotland, probably the Reay Fencibles.

1815	03	*Amethyst* of Aberdeen	Greig, H.	29	Aberdeen	Halifax

NAS E504/1/25.
Vessel Details: sw, 132 tns., built Aberdeen, 1812, A1.

Year	Mth	Vessel	Master	Psgr. Nos.	Departure Port	Arrival Port
1815	03	*Fame* of Aberdeen	Masson, George	4	Aberdeen	Halifax

NAS E504/1/25.
Vessel Details: bg, 141 tns., built Stockton, 1810, A1.

1815	03	*Mary* of Aberdeen	Oswald, James	35	Aberdeen	Halifax

NAS E504/1/25.

1815	04	*Carolina* of Aberdeen	Dunoon, A.	24	Aberdeen	Quebec

NAS E504/1/25.

1815	04	*Charlotte*	Dunlop	6	Glasgow	Quebec

QG June 21.
Passengers: Messrs McNighter, Roxbury, Clerk, Robertson, Fraser and Gibson.

1815	04	*Dunlop*	Abrams	4	Grnk	Quebec

QG May 18.
Passengers: Messrs Burnside, Lindsay, Gray and Captain Boag.

1815	04	*Earl of Buckinghamshire*	Phillips	16	Grnk	Quebec

QG July 20.
Passengers: Messrs Gibb, n/k, Burnett, Campbell, Dunlop, Clerk, Brown, Carmack, Black, Wishart, Rennings, n/k, plus four ladies.
Vessel Details: s, 593 tns., built Quebec, 1814, A1.

1815	04	*Glasgow* of Dundee	Kidd	2	Dundee	Quebec

QG May 18.
Passengers: Messrs Anderson and Bowley.
Vessel Details: bg, 168 tns.. built Quebec, 1800, E1.

1815	04	*Halifax Packet* of Aberdeen	Hogg, John	3	Aberdeen	Halifax

NAS E504/1/25.
Vessel Details: sw, 185 tns., built Sunderland, 1814, A1. 76' 8" x 24' x 15'.

1815	04	*John* of Berwick	Forster, Joseph	n/k	Fort George (near Inverness)	Halifax

IJ Apr. 7.
Agents were: John Stevenson, Fortrose; James Lyon, merchant, Inverness.

Year	Mth	Vessel	Master	Psgr. Nos.	Departure Port	Arrival Port
1815	04	*Perseverance* of Aberdeen	n/k	n/k	Cromarty	Halifax

IJ Apr 7.
Agents were: George Logan from America, Dornoch; James Campbell, Star Inn Inverness.

| 1815 | 04 | *Prescott* of Leith | Young, Robert | 12 | Leith | Quebec |

NAS E504/22/69; *QG* June 15.
Passengers: Mr White and eleven steerage passengers.
Vessel Details: bg, 163 tns., built Leith, 1799, repaired 1815, E1.

| 1815 | 04 | *Seven Sisters* of Aberdeen | Brown, A. | 19 | Aberdeen | Halifax |

NAS E504/1/25.

| 1815 | 05 | *Phesdo* of Aberdeen | Pennan, Andrew | 16 | Aberdeen | Saint John & St. Andrews |

NAS E504/1/25; *CG.* July 27, *IJ* May 5.
Vessel Details: bg, 245 tns., built Aberdeen, 1815, A1, 87' x 26' 1" x 16' 9".

| 1815 | 06 | *Prince of Wales* | n/k | 84 | Thurso | York Fort |

Passenger List: LAC SP(C–2),1659–61.
NAS E504/1/25; *IJ* July 28.
Passengers: Red River settlers who originated mainly from Sutherlandshire. Vessel took on some passengers at Gravesend.

| 1815 | 06 | *Wellington* of Aberdeen | Stephens, Alexander | 6 | Aberdeen | Miramichi |

NAS E504/1/25.
Vessel Details: bg, 211 tns., built Aberdeen, 1815. A1.

| 1815 | 07 | *Atlas* | Turnbull | 242 | Grnk | Quebec |

Passenger List: List for *Atlas, Baltic, Dorothy* and *Eliza* in NAB CO385/2.
McLean, *People of Glengarry*, 155–57.
   One of four ships taking settlers who received government assistance.
Vessel Details: s, 435 tns., built Shields, 1801, E1.

| 1815 | 07 | *Baltic Merchant* | Jeffreys | 140 | Grnk | Quebec |

See *Atlas.*

| 1815 | 07 | *Dorothy* | Spence | 194 | Grnk | Quebec |

See *Atlas.*
Vessel Details: s, 530 tns., built Denmark, prize, E1.

Year	Mth	Vessel	Master	Psgr. Nos.	Departure Port	Arrival Port
1815	07	*Eliza*	Telfer	123	Grnk	Quebec

See *Atlas.*

Year	Mth	Vessel	Master	Psgr. Nos.	Departure Port	Arrival Port
1815	07	*Margaret* of Peterhead	Shand, J.	16	Leith	Quebec

NAS E504/22/70.
Vessel Details: sw, 201 tns., built Peterhead, 1811, A1.

Year	Mth	Vessel	Master	Psgr. Nos.	Departure Port	Arrival Port
1815	07	*Ruby* of Aberdeen	Love, Thomas	2	Aberdeen	Halifax

NAS E504/1/25.
Vessel Details: sw, 128 tns., built Aberdeen, 1805, A1,
67' 9" x 21' 5" x 11' 1".

Year	Mth	Vessel	Master	Psgr. Nos.	Departure Port	Arrival Port
1815	08	*Glentanner* of Aberdeen	Laird, James	17	Aberdeen	Halifax & Pictou

NAS E504/1/25.
Vessel Details: bg, 160 tns.; built Aberdeen, 1811; A1;
77' 10" x 22' 2" x 13' 6".

Year	Mth	Vessel	Master	Psgr. Nos.	Departure Port	Arrival Port
1815	08	*Helen*	Moore, James	4	Aberdeen	Halifax

NAS E504/1/25.
Vessel details: bg, 185 tns., built 1804.

Year	Mth	Vessel	Master	Psgr. Nos.	Departure Port	Arrival Port
1815	08	*Union*(3)	Henry	15	Grnk	Quebec

QG Sept. 21.
Passengers: Mr. C. Stewart, plus 14 settlers–men, women and children.
Vessel details: s, 231 tns., built 1807, America, E1.

Year	Mth	Vessel	Master	Psgr. Nos.	Departure Port	Arrival Port
1815	10	*Favourite* of Saint John	Hyndman, John	133	Port Glasgow	Saint John

Passenger List: PANB MC300 MS17/40.
Arrived in December. The passengers had their fares paid by the House of Assembly. The *Royal Gazette* stated that the *Favourite* had sailed with "126 settlers for this province" who had left "for want of employment and the providence of New Brunswick" (*RG* Dec. 3).

Appendix II

SCOTTISH PETITIONERS WHO SOUGHT HELP FROM THE COLONIAL OFFICE FOR ASSISTANCE TO EMIGRATE TO BRITISH NORTH AMERICA, 1826–27.

[Source: Parliamentary Papers: Reports from the Select Committee appointed to inquire into the expediency of encouraging emigration from the United Kingdom, 1826–27.]

Date	Place of Residence	Description	Number of People/Families	Desired Destination
1826				
June 5	Glasgow	weavers	140 persons	Upper Canada
" 5	Paisley	paupers	50 families	Ditto
" 9	Uist & Barra	paupers	400/ 500 people	Cape Breton.
	[To join friends, who were assisted to emigrate to Cape Breton in 1817.]			
" 12	Paisley	Chelsea pensioners	n/k	Upper Canada
" 16	Hebrides	paupers	300 people	Cape Breton.
July 15	Paisley	manufacturers	100 families	Upper Canada
" 19	Aberdeen	old soldier	wife	Canada.
	[Requesting grant of land.]			
Aug. 26	Glasgow	weavers	242 families	Upper Canada.
	[Having formed themselves into an Emigration Society, request assistance to emigrate.]			
" 29	Springburn	weavers	many families	Ditto.
Sept. 4	Rutherglen	weavers	100 families	Ditto.
" 6	Roxburghshire	farmer	wife, 6 children	North America
" 6	Glasgow	weavers	150 families	Upper Canada
" 9	Glasgow	weavers	many families	Upper Canada
" 9	Glasgow	weavers	250 families	Upper Canada
" 14	Glasgow	various trades	50 families	Upper Canada
" 21	Glasgow	weavers	50 families	Upper Canada
" 21	Glasgow	weavers	150 families	Upper Canada

Date	Place of Residence	Description	Number of People/Families	Desired Destination

1826 continued

Sept. 21	Glasgow	weavers	200 people	Upper Canada

[Praying, on their behalf, for assistance to emigrate, and to be furnished with implements of husbandry.]

| " 23 | Glasgow | weavers | 100 families | Ditto |
| " 23 | Glasgow | weavers | 50 families | Upper Canada |

[Praying assistance to emigrate and to be provided with the means of subsistence until the first crops may be gathered.]

" 25	Glasgow	weavers	100 families	Ditto
" 25	Glasgow	weavers	100 families	Ditto
" 30	Glasgow	weavers	50 families	Ditto
" 30	Ards	Presbyterian minister	many families	Lake Erie, N. America

[Applies on their behalf, and would be desirous of accompanying them, as settlers, to the borders of Lake Erie, N. America.]

| Oct. 4 | Glasgow | manufacturers | 400 people | Upper Canada |

[Having received favourable accounts, would prefer Upper Canada for emigration, and praying assistance to accomplish their object.]

| " 13 | Glasgow | manufacturers | 95 people | Canada |

[Applies, on their behalf, for assistance to emigrate, and that they may be provided with the means of subsistence until their first crops be gathered.]

" 14	Balfron	manufacturers	119 people	Ditto
" 18	Glasgow	manufacturers	70 families	Ditto
" 19	Paisley	manufacturers	60 people	Ditto
" 23	Paisley	paupers	622 people	Sent list of applicants
" 25	Ayrshire	manufacturers	52 families	Upper Canada
" 25	Glasgow	manufacturers	wife, 4 children	N. America
" 31	Ayrshire	cotton spinners	43 families	Upper Canada
" 31	Glasgow	manufacturers	40 families	Upper Canada
Nov. 1	Paisley	pensioner of. 15th Reg't.	wife, 2 sons 1 daughter	Upper Canada
" 6	Perth	weavers	27 families	Upper Canada

[Praying assistance to emigrate, in consequence of the distress of the times.]

" 6	Ayrshire	weavers	42 families	Ditto
" 8	Glasgow	mechanics	260 people	Ditto
" 17	Glasgow	late Glengarry fencibles	11 people	Ditto
" 17	Hamilton	weaver		Ditto

Date	Place of Residence	Description	Number of People/Families	Desired Destination
1826 continued				
Nov. 17	East Kilbride	weavers	20 people	Van Diemen's Land
" 8	Glasgow	manufacturers	4,000 families	

[Encloses a petition to the House of Commons from 4,000 individuals, members of certain Emigration Societies, praying assistance to emigrate.]

" 8	Glasgow	manufacturers	250 families	

[Ditto from Clydesdale Emigration Society, for the same purpose.]

" 13	Lanarkshire	manufacturers	158 families	

[Encloses three petitions, to the same purport.]

" 23	Glasgow	manufacturers	162 families	

[Enclose petition for the same purpose.]

Dec. 4	Glasgow	pensioners	families	America
" 8	Glasgow	pensioner	wife, 3 children	N. America

[Having served in N. America, is desirous of proceeding there as a settler.]

" 9	Lanark	paupers		Seeking assistance to emigrate.
" 12	Glasgow	pensioner	wife and child	Ditto
" 12	Castle Douglas	pensioner	family	Ditto
" 19	Glasgow			
" 30	Lanark	manufacturers	40 families	Upper Canada.

[Praying assistance to emigrate on condition of repaying to H. M. government, expense: stating that their petition will be presented to the House of Commons by Lord A. Hamilton, and praying assistance to emigrate.]

" 30	Breadalbane	labourers	families	
1827				
Jan. 4	Paisley	late serjeant 94th Reg't.	wife, 4 children	Canada

[Is desirous of emigrating and is willing to pay his passage, provided the same privileges were insured to him on his arrival which a serjeant discharged in that country would be entitled to.]

" 9	Paisley	labourers	100 families	Upper Canada
" 19	Glenelg	labourers	families	British North America
" 22	Aberdeen	Capt. and Adj. Aberdeenshire militia	family	Upper Canada

[Is anxious to join some friends in Upper Canada; has served in several regiments and purchased all his commissions; and he wishes to know if he can obtain a grant of land according to the rank he holds.]

Date	Place of Residence	Description	Number of People/Families	Desired Destination

1827 continued

Date	Place of Residence	Description	Number of People/Families	Desired Destination
Jan. 22	Paisley	labourers	families	Upper Canada
" 23	Western Highlands	labourers	104 families, 550 people	British North America

[All are natives of the western Highlands, who have suffered from the introduction of the sheep system in those parts.]

Date	Place of Residence	Description	Number of People/Families	Desired Destination
" 31	Glasgow & vicinity	weavers & labourers	3586 people	British colonies

[Apply for the loan of a sufficient sum to enable them to emigrate, as the only means by which they can be saved from perishing.]

Date	Place of Residence	Description	Number of People/Families	Desired Destination
Feb. 3	Paisley	weavers	130 families, 628 people	Upper Canada.

[Petitions to the House of Lords and the King under the name of "Fourth Canadian Agricultural Emigration Society," praying for a free passage to Upper Canada.]

Date	Place of Residence	Description	Number of People/Families	Desired Destination
" 5	Paisley	weavers	100 families	Canada

[Members of "Irish Friendly Emigrant Society."]

Date	Place of Residence	Description	Number of People/Families	Desired Destination
" 10	Kirkfield Bank, near Lanark	weavers	families	As above
" 14	East Kilbride	weavers	families	Canada
Jan. 12	Arisaig	labourers	61 people	Canada
" 31	Kilmarnock	paupers	families	Chaleur Bay, N. B.

[Petition to be granted the means of emigrating to Chaleur Bay, or elsewhere in that province, and promise to repay any expense incurred on that account.]

Date	Place of Residence	Description	Number of People/Families	Desired Destination
Feb. 5	Edinburgh	pauper	family	
" 18	Glasgow	labourers & mechanics	250 families	Canada

[Apply, in behalf of these families, under the name of the Clydesdale Emigration Society, for assistance to enable them to emigrate this Spring. They will refund any sums advanced them for this object.]

Date	Place of Residence	Description	Number of People/Families	Desired Destination
" 26	Lymington	labourer	wife and child	Canada
" 26	Glasgow	calico printer	wife, 9 children	Canada

[Solicits a grant of land in Canada. He has been in an extensive way of business for twenty-five years, but, owing to the commercials distress, now ruined. Has commanded several volunteer regiments, and has some knowledge of agriculture.]

Date	Place of Residence	Description	Number of People/Families	Desired Destination
Mar. 2	Dornie, Kintail	paupers	20 families	Canada

[Applies, in their behalf, for aid to enable them to remove to Canada, as they can get no work, and have nothing but a few potatoes to subsist upon.]

Date	Place of Residence	Description	Number of People/Families	Desired Destination

1827 continued

Mar. 3	Berwick	pensioner 68th Reg't	wife, 2 children	Upper Canada
" 7	Hamilton			Upper Canada/New Brunswick

[Applies, in behalf of the Hamilton Emigration Society, to know what allowance government will make to persons emigrating to Upper Canada or New Brunswick.]

" 9	Breadalbane	husbandmen	families	Upper Canada

[Applies for himself, and a few others in his neighbourhood, for conveyance to Upper Canada whither they wish to proceed to join some friends and relatives, from whom they have received encouraging accounts.]

" 9	Paisley	labourers & mechanics	families	British America

[Apply in the name of First Paisley Emigration Society, to be conveyed to, and located in, the British American Settlements, and to be allowed rations & c.; and undertake, at the expiration of seven years, to repay, by instalments of £3 10s. 9d. per annum, the sums expended on that account.]

" 10	Upper Cotton	road contractor	family	
" 12	Paisley	labourers	families	Upper Canada

[Undertake, in the name of the Irish Friendly Emigrant Society, to repay whatever expense may be incurred by government in settling them in Upper Canada.]

" 12	Paisley	labourers & mechanics	60 families	Canada
" 16	Gatehouse of Fleet	pensioner from royal artillery	wife, 3sons 2 daughters	British North America
" 16	Edinburgh	various trades	11 families, 53 people	Upper Canada

1826

Dec. 23	Wilsonstown, Lanark	chiefly agricultural labourers	21 families, 108 people	Upper Canada

[request a free passage, and grant of land in Upper Canada, with provisions, implements of husbandry etc.]

Date	Place of Residence	Description	Number of People/Families	Desired Destination
1827 continued				
Feb. 10	Kirkfield Bank	weavers	families	N. America
Feb. 14	Aberdeen	Capt. & Adj. Aberdeenshire Militia	family	Upper Canada.

[Desirous of joining some friends in Upper Canada; has served as a captain in regular army, and wishes to know if he can obtain a grant of land according to that rank.]

Date	Place of Residence	Description	Number of People/Families	Desired Destination
" 15	Fort Augustus	paupers	328 people	Canada
Mar. 2	Paisley	labourers	130 families	Canada

[Applies to the Committee on Emigration in the name of the "Fourth Paisley Emigration Society" for assistance to enable them to emigrate.]

Date	Place of Residence	Description	Number of People/Families	Desired Destination
" 3	Dunning, Perthshire	weavers	5 families, 33 people	Canada
" 9	Kilmarnock	labourers & pensioners	4 families, 21 people	British America
" 10	Kilmarnock	late 36th Reg't of foot	family	Ditto
" 12	Paisley	pensioner from 15th Reg't of foot	wife, family	Upper Canada
" 19	Stirling	shoemaker	wife, 2 children	British North America
" 21	Edinburgh	landowner in Coll	several thousand	Canada

[Applies in behalf of several thousand souls in the Hebrides for aid towards emigration. He himself last year sent out 300 souls from one of his own islands, and he can now spare 1,500 from his estates, and would be willing to pay, for a limited number of years, the interest of money expended in the emigration; the emigrants themselves afterwards paying it, or an annuity.]

Date	Place of Residence	Description	Number of People/Families	Desired Destination
" 23	Dunning	n/k	n/k	Canada
" 23	Hamilton	weaver, late 15th Regiment of foot	n/k	Canada
" 28	Leith	n/k	n/k	British America.

[Requests information as to the quantity of land an emigrant possessed of £600 is entitled to in British America.]

Date	Place of Residence	Description	Number of People/Families	Desired Destination
" 31	Kilmarnock	n/k	30 families	Chaleur Bay, N.B.
Apr. 2	Glasgow	tailor	wife, 5 children	British North America
" 2	Paisley	mechanics	families	Upper Canada

[Applies in behalf of the "Paisley Hibernian Protestant Emigration Society" for aid to enable them to emigrate to Upper Canada.]

Date	Place of Residence	Description	Number of People/Families	Desired Destination
1827 continued				
Apr. 3	Aberdeen	n/k	n/k	Canada
" 12	Tradestown	tradesman	4 children	Ditto
" 13	Lanark	weaver, late of 70th Reg't Foot	wife, 2 children	Ditto
" 14	Kilmarnock	late 36th Reg't	wife, 2 children	Ditto
" 16	Kilmarnock	n/k	36 families	Canada

[Apply, in behalf of the Society, for aid to enable them to emigrate.]

" 16	Paisley	n/k	16 families	Upper Canada

[Applies for information whether a passage and provisions will be found for them to go to Upper Canada, where they propose to work at the Welland Canal.]

" 20	Greenock	weavers	17 families, 90 people	Upper Canada

[Transmits the petition of these families, under the name of the "West Kilbride Emigration Society," for assistance to enable them to emigrate to Upper Canada.]

Mar. 3	Edinburgh	mason, former farmer	wife, child	Any of colonies

[Applies for a certificate to emigrate to any of the Colonies; and will come bound, in any manner which the Government pleases, to repay expenses; understands architecture, and was taught geometry, mensuration, etc.; will produce certificates of good character.]

Apr.7	Glasgow	weaver, late 23rd Light Dragoons	numerous family	Canada
" 27	Glasgow	weavers & mechanics	250 families	Upper Canada

[The president, secretary. and eleven directors of the Clydesdale Emigration Society, consisting of 250 families, apply for a grant of land, the means of conveyance, implements of agriculture, and provisions for twelve months to accompany the grant in Upper Canada. Are led to believe this grant is chiefly to hand-loom weavers; and that in the present bad state of trade there are many mechanics and other operatives suffering severely for want of employment, and that even those that are employed receive such low wages, as are insufficient to procure the common necessaries of life, ... It is too painful to enter into minute details of all their sufferings. There are 30 heads of families anxiously depending upon the grant since August 1826.]

Date	Place of Residence	Description	Number of People/Families	Desired Destination

1827 continued

Date	Place of Residence	Description	Number of People/Families	Desired Destination
Apr. 12	Glasgow	Adj. of local militia, on half-pay	wife, 10 children	Canada

[His half-pay will not support his family and he is in great distress.]

Date	Place of Residence	Description	Number of People/Families	Desired Destination
" 26	Edinburgh	mason	wife, 5 children	Canada

[Seeks permission to join the emigrants proceeding from Renfrew and Lanark to Canada (to whom he is informed the grant is confined this season) as his family are suffering the greatest distress for want of food and clothing, and the impossibility of obtaining employment.]

Date	Place of Residence	Description	Number of People/Families	Desired Destination
May 1	Glasgow	weaver, former labourer		Canada
April 16	by Lanark	pensioner, 21st Reg't of Foot	family of 9	Canada

[his pension is not sufficient to support his family.]

Date	Place of Residence	Description	Number of People/Families	Desired Destination
" 28	Campsie	pensioner		Upper Canada
" 12	Breadlbane	n/k	self and friends	Canada
" 14	Glasgow	tailor	4 sons, 1 daughter	Upper Canada

[Prays for a hundred acres of land and free passage to Upper Canada, as the want of employment and high price of the necessities of life prevent him supporting his family, whom he trusts will become successful cultivators, when in Canada.].

Date	Place of Residence	Description	Number of People/Families	Desired Destination
" 27	Aberdeen	major of local militia		Canada

[Applicant does not wish for any assistance from Government, but requests grant of land.]

Date	Place of Residence	Description	Number of People/Families	Desired Destination
May 8	Leith	late private in Lanarkshire militia	wife, 7 sons	Canada

[Transmitted by Lord A. Hamilton; praying for aid from the Government to enable him to emigrate with his family (the three eldest sons being tradesmen) to Canada as they are suffering great distress, from the want of employment.]

Date	Place of Residence	Description	Number of People/Families	Desired Destination
April 2	Isle of Skye	late capt. in army	many families	Canada

[Refers to his former communication upon the subject of grants of land to be given by Government to a number of the poor agriculturalists of the parish of Bracanish, Isle of Skye, who are in great distress, and most anxious to emigrate to Canada, and requests information whether the terms offered by applicant in former letters will be acceded to.]

Date	Place of Residence	Description	Number of People/Families	Desired Destination

1827 continued

Date	Place of Residence	Description	Number of People/Families	Desired Destination
Apr. 22	Millerstown	weaver	n/k	Canada

[Requests a free passage to Canada, in order that he may join relations.]

| " 25 | Glasgow | n/k | 2 families | Canada |

[Requests a grant of land in Canada, as applicants are able to pay their passage; but solicit assistance in procuring agricultural instruments.]

| " 25 | Inverkip | labourer | wife, 3 sons 1 daughter | Canada |

| " 30 | Islands of Mull, Benbecula, Barra and N. Uist | 1600 people | British America | |

[Applies on behalf of 1600 persons, to know if they will receive any aid from Government to emigrate to British America this season, as they are in great distress; and refers to their former petition, presented by Lord Archibald Hamilton.]

| May 2 | Caledon | n/k | man and wife | Canada |
| " 3 | Kirkfield Bank, Lanark | n/k | | |

[The president of Kirkfield Bank (near Lanark) Emigration Society applies on behalf of that society, praying, that the object of their petition, which they had presented a long time back, may be granted, as their miseries are increasing and their only hope is emigration.]

| " 6 | Calton, Glasgow | n/k | 10 people | Upper Canada |

[Applicants state that they belong to an Emigration Society, but that as they have relations in Upper Canada who will assist them upon their arrival, they pray their peculiar circumstances may be taken into consideration, and that aid may be given, in order to convey them to the townships where their friends are settled.]

| " 7 | Edinburgh | lately in militia | | Canada |

[Applies for a temporary employment as a subordinate superintendant of emigrants going to Canada, and requests leave to present testimonials.]

| " 10 | Annan | pensioner, 25th foot | 1 son | Canada |

Date	Place of Residence	Description	Number of People/Families	Desired Destination

1827 continued

Date	Place of Residence	Description	Number of People/Families	Desired Destination
May 11	Kilmarnock	6 emigration societies	212 families	Canada

[The President and Secretary of the Kilmarnock Emigration Society …
state that all the Societies in Ayrshire are in communication with each
other, and that Kilmarnock is the centre of communication; that the
idea of 92 families in Ayrshire only having petitioned for emigration is
a mistake, as the number of the Societies is six, containing 212 heads
of families, who are most anxious to emigrate, as a means of relieving
them from their present distress. Request information as to what
qualifications are necessary that will constitute them a fit object for
emigration in the event of a grant being given.]

Date	Place of Residence	Description	Number of People/Families	Desired Destination
" 16	Edinburgh	out-pensioner, Chelsea Hospital	1 son	Upper Canada

[Prays for a free passage to Upper Canada.]

Date	Place of Residence	Description	Number of People/Families	Desired Destination
" 19	Paisley	late 72nd reg't, 14 years service receives no pension	3 sons	Canada

[Petitioners beg for a grant of land and implements of husbandry in
Canada, as they have collected sufficient money to pay for their passage.]

Date	Place of Residence	Description	Number of People/Families	Desired Destination
" 19	Barry, Forfar	agriculturalist	wife, 2 sons 4 daughters	Upper Canada

[Wishes to join his son, who has been located on Amherst Island,
Lake Ontario, in consequence of his son's requesting him and the
family to emigrate; hearing that some arrangements will be made to
facilitate a free passage, applies for information.]

Date	Place of Residence	Description	Number of People/Families	Desired Destination
" 24	Glasgow	president, clerk and 3 committee members		Canada

[They compose the Committee of the Clydesdale Emigration Society,
and apply on behalf of that Society for information how they may avail
themselves of the grant by Parliament, (agreeable to the information
they have received through Newspapers,) fully answering their
expectations of emigration.]

Date	Place of Residence	Description	Number of People/Families	Desired Destination

1827 continued

| May 14 | Glasgow | tradesmen | n/k | Canada |

[Applicant states that a number of tradesmen connected with Emigration Societies feel great alarm that weavers only are likely to be recommended as fit persons to extend the grant of emigration; therefore pray that their deep distress may be taken into favourable consideration; that they are starving, and will be ejected from their dwellings in a few days.]

| " 28 | Paisley | n/k | 60 families | Upper Canada |

[Applicants compose an Emigration Society in Paisley; state their despair at finding that no money will be granted towards emigration this season; their extreme distress, having large families, and the badness of trade and the advance in the price of provisions; state that many of the Society have friends in Canada whom they wish to join. A number of Societies, in addition to theirs, relied upon a grant of land and means to emigrate to Upper Canada, and they therefore pray that their distressed case may yet be taken into consideration, by which they may be relieved from their mournful condition.]

| " 29 | Johnstown, | n/k | 31 families | Upper Canada |

[They are labourers and natives of Scotland; that in consequence of the want of employment during the last six months, they are reduced to the most abject state of misery that is possible. …. 25 of their society are destitute of either house or bedding, their little having all been taken by their landlords, they are now depending for shelter from the storm, to the charity of their neighbours; that their misery is increasing from the great quantity of labour performed by the unemployed operative weavers, so that by even travelling for 20 miles around, they are not able to obtain a days employment. … Pray that endeavours may be made to relieve them from their awful situation.]

| " 24 | Dornie, Kintail | late in 78th Reg't but has no pension | 3 sons | British America. |

[Applying on behalf of himself and neighbours in the Western Highlands.]

| " 24 | Maxwell's Town, Paisley | weavers | 2 families | Upper Canada |

[Applicants have joined the 2nd Paisley Emigration Society, for the purpose of emigrating to Upper Canada. They are to be ejected from their dwellings on 28th May.]

Date	Place of Residence	Description	Number of People/Families	Desired Destination
1827 continued				
May 29	Corrokin, Breadalbane, Perthshire	n/k	n/k	Upper Canada
Mar. 2	West Kilbride	weavers	17 families	Upper Canada

[They are members of the West Kilbride Emigration, and inhabitants of Ayrshire; … they are most anxious to emigrate to Upper Canada. State, that owing to the badness of trade, thousands are thrown out of employment and reduced to a state of wretchedness hitherto unknown; Pray for assistance, and the same allowance as formerly given to distressed artisans on emigrating.]

Date	Place of Residence	Description	Number of People/Families	Desired Destination
1826				
Oct. 20	Topo, Colombia	labourers	44 families	British North America

[Petitioners emigrated under the auspices of the Colombian Agricultural Association where they were to be placed on elevated land that would produce European grain; to be supported for eight months, and to be supplied with implements of husbandry... After the total failure of their first crops, the Agent of the Association promised them 2 rials a day each, if they would make a trial for a second; to which they agreed, but at the end of three weeks, they were told that no more money or provisions would be forthcoming. … Pray for assistance that they may be enabled to emigrate to the British dominions in North America.]

Appendix III:

CHARACTERISTICS OF THE SAILING VESSELS THAT CARRIED AT LEAST 150 PASSENGERS IN ATLANTIC CROSSINGS, 1770–1855.

Explanatory Notes

Passenger Data
Cumulative passenger totals and the number of crossings are provided for each vessel.

Vessel Details
Information on the tonnage, vessel type, year built, place built and the Lloyd's Code have been taken from the *Lloyd's Shipping Register.*

Tonnage
This was a standard measure used to determine customs dues and navigation fees. Because it was a calculated figure, tonnage did not necessarily convey actual carrying capacity. Before 1836, the formula used to calculate tonnage was based only on breadth and length but after 1836 it incorporated the vessel's depth as well.

Vessel Type
The word "ship" can signify a particular vessel type as well as having a generic usage in denoting all types of sea-going vessels. Sailing ship rigs were many and varied. A major distinction was the alignment of the sails. There were the square-rigged vessels in which the sails were rigged across the vessel and the fore-and-aft rigs, which followed the fore-and-aft-line of the vessel. The square rig was normally used on ocean-going vessels:

Brig (bg):   a two masted vessel with square rigging on both masts.

Snow (sw):   rigged as a brig, with square sails on both masts but with a small triangular sail mast stepped immediately towards the stern of the main mast.

Barque (bk):   three-masted vessel, square rigged on the fore and main masts and fore-and-aft rigged on the third aftermost mast.

Ship (s):   three-masted vessel, square rigged on all three masts.

Schooner (sr):   fore-and-aft sails on two or more masts. Some had small
square topsails on the foremast. They were largely used in
the coasting trade and for fishing, their advantage being
the smaller crew than that required by square rigged
vessels of a comparable size.

Lloyd's Shipping Codes

These were assigned to vessels after periodic surveys according to their quality of construction, condition and age:

A   first-class condition, kept in the highest state of
repair and efficiency and within a prescribed age
limit at the time of sailing.

AE   "second description of the first class," fit for safe
conveyance, no defects but may be over a prescribed age
limit.

E   second-class vessels, which, although unfit for carrying dry
cargoes, were suitable for long distance sea voyages.

I   third-class vessels only suitable for short voyages (i.e. not
out of Europe).

The letters were followed by the number 1 or 2, which signified the condition of the vessel's equipment (anchors, cables and stores). Where satisfactory, the number 1 was used, and where not, 2 was used.

Failure to locate vessels in the *Register* does not in itself signify its exclusion from the Lloyd's classification system. To select the relevant vessel from the *Register* it is usually necessary to know the tonnage and captain's name, information that is often elusive and problematic because of gaps in the available shipping and customs records.

Vessel/	Type	Tons	Year(s) Sailed	Depart	Arrive	Psgr Nos & crossings	Year & place built	Lloyd's Code
Abeona of Glsgw	n/k	611	1874	Glsgw	Qbc	216 [1]	Qbc	n/k
Aberdeen-shire of Ab'n	bg	240 –35	1827	Ab'n	H'fx	246 [13]	1825, Ab'n	A1
						[Dimensions: 89' x 25' 2" x 17']		
Active	s	351	1827	Tober-mory	C. B. & Qbc	200 [1]	1826, N. S.	A1
Admiral of Glsgw	s	707	1851	Storn-oway	Qbc	413 [1]	1850, Dumb-arton	A1
Agamem-non	n/k	n/k	1818	Leith	Qbc	192 [1]	n/k	n/k

Vessel/	Type	Tons	Year(s) Sailed	Depart	Arrive	Psgr Nos & crossings	Year & place built	Lloyd's Code
Agincourt of Leith	s	347	1817 –19	Leith	H'fx & Qbc	400 [3]	1804, North Shields	E1
Aimwell of Ab'n	sw	232	1816 –32	Thurso & Ab'n	H'fx & Qbc	228 [4]	1816, Ab'n	A1
					[Dimensions: 85' x 25' 10" x 16' 9"]			
Albion	n/k	n/k	1802	Fort William	Qbc	167 [1]	n/k	n/k
Albion of Ab'n	bg	266	1829 –52	Ab'n	H'fx & Qbc	522 [29]	1826, Ab'n	A1
					[Dimensions: 94' 2" x 25' 6" x 17' 2"			
Albion of Glsgw	bg	190 –33	1832	Loch Indaal (Islay) & Tobermory, Glsgw	Sydney & Qbc	329 [4]	1826, Campbel-town	E1
Albion of Grnk	s	414	1846 –52	Glsgw	Qbc	392 [7]	1845, Grnk	A1
Alexander	n/k	n/k	1772	Arisaig & Loch-boisdale	P.E.I.	214 [1]	n/k	n/k
Alexander & 2 other ships	n/k	n/k	1803	Storno-way	Pictou	600 [1]	n/k	n/k
Alexander	bg	169	1820	Grnk	P.E.I. & Qbc	293 [2]	1818, New Carlisle, Qbc	A1
Alfred	n/k	n/k	1834	Leith	Qbc	243 [1]	n/k	n/k
Amity of Glasgow	n/k	n/k	1831 –34	Tober-mory, Glsgw	Ship Harbour	451 [5]	n/k C.B. & Qbc	n/k
Anacreon of Newcastle	s	443	1817	Tober-mory	Pictou & Qbc	166 [1]	1799, Sunderland	E1
Ann	bg	n/k	1828	Storn-oway	Sydney	209 [1]	n/k	n/k
Ann Harley of Glsgw	bk	455	1844	Glsgw	Qbc	206 [1]	1844, Miramichi	AE1
Ann Rankin of Glsgw	s	466 –52	1847	Glsgw	Qbc	642 [3]	1840, Quebec	n/k
Argyle	bg	139	1793	Glenelg	P.E.I. & Qbc	150 [1]	1790, N. S.	A1
			Year(s)			Psgr	Year &	Lloyd's

Vessel/	Type	Tons	Sailed	Depart	Arrive	Nos & crossings	place built	Code
Atlantic	s	n/k	1849	Ardro-ssan	Qbc	366 [1]	n/k	n/k
Atlas	s	435	1815	Grnk	Qbc	242 [1]	1801, Shields	E1
Augusta of Dumfries	s	370 –19	1817	Dumfries	Pictou, Miramichi & Saint John	538 [4]	1796, Whitby	E1
Aurora of Ab'n	s	709	1854 –55	Ab'n	Qbc	710 [3]	1843, Miramichi	AE1
Balfour of White-haven	bg	310	1833	White-haven	Qbc	272 [1]	1809, Whitehaven	E1
Banffshire of Dundee	s	471	1841	Loch-maddy	Cape Breton	450 [1]	1837, Pictou	A1
Barlow	bk	436	1849 –51	Loch Reag & John Stornoway, Grnk	Qbc	533 [3]	1834, Saint John N. B.	AE1
Baronet	n/k	n/k	1831	Cromarty	Qbc	187 [1]	n/k	n/k
Ben-lomond	s	345	1820 –53	Grnk	Qbc	606 [2]	1815, N. B.	A1
Benson	s	265	1821	Grnk	Qbc	287 [1]	1798, Lancaster	E1
Berbice of Ab'n	bk	340	1848 –55	Ab'n	Qbc	1225 [14]	1847, Miramichi	AE1
Birman of Grnk	bk	448	1851 –52	Grnk	Qbc	299 [2]	1840, Grnk	A1
Blanche of Liverpool	s	966	1852	Storno-way	Qbc	453 [1]	1850, Saint John N. B.	A1
Blonde of M'tl	bk	604	1842 –49	Glsgw	Qbc	1865 [6]	1841, M'tl	A1
Bona Dea	n/k	n/k	1843	Grnk	Qbc	446 [1]	n/k	n/k
Bowes	n/k		1834	Cromarty	Qbc	172 [1]	n/k	n/k
Bowling of Glsgw	bk	242	1842	Glsgw	Qbc	157 [1]	1842, n/k	A1
Breese	n/k	n/k	1831	n/k	Sydney	267 [1]	n/k	n/k
Brilliant of Ab'n	s	332	1828 –46	Ab'n	Qbc	1709 [24]	1814, Ab'n	AE1
			Year(s)			Psgr	Year &	Lloyd's

Vessel/	Type	Tons	Sailed	Depart	Arrive	Nos & crossings	place built	Code
Britannia of Dumfries	sw	200 -24	1820	Dumfries	P.E.I., Miramichi, Richibucto	158 [3]	1809 White- haven	E1
Britannia of New- castle	s	542	1847	Glsgw	Qbc	388 [1]	1840, N. B.	AE1
British King of Dundee	bg	239	1826 -40	Cromarty	Pictou & Qbc	166 [2]	1825, Sunderland	AE1
Broke	s	252	1820	Grnk	Qbc	176 [1]	1812, Salem	A1
Brooksby of Glsgw	s	423	1851	Loch- Boisdale	Qbc	285 [1]	1843, Grnk	A1
Caledonia	bg	160	1827 -29	Grnk	Qbc	299 [3]	1806, Scotland	E1
Caledonia of Grnk	s	383	1841 -55	Grnk	Qbc	944 [18]	1841, Grnk	A1
California of Grnk	bk	563	1843 -55	Glsgw	Qbc	975 [6]	1841, N.B.	A1
Cambria of Grnk	s	397	1846 -54	Glsgw	Qbc	421 [9]	1846, Grnk	A1
Canada	s	269	1830 -32	Cromarty	Pictou & Qbc	355 [2]	1811, M'tl	E1
Canada of Greenock	s	330 -48	1834	Grnk	Qbc	999 [15]	1831, Grnk	A1
Carleton	n/k	n/k	1842	Glsgw	Qbc	400 [1]	n/k	n/k
Cartha	bg	358	1830 -35	Grnk	Qbc	427 [4]	1827, N. B.	A1
Catherine	s	448	1843	Tober- mory	Ship Harbour & Qbc	275 [1]	n/k	n/k
Champion of Grnk	bk	673	1849 -54	Glsgw	Qbc	497 [2]	1838, Canada	AE1
Charles Hamerton of Liverpool	n/k	640	1843	Tober- mory	C. B.	405 [1]	n/k	n/k
Charlotte	n/k	1000	1849	Glsgw	Qbc	333 [1]	n/k	n/k
Charlotte Harrison of Grnk	bk	557 -55	1847	Grnk	Qbc	569 [2]	1841, Qbc	AE1
			Year(s)			Psgr	Year &	Lloyd's

Vessel/	Type	Tons	Sailed	Depart	Arrive	Nos & crossings	place built	Code
Cherokee of Glsgw	bk	278 –47	1834	Grnk	Qbc	157 [6]	1834, Grnk	A1
Chieftain of Kirkaldy	bk	333 –35	1832	Crom- arty, Leith	Pictou & Qbc	414 [3]	1832, Leith	A1
					[Dimensions: 100' 6" x 27' 9" x 19' 6"]			
Circassian of Grnk	bk	520	1848 –49	Glsgw	Qbc	315 [2]	1839, N. B.	A1
Clansman of Glsgw	bk	348 –49	1836	Grnk	Sydney & Qbc	464 [3]	1823, N. B.	E1
Clarendon of Hull	s	416	1808	Oban	P.E.I.	208 [1]	1783, Bristol	E1
Cleopatra	bg	267	1831	Crom- arty	Qbc	246 [1]	1817, Whitby	E1
Clutha of Grnk	bk	462	1851 –53	Glsgw	Qbc	612 [3]	1839, N. B.	AE1
Columbus	bg	322	1827	Tober- mory	C. B.	228 [1]	1825, Pictou	A1
Commerce of Grnk	s	425	1821 –24	Grnk	Qbc	839 [3]	1813, Quebec	A1
Conrad of Grnk	s	759	1850 –51	Glsgw	Qbc	588 [2]	1847, Quebec	A1
Corsair of Grnk	bg	276	1825 –38	Crom- arty, Tober- mory	Pictou, C. B. & Qbc	907 [8]	1823, N. B.	AE1
Cruickston Castle of Grnk	bk	382	1839	Storn- oway	Sydney & Qbc	260 [3]	1822. N. B.	AE1
Cumber- land	s	n/k	1831	n/k	Sydney	392 [1]	n/k	n/k
Curlew	bg	260	1818	Grnk	Qbc	205 [1]	1815, Newcastle	A1
Dalmar- nock	s	315	1831 –32	Berwick	Qbc	282 [3]	1828, Workington	E1
David of London	s	390	1821	Grnk	Qbc	364 [1]	1812, Pictou	E1
Deveron of Glsgw	bg	333 –40	1830	Loch- inver Loch Indaal, Grnk	Pictou, Qbc	737 [5]	1824, N. S.	AE1

| | Year(s) | | | | | Psgr | Year & | Lloyd's |

Vessel/	Type	Tons	Sailed	Depart	Arrive	Nos & crossings	place built	Code
Donegal	sw	190	1831 –32	Mary- port	Qbc	302 [2]	1808, Belfast	E1
Dorothy	s	530	1815	Glsgw	Qbc	194 [1]	Prize, Denmark	E1
Dove of Ab'n	n/k	186	1801	Fort William	Pictou	219 [1]	n/k	n/k
Duchess of Richmond	s	324 –32	1820	Grnk & Oban	Qbc	761 [5]	1807, Dublin	E1
Dunken- field and one other vessel	s	400	1791	n/k	Pictou	650 [1]	1783, n/k	A1
Dunlop	bg	331	1810 –30	Tober- mory, Glsgw	Sydney, Pictou & Qbc	290 [6]	1805 Montreal	E1
Dykes of Maryport	sw	235 –33	1803	Maryport	Qbc	389 [3]	1798, Maryport	A1
Earl of Bucking- hamshire	s	593 –21	1815	Grnk	Qbc	823 [3]	1814, Qbc	A1
Economy of Ab'n	n/k	n/k	1819	Tober- mory	Pictou	258 [1]	n/k	n/k
Eleutheria of South Shields	bk	340	1843	Glsgw	Qbc	160 [1]	1835, Shields	A1
Elisa of Cardiff	bk	384	1847	Glsgw	Qbc	269 [1]	1846, Qbc	AE1
Elizabeth and Anne	sw	296	1831	Grnk	Qbc	296 [1]	1779, Shields	E1
Elizabeth of Dumfries	n/k	n/k –22	1817	Dum- fries	St. John	576 [5]	n/k	n/k
Ellen of Liverpool	bk	397	1848 Loch Laxford	Loch	Pictou	154 [1]	1834, N. B.	AE1
Emperor Alexander of Ab'n	sw	236	1823	Cromarty, Tober- mory	Sydney & Qbc	160 [1] [Dimensions: 83' 11" x 25' 8" x 15' 11"]	1814, Sunderland	A1
Energy of Dundee	bg	224	1838	Storn- oway	Qbc	210 [1]	1832, Dundee	A1
Erromanga of Grnk	bk	351	1845 –54	Glsgw	Qbc	473 [8]	1845, Grnk	A1

Vessel/	Type	Tons	Year(s) Sailed	Depart	Arrive	Psgr Nos & crossings	Year & place built	Lloyd's Code
Euclid of Liverpool	bk	501	1847	Glsgw	Qbc	330 [1]	1841, Pictou	AE1
European n/k	n/k	n/k	1833	Leith	Qbc	155 [1]	n/k	n/k
Fairy of Dundee	s	248 41	1833,	Dundee	Qbc	173 [2]	1801, York	E1
Favourite of Grnk	bk	355	1841 –49	Glsgw	Qbc	692 [13]	1839, M'tl	A1
Favourite of Kirkaldy & one other vessel	bg	165	1803	Isle Martin	Pictou	500 [1]	1797, Kirkaldy	A1
Favourite of M'tl	bg	296	1826 –36	Grnk	Qbc	550 [13]	1825, M'tl	A1
Forth	sw	369	1827	Grnk	Qbc	150 [1]	1826, Leith	A1
Foundling	bg	205	1829 –31	Grnk	Qbc	331 [2]	1810, America	E1
George Canning	s	482 –31	1821	Grnk	Qbc	1377 [6]	1812, M'tl	A1
George of Dundee	s	676 –50	1841	Cromarty Loch Laxford & Thurso	Pictou, Qbc	707 [4]	1839, Pictou	n/k
					[Dimensions: 125' 3" x 27' 4" x 21']			
Glencairn of Glsgw	s	850 –54	1851	Glsgw	Qbc	651 [5]	1850, Quebec	A1
Gleniffer	bg	318	1826 –35	Grnk	Qbc	458 [6]	1826, Saint John N. B.	E1
Glentan-ner of Ab'n	bg	160	1815, 1820	Ab'n, Tober mory	H'fx, Pictou & C. B.	158 [3]	1811, Ab'dn	A1
					[Dimensions: 77' 10" x 22' 2" x 13' 6"]			
Greenock	n/k	n/k	1848	Loch Laxford	Qbc	399 [1]	n/k	A1
Hamilton of Glsgw	s	589	1843	Grnk	Qbc	283 [1]	1842,Restigouche	A1
Harlequin of Glsgw	bk	702	1852	Glsgw	Qbc	835 [4]	1851, Quebec	A1
Harmony n/k	n/k	n/k	1817 –19	Grnk	Qbc	369 [2]	n/k	n/k

Vessel/	Type	Tons	Year(s) Sailed	Depart	Arrive	Psgr Nos & crossings	Year & place built	Lloyd's Code
Harmony of White- haven	bg	244	1827	Storn- oway	H'fx & Qbc	236 [1]	1812, Whitehaven	A1
Harper	n/k	n/k	1842	Glsgw	Qbc	235 [1]	n/k	n/k
Hector	s	200	1773	Loch Broom	Pictou	190 [1]	Dutch Prize	I2
Hector	n/k	n/k	1835 –44	Islay, Glsgw	Qbc	199 [3] [Dimensions: 83' x 24' x 10']	n/k	n/k
Hedleys of New- castle	bk	279 –33	1832	Cromarty	Qbc	347 [2]	1823, Newcastle	E1
Helen of Irvine	sw	157	1802	Fort William	Qbc	166 [1]	1775, Leith	A1
Henry	n/k	n/k	1834, 1836	Glsgw	Qbc	214 [2]	n/k	n/k
Herald of of Grnk	s	801	1843	Grnk	Qbc	319 [1]	1840, N. B.	AE1
Hercules of Ab'n	bk	250	1834 –37	Ab'n	Qbc	590 [6] [Dimensions: 88' 6" x 26' 2" x 6' 3" between decks]	1781, Stockton	E1
Hero	bg	321	1829	Grnk	Pictou	157 [1]	1823, N. B.	E1
Heroine of Ab'n	s	387	1840 –47	Storn- oway & Ab'n	P.E.I. & Qbc	637 [7]	1831, Dundee	AE1
Highl- ander of Ab'n	bg	174	1817 –36	Ab'n, Cromarty	Saint John H'fx, Qbc	223 [3] [Dimensions: 79' 1" x 22' 11" x 14' 11"]	1817, Aberdeen	E1
Hope	n/k	n/k	1817	Grnk	Sydney	[1] 161	n/k	n/k
Hope of Glasgow	bk	513	1848, –51	Glsgw	Pictou Qbc	165 [2]	1839, N. B.	AE1
Hope of Grnk	bk	231	1819	Oban	Qbc	184 [1]	n/k	n/k
Indepen- dence of Belfast	s	584	1841	Liverpool	Qbc	245 [1]	1839, Quebec	A1
Industry	bk	291	1831 –32	Cromarty, Dundee	Pictou & Qbc	187 [2]	Prize, 1808	n/k

Vessel/	Type	Tons	Year(s) Sailed	Depart	Arrive	Psgr Nos & crossings	Year & place built	Lloyd's Code
Iris	bk	n/k	1831 –32	Grnk	Qbc	404 [2]	n/k	n/k
Isabella of Glsgw	bk	376 –42	1828	Grnk	H'fx, Sydney & Pictou	570 [9]	1828, N. B.	AE1
Jamaica of Glsgw	s	334 –51	1840	Grnk	Qbc	801 [7]	1796, Grnk	AE1
Jane	n/k	n/k	1790	Drimin- darich	P.E.I.	186 [1]	n/k	n/k
Jane Boyd of Ab'n	bk	387	1853 –54	Ab'n	Qbc	379 [3]	1843, Aberdeen	n/k
Jane Duffus of Irvine	bk	352	1843	Glsgw	Qbc	257 [1] [Dimensions: 99' 2" x 24'1" x 17' 2"]	1840, Pictou	A1
Jane Kay	sw	235	1833	Cromarty & Thurso	Pictou & Qbc	170 [1]	1831, Sunderland	A1
Janet of Glsgw	bk	444	1852	Glsgw	Qbc	190 [1]	1830, Qbc	AE1
Jean of Irvine	s	167 –5	1802	Fort William	Qbc	274 [2]	1799, Saltcoats	A1
Jessie	n/k	n/k	1832	Tober- mory	Sydney C.B.	313 [1]	n/k	n/k
Jessie of Dumfries	bg	209 –20	1816	Dumfries	P.E.I.. & N.B.	346 [6]	1814, Dumfries	A1
Joseph Green of Peterhead	s	353	1842	Cromarty Thurso & Lochinver	Qbc	239 [1]	1819, Sunderland	AE1
Justyn of Leith	bk	803	1851	Grnk	Qbc	313 [1] [Dimensions: 145' 2" x 29' 8" x 22']	1849, Quebec	A1
Lady Emily of Sunderland	sw	285	1842	Cromarty, Thurso, Loch Laxford	Pictou & Qbc	150 [1]	1840, Sunderland	A1
Lady Falkland	n/k	n/k	1842	Glsgw	Qbc	361 [1]	1846, N. S.	AE1
Lady Grey of North Shields	sw	285	1841	Cromarty & Thurso	Pictou & Qbc	240 [1]	1841, Sunderland	A1
Liskeard of Liverpool	bk	648	1849 –51	Inverness & Storn oway	Qbc	445 [2]	1847, N. S.	AE1

Vessel/	Type	Tons	Year(s) Sailed	Depart	Arrive	Psgr Nos & crossings	Year & place built	Lloyd's Code
Lord Middleton of North Shields	sw	341	1817	Leith	Qbc	163 [1]	n/k, Carolina	E1
Louisa of Ab'n	sw	213	1816 –29	Tober-mory, Storn-oway	H'fx, Pictou, Sydney & Miramichi	472 [10]	1816, Ab'n	E1
					[Dimensions: 85' 3" x 24' 2" x 15' 9"]			
Lulan of Pictou	bk	473 –52	1848	Glsgw	Pictou	209 [4]	1848, New Glsgw	A1
Macdonald	n/k	n/k	1786	Knoydart	Qbc	539 [1]	n/k	n/k
Mahaica of Grnk	bk	256	1842 –43	Glsgw	Qbc	184 [2]	1837, Grnk	A1
Malay	bg	215	1830	Skye	Sydney	211 [1]	1818, Grnk	E1
Mally of Grnk	bg	148	1791	Grnk	P.E.I.	236 [1]	1784, Grnk	A1
Margaret	bg	218	1821 –32	Grnk	H'fx, Saint John & Qbc	290 [2]	1820, Kirkaldy	A1
Margaret Bogle of Leith	s	324	1824 –43	Leith, Thurso	Qbc & Pictou	518 [8]	1804, Ayr	E1
					[Dimensions: 104' 2" x 27' x 18' 11"]			
Margaret of Grnk	bk	566	1843	Glsgw	Qbc	238 [1]	1839, Miramichi	AE1
Mariner of Sunderland	n/k	255	1836, 1841	Thurso & Loch Eriboll, Glsgw	C.B. Qbc, H'fx	180 [2]	n/k	n/k
Marion of Glasgow	s	670	1852	Glsgw	Qbc	297 [2]	1848, Qbc	A1
Marquis of Stafford	n/k	n/k	1851	Storno-way & Troon	Qbc	500 [1]	n/k	n/k
Mars	sw	208	1808 –19	Oban, Mull, Grnk	P.E.I., Qbc, Saint John	363 [3]	1806, Sunderland	A1
Mary Ann of London	bk	275	1841	Grnk	Qbc	220 [1]	1827, Bridlington	AE1
Mary Kennedy	n/k	n/k	1829	Skye	Sydney & P.E.I.	400[1]	n/k	n/k

Vessel/	Type	Tons	Year(s) Sailed	Depart	Arrive	Psgr Nos & crossings	Year & place built	Lloyd's Code
Mary of Newcastle	bg	n/k	1830	Loch Snizort & Tobermory	Qbc	330 [1]	n/k	n/k
Melissa	s	652	1855	Lewis Loch	Qbc	330 [1]	1843, Qbc	AE1
Melissa of Grnk	n/k	n/k	1852	Glsgw	Qbc	350 [1]	n/k	n/k
Mennie of N. B.	s	274	1802	Port Glsgw	P.E.I.	274 [1]	1802, N.B.	A1
Merlin	n/k	n/k	1842	Grnk	Qbc	185 [1]	n/k	n/k
Mohawk of Grnk	s	426	1841 –43	Glsgw	Qbc	161 [4]	1840, Grnk	A1
Molson of Dundee	sw	214	1831 –33	Dundee	Qbc	300 [3]	1830, Dundee	AE1
Monarch	n/k	n/k	1823	Tobermory	Qbc	259 [1]	n/k	n/k
Montezuma of Liverpool	bk	462	1851	Loch Boisdale	Qbc	440 [1]	1846, Qbc	A1
Morningfield of Ab'n	bg	141	1819	Tobermory	Pictou & P.E.I.	264 [1]	1816, Aberdeen	A1
Mount Stewart Elphinstone of Glsgw	s	387	1849	Loch Boisdale	Qbc	129 [1]	1826, Grnk	AE1
Nailer	s	313	1830 –33	Grnk	Qbc	379 [4]	1828, Qbc	A1
Nancy of Dumfries	bg	208	1818	Dumfries	P.E.I., Saint John & Miramichi	164 [2]	1817, Dumfries	A1
Nancy of South Shields	s	330	1817	Leith	H'fx & Qbc	164 [1]	1772, Scarborough	E1
Neptune	bg	n/k	1821 –30	Leith	Qbc	207 [2]	n/k	n/k
Neptune of Grnk	s	308	1802	Loch Nevis	Qbc	600 [1]	1802, N. B.	A1

Vessel/	Type	Tons	Year(s) Sailed	Depart	Arrive	Psgr Nos & crossings	Year & place built	Lloyd's Code
Nichol- son	n/k	n/k	1832	Maryport	Qbc	183 [1]	n/k	n/k
Nith of Liverpool	n/k	650	1840	Uig & Tober- mory	P.E.I., Sydney	550 [1]	n/k	n/k
Nora	n/k	372	1801	Fort William	Pictou	500 [1]	n/k	n/k
Northern Friends of Clyde	s	240	1802	Moidart	Sydney	340 [1]	1795, Finland [A prize.]	E1
Northum -berland	bk	361	1832	Tober- mory	St. Andrews	355 [1]	1828, N.B.	E1
Ocean of Liverpool	n/k	n/k	1841	Portree, Skye	P.E.I.	335 [1]	n/k	n/k
Osprey of Leith	s	382	1840	Cromarty & Thurso	Pictou & Qbc	150 [1]	1819, Grnk	AE1
Ossian of Leith	bg	194	1821 –22	Cromarty & Fort William	Pictou & Qbc	235 [2]	1813, Leith	A1
Oughton	bg	207	1803 –04	Uist, Kirk- cudbright	P.E.I. & Qbc	302 [2]	1787, Leith	E2
Oxford	s	401	1832	Leith	Qbc	300 [1]	1804, Whitby	E1
Pacific of Ab'n	bk	386	1835 –43	Cromarty, Thurso, Ab'n	Qbc & Pictou	495 [6]	1826, Ab'n	AE1
					[Dimensions: 102' x 26' 2" x 18' 7"]			
Pactolus	n/k	n/k	1842	Glsgw	Qbc	182 [1]	n/k	n/k
Panama of Liverpool	n/k	n/k	1847	Loch Laxford	Qbc	279 [1]	n/k n/k	n/k
Pekin of Liverpool	bg	288	1839	Storn- oway	P.E.I.	266 [1]	1833, Qbc	AE1
Persever- ence of Ab'n	bg	116	1814 –18	Cromarty, Storn- oway	Pictou, Qbc	202 [4]	n/k, Foreign	n/k
					[Dimensions: 65' 4" x 20' 10' x 11' 6"]			
Perthshire of Grnk	bk	459	1851	Loch- boisdale	Qbc	437 [1]	1841, N. S.	A1
Philadel- phia	s	300	1785	n/k	Qbc	300 [1]	1773, Hull	E1

Vessel/	Type	Tons	Year(s) Sailed	Depart	Arrive	Psgr Nos & crossings	Year & place built	Lloyd's Code
Polly	s	281	1803	Grnk	P.E.I.	400 [1]	1762, Whitby	E1
Polly of Glsgw	bk	629	1852 –55	Glsgw	Qbc	409 [3]	1845, Quebec	AE1
Portaferry	bg	283	1832 –33	Grnk	Qbc	319 [2]	1819, Workington	E1
Portia	bk	n/k	1834	Grnk	Qbc	171 [1]	n/k	n/k
Prince George of Alloa	bg	312 –51	1832	Alloa, Leith, Stornoway	Qbc	267 [4]	1789, London	AE1
Prince of Wales	s	342	1812 –15	Stromness, Stornoway	Hudson's Bay	272 [4]	1793, n/k	E1
Prompt of Bo'ness	s	333 –20	1817	Leith	H'fx & Qbc	521 [3]	1816, M'tl	A1
Queen of Grnk	bg	200	1791	Grnk	P.E.I.	300 [1]	1782, Hull	A1
Rambler of Leith	bg	296	1806 –07	Stromness, Tobermory	Pictou, P.E.I.	260 [2]	1800, Leith	A1

[Ship wrecked in 1807 with the loss of 138 people.]

Vessel/	Type	Tons	Year(s) Sailed	Depart	Arrive	Psgr Nos & crossings	Year & place built	Lloyd's Code
Rebecca of Grnk	s	305	1817 –32	Grnk	Qbc	364 [11]	1816, Grnk	E1
Renfrewshire	n/k	n/k	1842	Glsgw	Qbc	568 [1]	n/k	n/k
Renown of Ab'n	bk	289	1854 –55	Ab'n	Qbc	228 [3]	1842, Ab'n	AE1
Retrench of Grnk	bg	314	1833	Grnk	Qbc	299 [1]	1826, N. B.	AE1
Rival	bg	335	1831	Grnk	Qbc	333 [1]	1825, N. B.	E1
Roger Stewart	s	300	1832 –43	Grnk	Qbc	179 [2]	1811, Mass.	E1
Romulus of Grnk	bk	467	1831 –43	Grnk	H'fx, Qbc	223 [3]	1831, N.B.	AE1
Rosina of Campbeltown	bk	614 –53	1848	Grnk	Qbc	622 [3]	1845, Qbc	A1
Rother	sr	270	1840	Tobermory	P.E.I.	229	1835, Sunderland	A1

Vessel/	Type	Tons	Year(s) Sailed	Depart	Arrive	Psgr Nos & crossings	Year & place built	Lloyd's Code
Royal	bk	417	1836	Grnk	Saint	493 [2]	1830, N.B.	AE1
Salmes	bg	287	1831	Inverness	Qbc	250 [1]	1826, Qbc	A1
Saphiras of Whitby	sw	277	1841	Loch Laxford	Qbc	202 [1]	1838, Sunderland	A1
Sarah	n/k	n/k	1832	Maryport	Qbc	165 [1]	n/k	n/k
Sarah Botsford of Glsgw	bk	306 –51	1841	Glsgw	Pictou, Qbc	287 [3]	1840, N. B.	A1
Sarah Mariana	sw	194	1831	Maryport	Qbc	164 [1]	1816, Chester	E
Sarah of Ab'n	bg	232	1840 –52	Aberdeen	Qbc	303 [9]	1839, Ab'n	n/k
Sarah of Liverpool	n/k	372	1801	Fort William	Pictou	350 [1]	n/k	n/k
Scotia of Belfast	s	624 –49	1848	Loch Eribol	Qbc	390 [2]	1844, Richibucto	AE1
Sesostris of Glsgw	s	632	1851	Glsgw	Qbc	302 [1] [Dimensions: 139' x 28' x 21']	1840, N. S.	AE1
Sharp	sw	240	1832	Cromarty	Qbc	206 [1]	1831, Sunderland	A1
Sillery of Liverpool	s	994	1853	Skye	Qbc	339 [1]	1853, Qbc	A1
Sir William Wallace of Ab'n	bg	183 –55	1836	Ab'n	Qbc	325 [6]	1835, Ab'n	n/k
Six Sisters	sr	123	1831 –32	Stornoway	Wallace, N.S.	242 [2]	1830, Scotland	A1
Skeene of Leith	bg	250	1817 –19	Leith	H'fx	335 [3] [Dimensions: 86' x 24' 2" x 14' 7"]	1815, Leith	A2
Spartan of Grnk	s	681	1851	Glsgw	Qbc	244 [1]	1845, N. B.	AE1
Speculation	s	205	1819 –20	Oban, Fort William	H'fx, Pictou, Saint John & Qbc	270 [2]	n/k, America	E1
Springhill of Irvine	bk	348 –52	1834 ossan	Ardr-	Qbc	252 [5]	1826, N. B.	E1

Vessel/	Type	Tons	Year(s) Sailed	Depart	Arrive	Psgr Nos & crossings	Year & place built	Lloyd's Code
St Lawr- *ence* of Ab'n	bk	352 –54	1842	Ab'n	Qbc	1896 [22]	1841, Ab'n	A1
St. Lawr- *ence* of Newcastle	s	335	1828	Leith	Ship Harbour N.S.	208 [1]	1825, Newcastle	A1
Staffa	bg	268	1831	Grnk	P.E.I.	221 [2]	1830, P.E.I.	A1
Stephen	n/k	n/k	1827	Tober- mory	C,B., N.B.	193 [1]	n/k	n/k
Stephen *Wright* Newcastle	sw of	262	1827	Tober- mory	Sydney	170 [1]	1820, Newcastle	A1
Stirling	n/k	203	1841	Glsgw	Qbc	154 [1]	n/k	n/k
Stirling *Castle* of Grnk	bg	351	1830 –34	Grnk	Qbc	582 [2]	1829. Miramichi	AE1
Stranraer	n/k	n/k	1833 –36	Stranraer	Qbc	175 [5]	n/k	n/k
Superb of Grnk	bk	599	1838 –43	Grnk	Qbc	211 [2]	1837, N. B.	A1
Superior of Peter- head	bk	306	1842	Cromarty & Thurso	Pictou & Qbc	191 [1]	1813, Shields	AE1
Susan of Glsgw	bk	321 –54	1851	Glsgw	Qbc	477 [4]	1847, P.E.I.	A1
Swift of Sunderland	sw	280	1857	Cromarty	Qbc	215 [1]	1837, Sunderland	A1
Sylvanus of North Shields	sw	263	1832	Cromarty	Pictou, Qbc	237 [1]	1826, Sunderland	A1
Tamerlane of Grnk	s	390	1825 –33	Grnk	Qbc, Sydney	950 [6]	1824, N. B.	A1
Tay of Glsgw	bk	470	1841 –52	Loch- maddy, Glsgw	C. B., Qbc	1157 [4]	1840, N.B.	AE1
Thomp- *son's* *Packet* of Dumfries	bg	201	1821 –22	Dum- fries	Pictou & Qbc	213 [2]	1817, n/k	A1

Vessel/	Type	Tons	Year(s) Sailed	Depart	Arrive	Psgr Nos & crossings	Year & place built	Lloyd's Code
Three Bells s of Glsgw		730	1850 –54	Glsgw	Qbc	381 [4]	1850, Dumbarton	A1
Three Brothers of Hull	s	357	1816	Stornoway	Pictou & Miramichi	306 [1]	1801, Sweden	E1
Traveller of Ab'n	bg	195	1819 –20	Ab'n & Tobermory	Qbc	163 [2]	1819, Ab'n	n/k
Troubadour of Irvine	bk	298	1842	Glsgw	Qbc	224 [1]	1840, N. S.	A1
Tuskar of Liverpool	s	900	1849	Stornoway	Qbc	496 [1]	1845, N. B.	AE1
Tweed	bk	n/k	1836	Cromarty	Qbc	245 [1]	n/k	n/k
Two Sisters	bg	139	1828 –29	Grnk	Sydney	190 [2]	1827, Pictou	A
Unity	s	219e	1792	Grnk	Qbc	200 [1]	1791, Ayr	A1
Universe of Ab'n	bk	281	1828 –41	Stornoway	Sydney	588 [2]	1826, Ab'n	A1
Urgent of Belfast	s	592	1851	Stornoway	Qbc	370 [1]	1839, Qbc	AE1
Vestal	n/k	n/k	1829	Tobermory	Sydney & P.E.I.	301 [1]	n/k	n/k
Victoria of Dundee	sw	252	1832 –40	Dundee & Leith	Qbc	218 [6]	1832, Dundee	AE1
Viewforth of Kirkaldy	bk	289	1836	Cromarty	Qbc	150 [1]	1830, Shields	A1
Wandsworth s of Glsgw		767	1850	Grnk	Qbc	377 [1]	1839, Qbc	A1
Washington of Liverpool	n/k	n/k	1841	Skye	P.E.I.	551 [1]	n/k	n/k
Waterhen of London	bk	355	1849	Grnk	Qbc	167 [1]	1825, Hull	AE1
Wexford of Wexford	s	254	1842	Grnk	Qbc	200 [1]	1829, Qbc	AE1
William Glen Anderson of Glsgw	bk	389	1842	Ab'n	Qbc	152 [1]	1827, N. B.	AE1

Vessel/	Type	Tons	Year(s) Sailed	Depart	Arrive	Psgr Nos & crossings	Year & place built	Lloyd's Code
William Shand	n/k	n/k	1831	Berwick	Qbc	299 [1]	n/k	n/k
William Tell	n/k	n/k	1817	Grnk	C.B.	221 [1]	n/k	n/k
Wingrove of New-castle	sw	261	1842	Glsgw	Qbc	160 [1]	1839, Sunderland	A1
Wolfville of Ardrossan	bk	415 –2	1851	Loch Roag	Qbc	328 [2]	1841, N. S.	AE1
Zealous	n/k	n/k	1831	Leith	Qbc	182 [1]	n/k	n/k
Zephyr	n/k	650	1833	Cromarty	Pictou	150 [1] & Qbc	n/k	n/k

Appendix IV

ADULT TRANSATLANTIC FARES FROM SCOTTISH PORTS TO QUEBEC AND MARITIME PORTS, 1816–1854

c cabin fare; **I** intermediate fare; **s** steerage fare.
* denotes fare when provisions provided by shipper.

Year	Ship	Depart	Arrive	Fares	Sources
1804	*Commerce*	Oban	Quebec	£10 10s	NAS GD 202/70/12
1808	n/k	Highlands	Charlotte-	s £9	NLS MS 11976 ff3–4
1810	*Phoenix*	Tobermory town	Charlotte-	s £10 10s	LAC MG25–G426
1816	*North Star*	Dumfries	Richibucto	c £10 10s s £6 - £9 9s	*DGC* July 15
1819	*Good Intent*	Cromarty	Pictou	c £10 10s s £7 7s	*IJ* Jan. 15, March 3
1822	n/k	Clyde	Quebec	c £18 s £3 10s–£6 6s	Cameron, *Upper Canada*, 516
Early 1820s	n/k	Highlands	Cape Breton	s £3 10s–£4	Select Com. Emig. 1826, A329
1828	*Caroline* of Liverpool	Inverness	Pictou	s £3 10s	*IJ* Feb. 29
1832	n/k	Greenock	Quebec or New Brunswick	s £2–£2 10s s £4* - £5*	NAS GD 46/13/184
1840	*Percy* of Sunderland	Thurso	Quebec	s £2 10s	*JJ* March 20, 27

Year	Ship	Depart	Arrive	Fares	Sources
1841	n/k	Clyde	Quebec	s £3 10s–£4	Select Com. Emig. 1841, A1507
1841	n/k	Western Highlands	Quebec, Cape Breton, P.E.I.	s £4 1s (Inc. food)	Select Com. Emig. 1841, A192
1842	n/k	Leith	Quebec	c £10*–£12* I £5*–£6* s £2 10s–£3	Aberdeen University Special Collection (K61) *Information for Emigrants to British North America (1842)* 7–8.
1842	n/k	Leith	Halifax	c £12*–£15* I £5*–£7* s £4 4s–£4 10s	Ditto
1842	n/k	Greenock	Quebec	c £20* I £5*–£7* s £3 10s	Ditto
1842	n/k	Greenock I £5*–£7* s £3 10s	Halifax	c £16*	Ditto
1843	n/k	Clyde	Quebec	I £4 s £2	Cameron, *Upper Canada*, 516
1850	n/k	Clyde	Quebec	Ditto I £3 10s*–£4 10s* s £3*–£3 10s*	
1854	*John Mackenzie*	Glasgow Montreal	Quebec/	s £4 4s*	*AH* June 24
1854	Steamships inc. railway from Portland USA to Montreal	Greenock	Montreal	c £21* I £13 13s*–£15 15s* s £7 7s*	*IC* Feb. 9

NOTES

Chapter 1: Canada's Appeal

1. J.M. Bumsted (ed.), *The Collected Writings of Lord Selkirk*, vol. I (1799–1809): *Observations on the Present State of the Highlands of Scotland, with a View of the Causes and Probable Consequences of Emigration* (Winnipeg: Manitoba Record Society, 1984) 169; hereinafter *Selkirk's Observations*.
2. Maureen Williams, "John MacLean: His Importance as a Literary and Social Personality," paper for the Antigonish Heritage Society, Sept. 9, 1985.
3. Highland emigration poetry is discussed in Michael Kennedy, "Lochaber No More: A Critical Examination of Highland Emigration Mythology," in Marjory Harper and Michael E. Vance (eds.), *Myth, Migration and the Making of Memory* (Halifax and Edinburgh: Fernwood & John Donald, 1999) 267–97.
4. LAC SP (C–14) 14899–900: James Williams to Governor Fanning, Aug. 4, 1805.
5. For general background on the factors that induced Scots to emigrate, see Marjory Harper, *Adventurers and Exiles: The Great Scottish Exodus* (London: Profile Books, 2003) 71–111.
6. J.M. Bumsted, *The People's Clearance: Highland Emigration to British North America 1770–1815* (Edinburgh: Edinburgh University Press, 1982) 229.
7. *1827 Emigration Select Committee*, A142–145: Evidence of James Foster and James Little, both members of the Glasgow Emigration Society.
8. John Hart, *Diary of a Voyage of John Hart of Perth Ontario, who left Glasgow, Scotland ... on the 15th April, 1842 ... arriving in Quebec, 5th June, 1842* (W.A. Newman, 1940) 14.
9. The official figures show that a total of 123,805 Scots arrived at Canadian ports between 1825 and 1855 (British Parliamentary Papers: Emigration Returns from British North America, 1839–40; Colonial Land and Emigration Commissioners, *Annual Reports*, 1841–55). However, Canada was often used as a backdoor entry route to the United States. As a consequence, port arrival statistics will overstate the actual numbers who emigrated to Canada. Philip Buckner, *English Canada – the Founding Generations: British Migration to British North America, 1815–1865* (Canada House, Lecture Series no. 54 (ISBN 0265–4253), Canadian High Commission, London) 9–13.
10. Australia attracted Scots in large numbers only between 1852 and 1864, when emigration schemes offering free transport were available.
11. N.H. Carrier and J.R. Jeffrey, *External Migration: A Study of the Available Statistics 1815–1950* (London: HMSO, 1953) 27, 95–6; Michael W. Flinn (ed.), *Scottish Population History from the Seventeenth Century to the 1930s* (Cambridge: Cambridge University Press, 1977) 441–55.
12. With the ending of hostilities in 1763, many Acadians returned to the eastern Maritimes, although they were confined mainly to remote areas and to relatively poor land. W.S. MacNutt, *The Atlantic Provinces: The Emergence of Colonial Society 1712–1857* (London:

Oxford University Press, 1965) 62, 63, 113; Phillip Buckner and John G. Reid (eds.), *The Atlantic Region to Confederation: A History* (Toronto: University of Toronto Press, 1993) 144–47, 164–65, 198–99. One thousand people from Yorkshire, all tenants of the Duke of Rutland's, also emigrated to Nova Scotia during the 1770s.

13. This policy led to bloodshed in the Maritime provinces but was carried through in Upper and Lower Canada with little disturbance, owing to the greater abundance of land there.

14. Lower Canada was by far the largest of the British colonies, having a population of 250,000 by 1806. They were the descendents of the 3,000 or so French immigrants who had settled in New France by the mid-seventeenth century. For population figures, see Joseph Bouchette, *The British Dominions in North America: A Topographical and Statistical Description of the Provinces of Lower and Upper Canada, New Brunswick, Nova Scotia, the Islands of Newfoundland, Prince Edward Island and Cape Breton,* vol. II (London, 1832) 235.

15. J.M. Bumsted, *The Peoples of Canada, a Pre-Confederation History,* vol. I (Toronto: Oxford University Press, 1992) 65–79, 91–93.

16. Lucille H. Campey, *Les Écossais: The Pioneer Scots of Lower Canada, 1763–1855* (Toronto: Natural Heritage Books, 2006) 60–64

17. Lilian F. Gates, *Land Policies of Upper Canada* (Toronto: University of Toronto Press, 1968) 303–07.

18. Helen Cowan, *British Emigration to British North America: The First Hundred Years* (Toronto: University of Toronto Press, 1961) 7–12.

19. Buckner and Reid, *The Atlantic Region to Confederation,* 184–209; Bumsted, *The Peoples of Canada,* 166–78.

20. The old province of Quebec was partitioned in 1791 into Upper and Lower Canada; Fernand Ouellet, *Le Bas Canada 1791–1840; changements structuraux et crise* (Ottawa: Ottawa University, 1976), translated and adapted by Patricia Claxton as *Lower Canada, 1791–1840: Social Change and Nationalism* (Toronto: McClelland & Stewart, 1980) 22–36.

21. Lucille H. Campey, *After the Hector: The Scottish Pioneers of Nova Scotia and Cape Breton, 1773–1852* (Toronto: Natural Heritage Books, 2004. 34–55.

22. Esther Clark Wright, *The Loyalists of New Brunswick* (Fredericton, NB: nk, 1955) 120, 196–200.

23. Colonization was greatly assisted in Upper Canada by the establishment of the Canada Company in 1826 and in Lower Canada by the creation of the British American Land Company in 1834. These enterprises bought large tracts of land and sold them to bona fide settlers, on the understanding that they would be provided with an infrastructure of buildings and roads within which to develop their communities.

24. Church registers indicate that only about 8 per cent of eighteenth- and nineteenth-century emigrants were Scottish-born and originated mainly from the Clyde. W.G. Handcock, "Spatial Patterns in a Transatlantic Migration Field: The British Isles and Newfoundland during the Eighteenth and Nineteenth Centuries," in Brian S. Osborne (ed.), *Proceedings of the 1975 British-Canadian Symposium on Historical Geography. The Settlement of Canada: Origins and Transfer* (Kingston, ON: Queen's University Press, 1976) 13, 19, 32.

25. Kelp, which was extracted from seaweed, was used in the production of soap and glass.

26. Emigration Select Committee, 1826–27, Abstract of Petitions.

27. After sailing from Quebec to Montreal, the journey inland for emigrants became cumbersome. Passengers were first transferred to steamboats and then were moved onto large Durham boats that were dragged up the river to Prescott in Upper Canada. At the various rapids, people had to get off and proceed on foot. John Murray Gibbon, *Scots in*

Canada: A History of the Settlement of the Dominion from the Earliest Days to the Present Time (London: Kegan Paul, Trench, Trubner & Co. Ltd, 1911) 99–100. See also NAS GD 46/13/184: *Information published by His Majesty's Commissioners for Emigration respecting the British Colonies in North America* (London, Feb., 1832) 7–8.

28. Ralph Davis, *The Industrial Revolution and British Overseas Trade* (Leicester: Leicester University Press, 1979) 48–49. Duties increased from 25 shillings per load in 1804 to 54s. 6d. per load in 1811. Between 1814 and 1843, Baltic timber was sometimes shipped to North America and then back to Britain, as the saving of duty more than compensated for the double freight.

29. The timber trade had less impact in western Upper Canada. Potash and pearl ashes, which could be shipped more economically, had a market in Britain, but not the timber itself. A.R.M. Lower, "Settlement and the Forest Frontier in Eastern Canada," in W.A. Mackintosh and W.L.G. Jaerg (eds.), *Canadian Frontiers of Settlement*, vol. IX (Toronto: Macmillan, 1936) 40–47.

30. Lucille H. Campey, *'A Very Fine Class of Immigrants': Prince Edward Island's Scottish Pioneers, 1770–1850* (Toronto: Natural Heritage Books, 2001) 66–79.

31. John S. Moir, *The Church in the British Era, from the British Conquest to Confederation* (Toronto: McGraw-Hill Ryerson, 1972) 135–37.

32. Father MacEachern's patch also included Saint John, Fredericton, and the Miramichi in New Brunswick. SCA BL 5/81/18, Angus MacEachern to Dr A. Cameron, June 23, 1820.

33. The Society, in connection with the Established Church of Scotland, for Promoting the Religious Interests of Scottish Settlers in British North America was founded in 1825. Having been established by Glaswegians, it later came to be known by its condensed name – "the Glasgow Colonial Society."

34. Rev. William Bell, *Hints to Emigrants in a Series of Letters from Upper Canada* (Edinburgh: Waugh & Innes, 1824) 102–04.

35. Isabel Skelton, *A Man Austere* (Toronto: Ryerson Press, 1947) 118–19.

36. Having built their new Presbyterian church in Charlottetown, the church elders needed financial help to pay a minister's salary and debts. The Established Church congregation was too small to support the church. LAC M–1352: Elders of St. James Church, Charlottetown, to Rev. Burns, April 30, 1833.

37. S.D. Clark, *Church and Sect in Canada* (Toronto: University of Toronto Press, 1948) 178–80.

38. Martin Hewitt, "The Itinerant Emigration Lecturer: James Brown's Lecture Tour of Britain and Ireland, 1861-2," in *British Journal of Canadian Studies*, 10, no. 1 (1995) 103–19.

39. PANB MC295/3/305: James Brown to A.H. Gilmour, June 5, 1862.

40. CO 384/34 ff. 261, 271: Isabella MacKenzie to the Colonial Office, Feb. 12 and March 5, 1834.

41. Lucille H. Campey, *With Axe and Bible: The Scottish Pioneers of New Brunswick, 1784–1874* (Toronto: Natural Heritage Books/Dundurn Group, 2007) 105–13.

42. PANB RS24 1838/pe, file 4, petition no. 77: petition of thirty-three Skye families in 1838.

43. Emigrants had access to wider-ranging advice from emigration guidebooks and travelogues, although these varied greatly in quality and reliability. See Marjory Harper, "Image and Reality in Early Emigrant Literature," in *British Journal of Canadian Studies*, 7 (1992) 3–14.

44. AO F495 MU 2659 Acc 6122: Extract of a paper by Dr Angus Campbell, Feb. 22, 1961.

Chapter 2: Emigration Frenzy

1. *EA*, Sept. 28, 1773.
2. However, between 1763 and 1775 the numbers leaving the Highlands and leaving the Islands were nearly equal. For a detailed breakdown of figures, see Bumsted, *The People's Clearance*, 229.
3. *SM*, vol. XXXII (1770) 457, gives figures for the Western Isles and Highlands; vol. XXXIII (1771) 325, 500, for Islay and Skye; vol. XXXIV (1772) 395, 515–16, for Sutherland and the Western Isles; vol. XXXV (1773) 499, 557, for west Inverness-shire, Sutherland, and Lewis; vol. XXXVI, (1774) 157–58, 558, for Sutherland and Orkney; vol. XXXVII (1775) 340, 690, for Argyll and the north Highlands, including west Inverness-shire, Caithness, and Orkney; NAS RH.1/2/933 (1–13): The Lord Justice Clerk's Report to the Earl of Suffolk in April 1774, "Scottish Emigration to North America, 1769–1773," provides detailed parish figures for Argyll and Bute, Ross-shire, Morayshire, and Nairnshire. Passenger lists giving the geographical origins of emigrants were produced in 1774–75. These have been reprinted by Viola Root Cameron in *Emigrants from Scotland to America 1774–1775* (London, 1930, reprinted Baltimore: Genealogical Publishing Co., 1965).
4. Bumsted, *People's Clearance*, 228.
5. T.M. Devine, *Exploring the Scottish Past: Themes in the History of Scottish Society* (East Linton: Tuckwell Press, 1995) 33–181; T.M. Devine, *The Great Highland Famine, Hunger, Emigration and the Scottish Highlands in the Nineteenth Century* (Edinburgh: John Donald, 1988) 1–33.
6. Sir John Sinclair, *First Statistical Account of Scotland*, vol. XII (21 vols.) (Edinburgh: 1791–99) 155.
7. Ibid.
8. *SA*, vol. XVII, 76.
9. Eric Richards, *A History of the Highland Clearances: Emigration, Protest, Reasons* (London: Croom Helm, 1982–85) 196–204; Malcolm Gray, *The Highland Economy 1750–1850* (Edinburgh: Oliver & Boyd, 1957) 86–104.
10. T.M. Devine, "Temporary Migration and the Scottish Highlands in the Nineteenth Century," in *Economic History Review*, 32 (1979) 344–59; T. M. Devine, "Highland Migration to Lowland Scotland 1760–1860," in *Scottish Historical Review*, 62 (1983) 347–51.
11. The industry was highly profitable from the late eighteenth century on, reaching its high point about 1810. Bumsted, *The People's Clearance*, 41–43, 84–88.
12. Robert Brown, *Strictures and Remarks on the Earl of Selkirk's Observations on the Present State of the Highlands* (Edinburgh: Abemethy & Walker, 1806) 94.
13. Ian McGowan (ed.), *Samuel Johnson, A Journey to the Western Isles of Scotland* (Edinburgh: Canongate, 2001) 51.
14. In 1773, some eight hundred people from Skye and North Uist were intending to emigrate to America: National Library of Scotland (NLS) MS1306, 54, 55, 68. McGowan (ed.), *Samuel Johnson*, 58. Ian Adams and Meredyth Somerville, *Cargoes of Despair and Hope: Scottish Emigration to North America 1603–1803* (Edinburgh: John Donald, 1993) 96.
15. *SA*, vol. XX, 160–61.
16. NAS RH.1/2/933 (12).
17. *AJ*, Sept. 27, 1773. SM (1773), 557. The Lewis emigrants sailed to New York.
18. Kenneth MacKenzie, who had the title of Viscount Fortrose, was made Earl of Seaforth in 1771. He left no male heirs.
19. *AJ*, Sept. 27, 1773.

20. NLS MS 10787: Letter book of John Davidson of Stewartfield, ff. 1–2: letter to George Gillanders, factor to Earl Seaforth, May 16, 1774; see also letter to John Mackenzie, May 16, 1774.
21. Ibid, letter to John Mackenzie, Aug. 20, 1774.
22. Ibid, letter to George Gillanders, May 16, 1774.
23. *SA*, vol. XX, 117, 118.
24. Ibid.
25. Bishop George Hay was a leading supporter of the emigration scheme. For details of the Scottish Catholic Church's involvement, see J.M. Bumsted, *Land Settlement and Politics on Eighteenth Century Prince Edward Island* (Kingston: McGill-Queen's University Press, 1987) 55–61.
26. Tacksmen were an elite class in the Scottish feudal system who acted as factors or farm managers under a laird. They usually sublet much of their own land to sub-tenants who did most of the work on the great Highland estates.
27. The Jacobites suffered a bloody and savage defeat on the battlefield of Culloden in 1745–46. In addition to the seizure of some Highland estates, other reprisals were introduced, including the proscription of Highland dress.
28. Donald MacKay, *Scotland Farewell: The People of the 'Hector'* (Toronto: Natural Heritage Books, 1996) 44–59. The estates, which were forfeited after the Jacobite uprising of 1745–46, were returned to their original owners in the 1780s.
29. NAB CO 217/50, 62: Francis Legge to Earl of Dartmouth, May 10, 1774.
30. NLS MS 3431 f.180 (Lee Papers): "Observations or remarks upon land and islands which compose the barony called Harris" – a prospectus of 1772 drawn up apparently for the projected sale of Harris by Norman MacLeod of MacLeod.
31. *SM*, vol. XXXIV (1772), 515.
32. *SM*, vol. XXXV (1773), 667.
33. NAS RH.1/2/933, 1–13.
34. The passenger lists produced from this exercise have been reprinted in Viola Root Cameron, *Emigrants from Scotland to America 1774–1775* (Baltimore: Genealogical Publishing Co., 1965).
35. Bumsted, *The People's Clearance*, 23.
36. Marianne McLean, *People of Glengarry 1745–1820: Highlanders in Transition* (Montreal: McGill-Queen's University Press, 1991) 78–97.
37. NLS MS 9646, "On Emigration from the Scottish Highlands and Islands," attributed to Edward Fraser of Reelig (1801–1804), ff. 19, 21, 23, 27.
38. *SA*, vol. XIII, 14, 16; vol. XVII, 74–76. The west Inverness-shire settlers had sailed to Quebec on the *Macdonald* (1786), *Neptune* (1788), *British Queen* of Greenock (1790), *Unity* (1792), *Argyle* (1793), *Helen* of Irvine, *Jean* of Irvine, *Neptune* of Greenock, and *Friends of John Saltcoats* (1802); for further details of the crossings, see Appendix I.
39. NLS Adv MS 35.6.18 f. 10: Melville Papers, "State of Emigration from the Highlands of Scotland, its extent, causes and proposed remedy, London, March 21, 1803," ff. 10–11.
40. Passenger data account for a total Scottish influx of about 4,000 people, of whom roughly 3,000 had Inverness-shire origins.
41. Joseph Bouchette, *British Dominions in North America*, vol. II, 235.
42. Marjory Harper, *Emigration from North-East Scotland*, vol. I, *Willing Exiles* (Aberdeen: Aberdeen University Press, 1988) 156–90; Devine, *Exploring the Scottish Past*, 107–13; Eric Richards, "Varieties of Scottish Emigration in the Nineteenth Century," *Historical Studies*, 21 (1985) 473–94.

43. NLS MS 6602 ff. 21–5: George Dempster to Henry Dundas, 1784.
44. NAB CO 42/82 ff. 2–21: Council Minutes, Jan. 11, 1791.
45. The emigrants also received food supplies from Montreal merchants.
46. NAB CO 42/82 ff. 6–7.
47. James Barron, *The Northern Highlands in the Nineteenth Century Newspaper Index and Annals*, vol. III (3 vols.) (Inverness: R. Carruther & Sons, 1903–13) 400.
48. *SA*, vol. XIX, 93–4. Initially, Orcadians went out to work for the Hudson's Bay Company as indentured servants, remaining for a minimum of three years, then returning home. But from 1821 onwards, many became permanent residents of the Red River settlement, which was founded by Scots under the direction of Lord Selkirk (see chapter 4).
49. Patrick Campbell, *Travels in the Interior: Inhabited Parts of British North America in 1790 and 1792*, vol. XXIII (Toronto: Champlain Society, 1937) 49.
50. NLS MS 9646 f. 41.
51. Brown, *Strictures and Remarks*. See the Appendix, "State of Emigrations, 1801, 1802 and 1803," which names the shipping agents who provided crossings to the various emigrant groups between 1801 and 1803.
52. NAB CO 217, vol. 63: John Parr to Henry Dundas, Sept. 27, 1791.
53. Ibid., John Parr to Evan Nepean, 1791.
54. *CM*, Dec. 22, 1791.
55. The British government would have preferred to have English-speaking Anglican colonizers. However, most of the British arrivals to Nova Scotia before 1803 were Gaelic-speaking Catholic Highlanders.
56. Father Alexander MacDonald, writing in 1802, quoted by Bumsted, *The People's Clearance*, 75.
57. NLS MS 9646 ff. 15–49, Adv. MS.35.6.18 ff. 8–19: Much emigration was taking place from Inverness-shire and Sutherland.
58. NAS RH 4/188/2 f. 476: Highland Society of Edinburgh, Report of the Committee on Emigration, Jan. 1802.
59. NAS GD 9/166/23, 23A: Dr William Porter to John MacKenzie, Dec. 27, 1802.
60. NAS GD 248 3410/10: Duncan Grant to Sir James Grant, March 2, 1801.
61. NLS TD219/12/3: Campbell of Succoth family records, John MacNeill (senior) to John MacNeill (junior), May 2, 1803.
62. NAS GD 248/3416/3/25. For example, the customs collector at Dundee was directed in May 1803 "to provide an account of the number of vessels carrying more than 30 passengers cleared in 1802" for ports in North America. See DCA CE 70/1/10, no. 53.
63. NAS RH 4/188/2 ff. 531–35. The four ships from Port Glasgow and Greenock were the *Northern Friends* of Clyde, which sailed to Sydney, Cape Breton; the *Neptune* of Greenock, which sailed to Quebec; the *Elora* (probably the *Aurora*), which sailed to Quebec; and the *Mennie*, which sailed to Charlottetown, Prince Edward Island. The additional three ships that sailed from Fort William were the *Friends of John Saltcoats*, the *Jean* of Irvine and the *Helen* of Irvine, which went to Quebec (see NLS MS 9646 ff. 21, 23).
64. NAS RH 4/188/2 ff. 642, 644: Third Report of the Committee on Emigration, March 25, 1803.
65. NLS Adv.MS.73.2.15 ff. 43–5: Royal Highland and Agricultural Society of Scotland Papers, notes of Edward Fraser of Reelig, March 1803.
66. RH 4/188/2 ff. 643.
67. NAS RH 4/188/2: Prize essays and transactions of the Highland Society of Scotland, 3 (1802–03) ff. 475–92. Report of the Committee on Emigration, Jan. 1802.

68. NAS RH 2/4/87 ff. 66–75.
69. The Select Committee relied on Thomas Telford, *A Survey and Report of the Coasts and Central Highlands of Scotland* (London: 1803), which was published by the government in April of that year. It set out the scale of the exodus and made various recommendations.
70. Bumsted, *The People's Clearance*, 142–3.
71. Lucille H. Campey, *Fast Sailing and Copper-Bottomed: Aberdeen Sailing Ships and the Emigrant Scots They Carried to Canada* (Toronto: Natural Heritage Books, 2002) 99–113.
72. NAS GD 46/17/vol. 23: Seaforth papers, E. Fraser to Lord Seaforth, Aug. 1803.
73. Bumsted, *The People's Clearance*, 129–54.
74. Alexander Irvine, *An Enquiry into the Causes and Effects of Emigration from the Highlands and Western Isles of Scotland with Observations on the Means Employed for Preventing it* (Edinburgh: 1802) 19, 54, 64–67.
75. The British Fisheries Society established fishing villages from the 1780s on as a means of extending employment opportunities in the Highlands.
76. NAS GD 9/166/2: Dr William Porter to Sir William Pulteney, Jan. 18, 1802.
77. Ibid.
78. NAS GD 9/166/23, 23A: Dr.William Porter to John MacKenzie, Dec. 27, 1802.
79. Scotland produced a remarkable number of world-renowned intellectuals within decades of the Act of Union with England in 1707. They contributed greatly to diverse fields of study, including science, law, philosophy, economics, and medicine. The term "Scottish Enlightenment" was first introduced by William Robert Scott in 1900 to describe this extraordinary phenomenon.
80. *Selkirk's Observations*, 102–03.
81. Similarly, an anonymous writer, author of *Eight Letters on the Subject of the Earl of Selkirk's Pamphlet on Highland Emigration as They Lately Appeared under the Signature of AMICUS in One of the Edinburgh Newspapers* (Edinburgh: J. Anderson; London: Longman, Hurst, Rees, and Orme, 1806), presented anti-North American sentiments coupled with overly optimistic accounts of the Highland economy.
82. In addition to Belfast, Lord Selkirk also founded Highland settlements at Baldoon (later Wallaceburg) in Upper Canada in 1804 and at Red River (later Winnipeg) in 1811.
83. For details of the Belfast settlers of 1803, see Lucille H. Campey, *'A Very Fine Class of Immigrants': Prince Edward Island's Scottish Pioneers, 1770–1850* (Toronto: Natural Heritage Books, 2001) 32–47.
84. LAC SP (A–27) 390H, 390J: Lady Selkirk to Lord Selkirk, Montreal, Hogmanay 1816.
85. The eight hundred Highlanders sailed on three ships: the *Polly*, the *Dykes*, and the *Oughton*. NAS GD 46/17/vol. 23: E. Fraser to Lord Seaforth, Aug. 1803.
86. *IJ*, Dec. 28, 1810; Feb. 1, 1811.
87. NLS MS 11976 ff. 3–4: comments in a journal, July 1808, of Gilbert, second Earl of Minto, recorded during a visit to Blair Atholl on extensive current emigration from the district to Prince Edward Island and its deliberate stimulation by emigration agents.
88. For details of the influx to Prince Edward Island between 1804 and 1810, see Lucille H. Campey, *The Silver Chief: Lord Selkirk and the Scottish Pioneers of Belfast, Baldoon and Red River* (Toronto: Natural Heritage Books, 2003) 24–50.
89. The *Clarendon* passenger list is in NAB CO 226/23; the remainder are to be found in PAPEI MSS 2702.
90. *IC*, Oct. 9, 1807; Feb. 8, 1808.
91. *Weekly Recorder of Charlottetown, Prince Edward Island*, no. 17 (Sept. 1810).
92. For a description of John Campbell's political and business life, see M.E. Vance, "Emigra-

tion and Scottish Society: The Background of Government Assisted Emigration to Upper Canada, 1815–21" (University of Guelph, unpublished Ph D thesis, 1990) 15–44.
93. NAB CO 42/165 ff. 180–5: Campbell to Bathurst, Oct. 14, 1815.
94. Similar schemes were offered to Scots in 1818 and in the early 1820s, although they were far less generous. Lucille H. Campey, *The Scottish Pioneers of Upper Canada, 1784–1855: Glengarry and Beyond* (Toronto: Natural Heritage Books, 2005) 35–68.

Chapter 3: Push, Pull, and Opportunity

1. MM PO21/3: William Brodie to Hugh Brodie, June 12, 1820.
2. Cotton was also being manufactured in Stirlingshire, the mid- and west Lothians, and the southwest Borders. R.H. Campbell, *Scotland since 1707: The Rise of an Industrial Society* (Edinburgh: Donald, 1985) 81–94; Ian Levitt and Christopher Smout, *The State of the Scottish Working Class in 1843: A Statistical and Spatial Enquiry Based on Data from the Poor Law Commission Report of 1844* (Edinburgh: Scottish Academic Press, 1979) 16–18, 236–58.
3. The economic vitality of the Clyde area attracted huge numbers of Irish workers who were concentrated in the lowest-paid sectors of the labour market.
4. Campbell, *Scotland since 1707*, 135–42. See also Bruce Lenman, *An Economic History of Modern Scotland 1600–1976* (London: Batsford, 1977) 116–21.
5. Some Scottish landowners, including the Duke of Hamilton, considered adopting a scheme that would have enabled distressed weavers to obtain small allotments of land. However, the Scottish laws of entail, which ensured that estate property remained within families, proved to be an insuperable barrier, and the scheme had to be dropped. Vance, "Emigration and Scottish Society," 147–8.
6. H.J.M. Johnston, *British Emigration Policy 1815–1830: Shovelling Out Paupers* (Oxford: Clarendon Press, 1972) 10–31. Although the scheme was not publicized in England, thirty English people submitted applications and were accepted.
7. Although it was intended that they would settle in the Rideau Valley, they insisted on joining their friends and relatives in Glengarry County.
8. NAB CO 42/165 ff. 134.
9. Johnston, *British Emigration Policy*, 17–27.
10. The 1815 group settled in the townships of Bathurst, Drummond, and Beckwith (in Lanark County), which formed the Perth military settlement. See Campey, *Scottish Pioneers of Upper Canada*, 35–51.
11. W.F. Ganong, "Monograph of the Origins of Settlements in the Province of New Brunswick," *Transactions of the Royal Society of Canada*, 2nd series (10), sections 1–2 (1904) 73.
12. *RG*, Dec. 3, 1815. Passenger list for the *Favourite* of Saint John is in PANB MC 300 MS 17/40 (m/f F9798). The fare was £7.10s.
13. Lucille H. Campey, *With Axe and Bible: The Scottish Pioneers of New Brunswick, 1784–1874* (Toronto: Natural Heritage Books/Dundurn Group, 2007) 78–81.
14. NAB CO 42/165 ff. 142–3: John Campbell to Lord Bathurst, May 6, 1815.
15. Notices in Bathurst's name appeared, for example, in the *Dumfries and Galloway Courier* (April 2, 1816) and the *Aberdeen Journal* (April 3, 1816).
16. MM PO21/3: William Brodie to Hugh Brodie, April 22, 1816.
17. *AJ*, April 3, 1816.

18. The Passenger Act of 1817 allowed vessels to carry less food, and the new space require-ment was calculated at one person for every one-and-a half tons.
19. Richards, *Highland Clearances*, 113, 116, 187. For a detailed analysis of the economic prob-lems being experienced on the Breadalbane estate, see Vance, "Emigration and Scottish Society," 45–124.
20. NAB CO 384/1 ff. 317–18: McDermid to Lord Bathurst, March 18, 1817.
21. NAB CO 384/1 ff. 71–2: Campbell to Goulburn, Feb. 11, 1817. The group also included people from Blair Atholl and Kincardine.
22. They sailed on three ships provided by the government – the *Curlew*, with 205 passen-gers; the *Sophia* of Ayr, with 106; and the *Jane* of Sunderland, with 131 (see NAB CO 384/3 ff. 123–7, 133–4, CO 226/36 f. 19). Passenger lists can be found in Campey, *Scot-tish Pioneers of Upper Canada*, 49–51, 197–99.
23. The 1818 groups settled in Beckwith and Goulbourn townships in Lanark County and in Osgoode Township in Carleton County.
24. They are thought to have settled at lots 26 and 27 in Seven Mile Bay. For their petition seeking help from the government see NAB CO 226/36 ff. 19. For further details of their settlement, see *The Scottish Catholics in Prince Edward Island 1772–1922*, Memorial Volume (Summerside, PEI: Journal Publishing Co., 1922) 58–59, and Cowan, *British Emigration to British North America* 44–45.
25. Richards, *Highland Clearances*, 119–79.
26. See chapter 6.
27. See chapter 5.
28. Hugh Miller, *Sutherland As It Was and Is: How a Country May Be Ruined* (Edinburgh: John Johnstone, 1843) 21.
29. Ibid., 16.
30. NLS SP Dep 313/1128/29: William Young to Earl Gower, May 1813.
31. While most Sutherlanders opted for Nova Scotia, some Kildonan people signed up with Lord Selkirk in 1813 and 1815 to go to the Red River Colony.
32. NLS SP Dep 313/1468: Francis Suther to James Loch, Dec. 24, 1817.
33. Ibid., Francis Suther to James Stuart, July 21, 1819; Francis Suther to James Loch, April 4, 1818.
34. NLS SP Dep 313/1139: James Loch to Francis Suther, Sept. 23, 1819.
35. Ibid., James Loch to Francis Suther, Sept. 23, Dec. 24, Dec. 28, 1819.
36. John Prebble, *The Highland Clearances* (London: Penguin, 1969), 117–29.
37. The unknown sources in Bengal were probably people connected with the East India Company, suggesting that the emigrants' benefactors were in commerce and trade.
38. NAS E.504/17/9; *IJ*, July 12, 1822. A passenger list for the *Ossian* crossing appears in *IJ*, June 29, 1821.
39. *IJ*, July 12, 1822.
40. Norman Murray, *The Scottish Hand Loom Weavers 1790–1850* (Edinburgh: John Donald, 1978) 141–47.
41. *GC*, June 10, 1819. Johnston, *British Emigration Policy*, 33–90.
42. *IC*, July 1, 1819.
43. Johnston, *British Emigration Policy*, 36, 37.
44. MM PO 21/7: Robert Brodie to Hugh Brodie, April 4, 1820.
45. The rebels were mainly unemployed artisans, including many impoverished weavers. T.M. Devine, *The Scottish Nation, 1700–2000* (London: Allen Lane, Penguin, 1999) 196–230; Vance, "Emigration and Scottish Society," 125–55.

46. The emigration societies had to act as guarantors for charitable donations and all advances of money paid by the government. Robert Lamond, *A Narrative of the Progress of Emigration from the Counties of Lanark and Renfrew to the New Settlements in Upper Canada on Government Grant* (Ottawa, ON: Canadian Heritage Publications, 1978), first published 1821.

47. NAB CO 384/6 ff. 788–9: Note on behalf of Lanarkshire Emigration Societies, April 27, 1820.

48. There were only three English emigration societies. Unlike English local authorities, which were required to provide poor relief for people capable of working, Scottish parishes had no similar obligation under the Scottish Poor Law. Thus, while English parishes might have had an incentive to use their funds to assist paupers to emigrate, Scottish parishes did not. This explains why emigration societies were confined largely to Scotland. See Johnston, *British Emigration Policy*, 5, 6, 40, 102–3.

49. The cost to the government was £31,200, and the Glasgow committee paid £6,800. This was far less that the £111,000 spent on 3,500 emigrants who went to the Cape of Good Hope. The 1820–21 groups settled in the townships of Lanark, Dalhousie, North Sherbrooke, and Ramsay, which formed the Lanark Military Settlement. See Campey, *Scottish Pioneers of Upper Canada*, 52–68.

50. Lamond, *Emigration from Lanark and Renfrew to Upper Canada*, 102.

51. Miller had been a member of the Anderston and Rutherglen Emigration Society. Letter quoted in Carol Bennett, *The Lanark Society Settlers, 1820–1821* (Renfrew, ON: Juniper Books, 1991) 49.

52. They would have included many tenants who had been cleared from Lowland estates from the late eighteenth century on. See Malcolm Gray, "The Social Impact of Agrarian Change in the Rural Lowlands," in T.M. Devine and Rosalind Mitchison (eds.), *People and Society in Scotland 1760–1830*, vol. I (Edinburgh: John Donald, 1988) 53–69. Also see Peter Aitchison and Andrew Cassell, *The Lowland Clearances, Scotland's Silent Revolution* (East Linton: Tuckwell, 2003) 127–41.

53. *Reports from the Select Committee appointed to inquire into the expediency of encouraging emigration from the United Kingdom, 1827* (A52–53).

54. John MacTaggart, *Three Years in Canada: An Account of the Actual State of the Country in 1826-7-8, Comprehending Its Resources, Productions, Improvements and Capabilities and including Sketches of the State of Society, Advice to Emigrants, etc.* (London: 1829) vol. I, 243.

55. A. Boag to his sister, Aug. 24, 1821, in Lamond, *Emigration from Lanark and Renfrew to Upper Canada*, 103.

56. Emigrant Scot writing home, May 5, 1821, in ibid, 104.

57. *GC*, April 18, 1820.

58. Ibid.

59. Lamond, *Emigration from Lanark and Renfrew to Upper Canada*, 64, 65.

60. They requested one hundred acres per family, "the means of subsistence for a few months… £6 for every adult and £3 for children under 14." NAB CO 384/7 ff. 643–45: Alexander McCallum to the Colonial Office, Feb. 1821; see also Ayrshire petition in NAB CO 384/15, 623.

61. NAB CO 384/11 f.1123: Archibald McNiven to Lord Bathurst, Dec. 13, 1825.

62. NAB CO 384/8 f. 435.

63. There are no official statistics for this period. The total number of people who emigrated between 1815 and 1821 can be estimated to be about 20,000. This figure is derived from newspaper shipping reports and customs records. However, given the under-recording of

passenger data in these sources this figure will be far short of the actual total.

64. Lord Dalhousie went out of his way to help immigrant weavers. For instance, he donated books to a library founded by former weavers in Dalhousie Township, Upper Canada (Campey, *Scottish Pioneers of Upper Canada*, 87).

65. Edward Ellice acquired the land as a result of purchases made by his father of land that had been granted previously by the government to veterans of the American War of Independence.

66. Robert Sellar, *History of the County of Huntingdon and of the Seigneuries of Chateauguay and Beauharnois from Their First Settlement to the Year 1838* (Huntingdon, QC: Canadian Gleaner, 1888) 149, 158, 159, 163, 166, 413–15.

67. Elgin Township was created from Hinchinbrook Township in 1855.

68. An early cemetery was located on an island near the Dalhousie settlement, east of Port Lewis. Following the construction of the Old Beauharnois Canal, the level of St. Francis Lake was raised and the island became submerged.

69. Sellar, *History of Huntingdon*, 163.

70. Burton Lang, *Place Names of South Western Quebec* (Howick, QC: self-published, 2001) 8, 26, 63.

71. The seigneuries were occupied mainly by indigenous French Canadians, who paid rents as tenants to a proprietor. Generally, settlers in seigneuries could not purchase any land.

72. Norman MacDonald, *Canada, Immigration and Settlement 1763–1841* (London: Longmans & Co., 1939) 482–3.

73. NAS GD 45/3/534/12: Petition from the inhabitants of New Glasgow, submitted Dec. 11, 1827.

74. Scotland's woollen industry was concentrated largely in the Scottish Borders, Perthshire, and Aberdeenshire. The major centres of linen manufacture were in Fife and Angus.

75. Wages were significantly higher in the eastern Borders, since it attracted few Irish migrants.

76. His letter, first published in Dumfriesshire newspapers, was reprinted in *GC*, June 15, 1817.

77. Ibid. Some of the families who emigrated under the government's assisted scheme of 1815 originated from the Border counties of Berwickshire, Dumfriesshire, Peeblesshire, and Roxburghshire.

78. *DGC*, April 13, 1819.

79. *GH*, April 13, 1821.

80. For further details of the Dumfriesshire communities in New Brunswick, see Lucille H. Campey, *With Axe and Bible: The Scottish Pioneers of New Brunswick, 1784–1874*, 52, 53, 58, 67, 75, 85, 88, 89, 94, 143–48.

81. J.F.W. Johnston, *Notes on North America: Agricultural, Economical and Social*, vol. I (Edinburgh: William Blackwood & Sons, 1851) 110. Although timber shipments would have arrived at the port of Annan, it is likely that emigrants left from the much bigger port of Dumfries.

82. George Patterson, *History of the County of Pictou, Nova Scotia* (Montreal: Dawson Bros., 1877) 278. Lucille H. Campey, *After the Hector: The Scottish Pioneers of Nova Scotia and Cape Breton, 1773–1852*, 90. The Scottish customs records (NAS E.504/9/9) show that four ships arrived at Pictou or the Miramichi from Dumfries in the period from 1816 to 1818.

83. Walter Johnstone, "A Series of Letters descriptive of Prince Edward Island, in the Gulf of St. Lawrence addressed to the Rev. John Wightman, minister of Kirkmahoe, Dumfriesshire." An extract from one of the nine letters has been taken from Daniel Cobb

Harvey (ed.), *Journeys to the Island of Saint John or Prince Edward Island, 1775–1832* (Toronto: Macmillan Co. of Canada, 1955) 142–3.

84. Emigration Select Committee, 1827 (A 2391–2419).
85. Patterson, *History of the County of Pictou*, 280.
86. Ibid.
87. For details of Prince Edward Island's Scottish communities, see Campey, *Very Fine Class*, 66–79.
88. The figures are taken from the Parliamentary Papers: Emigration Returns, 1830–40; Colonial Land and Emigration Annual Reports, 1841–55; Annual Reports of the Immigration Agent at Quebec, 1830–55. There are problems in interpreting these figures. Some Scots sailed to New York because it was usually a quicker sea voyage than was the crossing to Quebec. Thus they would be excluded. Moreover, these figures include Scots who did not necessarily settle in British North America. The United States, with its cheaper land and better economic opportunities, attracted a good many of the British immigrants – Scots included.
89. Emigration Select Committee, 1826–27, Appendix to the Third Report: Abstracts of Scotch Petitions and Memorials.
90. NAB CO 384/15 f. 623. In all, six emigration societies formed in Kilmarnock in 1827, representing 212 families. Many of the family heads would have been unemployed weavers.
91. The deliberations of the Emigration Select Committee of 1826–27 are discussed in Johnston, *British Emigration Policy*, 91–108.
92. A great many petitions for help were considered by the Select Committee in 1826–27, including one sent on behalf of 3,586 individuals from Glasgow and Paisley. NAB CO 384/15, 571–83. The committee considered that the large numbers of Irish workers in the Glasgow area were largely responsible for the economic distress being experienced there and recommended that measures be taken to stem the flow of Irish migrants
93. NAB CO 384/15 ff. 587–9.
94. Ibid., f. 553.
95. Emigration Select Committee, 1826–27, Abstract of Petitions.
96. Ibid.
97. NAS GD 201/4/97: Duncan Shaw to Alexander Hunter – application to government for assistance in sending the extra population of Benbecula to America.
98. Ibid.
99. Evidence given by Rev. Norman MacLeod to the Select Committee on Emigration in 1841 (A826). Also see Richards, *Highland Clearances*, 191.
100. A total of five hundred people were reported to have been "sent away " from Rum. See John Bowie's evidence to the Select Committee on Emigration of 1841 (A209–A216); also see John L. MacDougall, *History of Inverness County* (Truro, NS: New Pub. Co. Ltd., 1922) 126–31.
101. For example, James Hunter, in *A Dance Called America* (Edinburgh: Mainstream Publishing, 1994) 114, argues that because MacNeil's sheep-farm tenants were charged much higher rents for the land previously occupied by his departed tenants, his motive in offering an assisted emigration scheme must have been purely mercenary.
102. Emigration Select Committee, 1826–27, Abstract of Petitions (see, for example, the Hebridean petition dated April 30, 1827).
103. *IJ*, May 13, 1831.
104. NAS GD 46/11/9: Extracts of letters (1835) from Rev. John Stewart, Presbyterian minister in Cape Breton.

Chapter 4: Settlement Growth in Eastern Canada

1. Anon., *A Statement of the Satisfactory Results Which Have Attended Emigration to Upper Canada from the Establishment of the Canada Company until the Present Period* (London: 1841) 14–15. Extracts of Dr Alling's letter to the commissioners of the Canada Company, dated December 16, 1840, were quoted in this pamphlet published by the Canada Company in 1841.
2. Ibid.
3. Parliamentary Papers, *Emigration Returns for British North America* (1830–40); *Colonial Land and Emigration Commissioners, Annual Reports* (1841–55). Although some Highlanders would have sailed from the Clyde, their numbers were relatively small.
4. Andrew Hill Clark, *Three Centuries and the Island: A Historical Geography of Settlement and Agriculture in Prince Edward Island, Canada* (Toronto: University of Toronto Press, 1959) 42–57.
5. Bumsted, *Eighteenth Century Prince Edward Island*, 45–64.
6. Andrew B. MacEwan, "The *Falmouth* Passengers," *Island Magazine*, 10 (1981) 12–19.
7. Bumsted, *Eighteenth Century Prince Edward Island*, 53.
8. LAC MG23–J1: Rev. William Drummond fonds, ff. 6, 7.
9. After serving a four-year indenture, those who remained would have been entitled to two hundred to five hundred acres of wilderness land per man on easy terms.
10. Campey, *Very Fine Class*, 16–21.
11. Stewart's Argyll settlers sailed in the *Annabella*. Another group arrived in the *Edinburgh* in 1771 (see Appendix I).
12. Campey, *Very Fine Class*, 21, 22, 55, 58, 64.
13. Argyll emigrants later established major settlements at Flat River (lot 60) and Wood Islands (lot 62). Mike Kennedy, "The Scottish Gaelic Settlement History of Prince Edward Island" (unpublished PhD thesis, University of Edinburgh, 1995) 307, 308.
14. Bumsted, *The People's Clearance*, 59–61.
15. SCA BL 3/258/3: Father James McDonald to John Grant, June 9, 1773.
16. SCA BL 3/269/3: Bishop John MacDonald to George Hay, Oct. 25, 1774.
17. The emigrants originated mostly from South Uist, Barra, Moidart, and Morar. They came to the Island on four vessels: *Jane*, *Lucy*, *Mally* of Greenock, and *Queen* of Greenock. See J. Orlo and D. Fraser, "Those Elusive Immigrants, Part 1," *Island Magazine*, no. 16 (1984) 36–44.
18. NLS Adv. MS. 73.2.13 f. 27: Letter to Colin MacDonald, Oct. 22, 1791.
19. NAS RH 4/188/2 f. 486: Highland Society of Edinburgh, Report of the Committee on Emigration, Jan. 1802.
20. Anon., *Scottish Catholics in Prince Edward Island*, 47–54.
21. Prince Edward Island Census Abstract, 1848.
22. Campey, *After the Hector*, 56–65.
23. D.F. Campbell and R.A. MacLean, *Beyond the Atlantic Roar: A Study of the Nova Scotia Scots* (Toronto: McClelland & Stewart, 1974) 210–13; Moir, *The Church in the British Era*, 135–37.
24. Donald MacKay, *Scotland Farewell*, 75–105.
25. Campey, *After the Hector*, 18–33.
26. Alexander MacKenzie, "First Highland Emigration to Nova Scotia: Arrival of the Ship *Hector*," in *The Celtic Magazine*, vol. VIII (1883) 141–44.
27. LAC MG31–B4: "Rough Draft of the Pictou Highlanders," 123.

28. Thomas Chandler Haliburton, *An Historical and Statistical Account of Nova Scotia* (2 vols.) (Halifax: J. Howe, 1829) 50–58. Anon, *A General Description of Nova Scotia*, vol. I (Halifax: Clement H. Belcher, 1825) 88, 91.

29. The land in question, which belonged to Alexander McNutt, later reverted to the Crown, enabling the settlers eventually to acquire it legally.

30. MacKenzie, "First Highland Emigration," 143.

31. Clark, *Three Centuries and the Island*, 99–102, 211–14, 263–69.

32. Cape Breton was separated from Nova Scotia in 1784 and was re-annexed to it in 1820. During this period Cape Breton was made an adjunct colony of Nova Scotia, which seriously weakened its ability to organize its own affairs. It had an appointed council, no elected house of assembly, and no power to collect taxes.

33. Stephen J. Hornsby, *Nineteenth Century Cape Breton: An Historical Geography* (Montreal: McGill-Queen's University Press, 1992) 19, 20, 23, 48, 120, 121.

34. Campey, *Very Fine Class*, 32–47.

35. Skye settlers went to North Carolina in several spurts from 1771 to 1775; large numbers originated from Duirinish and Bracadale. Ian Charles Cargill Graham, *Colonists from Scotland: Emigration to North America 1707–83* (New York: Cornell University Press, 1956) 76; Adams and Somerville, *Cargoes of Despair*, 96; *SA*, vol. XX, 155,160, 161; *Colonial Records of North Carolina*, vol. VIII (1771) 620–21.

36. *SM*, vol. XXXIII (1771) 500, 501; *Colonial Records of North Carolina*, vol. IX (1772) 364; Adams and Somerville, *Cargoes of Despair*, 91–97.

37. Selkirk, *Observations on the Present State of the Highlands*, 168.

38. Prince Edward Island may have acquired Skye settlers before 1803. Many Bracadale and Duirinish emigrants had previously gone to North Carolina in the early 1770s. Possibly some of them, or their descendants, relocated to the Island as Loyalists following the end of the American War of Independence.

39. McLean, *People of Glengarry*, 78–167.

40. LAC MG24 I183: McMillan to Duncan Cameron, Sept. 30, 1803, and to Ewan Cameron, Oct. 20, 1805.

41. An endowment system was introduced in 1792 for Protestant clergymen (interpreted as Church of England only) and the Crown, thus creating reserves that could be acquired by settlers only through renting.

42. McLean, *People of Glengarry*, 195–97.

43. Lucille H. Campey, *Les Écossais: The Pioneer Scots of Lower Canada, 1763–1855* (Toronto: Natural Heritage Books, 2006) 33–55.

44. McLean, *People of Glengarry*, 191, 192.

45. Joseph Bouchette, *A Topographical Dictionary of the Province of Lower Canada* (London: Longman & Co, 1832), entries for Lochaber and Grenville.

46. Campey, *Les ?cossais*, 53, 54.

47. LAC MG24 I183 ff. 7–9, 11. For details of the crossing, see Rae Fleming (ed.), *The Lochaber Emigrants to Glengarry* (Toronto: Natural Heritage Books, 1994) 5–16.

48. Campey, *Fast Sailing and Copper-Bottomed*, 106–9. The new space limit was one person for every 1.5 tons. Government attempts to protect emigrants from over-zealous shipowners and agents made little practical difference. In the end emigrant travel was transformed for the better not by legislation but through the arrival in the 1850s of specialist steamships. It was then that technology combined with capital investment and competition to bring affordable, consumer-friendly services to the masses.

49. *DWJ*, April 15, 1817.

50. Patrick Cecil Telford White (ed.), *Lord Selkirk's Diary 1803–04: A Journal of His Travels through British North America and the Northeastern United States* (Toronto: Champlain Society, 1958) 44.
51. The great gaps in the customs and shipping records for Pictou and Halifax prevent any precise or meaningful statistical assessment of the scale of the influx, but the likelihood is that several thousand Scots had emigrated to eastern Nova Scotia by the late 1830s. See J.S. Martell, *Immigration to and Emigration from Nova Scotia 1815–1838* (Halifax: PANS, 1942) 91–95.
52. David S. Macmillan, "Scottish Enterprise and Influences in Canada 1620–1900," in R.A. Cage, *The Scots Abroad* (London: Croom Helm, 1985) 46–79.
53. Campey, *With Axe and Bible*, 20–25, 50, 58, 59, 97, 159, 166.
54. George Patterson, *Memoir of the Rev. James MacGregor* (Philadelphia: 1859) 252, 253, 319, 320; Campey, *After the Hector*, 83–85, 88, 299–303.
55. In the early days most lumbering operations were carried out by small family ventures. By the 1830s the highly diversified small family businesses, which dominated the timber trade, were declining, and in their place came the large, well-funded companies that quickly acquired a monopolistic control over the trade. The central role of merchants and storekeepers in the early nineteenth-century development of the New Brunswick timber trade is described in Graeme Wynne, *Timber Colony: An Historical Geography of Early Nineteenth Century New Brunswick* (Toronto: University of Toronto Press, 1981) 84–86, 110–11, 113–37.
56. Basil Greenhilll and Anne Giffard, *Westcountrymen in Prince Edward's Isle* (Toronto: University of Toronto Press, 1967) 46–51.
57. Barbara Kincaid, "Scottish Emigration to Cape Breton, 1758–1838" (Dalhousie University, Nova Scotia, unpublished Ph D thesis, 1964). The appendix (133–95) lists the surnames of Scottish householders who acquired land permits, together with their location on the Island and date of arrival.
58. White, *Lord Selkirk's Diary*, 198.
59. Father Alexander MacDonell, writing in 1808 to Bishop Plessis, quoted in McLean, *People of Glengarry*, 215. MacDonell became Upper Canada's first Roman Catholic bishop.
60. Ibid.
61. Emigration Select Committee, 1841: A1565. Dr Rolph was emigration agent from 1840 to 1843.
62. Ibid., A1566.
63. Raoul Blanchard, *L'Ouest du Canada français: Montréal et sa région* (Montreal: Librarie Beauchemin Limité, 1953) 68, 69.
64. Bouchette, *Topographical Dictionary, Lower Canada*, entry for Beauharnois.
65. Lieutenant J.C. Morgan, *The Emigrants Notebook and Guide with Recollections of Upper and Lower Canada during the Late War* (London: 1824) 110.
66. Rev. Walter Roach's report, published in the Eighth Annual Report of the Glasgow Colonial Society for promoting the religious interests of the Scottish settlers in British North America (Glasgow: 1835).
67. LAC M-1354: Rev. James Hannay to Rev. Burns, Dec. 30, 1834.
68. Campey, *With Axe and Bible*, 48–104.
69. Rev. Steven's report, appended to the Ninth Annual Report of the Glasgow Colonial Society, is reproduced in Rev. R.F. Binnington, "The Glasgow Colonial Society and Its Work in the Development of the Presbyterian Church in British North America 1825–1840" (University of Toronto, unpublished ThD thesis, 1960) 83–86.
70. Ganong, "Origins of Settlements in New Brunswick," 76.

71. Johnston, *Notes on North America*, vol. I, 394.
72. Ibid.
73. The impact of the government's land policies on settlers is discussed in Gates, *Land Policies of Upper Canada*, 303–7; MacDonald, *Canada: Immigration and Settlement*, 74, 75; and Cowan, *British Emigration to British North America*, 114, 132–43.
74. George R. Sutherland, *The Rise and Decline of the Earltown Community, 1813–1970* (Colchester: Colchester Historical Society and Colchester Historical Museum, 1980) 13, 98–136. Sutherland emigrants had also founded communities at New London (lot 20) and Granville (lot 21) in Prince Edward Island by 1806; both places continued to attract Sutherland people until the 1840s.
75. NSARM RG1 vol. 229, doc. 34.
76. NAC M-1352: Tour of Eastern Nova Scotia and Cape Breton, Nov. 1829, Rev. Kenneth MacKenzie to Rev. David Welsh, Nov. 19, 1829.
77. Campey, *After the Hector*, 134–37.
78. Rev. W.A. MacKay, *Pioneer Life in Zorra* (Toronto: William Briggs, 1899) 22, 64, 154, 155.
79. *IC*, June 23, 1830.
80. *AJ*, July 13, 1831.
81. Ibid.
82. Sovereigns cost 21 shillings each at this time.
83. LAC M-1353: Rev. John Geddes to Rev. Burns, Jan. 26, 1833. Zorra had its first Presbyterian church by 1833. For details about the church and school, see LAC MG24-J50: Donald McKenzie Fonds.
84. It is claimed that MacLeod intended that the emigrants should settle in Ohio and that St. Anns was chosen because they happened to catch sight of it as they passed Cape North on their way to the United States. It is more likely that the relaxation of land regulations prompted MacLeod to select a suitable site in Cape Breton.
85. Campey, *After the Hector*, 109–12.
86. Laurie Stanley, *The Well-Watered Garden: The Presbyterian Church in Cape Breton 1798–1860* (Sydney, NS: University College of Cape Breton Press, 1983) 160–63.
87. Flora McPherson, *Watchman against the World: The Remarkable Journey of Norman McLeod and His People from Scotland to Cape Breton Island and New Zealand* (Cape Breton: Breton Books, 1993) 24–32, 45–64, 127–62.
88. At least 6,245 Scots were recorded as having arrived at Sydney in the decade from 1821 to 1830, but, given the sizeable gaps in the customs records, the actual numbers would have been much larger. NAB CO 217/152, 413: Customs Returns, Sydney, June 1, 1831.
89. Emigration Select Committee, 1826, A 331. Uniacke's view that Nova Scotia could absorb many more emigrants was not universally shared in Nova Scotia. Many people were concerned about the high cost to the government of caring for destitute emigrants and were loath to see their numbers rise.
90. Rev. Farquharson, writing in 1827. Anon., *Sketch of Missionary Proceedings at Cape Breton from August 1833 to September 1836* (1833–36), Aberdeen University Library Special Collections, Thomson Collection, T326/13, 10.
91. The 1827 directive was ignored initially and was only complied with from 1832. Hornsby, *Nineteenth Century Cape Breton*, 51–57.
92. Ibid., 48–54. The new system of land sales at public auctions was introduced in 1827 but did not take effect until 1832.

93. Margaret Bennett, *The Last Stronghold: Scottish Gaelic Traditions of Newfoundland* (Edinburgh: Canongate, 1989) 34–41. Newfoundland still had a substantial population of Catholic Highlanders in 1884. SCA DA 9/44/21: Thomas Sears to Bishop of Argyll, Dec. 19, 1884.

94. In 1826–27, the London jewellers Rundell, Bridge and Rundell acquired the rights to virtually all of the province's mineral resources in payment for the Duke of York's debts. Taking its acquisition very seriously, the jewellers formed the General Mining Association and invested huge amounts of capital in state-of-the-art machinery.

95. Bill Lawson, *A Register of Emigrants from the Western Isles of Scotland 1750–1900* (2 vols.) (Northton, Isle of Harris: self-published, 1992). By 1850, most of the Cape Breton colliers were Scottish (see Hornsby, *Nineteenth Century Cape Breton*, 95–110).

96. Campey, *After the Hector*, 122, 126, 139, 148, 325.

97. Extract from the *Prince Edward Island Register and Gazette*, June 2, 1829, in Malcolm MacQueen, *Skye Pioneers and the Island* (Winnipeg, MB: Stovel Co., 1929) 96, 97.

98. *Report from the Commissioners Poor Laws (Scotland)*, Appendix, 421–23.

99. The *Prince Edward Island Gazette*, in Orlo and Fraser, "Elusive Immigrants," 34.

100. Ibid.

101. Campey, *After the Hector*, 119–21, 145–46, 156, 158. For details of the controversy concerning the North Uist removals, see chapter 6.

102. Ships are listed, with passenger numbers in parentheses. In 1847 the *Panama* of Liverpool (279) sailed to Quebec, and the *Serius* (117) to Pictou; in 1848 the *Greenock* of Glasgow (399) and *Scotia* of Belfast (196) sailed to Quebec and the *Ellen* of Liverpool (154) to Pictou. See PP1847–48 (964) XLVII; George MacLaren, *The Pictou Book: Stories of Our Past* (New Glasgow, NS: Hector Pub. Co., 1954) 108–10, 122; Devine, *Highland Famine*, 324.

103. Campey, *Scottish Pioneers of Upper Canada*, 75–80, 137, 254, 256, 258, 260; Campey, *After the Hector*, 141, 275.

104. The provincial government allowed Talbot to exercise these powers. It even permitted him to allocate land privately without registering transfers through the office of the surveyor general. Fred Coyne Hamil, *Lake Erie Baron: The Story of Colonel Thomas Talbot* (Toronto: Macmillan, 1955) 100–13.

105. See chapter 4.

106. Campey, *Scottish Pioneers of Upper Canada*, 109–26.

107. Donald E. Meek, "Evangelicalism and Emigration: Aspects of the Role of Dissenting Evangelicalism in Highland Emigration to Canada," in Gordon MacLennan (ed.), *Proceedings of the First North American Congress of Celtic Studies*, held at Ottawa, March 26–30, 1986, 15–37.

108. *Perth Courier*, Aug. 19, 1819.

109. Campey, *Scottish Pioneers of Upper Canada*, 137–39. Dumfries Township would later become the two townships of North Dumfries (in Waterloo County) and South Dumfries (in Brant County).

110. Ibid., 139–45.

111. Ibid., 91–108.

112. LAC M-1353: Rev. Peter MacNaughton to Rev. Burns, Aug. 27, 1833.

113. The Canada Company was established in 1826 to encourage settlement by newcomers able to fund their own emigration.

114. For the background to the setting up of the Canada Company, its operations, and the key people who promoted and directed it, see Robert C. Lee, *The Canada Company and the*

Huron Tract, 1826–1853: Personalities, Profits and Politics (Toronto: Natural Heritage Books, 2004).

115. PP 1827, V (550), 461–63: "Prospectus of terms upon which the Canada Company proposes to dispose of their lands."

116. Gates, *Land Policies of Upper Canada*, 168–70. In 1829, the average price per acre in the Huron Tract was 7s. 6d. The price rose steadily, and by 1840 it was 13s. 3d.

117. Robert MacDougall (Elizabeth Thompson, ed.), *The Emigrant's Guide to North America* (Toronto: Natural Heritage Books, 1998) 52. Originating from Perthshire, MacDougall had emigrated with his father and brother to the Huron Tract in 1836.

118. Ibid., 52. See, for example, the many positive reports in *A Statement of the Satisfactory Results Which Have Attended Emigration to Upper Canada*, a pamphlet issued by the company in 1841.

119. NAS GD 112/61/8: Peter McNaughton to Rev. D. Duff, Kenmore, Oct. 24, 1835.

120. Statistics gathered for the Scottish Poor Law Commission, which reported to the British Parliament in 1844, give details of the numbers of poor people who emigrated from individual parishes, their destinations, and the extent of any financial help they may have received. See Answers to Questions 30 to 32 in the Appendices of *Report from the Commissioners Appointed for Inquiring into the Administration and Practical Operation of the Poor Laws in Scotland* (London: HMSO, 1844). For emigration from the Perthshire parishes, see 210–87.

121. Nine ship crossings from the Clyde to Quebec were involved: the *Eliza* of Cardiff (269 passengers), the *Jamaica* of Glasgow (212), and the *Charlotte Harrison* of Greenock (305) sailed in 1847; the *Barlow* (246) and the *Charlotte* (333) in 1849; the *Conrad* of Greenock (200) in 1850; the *Birman* of Greenock (180) and *Conrad* of Greenock (388) in 1851; and the *Alan Kerr* (18) in 1853. See PP 1847–48 (964) XLVII, 1850 (173) XL, 1851 (348) XL, 1852 (1474) XXXIII, and 1852–53 (1650) LXVIII, and Devine, *Highland Famine*, 326.

122. E. Mairi MacArthur, *Iona: Living Memory of a Crofting Community 1750–1914* (Edinburgh: Edinburgh University Press, 1990) 102–4.

123. The Duke of Argyll spent a total of £6,500 of his own money in funding their transport. Cameron, "Scottish Emigration to Upper Canada," 332–45.

124. The Marquis of Lorne, writing in 1846, is quoted in Cameron, ibid., 338.

125. Colonel John Gordon's tenants left in 1848 in the *Canada* of Greenock (98 passengers), the *Erromanga* of Greenock (99), and the *Lulan* of Pictou (167); in 1849 in the *Atlantic* (366), the *Mount Stewart Elphinstone* of Glasgow (250), and the *Tuskar* of Liverpool (496); and in 1851 in the *Brooksby* of Glasgow (285), the *Montezuma* of Liverpool (440), the *Admiral* (413), the *Liscard* of Liverpool (104), and the *Perthshire* (437). Lord MacDonald's tenants left in 1849 in the *Cashmere* of Glasgow (115) and the *Waterhen* of London (167). See PP 1852 (1474) XXXIII; PP 1850 (173) XL; NAS GD221/4011/53; Devine, *Highland Famine*, 325–26.

126. The North Uist clearances were resisted by the people and provoked legal action and widespread newspaper publicity. Richards, *Highland Clearances*, 214–30.

127. *Scotsman*, Aug. 11, 1849, quoted in Richards, *Highland Clearances*, 215. Gordon of Cluny assisted his tenants to emigrate, while additional funds were provided by the Glasgow Destitution Board.

128. NAS RH1/2/612/9: Adam Hope to George Hope, Oct. 8, 1849.

129. The British American Land Company was modelled on the Canada Company. It acquired 850,000 acres of Crown land south of the St. Lawrence River, bordering on Vermont and New Hampshire. For an analysis of its role as a settlement promoter, see John Irvine Little, *Nationalism, Capitalism and Colonization in Nineteenth Century Quebec: The Upper St. Francis District* (Kingston, ON: McGill-Queen's University Press, 1989) 36–61.

130. Campey, *Les Écossais*, 96–110. The Lewis settlers were concentrated mainly in Bury, Hampden, and Lingwick townships in Compton County; Winslow and Whitton townships in Frontenac County; and Dudswell township in Wolfe County. For details of some of the individual Lewis families who emigrated to the Eastern Townships, see Bill Lawson, *A Register of Emigrant Families from the Western Isles of Scotland to the Eastern Townships of Quebec* (Eaton Corner, QC: Compton County Historical Museum Society, 1988). For further details of the historical background, see J.I. Little, "From the Isle of Lewis to the Eastern Townships: The Origins of a Highland Settlement Community in Quebec 1838–81," in Catherine Kerrigan (ed.), *The Immigrant Experience: Proceedings of a Conference Held at the University of Guelph, 8–11 June 1989* (Guelph, ON: University of Guelph, 1992) 31–55.

131. Six ships carried the Lewis settlers in 1851: the *Wolfville* of Ardrossan (69), *Barlow* (287), *Prince George* of Alloa (203), *Islay* (68), *Marquis of Stafford* (500), and *Urgent* of Belfast (370). See PP 1852 (1474) XXXIII; Devine, *Highland Famine*, 219, 220, 325. For details of the number of families who emigrated from the various Lewis districts in 1851 and their funding arrangements, see John Munro MacKenzie, *Diary, 1851, John Munro MacKenzie, Chamberlain of the Lews* (Inverness: Acair Ltd, 1994). The diary was published by MacKenzie's great-grandson.

132. PP 1852 (1474) XXXIII; Richards, *Highland Clearances*, 219–24.

133. Devine, *Highland Famine*, 212–23. Matheson probably took advantage of the Emigration Advances Act of 1851, which provided loans to landlords at reasonable rates to help them finance the relocation of their tenants.

134. John Ramsay documented his visit in the form of a diary that was published later and republished in 1970; the latter edition includes a biographical sketch compiled by his grandson's widow. Freda Ramsay, *John Ramsay of Kildalton: Being an Account of His Life in Islay and Including the Diary of His Trip to Canada in 1870* (Toronto: Peter Martin Associates, c. 1977) 61. A number of Islay families petitioned the Colonial Office for assistance to emigrate to Canada in 1850 (NAB CO 327/1, 102).

135. Ramsay, *John Ramsay of Kildalton*, 97.

136. Speech given at the Annual Meeting of the Islay Association, 1878, in Margaret Storrie, *Islay: Biography of an Island* (Port Ellen, ON: self-published, 1981) 147.

137. Campey, *With Axe and Bible*, 117–29.

Chapter 5: Settlement Growth in Western Canada

1. AO MU2659 Acc 6068: Alexander Campbell to friends, Oct. 30, 1870.
2. Ibid., Alexander Campbell letters, March 17, April 29, 1872.
3. EU La.II.202/38: Feb. 26, 1814.
4. Thomas Douglas, 5th Earl of Selkirk, *A Sketch of the British Fur Trade in North America with Observations Relative to the North West Company of Montreal* (London: 1816) 123, 124.
5. Alexander MacKenzie, John Inglis, and Edward Ellice had also bought £2,500 worth of

Hudson's Bay Company shares at this time, in the hope of gaining influence for the rival North West Company. Selkirk and his supporters obtained about one-third of the total shareholding interest. Selkirk's influence far exceeded that of any other individual or group and gave him control over the entire company.

6. EU La.II.202/1: Aug. 14, 1811.
7. EU La.II.202/ 26A: Selkirk to Charles McLean, Feb 20, 1813.
8. In 1812, the Orkney men formed two-thirds of the company's workforce. Edith I. Burley, *Servants of the Honourable Company: Work Discipline and Conflict in the Hudson's Bay Company, 1770–1879* (Toronto: Oxford University Press, 1997) 68–71. John Shearer, W. Groundwater, and J.D. Mackay (eds.), *The New Orkney Book* (Edinburgh: Nelson Printers, 1966) 63–9; J. Storer Clouston, "Orkney and the Hudson's Bay Company," in *Beaver: A Magazine of the North*, outfit 267, no. 4 (March 1937) 39–43; John Nicks, "Orkneymen in the Hudson's Bay Company, 1780–1821," in Carol M. Judd and Arthur J. Ray, *Old Trails and New Directions: Papers of the Third North American Fur Trade Conference* (Toronto, University of Toronto Press, 1980) 102, 103.
9. LAC SP (A–27) 10: Memorandum from Selkirk, n/d.
10. OLA D31/21/5: Orkneymen in HBC Service in Peace River, Athabasca, and the west of Canada.
11. OLA D31/22/1: Biographical Details, Orkneymen in HBC.
12. OLA D31/21/5.
13. Nicks, "Orkneymen in the Hudson's Bay Company," 115; LAC (C–2170): Red River Census, 1831, 1834–35.
14. LAC SP (A–27) 29–30: Simon McGillivray to the wintering partners of the North West Company, Fort William, April 9, 1812. Simon's brother, William, was head of the North West company. For more background, see Jean Morrison, *Superior Rendez-Vous Place: Fort William in the Canadian Fur Trade* (Toronto: Natural Heritage Books, 2001), reprinted 2007.
15. The men sailed on three Hudson's Bay Company ships: the *Prince of Wales*, the *Eddystone*, and the *Edward and Ann*.
16. EU La.II.202/15, 22: May 6, 1812.
17. LAC SP (A–27) 97–8: Selkirk to Miles MacDonell, June 12, 1813. Kildonan people reacted angrily to the plan to have them moved from their homes in the interior to the coast in 1813. There were riots in some areas.
18. Ibid., 99,100.
19. During their early years the Kildonan settlers also relied on buffalo meat as well. They moved to a winter encampment at Pembina (now in Minnesota), where large numbers of grazing buffalo were to be found.
20. Campey, *The Silver Chief,* 77–105.
21. Ibid., 96—7.
22. In June 1815, eighty-four people sailed to York Factory from Thurso on the *Prince of Wales*; thirty-four sailed at that time from Stromness on the *Hadlow,* which also carried the Orcadian men engaged that year as company workers.
23. Men could refund their debts by working for the Hudson's Bay Company for an agreed-upon period.
24. John Pritchett, *The Red River Valley, 1811–1849* (New York: Russell & Russell, 1942) 168–80.

25. The Swiss mercenaries were joined four years later by a further 170 Swiss immigrants. Ibid., 223–26. Having little success as farmers, they left Red River in 1826.

26. Campey, *The Silver Chief*, 106–19.

27. Selkirk was blamed for causing the North West Company's downfall. The North West Company's much longer, inland routes made its transport costs more than double those of the Hudson's Bay Company. As the beaver was hunted to extinction, in the westward progression of the fur trade, the competitive gap widened. The company's efforts in opposing Selkirk would have added to its financial difficulties, but in the end the company was bound to go under.

28. The French voyageurs were renowned for their ability to paddle canoes at great speed over long periods.

29. The Native population consisted mainly of the Cree and Saulteaux peoples. The Saulteaux were of the Ojibwa people, who had relocated themselves from their ancient lands in the Great Lakes region during the late eighteenth century.

30. The Orcadians had worked mainly for the Hudson's Bay Company, and the French Canadians principally for the North West Company. Thomas Flanagan, *Métis Lands in Manitoba* (Calgary: University of Calgary Press, 1991) 13–27; Elaine Allan Mitchell, "The Scot in the Fur Trade," in Stanford W. Reid (ed.), *The Scottish Tradition in Canada* (Toronto: McClelland & Stewart, 1976) 27–48.

31. Before the merger, many Orkney men had returned home with their accrued savings, which usually amounted to about £60 after eight years of service. Although their wages were poor, this was sufficient money to buy a farm back in Orkney.

32. In addition to these recent arrivals, the colony had one hundred fifty-three Scots, forty-five de Meurons, and twenty-six Canadians. See LAC SP (A-27) 827–28: Captain Matthey to Selkirk, Aug. 30, 1818. Population figures for the Métis and Native people were not recorded.

33. Ibid., 825, 826.

34. LAC SP (C-1) 725: Selkirk to MacDonell, June 20, 1812.

35. Lewis G. Thomas (ed.), The *Prairie West to 1905* (Toronto: Oxford University Press, 1975).

36. Their land grants varied from thirty to two hundred acres, and all had river frontages. The new arrivals could buy their land outright, but if they leased it they had to provide labour for the upkeep of the colony's roads and bridges. Gerhard J. Ens, *Homeland to Hinterland: The Changing World of the Métis in the Nineteenth Century* (Toronto: University of Toronto Press, 1996) 30–35.

37. However, the Kildonan settlers had occasionally to hunt to supplement their food supplies.

38. Selkirk had persuaded the Church Missionary Society to send a chaplain to Red River. Subsequently, four churches were built on this site, with the last, built in 1926, becoming the present-day St. John's Cathedral.

39. Rev. Dr George Bryce and C.N. Bell, *Original Letters and Other Documents Relating to the Selkirk Settlement* (Winnipeg, MB: Historical and Scientific Society of Manitoba, 1889) Transaction No. 33. Many of the settlers spoke Gaelic.

40. OLA D31/21/6/3: Reminiscences of Sheriff Colin Inkster, c. 1960.

41. LAC SP (A-27), 1115: George Simpson to Andrew Colvile, Sept. 8, 1823.

42. *DCB*, vol. VIII, 765–68.

43. OLA D31/21/5; Robert J. Coutts, *The Road to the Rapids: Nineteenth Century Church and Society at St. Andrew's Parish, Red River* (Calgary, AB: University of Calgary Press, 1961) 101–3. The Swan River is to the east of Lake Winnipeg.

44. OLA Y1: James Sutherland to his brother John Sutherland, Aug. 10, 1828. The originals of this collection are stored at the Glenbow Foundation, Calgary, Alberta.

45. Ibid., Aug. 8, 1831.

46. LAC SP (A-27) 1139–41: George Simpson to Andrew Colvile, May 31, 1824.

47. The French Métis settled along the Assiniboine River, later forming the parishes of St. Charles, St. François Xavier and Baie St. Paul, and along the Red River at what would later become the parishes of St. Boniface, St. Vital, and St. Norbert.

48. George Bryce, *The Old Settlers of Red River* (Winnipeg: Manitoba Daily Free Press 1885), 8.

49. A. Shortt and A.G. Doughty (eds.), *Canada and Its Provinces: A History of the Canadian People and Their Institutions, by One Hundred Associates*, 20 vols. (Toronto: Publishers Association of Canada, 1913–17) vol. 20, 421.

50. NAS GD 46/1/530: Letter from Alexander Stewart to Mrs Stewart MacKenzie, June 26, 1832.

51. Each year from 1830 to 1890 some five hundred men would come to Rupert's Land to work for the company. Philip Goldring, "Lewis and the Hudson's Bay Company in the Nineteenth Century," in *Journal of the School of Scottish Studies* (University of Edinburgh), 22 (1978) 23–41; Burley, *Servants of the Honourable Company*, 96, 97.

52. Lawson, *Emigrants from the Western Isles of Scotland*, vol. III, Parish of Barvas (with Ness), Isle of Lewis, reveals few examples of men who emigrated to the prairies before the 1880s.

53. LAC SP (A-27) 1280.

54. Agriculture did not become firmly established in the new colony until 1827, the year after the great flood, and even then progress in cultivating land moved ahead very slowly. Ens, *Homeland to Hinterland*, 30–37.

55. LAC (C-2170): Red River Census Returns, 1834–35.

56. UBSC C C1 037/24: Subscription List for the Church Missionary Society, 1827.

57. LAC (C-2170): Red River Census Returns, 1834–35.

58. W.L. Morton, *Manitoba: A History* (Toronto: University of Toronto Press, 1967) 151.

59. PAM MG2 C14/203: Letter dated March 7, 1857.

60. Ibid.

61. Kennedy was the son of Aggathas (Cree) and Alexander Kennedy (Orcadian), a chief factor of the Hudson's Bay Company. The petition appears in Thomas, *The Prairie West*, 59–61. Also see Coutts, *Road to the Rapids*, 107–09.

62. Riel and his followers organized a "National Committee" and formed a provisional government to negotiate directly with Canada. Bumsted, *The Peoples of Canada*, vol. 1, 371–76.

63. Riel fled to the United States in 1870. He led the Métis in the North West Rebellion of 1885 and, following defeat, was hanged for treason.

64. Anon., *The Hudson's Bay Company: What Is It?* (London: A.H. Bailey, 1864) 47.

65. Martin, *Lord Selkirk's Work*, 180–84.

66. By 1886 Manitoba's population had soared to 109,000, with the Métis, both French- and English-speaking, representing only 7 per cent of the total. Coutts, *Road to the Rapids*, 110.

67. Land companies were established as a means to promote settlement in the prairies; twenty-seven had been formed by 1882. A.N. Lalonde, "Colonization Companies in the 1880s," *Saskatchewan History*, 24, no. 3 (1971) 101–14. The Dawson route, linking Canada with Red River, which opened in 1868, was built by a Scottish-born engineer, Simon Dawson.

68. Morton, *Manitoba*, 156.

69. Ibid., 151–87. Robert England, *Colonization of Western Canada: A Study of Contemporary Land Settlement (1896–1934)* (London: P.S. King & Son, 1936) 53–62, 280–87.

70. The Saskatchewan Trail was also known as the Carleton Trail. A branch of it went southwest from Beaver Hill to south Qu'Appelle. R.C. Russell, *Carleton Trail: The Broad Highway into the Saskatchewan Country from the Red River Settlement, 1840–80* (Saskatoon: Modern Press, 1965) 16–23.

71. MacArthur, *Iona*, 170, 171.

72. AO F495 MU 2659 Acc 6122.

73. Moffat was founded by English and Irish settlers from Ontario and Quebec. The later arrivals from Scotland eventually became the predominant settlers.

74. Kay Parley, "Moffat, Assiniboia, North-West Territories," *Saskatchewan History*, 20, no. 1 (1967) 32–36.

75. OLA D31/21/1/8; *DCB*, vol. XIII, 929–31. Binsgarth was known initially as "Colony Farm." The site was moved following the arrival of the North West Railway in 1886.

76. SCA DA 9/44/1: Rev. Corbett to Bishop Angus MacDonald, March 19, 1884.

77. OLA D31/21/1/6. The York Farmers Colonization Company was an Ontario land company.

78. LAC RG15-D-11-1, vol. 547 (microfilm T-13801): Alexander Begg Scheme. In 1887, Begg tried to establish Highland crofters in Vancouver Island, but his scheme was never implemented.

79. AO F495 MU 2659 Acc 6013: Letter from Lady Cathcart, Nov. 17, 1884. She offered £100 per family. Emily had married Sir Reginald Cathcart in 1880.

80. Alan R. Turner, "Scottish Settlement of the West," in W. Stanford Reid (ed.), *The Scottish Tradition in Canada* (Toronto: McClelland & Stewart, 1976) 82, 83.

81. AO MU 2659 Acc 6013.

82. Ibid.

83. *SH*, Oct. 13, 1887.

84. SCA DA 9/44/8: Rev. Gillies to Bishop Angus MacDonald, June 19, 1886.

85. *SH*, Oct. 13, 1887.

86. The Killarney scheme was administered by a board of commissioners, which had representatives from the Canadian and British governments and from private subscribers and land companies. The crofters were given additional financial help after they arrived.

87. The Saltcoats scheme was administered by the Imperial Colonization Board. The British government provided £10,000 for both the Killarney and Saltcoats schemes.

88. Wayne Norton, *Help Us to a Better Land: Crofter Colonies in the Prairie West* (Regina: University of Regina, 1994) 23–62; Kent Stuart, "The Scottish Crofter Colony, Saltcoats 1889–1904," *Saskatchewan History*, 24, no. 2 (1971) 41–50; James MacKinnon, "A Short History of the Pioneer Scotch Settlers, St. Andrews, Saskatchewan," *Courier*, Regina, 1921.

89. NAS GD40/16/57: Report from the Select Committee on Colonization, 1891.

90. Turner, "Scottish Settlement of the West," 83.

91. Harper, *Emigration from North-East Scotland*, vol. II, 28–31.

92. LAC RG76-1-A-1, vol. 405 (microfilm C-10294).

93. Norma J. Milton, "The Scots in Alberta," in Howard and Tamara Palmer (eds.), *Peoples of Alberta: Portrait of Cultural Diversity* (Saskatoon: Western Prairie Books, 1985) 109–22.

94. Jason Patrick Bennett, "The True Elixir of Life: Imagining Eden and Empire in the Settlement of Kelowna, B.C., 1904–1920" (Simon Fraser University, unpublished PhD thesis, 1996); Harper, *Emigration from North-East Scotland*, vol. II, 112–39.
95. The schemes operated under the auspices of the Empire Settlement Act of 1922.
96. Before sailing to Stornoway, the *Metagama* collected 1,100 men "from the ranks of the industrial workers on Clydeside" (*Glasgow Record*, April 23, 1923).
97. LAC RG76-1-A-1, vol. 632 (microfilm C-10447).
98. David Craig, *On the Crofter's Trail: In Search of the Clearance Highlanders* (London: Jonathan Cape, 1990) 246–47.
99. LAC MG29-D86: Article from *People's Journal*, June 2, 1923.
100. Ibid.
101. *People's Journal*, May 6, 1923.
102. LAC RG17, vol. 434, no. 47378.
103. Marjory Harper, *Emigration from Scotland between the Wars* (Manchester: Manchester University Press, 1998) 101–8.
104. LAC RG76-1-A-1, vol. 260 (microfilm C-7808): R.C.P. Croswell to Mr Benoit, March 3, 1954.

Chapter 6: Did They Go, Or Were They Sent?

1. Alexander Mackenzie, "The Editor in Canada Series," *The Celtic Magazine: A Monthly Periodical Devoted to the Literature, History, Antiquities, Folklore, Traditions, and the Social and Material Interests of the Celt at Home and Abroad/Conducted by Alexander Mackenzie and Alexander Macgregor* (Inverness: A. & W. Mackenzie, 1875–88), vol. V, 72.
2. Ibid., 24, 70.
3. Ibid., 20.
4. Ibid., 308.
5. PP1884, XXXII–XXXVI, *Report of H.M. Commissioners of Inquiry into the Condition of the Crofters and Cottars in the Highlands and Islands of Scotland: Report of the Commission*, 2 (hereinafter Napier Commission).
6. The famine was caused by a fungus (*phytophthora infestans*) that attacks the leaves and tubers of potatoes. By 1846 potatoes formed between three-quarters and seven-eighths of the diet of the average Highland family. The potato blight (or rot) devastated crops. Thousands of people became vulnerable to malnutrition and severe destitution.
7. R.C. MacDonald, *Sketches of Highlanders: With an Account of Their Early Arrival in North America; Their Advancement in Agriculture and Some of Their Distinguished Military Services in the War of 1812* (Saint John, NB: H. Chubb, 1843) Appendix A, ii–v.
8. 1841 Emigration Select Committee, A943.
9. Ibid., A2034.
10. Ibid., A222.
11. A survey carried out in 1836–37 by the Glasgow Destitution Committee indicated that about 60 per cent of Highlanders were interested in emigrating, but, of those, only 30 per cent would emigrate if financial assistance was provided. J.M. Cameron, "The Changing Role of the Highland Landlords Relative to Scottish Emigration during the First Half of the 19th Century," in *Proceedings of the Fourth and Fifth Colloquia on Scottish Studies* (Guelph, ON: University of Guelph, 1972) 80, 81.
12. AO F350 MU1145 #3927: Glengarry County Collections, Kippen, McDiarmid, and McEwen families.
13. NAB CO 42/170 ff.362–63: Donald MacCrummer, Nov. 20, 1816.

14. NAB CO 384/8 ff. 230–1: John McRa, Jan. 29, 1822.

15. NAB CO 384/5 f.7; CO 384/15 f. 485.

16. Alexander Beith, *Glenelg Parish: The New Statistical Account of Scotland/ by the Ministers of the Respective Parishes, Under the Superintendence of a Committee of the Society for the Benefit of the Sons and Daughters of the Clergy*, vol. XIV (Edinburgh and London: William Blackwood and Sons, 1845) 135, 136.

17. NAS HD 21/35: List of Glenelg tenants from J. Baillie's estate who are to emigrate to the Colonies. Baillie received funding from the Highland Destitution Committee.

18. Baillie's tenants sailed on the *Liskeard* of Liverpool, probably from Glenelg. PP 1850 (173) XL.

19. The Moidart people sailed on the *George* of Dundee from Oban to Quebec. PP 1851 (348) XL.

20. SCA OL1/45/1: Aeneas MacDonell to Bishop Murdoch, Jan. 26, 1851.

21. Some Moidart people were also settling north of the Ottawa River in Lower Canada. NLS MS 3952 ff. 23–5: Ronald Rankin to William Robertson MacDonald of Kinloch, Moidart, Oct. 16, 1850.

22. The group that sailed on the *Ellen* of Liverpool settled in Glengarry, Toronto, and Hamilton. PP 1852 (1474) XXXIII.

23. The Emigration Advances Act of 1851 made loans available to landlords at an interest rate of $6^1/4$ per cent. Devine, *Highland Famine*, 202, 204.

24. Mrs Macdonell's tenants sailed to Quebec from Isleornsay, Skye, on the *Sillery* of Liverpool. PP w/e, Sept. 17, 1853.

25. Richards, *Highland Clearances*, 260–64.

26. Donald Ross, *Glengarry Evictions or Scenes at Knoydart in Inverness-shire* (Glasgow, 1853) 6, 28, 29.

27. Money was raised to help the group survive the winter by charitable donations raised in London, Oxford, Manchester, Edinburgh, and Glasgow. Ibid., 1–4, 28, 29.

28. *Scotsman*, Oct. 20, 1853, quoted in Richards, *Highland Clearances*, 265.

29. Many Highlanders also responded at this time to government-financed schemes that offered free passages to Australia. The demand was so great in 1852 that Highlanders were required to make their own way to Glasgow or Liverpool, rather than be collected from a Highland port. See NAS HD4/1, 290: Highland and Island Emigration Society papers, 1852.

30. AO F350 MU1145 #3927: Duncan McDermid to Donald McKercher, Nov. 2, 1857.

31. Statistics gathered for the Scottish Poor Law Commission, which reported to the British Parliament in 1844, give details of the numbers of poor people who emigrated from individual parishes, their destinations, and the extent of any financial help they may have received. See Answers to Questions 30 to 32 in the Appendices of *Report from the Commissioners Appointed for Inquiring into the Administration and Practical Operation of the Poor Laws in Scotland* (London: HMSO, 1844) 421–23, 425. Lord MacDonald paid £1 per person, and his contribution was matched by funds paid by the Destitution Committees.

32. 1841 Emigration Select Committee, A 191.

33. NAS RH1/2/612/9: Adam Hope to George Hope, in Haddington, Scotland, Oct. 8, 1849.

34. 1841 Emigration Select Committee, A 1884–87.

35. The 1858 group sailed on the *William Gibb*. Both groups settled at Brooklyn and Glenmartin (lot 61), Glenwilliam (lot 63), and Caledonia (lots 60, 61, and 63). Personal interview quoted in Kennedy, "Gaelic Settlement History of Prince Edward Island," 458–89.

36. NAS GD 51/15/58: John Lawson, *Letters on Prince Edward Island* (Charlottetown: 1851), Letter X, 37.
37. Richards, *Highland Clearances*, 230–37.
38. Napier Commission, vol. I, A12734.
39. Campey, *After the Hector*, 118–21.
40. Patrick Cooper, *The So-called Evictions of the MacDonald Estates in the Island of North Uist, Outer Hebrides, 1849 (reprinted from the "Scotsman" of the 10ᵗʰ February, 1881)* (Aberdeen: 1881) 9, 10.
41. Ibid., 11.
42. Lord Thomson paid £1,160 on emigration costs for his North Uist tenants (*Report from the Poor Law Commissioners*, Appendix, 425).
43. Ibid., 13.
44. 1841 Emigration Select Committee, A 1369–72. *Report from the Poor Law Commissioners*, Appendix, 416.
45. *Report from the Poor Law Commissioners*, Appendix, 424.
46. 1841 Emigration Select Committee, A2647.
47. Ibid., A2651, 2654.
48. *Report from the Poor Law Commissioners*, Appendix, 182, 184. Cameron, "Scottish Emigration to Upper Canada," 382.
49. *Report from the Poor Law Commissioners*, Appendix, 210, 409.
50. For instance, the *Report from the Poor Law Commissioners*, Appendix, 210, 239, 407, gives examples of people from Halkirk Parish in Caithness and from Fortingall and Kilmadock parishes in Perthshire who emigrated without assistance.
51. Before 1845 an average of about seven hundred people sailed each year from Highland ports to Canada.
52. See the list of ship crossings in Campey, *After the Hector*, 234–77, and Campey, *Scottish Pioneers of Upper Canada*, 216–67.
53. Eric Richards, *Patrick Sellar and the Highland Clearances: Homicide, Eviction and the Price of Progress* (Edinburgh: Polygon, 1999) 83–137.
54. SCRO D593 P/22/1/7.
55. SCRO D593 P/22/1/22: Evander McIver, March 26, 1847.
56. SCRO D593 P/22/1/7: The Rev. William Findlater to the 2nd Duke of Sutherland, Oct. 6, 1841.
57. Ibid., April 2, 1847. Most of the emigrants originated from Elphin and Knockan.
58. NAS RH/1/2/612/8: Adam Hope to George Hope, Aug. 12, 1847.
59. PP 1847–48 (964) XLVII; PP 1849 (1025) XXXVIII; PP 1851 (348) XL; PP 1852 (1474) XXXIII. The duke spent £6,000 on assisting his tenants to emigrate during the late 1840s and early 1850s. Cameron, "Scottish Emigration to Upper Canada," 379.
60. 1841 Emigration Select Committee, A829.
61. NAB CO 384/28 ff. 24–26: Memorial of the inhabitants of Tiree, Jan. 24, 1831.
62. NAS GD 133/170/ 3, 4: Duke of Argyll to Robertson of Inches, June, 1840.
63. NLS Adv. MS.26.2.19: Papers relating to the British American Emigration Society.
64. NAS GD 133/170: Letters from the Duke of Argyll to Robertson of Inches, 1840.
65. Cameron, "Scottish Emigration to Upper Canada," 341–42.
66. PP 1850 (173) XL. They had sailed on the *Charlotte* (333 passengers) and *Barlow* (246 passengers). Campey, *Scottish Pioneers of Upper Canada*, 144–51.
67. *IA*, Oct. 23, 1849.
68. *IA*, Oct. 2, 1849.

69. A total of around five hundred people, who were mostly from Tiree, sailed to Quebec on the *Birman* of Greenock and the *Conrad* of Greenock in 1851. PP 1852 (1474) XXXIII.
70. George Douglas Campbell, Duke of Argyll, *Crofts and Farms in the Hebrides* (Edinburgh: David Douglas, 1883) 22.
71. The Tiree petition is printed in George Douglas Campbell, Duke of Argyll, *Scotland As It Was and As It Is* (Edinburgh: Douglas, 1887) 488, 489.
72. Cameron, "Scottish Emigration to Upper Canada," 345.
73. *AR*, Aug. 26, 1848.
74. A head tax of five shillings was payable by overseas passengers to enable the authorities to fund quarantine facilities.
75. Campey, *After the Hector*, 142, 143.
76. *AR*, Aug. 26, 1848.
77. PP 1852 (1474) XXXIII.
78. Ibid.
79. Richards, *Highland Clearances*, 207–25.
80. SCA OL/1/45/6, 7: Rev. J. Chisholm, Jan. 17, 1852; Rev. D. MacDonald, Jan. 13, 1852.
81. Richards, *Highland Clearances*, 221.
82. Ibid.
83. See the *Lloyd's Shipping Register* for the relevant years. Also see Appendix III for a further explanation of the Lloyd's shipping codes.
84. NAB CO 384/74, f. 278: letter dated Feb. 21, 1843.
85. NAB CO 384/ 79 ff. 261–65: letter dated July 14, 1848.
86. For example, see the Quebec Immigration Agent's Report, PP w/e June 11, 1843.
87. NAB CO 384/74, ff. 247–8: J.W. Campbell to Lord Stanley, May 6, 1843.
88. Ibid. Lord Stanley to the Lord Provost of Glasgow, May 15, 1843.
89. Richards, *Highland Clearances*, 189–91.
90. NAS GD 46/13/197: the Lord Advocate to Stewart Mackenzie [Earl of Seaforth], Nov. 29, 1836; NAS GD 46/9/6/26: Stewart Mackenzie to Hugh Innis Cameron, Aug. 11, 1838. 1841 Emigration Select Committee, A2176–78. The entries for Lewis in the *Report from the Poor Law Commissioners*, ix, fail to reveal any instances of assisted emigration from 1841 to 1843 (see pp. 426–27). The Lewis emigrants sailed on the *Charles* (145), the *Lady Hood* of Stornoway (78), and the *St. Andrew* of New Brunswick (133).
91. Campey, *Les Écossais*, 96–110.
92. Napier Commission, Appendix A, 161–2. Example after example was provided of crofters moving to vacant lots after small groups had emigrated.
93. Napier Commission, vol.II, A14299–A14304.
94. MacKenzie, *Diary, 1851*, 104, 117.
95. Napier Commission, Appendix A, 162, 165, 166.
96. Richards, *Highland Clearances*, 244–47.
97. AO F495 MU2659 Acc 6013: Kildalton Papers. The Islay tenants sailed on the SS *Damascus* from Glasgow to Quebec in June 1862 (passenger list survives). Thirty-one people paid their own passages.
98. Ibid., John Ramsay, July 13, 1863.
99. They sailed on the *Olympia* from Glasgow. NAS GD 371/313: Robert Shives to Captain Stewart, June 23, 1862.
100. PP 1863 (3199) XV 247.
101. NAB CO 180/137 ff. 185–6: Robert Shives to Samuel Tilley, Aug. 26, 1862.
102. Ibid.

103. *Edinburgh Daily Review*, July 10, 1862.
104. Thomas Rolph, *Emigration and Colonization: Embodying the Results of a Mission to Great Britain and Ireland during the Years, 1839, 1840, 1841 and 1842* (London: 1894) 23, 24 (also see the evidence given by Dr Norman MacLeod to the 1841 Select Committee, A 919). Under the Glasgow Destitution Board's scheme, the committee paid 10 shillings to each emigrant provided this sum was matched by the proprietor.
105. Alexander Mackenzie, quoting from Donald Ross in his *History of the Highland Clearances* (Edinburgh: Mercat Press, 1991) 221, first published in 1883.

Chapter 7: Emigration Myths and Realities

1. Thomas Samuel Mulock, *The Western Highlands and Islands of Scotland Socially Considered with Reference to the Proprietors and People: Being a Series of Contributions to the Periodical Press* (Edinburgh: J. Menzies, 1850) 69.
2. Miller, *Sutherland As It Was and Is*, 19. Elizabeth, Countess of Sutherland, married George Granville Leveson-Gower in 1785. He became the second Marquess of Stafford in 1803 and was made the first duke of Sutherland in January 1833.
3. See chapter 3.
4. Donald MacLeod's account is quoted in Prebble, *The Highland Clearances*, 79.
5. NC, vol. XXXII, 9, 97.
6. Beriah Botfield, *Journal of a Tour through the Highlands of Scotland, during the Summer of 1829* (Edinburgh: privately printed, 1830) 152–3.
7. Prebble, *The Highland Clearances*, 48.
8. Donald Ross, *The Russians of Ross-shire, or, Massacre of the Rosses in Strathcarron, Ross-shire, by Policemen, When Serving the Tenants in Strathcarron with Summonses of Removal in March Last by Donald Ross* (Glasgow: G. Gallie; London: Houlston and Stoneman, 1854) 36 – quoted by Cameron in "Scottish Emigration to Upper Canada," 322.
9. Donald MacLeod of Sutherland, *Gloomy Memories in the Highlands of Scotland: Versus Mrs. Harriet Beecher Stowe's Sunny Memories ... or A Faithful Picture of the Extirpation of the Celtic Race from the Highlands of Scotland* (Glasgow: A. Sinclair, 1892) 127.
10. Donald MacLeod, *History of the Destitution in Sutherlandshire* (Edinburgh, 1841) 9.
11. Rev. Thomas McLauchlan, *Recent Highland Ejections Considered in Five Letters* (Edinburgh: 1850) 12–16.
12. Rowland Hill MacDonald, *The Emigration of Highland Crofters* (Edinburgh: Blackwood & Sons, 1885) 33.
13. NAS HD 21/35: List of Glenelg tenants from J. Baillie's estate.
14. Richards, *Highland Clearances*, 310–30.
15. NAB CO 384/22 ff. 2–5.
16. One group settled in Reach Township, while a second group lived in Osgood Township. Each appealed to the Marquis of Breadalbane for funds to build a church. See NAS GD 112/61/5: Osgood petition in 1836 and Reach petition in 1848.
17. Napier Commission, Q11142–51.
18. Napier Commission, Q12081–12110.
19. NAS GD 46/13/184: Select Committee on Colonization (1890), Q4801–Q4806.
20. Ibid., Q4809, Q4812.
21. Alexander Mackenzie, *An Analysis of the Report of the Crofter Royal Commission* (Inverness: A. & W. MacKenzie, 1884) 71.

22. MacKenzie, *History of the Highland Clearances*, 236.
23. MacDonald, *Emigration of Highland Crofters*, 15.
24. Napier Commission, vol. IV, 2733–36.
25. *SH*, Sept. 1, 1887. Mackenzie later retracted his negative reporting when challenged by the Select Committee on Colonization in 1890 (Q5358–Q5376).
26. *SH*, Feb. 17, 1887.
27. Napier Commission, Appendix A, 129: L. McPherson to C. Cameron, Benbecula.
28. *SH*, Feb. 20, 1890.
29. Ibid.
30. *SH*, Feb. 27, 1890.
31. *SH*, May 15, 1890.
32. *Colonist* (Winnipeg), April 1890, reprinted in *Saskatchewan History*, 16, no. 2 (spring 1963) 78.
33. Ibid.
34. Select Committee on Colonization (1890) Appendix No. 6.
35. Ibid., Q4727–4732, Appendix No. 6.
36. Neil Gunn, *Butcher's Broom* (Edinburgh: Porpoise Press, 1934) 417–18.
37. Richards, *Patrick Sellar*, 367–68.
38. Ibid.
39. Craig, *On the Crofter's Trail*, 2–9.
40. Ibid., 88.
41. John MacLeod, *Highlanders: A History of the Gaels* (London: Hodder and Stoughton, 1996) 199.
42. *Scotsman*, July 24, 2007.

Chapter 8: What About the "Coffin" Ships?

1. John Rhind, "Ship Log, *Jane Boyd* crossing Aberdeen to Montreal, in 1854 (August 15 to October 8)," 31. This unpublished diary is the property of Mrs. Betty Rhind (née Brown) of Montreal, who is the widow of John Rhind's grandson, William Rhind. Her permission to use the document is gratefully acknowledged. I am also indebted to Gail Dever for bringing it to my attention.
2. Ibid., 25.
3. About 18 per cent of the 98,649 emigrants, mainly from Ireland, who boarded ship for Quebec in 1847 died before reaching their destination. André Charbonneau and André Sévigny, *1847 Grosse Île: A Record of Daily Events* (Ottawa: Parks Canada, 1997) 1–32.
4. Edwin C. Guillet, *The Great Migration: The Atlantic Crossing by Sailing Ships since 1770* (Toronto: University of Toronto Press, 1963) 10–19.
5. MacLeod, *Highlanders: A History of the Gaels*, 200.
6. Craig, *On the Crofter's Trail*, 101–2, 106, 107.
7. De Vere's report to the Emigration Commissioners is quoted in Norman MacDonald, *Canada: Immigration and Colonization, 1841–1903* (Aberdeen: Aberdeen University Press, 1966) 61.
8. Prebble, *The Highland Clearances*, 197.
9. Rhind, "Ship Log, *Jane Boyd* crossing," 6.
10. Ibid.
11. Rhind, "Ship Log, *Jane Boyd* crossing," 4.

12. Ibid., 15.
13. Ibid., 10.
14. *Glasgow Courier*, April 9, 1803.
15. Campey, *Very Fine Class*, 32–47.
16. No agency had been set up to enforce the new legislation. The existing authorities had insufficient personnel to adequately check all ship departures. Oliver Macdonagh, *A Pattern of Government Growth 1800–1860: The Passenger Acts and Their Enforcement* (London: Macgibbon & Kee, 1961) 337–50.
17. Aberdeen ships collected emigrants from Cromarty as early as 1784. See, for example, *AJ*, July 19, 1784.
18. For example, see M.A. Walpole, "The Humanitarian Movement in the Early 19th Century to Remedy Abuses on Emigrant Vessels," *Transactions of the Royal Historical Society*, 14 (1931) 197–224. See also W.S. Shepperson, *British Emigration to North America: Projects and Opinions in the Early Victorian Period* (Oxford: Oxford University Press, 1957) 197–224.
19. Prebble, *The Highland Clearances*, 187.
20. NAB CO 384/67 ff. 235–36: Archibald McNiven to Lord John Russell, Jan. 19, 1841.
21. By the 1830s steerage fares were as low as £2. 10 s. – £3 for people taking their own food.
22. Foden Frank, *Wick of the North: The Story of a Scottish Royal Burgh* (Wick: self-published, 1996) 16, 458, 459, 466–68.
23. Although MacLennan and Sutherland's voluminous newspaper articles and advertisements gave highly optimistic accounts of the agricultural and economic opportunities on offer in British North America, Sutherland was always on hand to be challenged. Having been made the Canada Company's principal Highland agents, the partners provided extensive details of its land holdings, taking their briefing documents to all parts of the Highlands.
24. Campey, *Fast Sailing and Copper-Bottomed*, 63–65, 67–69.
25. *John O'Groat Journal*, Sept. 25, 1840.
26. NAB CO 384/77 ff. 461–69: Memorial to the Colonial Office from John Sutherland, 1846.
27. Archibald MacNiven feared that the new immigration tax would end emigration entirely, but it failed to do so. Numbers did fall initially, but they recovered by the early 1840s. NAB CO 217/154, f. 877: A. MacNiven to Lord Goderich, April 5, 1832.
28. NAS RH1/2/908: *Mechanic and Farmer*, Pictou, NS, July 28, 1841. The *Mechanic and Farmer* was "devoted to the advancement of agriculture and the useful arts in the Colonies of Nova Scotia, Cape Breton, Prince Edward Island and New Brunswick, neutral in politics and religion."
29. *Halifax Times*, Aug. 22, 1843.
30. *Pictou Observer*, Sept. 6, 1842.
31. Ibid.
32. *JJ* article in *IJ*, July 1, 1842.
33. Ibid.
34. *Pictou Observer*, June 21, 1842.
35. The tribute is quoted in George A. MacKenzie, *From Aberdeen to Ottawa in 1845: The Diary of Alexander Muir* (Aberdeen: Aberdeen University Press, 1990) 19, 85.
36. *JJ*, June 15, 1849.
37. Ibid.

38. Ibid.
39. The *Lloyd's Shipping Register* is available as a regular series from 1775, apart from the years 1785, 1788, and 1817.
40. Still in use today and run by a Classification Society with a worldwide network of offices and administrative staff, the *Lloyd's Register* continues to provide standard classifications of quality for shipbuilding and maintenance.
41. The number of years that a ship could hold the highest code varied according to where it was built. In time, rivalries developed between shipowners and underwriters, and this led to the publication of two Registers between 1800 and 1833 –the Shipowners' Register (Red Book) and the Underwriters' Register (Green Book). Their coverage was similar but not identical. By 1834, with bankruptcies facing both sides, the two Registers joined forces to become the *Lloyd's Register of British and Foreign Shipping*.
42. Guillet, *Great Migration*, 19, 233.
43. Arthur R.M. Lower, *Colony to Nation: A History of Canada* (Toronto: Longmans, Green & Co., 1946) 98.
44. NAS GD 46/13/184, 6, 7.
45. Having extra sheathing, whaling ships could offer greater protection against ice.
46. NAS CE/57/11: Leith Shipping Registers.
47. Initially, Greenock was the more important port, but Glasgow overtook it in the late 1830s, when the River Clyde was opened up to large sailing ships.
48. A history of the Allan Line is provided in Thomas E. Appleton, *Ravenscrag: The Allan Royal Mail Line* (Toronto: McClelland & Stewart, 1974). See also Gerald J.J. Tulchinsky, *The River Barons: Montreal Business and Growth of Industry and Transport, 1837-53* (Toronto; Buffalo: University of Toronto Press, 1977) 79, 80.
49. Alan Kerr and Co. advertisement quoted in Appleton, *Ravenscrag*, 35.
50. David R. MacGregor, *Merchant Sailing Ships: Supremacy of Sail 1815-1850* (London: Conway Maritime Press, 1984) 163–70.
51. For example, the *Harlequin* (702 tons) took about 850 passengers in just four crossings, while the *Caledonia* of Greenock had carried a similar number in fifteen crossings.
52. Official figures are available from 1831 on. See PP, *Annual Reports of the Immigration Agent at Quebec*. However, because of gaps in some years these figures understate emigrant totals.
53. Cameron, "Scottish Emigration to Upper Canada," 458–74.
54. Because of gaps and inconsistencies in sources, the identification of shipping codes can never be an exact science. To locate a vessel's code from the *Register*, it is usually necessary to have the vessel name, the tonnage, and/or the captain's name. Such data are not always available and are highly problematict to locate. Some vessels may not have been offered for inspection, particularly in cases where a shipowner could rely on his personal contacts for business. The lack of a survey might arouse suspicions but is not necessarily conclusive proof of a poor quality ship.
55. **A** – first class condition, kept in the highest state of repair and efficiency and within a prescribed age limit at the time of sailing; **AE** – 'the second description of the first class,' fit, no defects but may be over a prescribed age limit; **E** – second class, although unfit for carrying dry cargoes were suitable for long distance sea voyages; **I** – third class, only suitable for short voyages (i.e. not out of Europe). These letters were followed by the number 1 or 2 which signified the condition of the vessel's equipment (anchors, cables and stores). Where satisfactory, the number 1 was used, and where not, 2 was used. George Blake, *Lloyd's Register of Shipping 1760-1960* (London, 1960) 12–13, 26–27.
56. MacLeod, *Highlanders: A History of the Gaels*, 200.

57. Lubbock is quoted in Guillet, *Great Migration*, 67.

58. ACA CE 87/11 (Aberdeen ship register); DCA CE 70/11 (Dundee register); NAS CE 57/11 (Leith register); SRA CE 59/11, CE 60/11(Glasgow and Greenock registers).

59. Eric Sager, with G.E. Panting, *Maritime Capital: The Shipping Industry in Atlantic Canada, 1820–1914* (Montreal: McGill-Queen's University Press, 1990) 51–62.

60. Campey, *Fast Sailing and Copper-Bottomed*, 80–98.

61. Rhind, "Ship Log, *Jane Boyd* crossing," 7.

62. For example, Alexander Leslie owned eight out of sixty-four shares in the *Albion*, the same number owned by James Oswald in the *Aberdeenshire* and John Morison in the *Pacific*. Alexander Anderson, in charge of the *Annandale, Carleton*, and *Quebec Packet*, held four out of sixty-four shares in the first two and five out of sixty-four in the third. ACA CE87/11/1, 2, 5.

63. Having been a major whaling port in the first two decades of the nineteenth century, Aberdeen's whaling interests went into decline by 1830. Gordon Jackson, *The British Whaling Trade* (London: A. and C. Black, 1978) 88, 89, 130, 144, 145.

64. *AJ*, June 29, 1836.

65. "Account of a Voyage from Aberdeen to Quebec," in MacKenzie, *The Diary of Alexander Muir*, 113–16. The original spelling has been modified to modern spelling. The *Hercules*, another former whaling ship, could offer 6'3" between decks.

66. Rhind, "Ship Log, *Jane Boyd* crossing," 5, 14.

67. Ibid., 17.

68. Hart, *Diary of a Voyage in 1842*, 20.

69. *Acadian Recorder*, Oct. 16, 1819; NAS E.504/35/2.

70. *IJ*, Nov. 23, 1820; *IJ*, Jan. 30, 1824; NAS E.504/35/2; *QM*, Aug. 25, 1820; *QM*, Oct. 7, 1823.

71. *IJ*, Dec. 10, 1830; *QM*, Sept. 4, 1830.

72. *DC*, Feb. 7, 1834. The *Fairy* carried fifty passengers, whose names are listed in the commendation printed in the *Dundee Courier*.

73. Walter Riddell, *Diary of a Voyage from Scotland to Canada in 1833 and the Story of St. Andrew's Presbyterian Church, Cobourg, Ontario* (Toronto: Assoc. Printers Ltd, 1932) 6.

74. Ibid., 8.

75. Thomas Fowler, *Journal of a Tour through British North America to the Falls of Niagara, Containing an Account of the Cities, Towns and Villages Along the Route in 1831* (Aberdeen, 1832) 252.

76. NAS GD 263/63/2/54.

77. The Passenger Act of 1803 required shippers to stock provisions for twelve weeks, expressed as the following daily allowance per person: one gallon of water, one-half pound of meat, one-and-one-half pounds of bread, biscuit, or oatmeal, and one-half pint of molasses. Also see NAB CO 384/6, ff. 27–8: William Allan to the Colonial Office, May 10, 1820.

78. Hart, *Diary of a Voyage in 1842*, 13.

79. *IC*, April 7, 1830.

80. NSARM RG1 vol. 252, doc. 88: John G. Marshall to T.W. James (Deputy Provincial Secretary), Sept. 14, 1836.

81. See chapter 6. The twenty-nine deaths on the *Eliza* of Cardiff's crossing represent nearly half of the total deaths of Scottish emigrants while crossing the ocean for 1847 (Charbonneau and Sévigny, *Grosse Île*, 59, 88, 159, 194, 218, 224).

82. For details of the quarantine arrangements at Grosse Île, see Cowan, *British Emigration to British North America*, 56–57, 152, 153, 192, 193.

83. PP 1850 (173) XL.
84. For example, Donald MacCrummer, a Skye-based emigration agent, told the Colonial Office that his potential clientele could not afford fares at £6 to £7, but if the tonnage restrictions were reduced from two tons per passenger to one ton per passenger, he could reduce his fares to £4 to £5, which they could afford. NAB CO 42/170, f. 362.
85. Macdonagh, *The Passenger Acts*, 54–62.
86. Ibid., 54–62.
87. Guillet, *Great Migration*, 13–19.
88. Martell, *Immigration and Emigration Nova Scotia*, 61. Long boats were used to ferry small groups of people to and from ships once they had anchored offshore.
89. NSARM RG1 vol. 336, doc. 48: John G. Marshall to R.D. George, Sept. 9, 1828.
90. ML MS106: The SS *Clyde*, 1857. However, she ran aground in the St. Lawrence in August of that year on her second voyage and had to be abandoned.
91. ML MS106/98.
92. Delays in sailing-ship departures at major ports such as Liverpool and Glasgow had sometimes been exploited by boarding-house owners who profited greatly by renting rooms to waiting emigrants. See Walpole, "The Humanitarian Movement in the Early 19th Century," 210.
93. Including the railway fare from Portland to Montreal, the first-cabin fare was twenty guineas, the second-cabin thirteen to fifteen guineas and steerage seven guineas. (*IC*, Feb. 9, 16, 1854).
94. All but three of the 130 passengers who sailed in the *Rambler* of Leith in 1807 from Stromness to Pictou perished in a shipwreck.
95. AO F350 MU1145 #3927: John Kippen to Robert Kippen, July 23, 1835 or 1838.
96. *AJ*, July 13, 1831.
97. Prebble, *The Highland Clearances*, 192, 193.
98. The emigrants were probably being taken by steamer from Brora to Cromarty.
99. Botfield, *Journal of a Tour through the Highlands*, 141, 142.
100. The full description, taken from the *Inverness Journal*, has been inscribed on the Emigration Stone at Cromarty.
101. William Bell's Journal, quoted in Skelton, *A Man Austere*, 85. Bell's Journals have been deposited in the Douglas Library of Queen's University, Kingston. There are seventeen volumes.
102. Anon., *The Scotch Colony: The Story of 1873* (Margate, England: Eyre & Spottiswoode, n.d.) 2.
103. *JJ*, June 15, 1849.
104. NLS MS 9656 ff.101–2: Murray Correspondence, letter to Capt. Murray from Ewan Cameron, on board ship, Saturday, April 7, 1841.
105. Hart, *Diary of a Voyage in 1842*, 24.

Chapter 9: Canada's Scottish Heritage

1. The English translation is taken from Kennedy, "Lochaber No More," 293, 294.
2. J.M. Bumsted, *The Scots in Canada*, Canada's Ethnic Group Booklet No. 1 (Ottawa: Canadian Historical Association, 1982) 10.
3. Pierre Berton, *The National Dream* (Toronto: McClelland & Stewart, 1971) 319.
4. John Kenneth Galbraith, *The Scotch* (Toronto: Macmillan of Canada, 1964) 141, 142.

5. Margaret Bennett, "Musical Traditions of the Scots in Newfoundland," *London Journal of Canadian Studies*, 9 (1993) 63–85. The milling process was referred to as "waulking" in Scotland.
6. Bennett, *The Last Stronghold*, 22–54.
7. Donald McKenzie McKillop, *Annals of Megantic County, Quebec* (Lynn, MD: D. McKillop, 1962) 37. Campey, *Les Écossais*, 77–88. The Arran emigrants were expected to go to the Rideau Valley, but Archibald Buchanan, the Quebec immigration agent, persuaded them to settle in Megantic County, south of Quebec City.
8. Bennett, *Oatmeal and the Catechism*, 16, 17.
9. Mackenzie, "The Editor in Canada Series," 24, 75, 107. The 1871 census returns show that Scottish ancestry was claimed by 76 per cent of the combined population of Antigonish and Pictou counties (mainland Nova Scotia) and 82 per cent of the combined population of Inverness and Victoria counties (Cape Breton).
10. The Gaelic half of the newspaper was devoted to songs, stories, and editorials. Philip Buckner, "The Transformation of the Maritimes, 1815–1860," *London Journal of Canadian Studies*, 9 (1993) 24.
11. Janet Adam Smith, *John Buchan: A Biography* (Oxford: Oxford University Press, 1985) 406.
12. The poem appears in Angus MacKay, *By Trench and Trail in Song and Story* (Seattle and Vancouver: MacKay Printing and Publishing, 1918) 116–19.
13. Laurel Doucette (ed.), "Cultural Retention and Economic Change: Studies of the Hebridean Scots in the Eastern Townships of Quebec," in *Canadian Centre for Folk Culture Studies* No. 34 (Ottawa: National Museums of Canada, 1980) 22–41.
14. Bennett, *Oatmeal and the Catechism*, 153.
15. LAC M-1353: Rev. James Souter to Rev. Burns, April 6, 1832.
16. *Seventh Annual Report of the Glasgow Colonial Society* (1833) 12.
17. McKillop, *Annals of Megantic County, Quebec*, 31.
18. Mackenzie, "The Editor in Canada Series," 306, 308–9.
19. Royce MacGillivray and Ewan Ross, *A History of Glengarry* (Belleville, ON: Mika, 1979) 276–7.
20. 1841 Emigration Select Committee, A921.
21. William J. Rattray, *The Scot in British North America*, 4 vols. (Toronto, 1880–83) vol. I, 197.
22. LAC M-1352: John McIntyre to Rev. Burns, Oct. 23, 1828; NAS GD 45/3/140/815: Lt Col. William Marshall to Earl Dalhousie, May 27, Sept. 3, 1828.
23. NLS MS3908/1: Charles Baillie to Sir Walter Scott, 1829.
24. Andrew Haydon, *Pioneer Sketches of the District of Bathurst* (Toronto: Ryerson Press, c. 1925) 188. The Dalhousie Library shut down sometime after 1880.
25. Ibid.
26. I. Allen Jack, *History of the Saint Andrews Society of St. John, New Brunswick, Canada, 1798–1903* (Saint John, NB: J. & A. McMillan, 1903) 179.
27. UNBA MG H17: Historical Background.
28. LAC MG24 I3: McGillivray family of Glengarry Papers; vol. 6: Report of the inaugural meeting of the Highland Society, held 10th November, 1818. It ceased to function by 1870.
29. The Highland Society of London had been founded in 1778. Thanks largely to its efforts, the wearing of the kilt, which had been banned following the Jacobite uprising of 1745–46, became the accepted national dress of Scotland.
30. Simon McGillivray, who was the London agent for the North West Company, had been

president of the Highland Society of London. Although most of Montreal's fur traders were Scottish, they conducted their business through London, not Scotland.

31. LAC MG24 I3: vol. 4, "Subscribers for life."

32. Ibid., vol. 6, 3, 15.

33. Fourteen of the sixty-nine members of the church's initial managing group were North West Company partners. Elizabeth Luther, *Pioneering Spirit: Ontario Places of Worship, Then and Now* (Toronto: Eastend Books, 2000) 30, 31.

34. Anon., *Constitution and First Annual Report of the Highland Society of Nova Scotia with a List of Members and Office Bearers for 1839* (Halifax: Nova Scotia, 1839) 13. Branches were later established at Pictou, Antigonish, and Lochaber (Guysborough County).

35. MacDougall, *History of Inverness County,* 502.

36. Highland Society of New Brunswick, Miramichi, "Gatherin' o' the Clans Banquet, Nov. 30, 1942" (Archives and Special Collections, UNB).

37. Walter Johnstone, *Travels in Prince Edward Island, Gulf of St. Lawrence, North America in the Years 1820-1821, Undertaken with a Design to Establish Sabbath Schools* (Edinburgh, 1823) 55.

38. Ted Cowan, "The Myth of Scotch Canada," in Marjory Harper and Michael E. Vance, eds., *Myth, Migration and the Making of Memory* (Halifax: Fernwood & John Donald, 1999) 49-72.

39. The Montreal Games, revived about thirty years ago, are now held annually, attracting forty to fifty pipe bands.

40. The games were organized by the Embro Highland Society, formed in 1856. After being disbanded, they were revived in 1937 with the formation of the current Zorra Caledonian Society.

41. AO F350 MU1145#3927: Glengarry County collections.

42. UNBA MG H17: file 14 (loose folders).

43. UNBA MG H17: box 12a, box 12c.

44. The Rev. Daniel Fraser, speaking at the centenary celebrations of the St. Andrew's Society of Saint John, *History of the Saint Andrews Society of Saint John,* 185.

45. Gerald Redmond, *The Sporting Scots of Nineteenth Century Canada* (London and Toronto: Associated University Presses, 1982) 121.

46. *Montreal Star,* Jan. 1934.

47. Redmond, *The Sporting Scots,* 112.

48. Curling's popularity is greatest in the west, with Manitoba now being Canada's principal curling centre.

49. Shinty is a Gaelic word. Originating in pre-Christian times, it is western Europe's oldest team game. Played with a ball and stick, it continues to be played today, as an amateur sport, mainly in the Highlands. For the connection between shinty and ice hockey, see Redmond, *The Sporting Scots,* 265-68.

50. Pipe bands and traditional Highland music flourish in the west. Winnipeg had a St. Andrew's Society by 1871, and Calgary's St. Andrew-Caledonian Society was formed in 1884. Alberta now hosts nine Highland Games annually.

51. David Frank, "Tradition and Culture in the Cape Breton Mining Community in the Early Twentieth Century," in Kenneth Donovan (ed.), *Cape Breton at 200: Historical Essays in Honour of the Island's Bicentennial, 1785-1985* (Cape Breton: University College of Cape Breton Press) 203-18.

52. George S. Emmerson, "The Gaelic Tradition in Gaelic Culture," in Stanford Reid, [ed?] *Scottish Tradition in Canada*, 240, 241; Bennett, "Musical Traditions of Scots in Newfoundland," 79–81.
53. LAC M-1354: Rev. James Souter to Rev. Burns, Jan. 26, 1836.
54. After the disruption of 1843 when the Free Church was formed in Scotland, it also won considerable backing in Canada from Scots who were keen to break free from the control exercised by the Established Church.
55. Malcolm Alexander MacQueen, *Hebridean Pioneers* (Winnipeg: Henderson Directories, 1957) 73, 74, 95.
56. John Howison, *Sketches of Upper Canada, Domestic, Local and Characteristic: To Which Are Added Practical Details for the Information of Emigrants of Every Class* (Edinburgh, 1822) 188.
57. Fowler, *Tour through British North America*, 152.

BIBLIOGRAPHY

Primary Sources (Manuscripts)

Aberdeen City Archives (ACA)
CE 87/11: Aberdeen Shipping Registers.

Archives of Ontario (AO)
F350 MU1145: Glengarry County Collection, Kippen, McDiarmid, McEwan families.
F495 MU 2659: Kildalton papers.

Dundee City Archives (DCA)
CE 70/11: Register of Ships.

Edinburgh University Special Collections (EU)
La.II.202: Laing Manuscripts.

Library and Archives Canada (LAC)
C-2170: Red River settlement Census returns.
M-1352, M-1353, M-1354, M-1355, M-1356: Glasgow Colonial Society Correspondence, 1829–37 (microfilm reels).
MG23–J1: Rev. William Drummond fonds.
MG24 I3: McGillivray of Glengarry family papers.
MG24 I183 (H-1099): Archibald McMillan's letter book, 1802–32.
MG24 I8: Alexander McDonell Papers
MG24 I183 ff. 2, 7–9, 11: Passenger lists, *Helen* of Irvine, *Jean* of Irvine and *Friends of John Salt-coats*, 1802 .
MG24–J50: Donald McKenzie Fonds.
MG25–G426: MacMillan & MacNeil fonds.
MG29–D86: Robert William Campbell fonds.
MG31–B4: Henry R. Beer collection.
RG15–D-11–1, vol. 547 (microfilm T-13801): Alexander Begg Scheme.
RG17 vol. 434 no. 47378: Sir Charles Tupper to J. H. Pope, 10 March, 1885; Scottish Emigrant's Aid Association.
RG76–1–A–1, vol. 260 (microfilm C-7808): R. C. P. Croswell to Mr. Benoit, March 3, 1954.
RG76–1–A–1, vol. 405 (microfilm C-10294): John McLennan Immigration Agent in Scotland, 1906–09.
Selkirk Papers (Microfilm Reels): A-27, C-1, C-2, C-3, C-4, C-6, C-13, C-14, C-15.

McCord Museum (MM)
P021: Brodie family papers.

Mitchell Library, Glasgow (ML)
MS106: The *S. S. Clyde*, 1857.

National Archives of Britain, Kew (NAB)
CO 42: Correspondence, Canada.
CO 180: War and Colonial Office papers.
CO 217: Nova Scotia and Cape Breton Original Correspondence.
CO 226: Prince Edward Island Correspondence.
CO 384: Colonial Office Papers on emigration containing original correspondence concerning North American settlers.
CO 385: Colonial Office Papers on emigration, Entry Books of correspondence.
T47/12: Passenger Lists *Lovelly Nelly*, 1774–75

National Archives of Scotland (NAS)
CE 57/11: Register of Ships, Leith.
CS 96: Court of Sessions Productions
E.504: Customs records, collectors quarterly accounts, 1776–1830
/1 Aberdeen, /4 Ayr, /7 Thurso, /9 Dumfries, /11 Dundee,/12 Fort William, /15 Greenock, /17 Inverness, /22 Leith, /25 Oban, /33 Stornoway, /35 Tobermory.
GD 9/166/2: Dr. William Porter to Sir William Pulteney, 18 Jan. 1802.
GD 9/166/23, 23A: Dr. William Porter to John MacKenzie, 27 Dec. 1802.
GD40/16/57: Lothian Muniments: (1) Western Highlands & Islands Commission report (1890); (2) Report from the Select Committee on Colonisation (1891).
GD 45: Dalhousie papers.
GD 46: Seaforth muniments.
GD 46/13/184: *Information published by His Majesty's Commissioners for Emigration respecting the British Colonies in North America* (London, Feb., 1832).
GD 51/15/50, 58: Melville Castle papers.
GD 112: Breadalbane papers.
GD 133: Robertson of Inches papers.
GD 201: Clanranald papers
GD 202: Campbell of Dunstaffinage papers.
GD 221: Lord MacDonald papers.
GD 248: Seafield papers.
GD 263: Heddle papers.
GD 371/313: Robert Shives to Captain Stewart, 23 June, 1862.
HD4/1: Highland and Island Emigration Society papers.
HD 21: Highland Destitution Board papers.
RH/1/2/612/8: Adam Hope to George Hope, 12 Aug., 1847.
RH1/2/612/9: Adam Hope to George Hope, 8 Oct., 1849.
RH1/2/908: *Mechanic and Farmer*, Pictou: N.S., 28 July, 1841.
RH1/2/933 (1–13): The Lord Justice Clerk's Report to the Earl of Suffolk in April, 1774, "Scottish emigration to North America, 1769–1773."
RH 2/4/87, ff. 66–75 Passenger Lists, *Sarah* of Liverpool and *Dove* of Aberdeen, 1801.
RH 4/188: Prize essays and Transactions of the Highland Society of Scotland, vol. III, 1802–03.

National Library of Scotland (NLS)

Adv. MS 35.6.18: Melville Papers. State of Emigration from the Highlands of Scotland, its extent, causes and proposed remedy, London, March 21, 1803.

Adv. MS.73.2.13 f. 27: Letter to Colin MacDonald, Oct. 22, 1791.

Adv. MS 73.2.15, f. 44: Royal Highland and Agricultural Society of Scotland Papers, Notes of Edwards Fraser of Reelig, 1803.

GD 46/13/184: *Information published by His Majesty's Commissioners for Emigration respecting the British Colonies in North America* (London, Feb., 1832).

Adv. MS 26.2.19: Papers relating to the British American Emigration Society.

MS 1053 ff.104–9: Passenger List, *Commerce*, 1803.

MS 3431 f. 180 (Lee Papers): "Observations or remarks upon land and islands which compose the barony called Harris."

MS3908/1: Charles Baillie to Sir Walter Scott, 1829.

MS 3952: Robertson-MacDonald papers.

MS 6602, ff. 21–5: George Dempster to Henry Dundas, 1784.

MS 9646: "On Emigration from the Scottish Highlands and Islands attributed to Edward S. Fraser of Inverness-shire (1801–04)."

MS 9656: Murray Correspondence.

MS 10787: Letter book of John Davidson of Stewartfield, 1774.

MS 11976: Minto Papers, Journal concerning emigration from Blair Atholl to Prince Edward Island, 1808.

SP Dep 313: Sutherland Papers

Nova Scotia Archives and Records Management (NSARM)

RG1: Bound volumes of Nova Scotia Records.

MG7: Log books, ships and shipping.

MG100: Miscellaneous.

Orkney Library and Archives (OLA)

D31/22/1 and D31/21/5: Orkneymen in the Hudson's Bay Company.

Y1: Letter from James Sutherland, in Montreal, to his brother John Sutherland in South Ronaldshay, Orkney, June 29, 1814.

Public Archives and Records Office of Prince Edward Island (PAPEI)

MSS 2702: Passenger lists, *Elizabeth and Anne*, *Spencer* of Newcastle, *Humphreys* of London and *Isle of Skye* of Aberdeen, 1806.

MSS 2704/4: 'Early British Emigration to the Maritimes. List of vessels carrying Scottish emigrants to the Maritimes' compiled by Mary Brehaut (1960).

RG9: Customs

Public Archives of Manitoba (PAM)

MG2 C14: Alexander Ross papers.

Public Archives of New Brunswick (PANB)

MC295/3/305: James Brown to A. H. Gilmour, 5 June, 1862.

MC 300 MS 17/40 (m/f F9798): Passenger list, *Favourite*, 1815.

MC 1672: Surveyor General's papers.

RS24 1838/pe File 4 petition #77: petition of 33 Skye families in 1838.

Scottish Catholic Archives (SCA)
BL: Blairs letters.
DA: Diocese of Argyll and the Isles papers.
OL: Oban letters.

Staffordshire County Record Office (SCRO)
D593: The Sutherland papers.

Strathclyde Regional Archives (SRA)
CE 59/11: Register of Ships, Glasgow.
CE 60/11: Register of Ships, Greenock.

University of Birmingham Special Collections (USBC)
Church Missionary Society Papers.

University of New Brunswick Archives (UNBA)
Highland Society of New Brunswick, Miramichi, "Gatherin' o' the Clans Banquet, Nov., 30,
    1942."
MG H17: Fredericton Society of Saint Andrew.

Private Collections
Rhind, John, "Ship Log, *Jane Boyd* crossing Aberdeen to Montreal, in 1854 (August 15 to
    October 8)."

Printed Primary Sources and Contemporary Publications

Anderson, J., "Essay on the Present State of the Highlands" in *The Transactions of the Highland
    and Agricultural Society of Scotland*, New Series II, 1831.
Anon, *A General Description of Nova Scotia*, (Halifax: Clement H. Belcher, 1825).
Anon., *A Statement of the Satisfactory Results which have attended Emigration to Upper Canada
    from the Establishment of the Canada Company until the Present Period* (London: 1841).
Anon., *Constitution and First Annual Report of the Highland Society of Nova Scotia with a List of
    Members and Office Bearers for 1839* (Halifax: Nova Scotia, 1839).
Anon., *Information for Emigrants to British North America* (1842).
Anon., *The Hudson's Bay Company, What is it?* (London: A. H. Bailey, 1864).
Anon., *The New Statistical Account of Scotland/by the Ministers of the Respective Parishes, under
    the Superintendence of a Committee of the Society for the Benefit of the Sons and Daughters of
    the Clergy* (Edinburgh and London : William Blackwood and Sons, 1845).
Anon., *Sketch of Missionary Proceedings at Cape Breton from August 1833 to September 1836*
    (1833–36).
Argyll, George Douglas Campbell, Duke of, *Crofts and Farms in the Hebrides* (Edinburgh:
    David Douglas, 1883).
Argyll, George Douglas Campbell, Duke of, *Scotland As It Was and As It Is* (Edinburgh:
    Douglas, 1887).
Atkinson, Rev. Christopher, *An Historical and Statistical Account of New Brunswick, British
    North America* (Edinburgh: 1844).
Bell, Rev. William, *Hints to Emigrants in a Series of Letters from Upper Canada*, (Edinburgh:

Waugh & Innes, 1824).

Botfield, Beriah, *Journal of a Tour through the Highlands of Scotland, During the Summer of 1829* (Edinburgh: privately printed, 1830).

Bouchette Joseph, *A Topographical Dictionary of the Province of Lower Canada* (London: Longman & Co, 1832).

Bouchette, Joseph, *The British Dominions in North America: a Topographical and Statistical Description of the Provinces of Lower and Upper Canada, New Brunswick, Nova Scotia, the Islands of Newfoundland, Prince Edward Island and Cape Breton*, Vols I, II (London: 1832).

Brown, Robert, *Strictures and Remarks on the Earl of Selkirk's Observations on the Present State of the Highlands* (Edinburgh: Abemethy & Walker, 1806).

Bryce, George, *The Old Settlers of Red River* (Winnipeg, Manitoba Daily Free Press, 1885).

Colonial Records of North Carolina, Vols viii (1771) and ix (1772)

Cooper, Patrick, *The So-called Evictions of the MacDonald Estates in the Island of North Uist, Outer Hebrides, 1849 (reprinted from the "Scotsman" of 10th February, 1881)* (Aberdeen: 1881).

Douglas, Thomas, 5th Earl of Selkirk, *A Sketch of the British Fur Trade in North America with Observations Relative to the North West Company of Montreal* (London: 1816).

Fowler, Thomas, *Journal of a Tour through British North America to the Falls of Niagara Containing an Account of the Cities, Towns and Villages along the Route in 1831* (Aberdeen: 1832).

Gesner, Abraham, *New Brunswick with Notes for Emigrants: Comprehending the Early History, Settlement, Topography, Statistics, Natural History, etc.*, (London: 1847).

Glasgow Colonial Society, *Seventh Annual Report of the Glasgow Colonial Society for Promoting the Religious Interests of the Scottish Settlers in British North America* (Glasgow: 1833).

Glasgow Colonial Society, *Eighth Annual Report of the Glasgow Colonial Society for Promoting the Religious Interests of the Scottish Settlers in British North America* (Glasgow: 1835).

Gordon, James, *Eight Letters on the Subject of the Earl of Selkirk's Pamphlet on Highland Emigration as They Lately Appeared under the Signature of AMICUS in one of the Edinburgh Newspapers*, (Edinburgh: J. Anderson; London: Longman, Hurst, Rees, and Orme, 1806).

Haliburton, Thomas Chandler, *An Historical and Statistical Account of Nova Scotia*, 2 Vols. (Halifax: J. Howe, 1829).

Howison, John, *Sketches of Upper Canada, Domestic, Local and Characteristic, to which are added Practical Details for the Information of Emigrants of Every Class* (Edinburgh, 1822).

Irvine, Alexander, *An Enquiry into the Causes and Effects of Emigration from the Highlands and Western Isles of Scotland with Observations on the Means Employed for Preventing it* (Edinburgh, 1802).

Johnston, J.F.W., *Notes on North America: Agricultural, Economical and Social, 2 vols.* (Edinburgh: William Blackwood & Sons, 1851).

Johnstone, Walter, *Travels in Prince Edward Island, Gulf of St. Lawrence, North America in the Years 1820–1821, Undertaken with a Design to Establish Sabbath Schools* (Edinburgh: 1823).

Lloyd's Shipping Register 1775–1855.

MacDonald, R.C., *Sketches of Highlanders; With an Account of their Early Arrival in North America; Their Advancement in Agriculture and Some of their Distinguished Military Services in the War of 1812* (Saint John, NB: H. Chubb, 1843).

MacDonald, Rowland Hill, *The Emigration of Highland Crofters* (Edinburgh: Blackwood & Sons, 1885).

MacKay, Rev. W.A., *Pioneer Life in Zorra* (Toronto: William Briggs, 1899).

Mackenzie, Alexander, *An Analysis of the Report of the Crofter Royal Commission* (Inverness: A& W. MacKenzie, 1884).

Mackenzie, Alexander, "First Highland Emigration to Nova Scotia: Arrival of the Ship *Hector*," in *The Celtic Magazine*, vol. VIII, 141–4.

Mackenzie, Alexander (ed.) *The Celtic Magazine: A Monthly Periodical Devoted to the Literature, History, Antiquities, Folk Lore, Traditions, and the Social and Material Interests of the Celt at Home and Abroad/conducted by Alexander Mackenzie and Alexander Macgregor* (Inverness: A & W Mackenzie, 1875–1888).

MacLeod, Donald, of Sutherland, *Gloomy Memories in the Highlands of Scotland: Versus Mrs. Harriet Beecher Stowe's Sunny Memories ... or A Faithful Picture of the Extirpation of the Celtic Race from the Highlands of Scotland.* (Glasgow : A. Sinclair, 1892).

MacLeod, Donald, of Sutherland, *History of the Destitution in Sutherlandshire* (Edinburgh: 1841).

MacTaggert, John, *Three Years in Canada: An Account of the Actual State of the Country in 1826-7-8, Comprehending its Resources, Productions, Improvements and Capabilities and including Sketches of the State of Society, Advice to Emigrants, etc.*, 2 vols. (London: 1829).

Mathison, John, *Counsel for Emigrants, and Interesting Information from Numerous Sources Concerning British America, the United States and New South Wales*, Third edition with a supp. (Aberdeen: 1838).

McCulloch, Thomas, *A Review of the Supplement to the First Annual Report of the Society for Promoting the Religious Interests of the Scottish Settlements in British North America in a Series of Letters to the Rev. Robert Burns* (Glasgow: Andrew Young, 1828).

McDonald, John, *Narrative of a Voyage to Quebec and Journey from thence to New Lanark in Upper Canada, detailing the Hardships and Difficulties which an Emigrant has to Encounter, before and after his Settlement; with an account of the Country, as regards its Climate, Soil and the Actual Conditions of its Inhabitants* (Edinburgh: 1823).

McLauchlan, Rev. Thomas, *Recent Highland Ejections Considered in Five Letters* (Edinburgh: 1850).

Miller, Hugh *Sutherland As It Was and Is: How a Country May Be Ruined* (Edinburgh: John Johnstone, 1843)

Morgan, Lieutenant J.C., *The Emigrants Notebook and Guide with Recollections of Upper and Lower Canada during the Late War* (London: 1824)

Mulock, Thomas Samuel, *The Western Highlands and Islands of Scotland Socially Considered with Reference to the Proprietors and People: Being a Series of Contributions to the Periodical Press* (Edinburgh: J. Menzies, 1850).

Patterson, George, *History of the County of Pictou, Nova Scotia* (Montreal: Dawson Bros., 1877).

Patterson, George, *Memoir of the Rev. James MacGregor* (Philadelphia: 1859).

Rattray, William J., *The Scot in British North America*, 4 vols. (Toronto: Maclear & Co., 1880–83).

Rolph, Thomas, *Emigration and Colonization; Embodying the Results of a Mission to Great Britain and Ireland during the Years, 1839, 1840, 1841 and 1842* (London: 1894).

Ross, Donald, *Glengarry Evictions or Scenes at Knoydart in Inverness-shire*, (Glasgow: 1853).

Ross, Donald, *The Russians of Ross-shire, or, Massacre of the Rosses in Strathcarron, Ross-shire by Policemen, when serving the Tenants in Strathcarron with Summonses of Removal in March last by Donald Ross* (Glasgow: G. Gallie; London: Houlston and Stoneman, 1854).

Sellar, Robert, *History of the County of Huntingdon & of the Seigneuries of Chateauguay and Beauharnois from their First Settlement to the Year 1838* (Huntingdon Que.: Canadian Gleaner, 1888).

Sinclair, Sir John, *First Statistical Account of Scotland*, 21 vols. (Edinburgh: 1791–99).

Telford, Thomas, *A Survey and Report of the Coasts and Central Highlands of Scotland* (London: 1803).

Parliamentary Papers

Annual Reports of the Immigration Agent at Quebec (1831–55).
Colonial Land and Emigration Commissioners, Annual Reports (1841–55).
Emigration Returns for British North America 1830–40.
Report from the Commissioners appointed for inquiring into the Administration and Practical Operation of the Poor Laws in Scotland (1844).
Reports from the Select Committee appointed to inquire into the expediency of encouraging emigration from the United Kingdom, 1826, IV; 1826–27, V.
Report from the Select Committee appointed to enquire into the condition of the population of the Highlands and Islands of Scotland, and into the practicability of affording the People relief by means of Emigration, 1841, VI.

Contemporary Newspapers

Aberdeen Herald
Aberdeen Journal
Acadian Recorder (Halifax)
Caledonian Mercury
Courier (Regina)
Dundee Courier
Dumfries and Galloway Courier
Dumfries Weekly Journal
Edinburgh Advertiser
Edinburgh Daily Review
Glasgow Chronicle
Glasgow Courier
Glasgow Herald
Glasgow Record
Greenock Advertiser
Halifax Times
Inverness Advertiser
Inverness Courier
Inverness Journal
John O'Groat Journal
Lloyd's List
Montreal Star
People's Journal
Perth Courier
Pictou Observer
Quebec Gazette
Quebec Mercury
Royal Gazette (New Brunswick)
Scottish Highlander
Scots Magazine
Scotsman
Weekly Recorder of Charlottetown, Prince Edward Island

Contemporary Material of Later Printing

Anon., *The Scotch Colony; The Story of 1873* (Margate, UK: Eyre & Spottiswoode, n.d.).

Bumsted, J.M. (ed.) *The Collected Writings of Lord Selkirk*, vol. I, (1799–1809): *Observations on the Present State of the Highlands of Scotland, with a View of the Causes and Probable Consequences of Emigration*, (Winnipeg: The Manitoba Record Society, 1984).

Cameron, Viola Root, *Emigrants from Scotland to America 1774–1775: Compiled from a loose bundle of Treasury Papers in the Public Record Office, London England* (Baltimore: Genealogical Publishing Co., 1965. First published 1930.

Campbell, Patrick, *Travels in the Interior; Inhabited Parts of British North America in 1790 and 1792* (Vol.23) (Toronto: Champlain Society, 1937).

Cooney, Robert, *A Compendious History of the Northern Part of the Province of New Brunswick and of the District of Gaspe in Lower Canada* (Chatham: 1896), First published Halifax, NS: Joseph Howe, 1832).

Elizabeth, Ann Kerr McDougall and John S. Moir (eds.), *Selected Correspondence of the Glasgow Colonial Society 1825–1840* (Champlain Society, Toronto, 1994).

Hart, John, *Diary of a Voyage of John Hart of Perth Ontario, who left Glasgow, Scotland ... on the 15th April, 1842 ... arriving in Quebec, 5th June, 1842* (W.A. Newman, 1940).

Lamond, Robert, *A Narrative of the Progress of Emigration from the Counties of Lanark and Renfrew to the New Settlements in Upper Canada on Government Grant* (Ottawa, ON.: Canadian Heritage Publications, 1978). First published 1821.

Mackenzie, Alexaander, *History of the Highland Clearances* (Edinburgh: Mercat Press, 1991). First published in 1883.

MacKenzie, George A., *From Aberdeen to Ottawa in 1845: The Diary of Alexander Muir* (Aberdeen: Aberdeen University Press, 1990).

MacKenzie, John Munro, *Diary, 1851: John Munro MacKenzie, Chamberlain of the Lews* (Inverness: Acair Ltd., 1994).

Riddell, Walter, *Diary of a Voyage from Scotland to Canada in 1833 and the Story of St. Andrew's Presbyterian Church, Cobourg, Ontario* (Toronto: Assoc. Printers Ltd., 1932).

White, Patrick Cecil Telford (ed.), *Lord Selkirk's Diary 1803–04; A Journal of his Travels through British North America and the Northeastern United States* (Toronto: The Champlain Society, 1958).

Secondary Sources

Adam, R. J. (ed), *Papers on Sutherland Estate Management* (2 vols.) (Edinburgh: Scottish History Society, 1972).

Adams, Ian and Somerville, Meredyth, *Cargoes of Despair and Hope: Scottish Emigration to North America, 1603–1803* (Edinburgh: John Donald, 1993).

Aitchison, Peter and Andrew Cassell, *The Lowland Clearances: Scotland's Silent Revolution* (East Linton: Tuckwell, 2003).

Allen, Robert S., *The Loyal Americans: The Military Role of the Loyalist Provincial Corps and their Settlement in British North America 1775–1784* (Ottawa: National Museum of Canada, 1983).

Andrews, Allen, *The Scottish Canadians* (Toronto: Van Norstrand Reinhold, 1981).

Anon., *The Scottish Catholics in Prince Edward Island 1772–1922,* Memorial Volume (Summerside: Journal Publishing Co., 1922).

Appleton, Thomas E., *Ravenscrag: The Allan Royal Mail Line* (Toronto: McClelland & Stewart, 1974).

Baines, Dudley, *Emigration from Europe, 1815–1930* (Basingstoke: Macmillan, 1991).

Barron, James, *The Northern Highlands in the Nineteenth Century Newspaper Index and Annals* (3 vols.) (Inverness: R. Carruther & Sons, 1903–13).

Bennett, Carol, *The Lanark Society Settlers, 1820–1821* (Renfrew, ON: Juniper Books, 1991).

Bennett, Jason Patrick, "The True Elixir of Life; Imagining Eden and Empire in the Settlement of Kelowna, B.C., 1904–1920" (Simon Fraser University, unpublished Ph.D. thesis, 1996).

Bennett, Margaret, "Musical Traditions of the Scots in Newfoundland," in *The London Journal of Canadian Studies,* vol. 9 (1993) 63–85.

Bennett, Margaret, *Oatmeal and the Catechism: Scottish Gaelic Settlers in Quebec* (Montreal: McGill-Queen's University Press; Edinburgh: John Donald, 1998).

Bennett, Margaret, *The Last Stronghold: Scottish Gaelic Traditions of Newfoundland,* (Edinburgh: Canongate, 1989).

Berton, Pierre, *The National Dream: The Great Railway, 1871–1881* (Toronto: McClelland & Stewart, 1971).

_____, *The Promised Land: Settling the West, 1896–1914,* (Toronto: McClelland & Stewart, 1984).

Bigwood, Frank, 'Two Lists of Intending Passengers to the New World, 1770 and 1771' in *SG,* vol. xliii (1996) 17–22.

Binnington, Rev. R.F., "The Glasgow Colonial Society and Its Work in the Development of the Presbyterian Church in British North America 1825–1840" (University of Toronto, unpublished Th.D. thesis, 1960).

Blake, George, *Lloyd's Register of Shipping 1760–1960* (London: Lloyd's, 1960).

Blanchard, Raoul, *L'ouest du Canada Francais – Montréal at sa region* (Montréal: Librarie Beauchemin Limitée, 1953).

Brander, Michael, *The Scottish Highlanders and their Regiments* (Haddington: The Gleneil Press, 1996).

Brock, William R., *Scotus Americanus: A Survey of the Sources for Links Between Scotland and America in the Eighteenth Century* (Edinburgh: Edinburgh University Press, 1982).

Brunger, A.G., "The Distribution of Scots and Irish in Upper Canada, 1851–71," in *Canadian Geographer,* vol. 34 (1990) 250–58.

Bryce, Rev. Dr. George and C.N. Bell, *Original Letters and other Documents Relating to the Selkirk Settlement* (Historical and Scientific Society of Manitoba, 1889) Transaction No. 33.

Buckner, Philip, *English Canada–The Founding Generations: British Migration to British North America, 1815–1865.* Canada House, Lecture Series no. 54 (ISBN 0265–4253) Canadian High Commission, Grosvenor Square, London.

Buckner, Phillip and John G. Reid (eds.), *The Atlantic Region to Confederation: A History* (Toronto: University of Toronto Press, 1993).

Bumsted, J.M., 'Highland Emigration to the Island of St. John and the Scottish Catholic Church' in *Dalhousie Review,* vol. 58 (1978) 511–27.

_____, *Interpreting Canda's Past* (Vol. I) (Toronto: Oxford University Press Canada, 1993).

_____, *Land Settlement and Politics on Eighteenth Century Prince Edward Island* (Kingston: McGill-Queen's University Press, 1987).

_____, *The Peoples of Canada: A Pre-Confederation History* (Vol. 1) (Toronto: Oxford University Press, 1992).

_____, *The People's Clearance: Highland Emigration to British North America 1770–1815,* (Edinburgh: Edinburgh University Press, 1982).

_____, *The Scots in Canada*, Canada's Ethnic Group Booklet No. 1 (Ottawa: Canadian Historical Association, 1982).

Burley, Edith I., *Servants of the Honourable Company, Work Discipline and Conflict in the Hudson's Bay Company, 1770–1879* (Toronto: Oxford University Press, 1997).

Cage R.A. (ed.), *The Scots Abroad: Labour, Capital, Enterprise, 1750–1914* (London: Croom Helm, 1985).

Cameron, J.M., "A Study of the Factors that Assisted and Directed Scottish Emigration to Upper Canada 1815–1855" (University of Glasgow, unpublished Ph.D. thesis, 1970).

Cameron, J.M., "The Changing Role of the Highland Landlords Relative to Scottish Emigration during the First Half of the 19th Century" in the Proceedings of the Fourth and Fifth Colloquia on Scottish Studies (University of Guelph, 1972) 80–81.

Campbell, D.F. and R.A. MacLean, *Beyond the Atlantic Roar: A Study of the Nova Scotia Scots* (Toronto: McClelland & Stewart, 1974).

Campbell, R.H., *Scotland Since 1707: The Rise of an Industrial Society* (Edinburgh: Donald, 1985).

Campbell, Wilfrid, *The Scotsman in Canada* Vols. I & II (London: Sampson Low & Co., 1911).

Campey, Lucille H., *"A Very Fine Class of Immigrants": Prince Edward Island's Scottish Pioneers, 1770–1850* (Toronto: Natural Heritage Books, 2001). Reprinted 2007.

_____, *After the Hector: The Scottish Pioneers of Nova Scotia and Cape Breton, 1773–1852* (Toronto: Natural Heritage Books, 2004). Reprinted 2007.

_____, *"Fast Sailing and Copper-Bottomed": Aberdeen Sailing Ships and the Emigrant Scots They Carried to Canada* (Toronto: Natural Heritage Books, 2002).

_____, *Les Écossais: The Pioneer Scots of Lower Canada, 1763–1855* (Toronto: Natural Heritage Books, 2006).

_____, *The Scottish Pioneers of Upper Canada, 1784–1855: Glengarry and Beyond* (Toronto: Natural Heritage Books, 2005).

_____, *The Silver Chief: Lord Selkirk and the Scottish Pioneers of Belfast, Baldoon and Red River* (Toronto: Natural Heritage Books, 2003).

_____, *With Axe and Bible: The Scottish Pioneers of New Brunswick, 1784–1874* (Toronto: Natural Heritage Books/The Dundurn Group, 2007).

Carrier, N.H. and J.R. Jeffrey, *External Migration: A Study of the Available Statistics 1815–1950* (London: H.M.S.O., 1953).

Charbonneau, André and André Sévigny, *1847 Grosse Île: A Record of Daily Events* (Ottawa: Parks Canada, 1997).

Clark, Andrew H., "Old World Origins and Religious Adherence in Nova Scotia," in *Geographical Review*, vol. 1 (1960) 317–44.

Clark, Andrew Hill, *Three Centuries and the Island: A Historical Geography of Settlement and Agriculture in Prince Edward Island, Canada* (Toronto: University of Toronto Press, 1959).

Clark, S.D., *Church and Sect in Canada* (Toronto: University of Toronto Press, 1948).

Clouston, J. Storer, "Orkney and the Hudson's Bay Company" in *The Beaver, A Magazine of the North*, Outfit 267, No. 4 (March 1937) 39–43.

Coutts, Robert J., *The Road to the Rapids: Nineteenth Century Church and Society at St. Andrew's Parish, Red River* (Calgary: University of Calgary Press, 1961).

Cowan, Helen, *British Emigration to British North America: The First Hundred Years* (Toronto: University of Toronto Press, 1961).

Cowan, Ted, "The Myth of Scotch Canada," in Marjory Harper and Michael E. Vance, (eds.) *Myth, Migration and the Making of Memory* (Halifax: Fernwood & John Donald, 1999) 49–72.

Craig, David, *On the Crofter's Trail: In Search of the Clearance Highlanders* (London: Jonathan Cape, 1990).

Creighton, D.G., *The Commercial Empire of the Saint Lawrence 1760–1850* (Toronto: The Ryerson Press, 1937).

Davis, Ralph, *The Industrial Revolution and British Overseas Trade* (Leicester: Leicester University Press, 1979).

Devine, T.M., *Exploring the Scottish Past: Themes in the History of Scottish Society*, (East Linton: Tuckwell Press, 1995)

————, "Highland Migration to Lowland Scotland, 1760–1860," in *Scottish Historical Review*, vol. LXII (1983) 347–51.

———— (ed.), *Scottish Emigration and Scottish Society* (Edinburgh: John Donald, 1992).

————, "Temporary Migration and the Scottish Highlands in the Nineteenth Century," in *Economic History Review*, vol. 32 (1979) 344–59.

————, *The Great Highland Famine: Hunger, Emigration and the Scottish Highlands in the Nineteenth Century* (Edinburgh: John Donald, 1988).

————, *The Scottish Nation, 1700–2000* (London: Allen Lane, Penguin, 1999).

Dictionary of Canadian Biography, Vols. V-XIII (Toronto: 1979–85).

Dobson, David, *Ships from Scotland to America 1628–1828* (3 Vols.) (Baltimore, Gen. Pub. Co., 1998).

Donaldson, Gordon, *The Scots Overseas* (London: Robert Hale, 1966).

Doucette Laurel (ed), "Cultural Retention and Economic Change: Studies of the Hebridean Scots in the Eastern Townships of Quebec" in *Canadian Centre for Folk Culture Studies*, No. 34 (Ottawa: National Museums of Canada, 1980).

Elliott, Bruce, "Emigrant Recruitment by the New Brunswick Land Company: The Pioneer Settlers of Stanley and Harvey," in *Generations*, the journal of the New Brunswick Genealogical Society, (Winter, 2004) 50–54, (Spring, 2005) 34–40, (Summer, 2005) 11–17.

Emmerson, George S., "The Gaelic Tradition in Gaelic Culture," in Stanford W. Reid (ed.), *The Scottish Tradition in Canada*, (Toronto: McClelland & Stewart, 1976) 232–47.

England, Robert, *Colonization of Western Canada: A Study of Contemporary Land Settlement (1896–1934)* (London: P. S. King & Son, 1936).

Ens, Gerhard J., *Homeland to Hinterland: The Changing World of the Métis in the Nineteenth Century* (Toronto: University of Toronto Press, 1996).

Flanagan, Thomas, *Métis Lands in Manitoba* (Calgary: University of Calgary Press, 1991).

Fleming, Rae (ed.), *The Lochaber Emigrants to Glengarry* (Toronto: Natural Heritage Books, 1994).

Flewwelling, Susan Longley (Morse), "Immigration to and Emigration from Nova Scotia 1839–51" in *Nova Scotia Historical Society (Collections)*, vol. xxviii (1949) 84–85.

Flinn, Michael W. (ed.), *Scottish Population History from the Seventeenth Century to the 1930s* (New York: Cambridge University Press, 1977).

Frank, David, "Tradition and Culture in the Cape Breton Mining Community in the early Twentieth Century," in Kenneth Donovan (ed.), *Cape Breton at 200: Historical Essays in Honour of the Island's Bicentennial, 1785–1985* (Cape Breton: University College of Cape Breton Press).

Frank, Foden, *Wick of the North, The Story of a Scottish Royal Burgh* (Wick: 1996).

Galbraith, John Kenneth, *The Scotch* (Toronto: Macmillan of Canada, 1964).

Ganong, W.F., "Monograph of the Origins of Settlements in the Province of New Brunswick," in *Transactions of the Royal Society of Canada*, 2nd series (10), sections 1–2 (1904).

Gates, Lilian F., *Land Policies of Upper Canada* (Toronto: University of Toronto Press, 1968).

Gentilcore, Louis R. (ed.), *Historical Atlas of Canada, vol. II: The Land Transformed, 1800–1891* (Toronto: University of Toronto Press, 1993).

Gibbon, John Murray, *Scots in Canada: A History of the Settlement of the Dominion from the Earliest Days to the Present Time* (London: Kegan Paul, Trench Trubner & Co. Ltd., 1911).

Gibson, John G., *Traditional Gaelic Bagpiping* (Montreal: McGill-Queen's University Press, 1998).

Goldring, Philip, "Lewis and the Hudson's Bay Company in the Nineteenth Century," in *The Journal of the School of Scottish Studies* (University of Edinburgh) vol. 22, 1978, 23–41.

Graham, Ian Charles Cargill *Colonists from Scotland: Emigration to North America 1707–83* (New York: Cornell University Press, 1956).

Gray, John Morgan, *Lord Selkirk of Red River* (London: Macmillan, 1963).

Gray, Malcolm, *The Highland Economy, 1750–1850* (Edinburgh: Oliver & Boyd, 1957).

Gray, Malcolm "The Social Impact of Agrarian Change in the Rural Lowlands" in T. M. Devine and Rosalind Mitchison (eds.), *People and Society in Scotland 1760–1830*, vol. I (Edinburgh, 1988) 53–69.

Greenhilll, Basil and Anne Giffard, *Westcountrymen in Prince Edward's Isle,* (Toronto: University of Toronto Press, 1967).

Guillet, Edwin C., *The Great Migration, The Atlantic Crossing by Sailing Ships Since 1770* (Toronto: University of Toronto Press, 1963).

Gunn, Neil, *Butcher's Broom* (Edinburgh: The Porpoise Press, 1934).

Hamil, Fred Coyne, *Lake Erie Baron: The Story of Colonel Thomas Talbot,* (Toronto: Macmillan, 1955).

Hamilton, Henry, *The Industrial Revolution in Scotland,* (Oxford: Clarendon Press, 1932).

Handcock, W.G., "Spatial Patterns in a Transatlantic Migration Field: The British Isles and Newfoundland during the Eighteenth and Nineteenth Centuries" in Brian S. Osborne (ed.), *Proceedings of the 1975 British-Canadian Symposium on Historical Geography: The Settlement of Canada: Origins and Transfer* (Kingston, ON: Queen's University Press, 1976).

Harper, Marjory, *Adventurers & Exiles: The Great Scottish Exodus* (London: Profile Books, 2003).

———, *Emigration from North-East Scotland (*2 Vols.) (Aberdeen: Aberdeen University Press, 1988).

———, *Emigration from Scotland Between the Wars* (Manchester: Manchester University Press, 1998).

———, "Image and Reality in Early Emigrant Literature," in *British Journal of Canadian Studies,* vol. 7 (1992).

Harper, Marjory and Michael E. Vance, (eds.) *Myth, Migration and the Making of Memory* (Halifax: Fernwood & John Donald, 1999).

Harvey, D.C., "Early Settlement in Prince Edward Island" in *Dalhousie Review*, vol. xi, no. 4 (1932) 458–9.

Harvey, Daniel Cobb, (ed.), *Journeys to the Island of Saint John or Prince Edward Island, 1775–1832* (Toronto: Macmillan Co. of Canada, 1955).

Haydon, Andrew, *Pioneer Sketches of the District of Bathurst* (Toronto: Ryerson Press, c. 1925).

Healy, W.J., *Women of Red River: Being a Book Written from the Recollections of Women Surviving from the Red River Era* (Winnipeg: Peguis Publishers Ltd., 1987).

Herman, Arthur, *The Scottish Enlightenment: The Scots' Invention of the Modern World* (London: Fourth Estate, 2001).

Hewitt, Martin, "The Itinerant Emigration Lecturer: James Brown's Lecture Tour of Britain and Ireland, 1861–2" in *The British Journal of Canadian Studies,* vol. 10, no. 1 (1995) 103–19.

Hill, Douglas Arthur, *The Scots to Canada* (London: Gentry Books, 1972).

Hill, Robert, *Voice of the Vanishing Minority: Robert Sellar and the Huntingdon Gleaner 1863–1919* (Montreal: McGill-Queen's University Press, 1998).

Hornsby, Stephen J., *Nineteenth Century Cape Breton: An Historical Geography* (Montreal: McGill-Queen's University Press, 1992).

Hunter, James, *A Dance Called America* (Edinburgh: Mainstream Publishing, 1994).

Hunter, James, *The Making of the Crofting Community* (Edinburgh: John Donald, 1976).

Jack I. Allen, *History of the Saint Andrews Society of Saint John, New Brunswick, Canada, 1798–1903* (Saint John, NB: J. & A. McMillan, 1903).

Jackel, Susan (ed.), *A Flannel Shirt and Liberty: British Emigrant Gentlewomen to the Canadian West, 1880–1914* (Vancouver: University of British Columbia Press, 1982).

Jackson, Gordon, *The British Whaling Trade* (London: A. and C. Black, 1978).

Johnson, Stanley Currie, *A History of Emigration from the United Kingdom to North America, 1763–1912* (London: Frank Cass & Co., 1966).

Johnston, Angus Anthony, *A History of the Catholic Church in Eastern Nova Scotia* (2 vols.) (Antigonish: St. Francis Xavier University Press, 1960).

Johnston, H.J.M., *British Emigration Policy 1815–1830: Shovelling Out Paupers* (Oxford: Clarendon Press, 1972).

Kennedy, Michael, "Lochaber No More: A Critical Examination of Highland Emigration Mythology," in Marjory Harper and Michael E. Vance, (eds.) *Myth, Migration and the Making of Memory* (Halifax & Edinburgh: Fernwood & John Donald, 1999).

Kennedy, Mike, "The Scottish Gaelic Settlement History of Prince Edward Island," (Edinburgh University, unpublished Ph.D. thesis, 1995).

Kincaid, Barbara, "Scottish Emigration to Cape Breton, 1758–1838" (Dalhousie, Nova Scotia, unpublished Ph.D. thesis, 1964).

Lalonde, A.N., "Colonization Companies in the 1880s" in *Saskatchewan History*, vol. XXIV, no. 3 (1971) 101–14.

Lang, Burton, *Place Names of South Western Quebec* (Howick, Quebec: self-published, 2001).

Lawson, Bill, *A Register of Emigrants from the Western Isles of Scotland 1750–1900* (2 vols.) (Northton, Isle of Harris: self-published, 1992).

Lawson, Bill, *A Register of Emigrant Families from the Western Isles of Scotland to the Eastern Townships of Quebec* (Eaton Corner, QC: Compton County Historical Museum Society, 1988).

Lawson, Rev. James, "Early Scottish Settlement on Prince Edward Island: The Princetown Pioneers, 1769–1771" in *SG*, vol. xli (1994) 112–30.

————, " 'Lucy, Jane and the 'Bishop,' A Study in Extant Passenger Lists" in *SG*, vol. xlii (1995) 1–13.

————, "Passengers on the *Alexander*, Arisaig to St. John's Island, April-June 1772" in *SG*, vol. xxxix (1992) 127–43.

Lawson, James, *The Emigrant Scots* (Aberdeen: Aberdeen & North East Scotland FHS, 1988).

Lee, Robert C., *The Canada Company and the Huron Tract, 1826–1853: Personalities, Profits and Politics* (Toronto: Natural Heritage Books, 2004).

Lenman, Bruce, *An Economic History of Modern Scotland 1600–1976* (London: Batsford, 1977).

Levitt, Ian and Christopher Smout, *The State of the Scottish Working Class in 1843: A Statistical and Spatial Enquiry Based on Data from the Poor Law Commission Report of 1844* (Edinburgh: Scottish Academic Press, 1979).

Lindsay, Virginia Howard, "The Perth Military Settlement: Characteristics of its Permanent and Transitory Settlers, 1815–22" (Ottawa, ON: Carleton University, unpublished M.A. thesis, 1972).

Little, J.I., "From the Isle of Lewis to the Eastern Townships: The Origins of a Highland Settlement Community in Quebec, 1838–81" in Kerrigan, Catherine (ed.) *The Immigrant Experience: Proceedings of a Conference held at the University of Guelph, 8–11 June 1989* (Guelph, ON: University of Guelph, 1992).

Little, John Irvine, *Crofters and Habitants: Settler Society, Economy, and Culture in a Quebec Township, 1848–81* (Montreal: McGill-Queen's University Press, 1991).

—————, *Nationalism, Capitalism and Colonization in Nineteenth-Century Quebec, the Upper St. Francis District* (Kingston, ON: McGill-Queen's University Press, 1989).

—————, "The Bard in a Community in Transition & Decline: Oscar Dhu & the Hebridean Scots in the Upper St. Francis District" in Donald H Akenson (ed.), *Canadian Papers in Rural History*, vol. X (Gananoque: Langdale Press, 1995).

Lower, Arthur R.M., *Colony to Nation: A History of Canada* (Toronto: Longmans, Green & Co., 1946).

—————, *Great Britain's Woodyard: British America and the Timber Trade 1763–1867* (Montreal: McGill-Queen's University Press, 1973).

—————, "Immigration and Settlement in Canada 1812–1820," in *Canadian Historical Review*, vol. iii (1922) 37-47.

—————, "Settlement and the Forest Frontier in Eastern Canada" in W. A. Mackintosh and W. L. G. Jaerg (eds.) *Canadian Frontiers of Settlement*, vol. IX (Toronto: Macmillan, 1936) 40–47.

Luther, Elizabeth, *Pioneering Spirit: Ontario Places of Worship, Then and Now* (Toronto: Eastend Books, 2000).

MacArthur, E. Mairi, *Iona: Living Memory of a Crofting Community, 1750–1914* (Edinburgh: Edinburgh University Press, 1990).

Macdonagh, Oliver, *A Pattern of Government Growth, 1800–1860: The Passenger Acts and Their Enforcement* (London: Macgibbon & Kee, 1961).

MacDonald, Colin S., 'Early Highland Emigration to Nova Scotia and Prince Edward Island from 1770 to 1853' in *Nova Scotia Historical Society (Collections)*, vol. xxiii (1936) 44.

MacDonald, Ewen J., "Father Roderick MacDonell, Missionary at St. Regis and the Glengarry Catholics" in *The Catholic Historical Review*, vol. XIX (1933) no. 3. 265-74.

MacDonald, Norman, *Canada, Immigration and Settlement 1763–1841* (London: Longmans & Co., 1939).

MacDonald, Norman, *Canada, Immigration and Colonization, 1841–1903* (Aberdeen: Aberdeen University Press, 1966).

MacDougall, Donald (ed.), *Scots and Scots Descendants in America* (New York: 1917).

MacDougall, John L., *History of Inverness County* (Truro: New Pub. Co. Ltd., 1922).

MacDougall, Robert, *The Emigrant's Guide to North America*, edited by Elizabeth Thompson (Toronto: Natural Heritage Books, 1998). First published 1841.

MacEwan, Andrew B., "The *Falmouth* Passengers," in *The Island Magazine*, vol. 10 (1981) 12-19.

MacGillivray, Royce, *The Mind of Ontario*, (Belleville, ON: Mika Pub. Co., 1985).

MacGillivray, Royce and Ewan Ross, *A History of Glengarry*, (Belleville, ON: Mika, 1979).

MacGregor, David R., *Merchant Sailing Ships: Supremacy of Sail 1815–1850* (London: Conway Maritime Press, 1984).

MacKay, Angus, *By Trench and Trail in Song and Story* (Seattle & Vancouver: MacKay Printing and Publishing, 1918).

MacKay, Donald, *The Lumberjacks* (Toronto: Natural Heritage Books, 1998).

MacKay, Donald, *Scotland Farewell, The People of the 'Hector'* (Toronto: Natural Heritage Books, 1996)

MacKenzie, A.E.D., *Baldoon: Lord Selkirk's Settlement in Upper Canada* (London, ON: Phelps Publishing Co., 1978).

MacLaren, George, *The Pictou Book: Stories of our Past* (New Glasgow, NS: Hector Pub. Co., 1954).

MacLennan, Gordon (ed.), *Proceedings of the First North American Congress of Celtic Studies,* (held at Ottawa from March 26–30, 1986) 15–37.

MacLeod, John, *Highlanders: A History of the Gaels* (London: Hodder and Stoughton, 1996).

MacLeod, Peter Kenneth, "A Study of Concentrations of Scottish Settlements in Nineteenth Century Ontario"(Ottawa:Carleton University, unpublished M.A. thesis, 1972).

Macmillan, David S., "Scottish Enterprise and Influences in Canada 1620–1900" in R.A. Cage, *The Scots Abroad* (London: Croom Helm, 1985) 46–79.

MacMillan, Somerled, *Bygone Lochaber: Historical and Traditional* (Glasgow: K. & R. Davidson, 1971).

MacNutt, W.S., *The Atlantic Provinces: The Emergence of Colonial Society, 1712–1857* (London: Oxford University Press, 1965).

MacQueen, Malcolm Alexander, *Hebridean Pioneers* (Winnipeg: Henderson Directories, 1957).

MacQueen, Malcolm, *Skye Pioneers and the Island* (Winnipeg: Stovel Co., 1929).

Malpeque Historical Society, *Malpeque and its People 1700–1982* (Malpeque, PE: 1982).

Martell, J.S., *Immigration to and Emigration from Nova Scotia 1815–1838* (Halifax, NS: PANS, 1942).

Martin, Chester, "Lord Selkirk's Work in Canada" in *Oxford Historical and Literary Studies,* vol. 7 (1916).

McGill, Jean S., *A Pioneer History of the County of Lanark* (Toronto: self-published, 1974).

McGowan, Ian (ed.), *Samuel Johnson: A Journey to the Western Isles of Scotland* (Edinburgh: Canongate, 2001).

McKillop, Donald McKenzie, *Annals of Megantic County, Quebec* (Lynn, MA: D McKillop, 1962).

McLean, Marianne, *People of Glengarry 1745–1820: Highlanders in Transition 1745–1820* (Montreal: McGill-Queen's, 1991).

McPherson, Flora, *Watchman Against the World, The Remarkable Journey of Norman McLeod and his People from Scotland to Cape Breton Island and New Zealand* (Cape Breton: Breton Books, 1993).

Meek, Donald E., "Evangelicalism and Emigration: Aspects of the Role of Dissenting Evangelicalism in Highland Emigration to Canada" in Gordon Messamore & Barbara J., *Canadian Migration Patterns* (Toronto: University of Toronto Press, 2004).

Meyer, D. Vane, *The Highland Scots of North Carolina* (Durham: University of Carolina Press, 1961).

Milton, Norma J., "The Scots in Alberta," in Howard and Tamara Palmer (eds.), *Peoples of Alberta: Portrait of Cultural Diversity* (Saskatoon: Western Prairie Books, 1985) 109–22.

Mitchell, Elaine Allan,"The Scot in the Fur Trade" in Stanford W. Reid (ed.), *The Scottish Tradition in Canada* (Toronto, McClelland & Stewart, 1976) 27–48.

Moir, John S., *Enduring Witness: A History of the Presbyterian Church in Canada* (Toronto: Presbyterian Publications, 1975).

Moir, John S., *The Church in the British Era: From the British Conquest to Confederation* (Volume Two of History of the Christian Church in Canada), John Webster Grant (gen. ed.) (Toronto: McGraw-Hill Ryerson Ltd., 1972).

Morton, W. L., *Manitoba: A History* (Toronto: University of Toronto Press, 1967).

Murdoch, Steve, "Cape Breton, Canada's 'Highland Island'?" in *Northern Scotland*, vol. 18 (1998) 31–42.

Murray, Norman, *The Scottish Hand Loom Weavers, 1790–1850* (Edinburgh: John Donald, 1978).

Nicks, John, "Orkneymen in the Hudson's Bay Company, 1780–1821" in Carol M. Judd and Arthur J. Ray, *Old Trails and New Directions: Papers of the Third North American Fur Trade Conference* (Toronto, University of Toronto Press, 1980) 102–03.

Norton, Wayne, *Help Us to a Better Land, Crofter Colonies in the Prairie West* (Regina: University of Regina, 1994).

Orlo, J. and Fraser D., 'Those Elusive Immigrants, Parts 1 to 3', in *The Island Magazine*, No. 16 (1984) 36–44; No. 17 (1985) 32–7; No. 18 (1985) 29–35.

Ouellet, Fernand, *Le Bas Canada 1791–1840, changements structuraux et crise* (Ottawa: Ottawa University, 1976). (Translated and adapted by Patricia Claxton, *Lower Canada, 1791–1840: Social Change and Nationalism* (Toronto: McClelland & Stewart, 1980).

Parley, Kay, "Moffat, Assiniboia, North-West Territories" in *Saskatchewan History*, vol. XX, no. 1 (1967) 32–36.

Patterson, George, *Memoir of the Rev. James MacGregor* (Philadelphia: Joseph M. Wilson, 1859).

Prebble, John, *The Highland Clearances* (London: Penguin, 1969).

Prince Edward Island Genealogical Society, *From Scotland to Prince Edward Island: Scottish Emigrants to Prince Edward Island from Death and Obituary Notices in Prince Edward Island 1835–1910* (n.d.).

Pritchett, John Perry, *The Red River Valley, 1811–1849* (New York: Russell & Russell, 1942).

Ramsay, Freda, *John Ramsay of Kildalton: Being an Account of his Life in Islay and Including the Diary of his Trip to Canada in 1870,* (Toronto: Peter Martin Associates, c.1977).

Redmond, Gerald, *The Sporting Scots of Nineteenth Century Canada* (London and Toronto: Associated University Presses, 1982) 162.

Reid, W. Stanford (ed.), *The Scottish Tradition in Canada* (Toronto: McClelland & Stewart, 1976).

Richards, Eric, *A History of the Highland Clearances: Emigration, Protest, Reasons* (London: Croom Helm, 1982–85).

————, "How Tame were the Highlanders During the Clearances?" in *Scottish Studies*, vol. 17 (1973) 35-50.

————, *The Highland Clearances: People, Landlords and Rural Turmoil* (Edinburgh: Birlinn Ltd., 2000).

————, *Patrick Sellar and the Highland Clearances: Homicide, Eviction and the Price of Progress,* (Edinburgh: Polygon, 1999).

————, "Varieties of Scottish Emigration in the Nineteenth Century" in *Historical Studies*, vol. 21 (1985) 473–94.

Rider, Peter E. and Heather McNabb (eds.) *A Kingdom of the Mind: How the Scots Helped Make Canada* (Montreal: McGill-Queen's University Press, 2006).

Roxborough, Henry, *One Hundred–Not Out: The Story of Nineteenth Century Canadian Sport* (Toronto: Ryerson Press, 1966).

Russell, R.C., *Carleton Trail: The Broad Highway into the Saskatchewan Country from the Red River Settlement, 1840–80* (Saskatoon: Modern Press, 1965).

Sager, Eric, with G.E. Panting, *Maritime Capital: The Shipping Industry in Atlantic Canada 1820–1914* (Montreal: McGill-Queen's University Press, 1990).

Shaw, Matthew, *Great Scots!: How the Scots Created Canada* (Winnipeg: Heartland Associates, 2003).

Shearer, John, W. Groundwater and J.D. Mackay (eds.) *The New Orkney Book* (Edinburgh: Nelson Printers, 1966).

Shepperson, W.S., *British Emigration to North America: Projects and Opinions in the Early Victorian Period* (Oxford: Oxford University Press, 1957).

Shortt, A. and A.G. Doughty, (eds.), *Canada and its Provinces. A History of the Canadian People and Their Institutions, by One Hundred Associates* (Toronto: Publishers Association of Canada, 1913–17).

Silverman, Elaine Leslau, *The Last Best West: Women on the Alberta Frontier, 1880–1930* (Calgary: Fifth House Publishers, 1998).

Skelton, Isabel, *A Man Austere* (Toronto: Ryerson Press, 1947).

Smith, Janet Adam, *John Buchan, A Biography* (Oxford: Oxford University Press, 1985).

Stanley, Laurie, *The Well-Watered Garden: The Presbyterian Church in Cape Breton 1798–1860* (Sydney, NS: University College of Cape Breton Press, 1983).

Stevenson, John A., *Curling in Ontario, 1846–1946* (Toronto: Ontario Curling Assoc., 1950).

Storrie, Margaret, *Islay: Biography of an Island*, (Port Ellen, ON: self-published, 1981).

Stuart, Kent, "The Scottish Crofter Colony, Saltcoats 1889–1904" in *Saskatchewan History*, vol. XXIV(2) (1971) 41–50.

Sutherland, George R., *The Rise and Decline of the Earltown Community, 1813–1970* (Colchester, NS: Colchester Historical Society and Colchester Historical Museum, 1980).

Thomas, Lewis G., (ed.) *The Prairie West to 1905* (Toronto: Oxford University Press, 1975).

Tulchinsky, Gerald J.J., *The River Barons: Montreal Business & Growth of Industry & Transport, 1837–53* (Toronto; Buffalo: University of Toronto Press, 1977).

Turner, Alan R., "Scottish Settlement of the West" in W. Stanford Reid (ed.), *The Scottish Tradition in Canada* (Toronto: McClelland & Stewart, 1976) 82, 83.

Vance, M.E., "Emigration and Scottish Society: The Background of Government Assisted Emigration to Upper Canada, 1815–21" (University of Guelph, unpublished Ph.D. thesis, 1990).

Walpole, M.A., "The Humanitarian Movement in the Early 19th Century to Remedy Abuses on Emigrant Vessels" in *Transactions of the Royal Historical Society*, vol. XIV (1931)197–224.

Warburton, A.B., *History of Prince Edward Island* (Saint John, NB: nk., 1923).

Williams, Maureen, "John MacLean, His Importance as a Literary and Social Personality," a paper read before the Antigonish Heritage Society, Sept. 9, 1985 (8 pages).

Wright, Esther Clark, *The Loyalists of New Brunswick* (Fredericton, NB: nk., 1955).

Wynne, Graeme, *Timber Colony: An Historical Geography of Early Nineteenth Century New Brunswick* (Toronto: University of Toronto Press, 1981).

INDEX

Photograph by Geoff Campey

ABOUT THE
AUTHOR

Dr. Lucille Campey is a Canadian, living in Britain, with over thirty years of experience as a researcher and author. It was her father's Scottish roots and love of history that first stimulated her interest in the early exodus of people from Scotland to Canada. Lucille's mother, Cécile Morency, was born in Quebec and had ancestors who came from France, settling in Île d'Orléans in 1659.

A Chemistry graduate of Ottawa University, Lucille worked initially in the fields of science and computing. After marrying her English husband, she moved to the north of England, where she studied medieval settlement patterns, acquiring a Master of Philosophy Degree from Leeds University. Later, they lived for five years at Tain, in Easter Ross in Scotland, while Lucille completed her doctoral thesis at Aberdeen University on "The Regional Characteristics of Scottish Emigration to British North America 1784 to 1854." Lucille and Geoff have returned to England, and now live near Salisbury in Wiltshire.

An Unstoppable Force is the eighth book in a series that Lucille has written about the Scottish exodus to Canada. As with the earlier titles, it is based on the research she undertook while studying for her Ph. D. but is augmented by a considerable amount of new material. Lucille has her own Web site: www.scotstocanada.com.